Michael J. Leitner, PhD
Sara F. Leitner, MA

·ure in Later Life

₁ ₁ᵈ᷍ᵢⁱᵒⁿ

Pre-publication
REVIEWS,
COMMENTARIES,
EVALUATIONS . . .

"Until recently, leisure has been considered somewhat frivolous in comparison to the more serious business of life, and has been commonly misunderstood in relation to the later phase of life. However, evidence suggests that this trend is changing and leisure, irrespective of its form, provides a context for self-expression, learning, challenge, and accomplishment. One's choice of leisure activities in later life is strongly influenced by cultural values, societal expectations, and geographic location as well as personal situations such as relationships, previous experiences, health status, and financial situation.

Considerable attention has been given to examining the relationship between age and leisure, including the search for patterns of and influence on continuity and change in activities across the life span. Despite the many theories about aging and leisure, the authors make it clear that this is a complex and complicated aspect of life about which much is yet to be learned. Hence, it is imperative that those who offer leisure services to older citizens realize that what occurs in later years is more about adaptation than evolution. This book provides insight into this important aspect of life, covers a multitude of practical ideas for activities, and encourages the reader to grapple with the many recent developments and issues associated with leisure in later life."

Bevan C. Grant, PhD
Professor of Sport and Leisure Studies,
University of Waikato, New Zealand

More pre-publication
REVIEWS, COMMENTARIES, EVALUATIONS . . .

"*Leisure in Later Life* by Michael Leitner and Sara Leitner is an excellent resource for current recreation professionals and students enrolled in recreation, sociology, or gerontology programs. The text provides insight into leisure and later life as well as practical examples that will be beneficial to readers. The book covers such topics as foundations of recreation service delivery for elders, current recreation service delivery, examples of resources for recreation programs for older adults, and how different countries have examined leisure and aging. The text also speculates on the future of leisure in later life.

This text will be an asset as well to students enrolled in leisure and aging, program planning, and therapeutic recreation courses. The book will be an excellent resource for therapeutic recreation professionals working with older adults in the community as well as in long-term care facilities. This book provides an excellent foundation for professionals and students who are or will be facilitating leisure opportunities for older adults."

Jerome F. Singleton, PhD
Professor of Leisure Studies,
School of Health and Human Performance,
Dalhousie University,
Halifax, Nova Scotia

The Haworth Press®
New York • London • Oxford

Leisure in Later Life

Third Edition

HAWORTH Leisure and Recreation
Michael J. Leitner, PhD and Sara F. Leitner, MA
Senior Co-Editors

Leisure Enhancement, Third Edition by Michael J. Leitner and Sara F. Leitner

Leisure in Later Life, Third Edition by Michael J. Leitner and Sara F. Leitner

Leisure in Later Life

Third Edition

Michael J. Leitner, PhD
Sara F. Leitner, MA

The Haworth Press®
New York • London • Oxford

The Haworth Press, Inc., 10 Alice Street, Binghamton, NY 13904-1580.

Cover design by Lora Wiggins.

Library of Congress Cataloging-in-Publication Data

Leitner, Michael J.
    Leisure in later life / Michael J. Leitner, Sara F. Leitner.—3rd ed.
        p. cm.
    Includes bibliographical references and index.
    ISBN 0-7890-1535-8 (Hard : alk. paper) — ISBN 0-7890-1536-6 (Soft : alk. paper)
        1. Aged—Recreation—United States. 2. Recreation centers—United States. 3. Recreation leaders—Training of—United States. I. Leitner, Sara F. II. Title.

GV184.L45 2004
790.1'926'0973—dc22
                                                                                            2003025496

CONTENTS

Chapter 4. Recreation in Residential Communities for Older Adults   **65**

Michael J. Leitner
Sara F. Leitner
Philip D. Shapiro
Nancy A. Shapiro

Chapter 5. Nursing Homes   **91**

PART II: FOUNDATIONS

Chapter 6. Recreation Leadership Principles   **113**

Chapter 7. Program Planning Principles   **135**

PART IV: ISSUES IN PROVIDING LEISURE SERVICES FOR ELDERS

ABOUT THE AUTHORS

Michael J. Leitner, PhD, is a Professor in the Department of Recreation and Parks Management at California State University in Chico, California. **Sara F. Leitner, MA,** is an instructor in Special Education and Adapted Physical Education at Butte College in Oroville, California. They are co-authors of the textbook *Leisure Enhancement,* Third Edition (Haworth) and *How to Improve Your Life Through Leisure.* They have co-authored numerous articles on the topic of leisure and aging, and have been invited to be speakers at conferences around the world.

Preface

Leisure in Later Life is intended for use as the following:

1. a basic textbook for students in college and university courses dealing specifically with the topic of leisure and aging;
2. a supplementary textbook for courses in the psychology of aging, social work with elders, health in later years, therapeutic recreation, introduction to special populations, adapted physical education, and courses in principles of recreation leadership and programming;
3. a reference text for fieldwork and practicum students working with elders;
4. a reference text for activity directors in nursing homes, recreation leaders in senior centers, adult day care centers, and retirement communities, and other personnel involved in the provision of leisure services to elders; and
5. a sourcebook for the in-service training of volunteers and entry-level personnel working with elders.

The third edition of this book has been revised a great deal, especially Chapters 1, 4, 11, and includes a new chapter (17) on the topic of global perspectives on leisure in later life.

The diversity of the older population is recognized in this book. The chapters on leadership, program planning, evaluation, techniques, exercise, adapted dance, programs, intergenerational activities, and leisure counseling are designed to provide useful information for work with elders in any setting. The chapters on the particular settings for recreational programs for elders are intended to supply information that will provide ideas on how to apply the material in the aforementioned chapters to work with elders in these various settings.

The first chapter presents a general overview of the older population and the importance of leisure in the lives of elders. The next four chapters constitute Part I of the book, Settings. Included in this section are chapters on senior centers, senior day care centers, nursing homes, and retirement housing. Part II, Foundations, includes chapters on leadership, program planning, evaluation, and leisure counseling. Part III, Resources for Recreation Programs for Elders, includes chapters on intergenerational activity, exercise, adapted dance, programs, and techniques. Part IV, Issues in Providing Leisure Services for Elders, includes chapters on the role of recreation in hospice care, sexuality in later life, global perspectives on leisure in later life, and leisure in later life in the future.

Leisure in Later Life covers a broad range of topics. Both theoretical information and material with clear practical applications are presented in this book. Thus, the book is truly a valuable sourcebook for the provision of recreation services to elders.

Acknowledgments

The authors wish to acknowledge the important contributions of numerous individuals and organizations to the successful completion of this book:

1. Phil and Nancy Shapiro, for their extensive contribution to Chapter 4;
2. the Department of Recreation and Parks Management at California State University, Chico, for their help and support;
3. Shalini Singh for her contributions to the section on India in Chapter 17;
4. Gilad Scher for his contributions to the section on Israel in Chapter 17;
5. Harumi Karel and Nozomi Sato of the Center on Aging at the University of Hawaii at Manoa for their contribution to the section on Japan in Chapter 17;
6. Mike Garmise, Shlomo Zidkiyahu, David Ben Sira, and others at the Zinman College of the Wingate Institute in Netanya, Israel, for their assistance;
7. Uri Schaefer, the director of the Wingate Institute in Netanya, Israel;
8. The University of Hawaii at Manoa for technical assistance;
9. The Department of Kinesiology and Leisure Science at The University of Hawaii at Manoa;
10. Crestwood Convalescent Hospital and Riverside Convalescent Hospital in Chico, California, for photographs;
11. Paul Shepherd and Ed Ansello for their contributions to the section in Chapter 11 on recreation and the rural elderly;
12. Yvonne Harahousou of the World Leisure and Recreation Association (WLRA) for her efforts on behalf of the WLRA Commission on Leisure in Later Life that made Chapter 17 possible;
13. Gloria Leitner for her assistance with the literature review for the third edition;
14. Don Penland of the College of Communication and Education at California State University, Chico, for computer assistance;
15. Kathryn Braun and Michael Cheang of the Center on Aging at the University of Hawaii at Manoa for assistance with Chapter 17; and

16. all of the very helpful and professional staff at The Haworth Press who have been instrumental in helping us produce quality textbooks over the years.

Last, but not least, special thanks to all of our family and close friends for their inspiration and interest in this book.

Chapter 1

Introduction to Leisure Services for Elders

INTRODUCTION

The topic of leisure services for elders is one of growing importance. One reason for the increased concern for leisure services for elders is the continuous growth in the population of older adults. According to the Administration on Aging (2003), there were 35 million adults in the United States age sixty-five and over in the year 2000, up 12 percent since 1990. Other reasons for the increased concern for leisure services for elders are that elders have more free time than other adult age groups and that research has demonstrated the strong influence of satisfaction with leisure activities on quality of life (Russell, 1990). The purpose of this chapter is to present an introduction to the field of leisure services for elders. Topics covered in the chapter include definitions of basic terminology used throughout the book, statistics on demographic characteristics of the older population, the current status of leisure and recreational services for elders, and research on the importance of leisure to elders. The learning objectives of this chapter are to be able to

1. define the terms *elders, leisure, recreation, therapeutic recreation, frail, high functioning, limited mobility,* and *low-functioning elders;*
2. cite statistics on the size, age, health status, education, economic status, and living conditions of elders, and the implications of these statistics for leisure services for elders;
3. contrast the present leisure activities of elders (as reported in research studies) with the optimal leisure activities for elders (based on needs and potential benefits);
4. identify five factors affecting the leisure activities of elders; and
5. cite a minimum of five research studies that provide evidence of the physiological and psychological benefits of recreation for elders.

TERMINOLOGY

Elders

The definition of the term *elder* for the purposes of this book is a difficult issue to address. Although age sixty-five does not necessarily denote a point in life at which dramatic biological or psychological changes occur, it is commonly used in research and in programs for elders as the minimum age. The ages sixty and even fifty-five are also often used as the minimum age for participation in recreational programs for older adults. However, should ages fifty-five, sixty, or sixty-five be used as markers of old age? Dychtwald (1997) explains that when Otto von Bismarck picked age sixty-five as the age for Germany's first pension plan in the 1880s, life expectancy was only forty-five years, about thirty years less than it is in the United States today!

The needs of younger retirees (ages fifty-five to seventy-nine) should not be ignored just because their health status is better than that of adults age eighty and over. In Chapter 11, many programs (e.g., travel programs) are discussed that meet the needs of this generally active, healthy population.

However, the main focus of this book is on adults age eighty and over, as these elders are most in need of special recreational programs and services. Most younger retirees can participate in the same recreational activities that people in younger age groups enjoy. Sometimes, younger retirees also choose to participate in leisure activities that are geared toward older partic- ipants (e.g., people in their sixties and seventies might choose to go to a senior dance where most of the attendees are age eighty and over). Never- theless, it is difficult and oftentimes inappropriate to try to program recre- ational activities for people in their sixties together with people in their eighties and nineties. The needs and ability levels tend to be different.

Therefore, in general, the term *elders* is used in this book to refer to peo- ple in the eighty and over age group—the fastest growing age group in the United States, also referred to as the "oldest-old" by gerontologists (Rimer, 1998). Based on longevity and health status statistics in developed nations, using age sixty or sixty-five as the marker of old age does not seem to make sense anymore. In practical terms, most of the participants in recreational activities in senior centers, senior day care centers, nursing homes, and vari- ous forms of retirement housing are eighty and over. The exercise (Chapter 12), adapted dance (Chapter 13), and other recreational activity ideas (Chapter 14) presented in this book are most appropriate for adults ages eighty and over.

The term *elder* is used in this book because it is both a familiar term and is one that is associated with a more positive and respectful attitude toward older adults. The terms *Golden Agers* and *the elderly* are avoided in this book, because they seem to have a negative connotation with older adults. Rimer (1999) cites a poll in which older Americans identified the label *the elderly* as the one they dislike the most, followed by the term *Golden Agers*. According to this poll, the terms most preferred were *older adults, older Americans,* and *seniors.* These terms, along with the term *elders* are used throughout the book to refer to persons age sixty-five and over.

High-Functioning, Limited-Mobility, Low-Functioning, and Frail Elders

Throughout the book, discussion on providing leisure services for elders focuses on three major categories of older adults: *high functioning;* elders with *limited mobility* or who are *moderately impaired;* and *low functioning.* For the purposes of this book, *high-functioning* elders are in good or excellent health with unrestricted mobility, and are physically, mentally, and emotionally capable of participating in most recreational programs for elders. The terms *limited mobility* or *moderately impaired* are utilized in this book to refer to older adults with chronic conditions that restrict their ability to participate in recreational activities involving a great deal of movement or strenuous exercise, but who are not necessarily confined to a wheelchair or bed. The term *low functioning* is used in this book to identify bedridden or wheelchair-bound elders with chronic conditions that limit their ability to participate in many physically and mentally demanding recreational activities. The term *frail older adult* is also used throughout this book. It refers to older adults with three or more of the following symptoms: muscle weakness, fatigue, declines in activity, a slow or unsteady gait, and weight loss (Kolata, 2002).

Leisure and Recreation

For the purposes of this book, the term *leisure* refers to free or unobligated time, time during which work, life-sustaining functions, and other obligatory activities are not performed. Although more elaborate theoretical constructs of leisure have been described in the literature (Leitner, Leitner, and Associates, 2004), the "discretionary time" definition of leisure is used for the purposes of this book because it is easier to use in attempting to identify and categorize different types of behavior. *Recreation* is defined for purposes of this book as activity conducted during leisure, usually for the purpose of enjoyment. The terms *leisure activity* and *recreation* are used synonymously in the book.

Leisure and Recreational Services, Therapeutic Recreation

The terms *leisure services* and *recreational services* are used interchangeably in this book to identify programs and activities designed to provide enjoyable experiences for people during their leisure. *Therapeutic recreation* is defined as a process that uses recreation to facilitate an improvement and/or maintenance in physical and/or mental functioning and/or to promote developmental growth (Leitner, Leitner, and Associates, 2004).

DEMOGRAPHY OF THE OLDER POPULATION

Size and Proportional Representation

The older population has increased greatly and is projected to continue to grow. Adults age sixty-five and over constituted 4 percent of the total U.S. population in 1900, and 12.4 percent by 2000 (Administration on Aging, 2003). The number of persons age eighty-five and over is projected to more than quadruple to nearly 20 million by the year 2050 (Knox, 1999). Certainly, this growth in the older population necessitates a growth in leisure services for elders.

However, the older population might grow far more rapidly (and leisure services would need to expand far more rapidly) if medical advances are made that enable people to live longer. Dr. James Vaupel, a Duke University demographer working with the National Institute on Aging, projects that by 2080 the average life span will be ninety-four for men and one hundred for women (Kolata, 1992). Vaupel's projections could very well come true if progress is made in research on cancer and heart disease (the two most prominent causes of death of people age sixty-five and over). Coupled with the trend toward a declining birth rate, it is possible that by the year 2050, elders will constitute 40 to 50 percent of the U.S. population, not 20 to 25 percent as is commonly projected. Imagine the expansion in leisure services for elders that would be needed for such a large older population!

Male/Female Ratio

Women greatly outnumber men in the older population, and the ratio gets more lopsided in the older age categories; more than 80 percent of centenarians are women ("You May Be Younger Than You Think," 2000). However, the gender gap might be narrowing in the future. Dembner (2003) cites the following statistics and projections on the gender gap among adults age sixty-five and over:

1. In 1990, there were only 67 men per 100 women, but in 2000, there were 70 men per 100 women.
2. By 2015, projections are that there will be 76 men per 100 women, and by 2025, there will be 79 men per 100 women.
3. For people born in 2000, the life expectancy is 74 years for males and 80 years for women.
4. About 40 percent of women but only 17 percent of men live alone. Whereas two-thirds of men over 75 are married, only one-quarter of women are married, although the percentage of widows dropped by 10 percent between 1980 and 2000.
5. Among those 85 and over, women outnumber men by a ratio of 5 to 2.

Because of the lopsided ratio of women to men and attitudinal barriers, such as a strong work ethic among older males, the participants in most recreation programs for elders, whether they are offered at senior centers, day care centers, nursing homes, or retirement communities or homes, are predominantly female. Therefore, recreation programs tend to be geared toward meeting the needs and interests of women. However, special efforts are also needed to encourage men to become involved in programs and activities. If programs are perceived as being female oriented, then men might not be inclined to participate.

The idea of making special efforts to meet the leisure needs of older men is extremely important. Too often, the leisure preferences of older men are ignored because they are a minority within the older population, and many people in the field of gerontology believe, as McPherson (1999) states, "aging is a woman's issue." Although some statistics support this statement (e.g., the disproportionate number of women in the older population, higher poverty rates for older women, and the greater likelihood of older women to be widowed), it is important to note that white males ages sixty-five to seventy-four commit suicide at a rate that is nearly five times greater than that of white women and fourteen times greater than that of black women (Bandon, 1997). These statistics should alert leisure services providers for elders to pay special attention to the needs of men. Because there are so many more single women than single men in the older population, and widowed men are much more likely than widowed women to remarry, people often joke that single older males "have it made," and that "the women are knocking down their doors." However, this seems to be a myth. Based on years of experience working with elders in a variety of settings, it seems that older men tend to suffer from depression and loneliness more often than do females. Rodriguez (2001) states that the number of elderly widowers increased 64 percent since 1950, and that loneliness is a major problem among these 2 million senior widowers because widowers struggle more than widows to live without a spouse, particularly in terms of social and emotional needs. Meanwhile, Dembner (2002b) cites research indicating that a majority of older women say that the experience of aging is better than they expected. Perhaps greater emphasis on meeting older men's leisure needs and preferences can help to reduce their loneliness and depression, and also lower their suicide rates.

In order to gain further insight into the leisure-related differences between males and females in later life, Exercise 1.1 follows.

After completing Exercise 1.1, answer the following questions. How similar were the responses of the males and females you interviewed? Did the males or the females seem more active? Did the males or the females seem happier? The responses to some of these questions can be utilized again in answering Exercise 1.2, presented later in the chapter.

Age and Health Status

There are more adults age sixty-five and over in the United States than ever before, and the population of older adults is also becoming older. Statistics indicate that from 1982 to 1995, the population of adults ages eighty-five and over rose nearly 50 percent, whereas the population of those ages sixty-five to seventy-four grew less than 20 percent (Kolata, 1996). The number of centenarians is also rising. Rimer (1998) cites projections for the U.S. population of centenarians rising from 72,000 in the year 2000 to over 100,000 by the year 2005; 447,000 by the year 2040; and 834,000 by the year 2080. It appears that the aging of the older population will necessitate an expansion in leisure services geared toward low-functioning or frail elders. Statistics indicate that whereas only 3 percent of adults aged sixty-five to sixty-nine are frail, 20 percent to 30 percent of those aged eighty or older are frail (Kolata, 2002). Similarly, the prevalence of memory loss and dementia varies greatly among different age groups within the population of older adults. At age sixty-five, only about 1 percent of people experience some mental decline; about 10 percent of those who live to age seventy-five experience some mental decline; the figure jumps to almost 50 percent for those who live to age eighty-five (Duenwald, 2003). Many of the oldest old have hearing and visual impairments, arthritis, or other impairments (Bizjak, 1993), although Hilts (1999) cites research indicating that

EXERCISE 1.1. Comparison of Leisure in Later Life of Males and Females

Instructions:

1. Try to interview at least two males and two females age eighty or over.
2. Try to find out information about current leisure activities, including frequency of participation, satisfaction with the activities, and desired activities.
3. Try to gain insight into attitudes toward leisure/work ethic.

Topic	Males' Responses	Females' Responses
Leisure activities		
Activity level/frequency of participation		
Satisfaction with leisure activities		
Most desired leisure activities		
Leisure attitudes/work ethic		

centenarians are surprisingly healthy, in many ways healthier than people twenty or thirty years younger than them.

Some of the differences in health status among different age groups within the older population are highlighted in Table 1.1.

The statistics in Table 1.1 illustrate the point made earlier in the chapter regarding the different needs and abilities of adults eighty and over versus younger retirees in their sixties and seventies. The percentage of adults with chronic conditions requiring them to need assistance with daily activities is more than double among those ages eighty and over compared to those ages seventy-five to seventy-nine. Compared to those in ages sixty-five to sixty-nine, the percentage of those ages eighty and over needing assistance is four times greater! Similarly, a much higher percentage of those in the eighty and over age group have severe disabilities as compared to the other age groups within the older population. Because the eighty and over age group is the fastest growing segment of the population and is also the one with the highest incidence of people having severe disabilities or needing assistance, it seems that there will be a strong need to expand therapeutic recreation services for older adults.

In addition to physical disabilities, there is the problem of depression, which affects approximately 35 percent of frail elders, and dementia, which is estimated to affect 40 percent of those age eighty and over (Kunstler, 2001). However, research indicates that dementia is *not* inevitable with old age. Many centenarians seem to survive the years in perfect mental health (Ferguson, 1998). Furthermore, dementia is sometimes caused by something curable, such as B-12 vitamin deficiency, medication for heart disease, or depression.

Related to the problem of depression are research findings indicating that older adults might be experiencing deeper emotions than younger adults even when they appear to be showing their feelings less than younger people

TABLE 1.1. Age Differences in Health Status

Age Category	% with Severe Disability	% Needing Assistance
65-69	30.7	8.1
70-74	28.3	10.5
75-79	38.0	16.9
80+	57.6	34.9

Source: Administration on Aging, 2003.

(Goldberg, 2002b). Older adults are obviously more prone to experiencing the loss of a loved one (e.g., a spouse, sibling, or close friend) and although they might not outwardly appear to be grieving, their grief is often much deeper than that of a young person.

However, some data indicates that older adults are becoming healthier and disability rates are declining. Recer (2001) cites a study by the National Institute on Aging which indicates that among adults age sixty-five and over, the percentage with a disability declined from 26 percent in 1982 to 19.7 percent in 1999. There is also research in progress which indicates that frailty is *not* an inevitable consequence of aging and that perhaps it can be prevented through healthy lifestyle habits, especially regular exercise (Kolata, 2002). Another study of 1939 and 1940 University of Pennsylvania graduates shows how older adults with healthier lifestyle habits tend to have lower rates of disability. The disability index was three times greater for seventy-five-year-olds in the high-risk lifestyle group as opposed to the low-risk lifestyle group (Brody, 1998). The lifestyle groups were based on weight, exercise, and use of tobacco. In this study, it was found that those in the low-risk group remained free of even minor disabilities for up to seven years longer than those in the high-risk group (Associated Press, 1998).

Another lifestyle habit that affects the health of older adults is alcohol consumption. There is an alarmingly high rate of heavy drinking and binge drinking among older Americans, and it is especially dangerous for those taking medications for conditions such as high blood pressure and arthritis (Tye, 1999).

Furthermore, alcohol consumption can increase the risk of falling, already a major problem among older adults. Studies indicate that about one-third of adults age sixty-five and over fall each year and that 10,000 of them die from injuries related to falls (Kleinfeld, 2003). However, falls can be prevented and are not a normal part of aging.

Education and Economic Status

The increasing level of education among elders might cause disability rates among older adults to decline further. According to Barringer (1993), several studies have found that higher levels of education are associated with higher incomes, better nutrition, and better health care. It is estimated that in 1980, more than 60 percent of U.S. adults ages eighty-five to eighty-nine had fewer than eight years of schooling, but by 2015, that figure will drop to 10 to 15 percent (Kolata, 1996). Thus, there is reason for hope that an active leisure lifestyle can be pursued in later life. According to Netz

(1989), elders with higher levels of education seem to have a greater command of their free time and a more optimistic attitude toward life.

Another way that increasing education levels can benefit older adults is that it will possibly reduce prejudice against elders (ageism). Research indicates that even older adults have widespread bias against elders (Goldberg, 2002a). Reducing this bias against elders can have significant implications for health. One study found that people age fifty and over who had a positive view of aging lived an average of seven years longer than those with more negative views (Goldberg, 2002a).

The economic status of elders points to the need for publicly provided leisure services for low-income elders and to the great potential of the market for private recreation enterprises, resorts, and tourism for the substantial number of wealthy elders. According to the Administration on Aging (2003), the poverty rate for adults age sixty-five and over in 2001 was at a historic low, 10.1 percent. The median income in 2001 for older adults was $19,688 for males and $11,313 for females. Racial and ethnic minority elderly, constituting 16 percent of the older population in the United States in 2000 and projected to comprise 25 percent in 2030 (Administration on Aging, 2003), are disadvantaged both in terms of economic status and education. According to Allison and Smith (1990), a higher percentage of Hispanic and black elders live at or below the poverty line. In terms of education, approximately 20 percent of Hispanic and black elders finished four years of high school or more, compared to 50 percent of white elders.

People over fifty control 75 percent of the nation's wealth and half the discretionary income (McCormick, 1991). In Canada, people ages fifty and over control 55 percent of all discretionary spending and 75 percent of all personal assets (Wengler, 1992). According to Hudson and Rich (1993), over 20 percent of all trips in the United States were taken by people fifty-five and over, which represents the third largest segment of the U.S. travel market. Adults fifty and over take 72 percent of recreational vehicle (RV) trips, 70 percent of bus trips, and constitute 70 percent of cruise passengers (Bandon, 1997).

It is hoped that the economic status of elders will improve as the educational level of the older population continues to rise. Higher educational levels combined with improved economic status should enable the provision of a broader range of leisure services for elders in the future.

Living Arrangements

Most elders live in the community. According to Kunstler (2001), 70 percent of older adults spend the rest of their lives where they were living at age sixty-five, and 86 percent say that they want to stay where they are as they grow older. Only 3.4 percent live in nursing homes, down from 6.2 percent in 1982 (Recer, 2001), although this figure rises to 20 percent for those eighty-five and older (Bizjak, 1993). There has been a sharp rise in the numbers and proportions of elders living alone in the United States, with 30 percent of all noninstitutionalized older adults living alone, including 50 percent of women age seventy-five and over (Administration on Aging, 2003).

Perhaps related to the increase in the proportion of elders living alone is the prominence of loneliness and depression as problems confronting elders. Riddick and Keller (1992) report that 12 to 30 percent of noninstitutionalized elders are lonely, and 10 to 25 percent have clinically diagnosed depression. The problems of loneliness and depression are reflected in suicide statistics, particularly the high suicide rates for older males (Barrow, 1989). As discussed in the next section, recreation can help to alleviate problems such as loneliness and depression. First, the following list is presented to summarize the demographic statistics on elders cited in this section of the chapter.

Proportional representation:	12.4 percent
Life expectancy:	77.2
Healthy life span:	63 for females; 60 for males
Disability life span:	15 for females; 12 for males
Health (for those 65-74):	73.9 percent have no limitations in their activities; only 3 to 10 percent of adults age 65+ are affected by dementia
Health (for those 80+):	26.4 percent have no limitations in their activities; about 40 percent of adults age 80+ are affected by dementia
Psychological well-being:	12 to 30 percent are lonely; 10 to 25 percent have clinically diagnosed depression
Ratio of females to males:	3 to 2; among those 85+: 5 to 2
Fastest growing segment:	The 85 and over age group
Economic status:	Majority ages 65 to 74 are low to middle income; ages 75+ are mostly low income
Living arrangements:	30 percent live alone; 50 percent of women 75+ live alone; 3.4 percent live in nursing homes

IMPORTANCE OF RECREATION FOR ELDERS

Numerous studies document the general benefits of recreation for elders, and other studies demonstrate the specific benefits of particular types of activities.

General Benefits of Recreation

Numerous studies indicate that leisure activity is an important quality-of-life factor for elders. For example, Lawton (1994) found a positive relationship to exist between activity participation and positive psychological well-being and contentment. In addition, less hostility was found to be associated with greater participation in spectator sports, visiting out of town, being visited, and vacationing. Higher levels of activity involvement were associated with less depression, less hostility, less anxiety, and less shyness. Conversely, life satisfaction seems to suffer when there is a lack of leisure participation. In Kim's (2000) study of older urban Korean immigrants, low levels of leisure participation were related to isolation and low levels of life satisfaction.

Russell (1990) reports that satisfaction with recreation is the only significant, direct predictor of quality of life in old age. Even though the variables of sex, education, religiosity, marital status, age, income, health, and frequency of recreation activity participation were found to have significant relationships, none were significantly related to quality of life. Russell (1990) states that the value of recreation activity is determined more by the participant's satisfaction than by frequency of participation.

Meanwhile, Beck and Page (1988) found in their study of over 2,000 retired men that more involvement in activities did result in higher levels of psychological well-being. In this study, informal activities were not found to be more important in determining psychological well-being than were formal involvements.

Riddick (1993) found that for older females leisure roles emerged as the most important factor in determining life satisfaction. In particular, the three types of activities found to be correlated the most with older women's well-being were informal activity/friendship interaction, participation in community and volunteer organizations, and solitary activity.

According to Mannell (1993), retirees who have higher life satisfaction have a greater level of involvement in freely chosen activities and activities that challenge their knowledge and skills and require an investment of effort (high-investment activities). These activities also usually involve commitment, obligation, discipline, and sacrifice.

Kaufman's (1988) study of 225 male and female retirees found that both greater leisure satisfaction and leisure participation are associated with lower levels of anxiety. Kaufman (1988) states that in order to encourage maximum participation in recreational pursuits, activity directors need to address participation barriers faced by older persons, the three most significant ones being fear of crime, inadequate free time, and health-related problems.

Purcell and Keller (1989) assert that reciprocity (balanced exchange) and perceived control (the feeling of being able to predict or control one's own environment) are key characteristics of leisure activities that help elders achieve life satisfaction. Activity directors can maximize feelings of control by giving participants input in planning, implementing, and evaluating activities, and by promoting participation in activities in which elders have proficiency and will feel in control. Reciprocity can be facilitated through the exchange of nontangibles such as information and compliments, and even small tangible gifts (Purcell and Keller, 1989).

Based on the findings of McContha and McContha's (1989) study, it appears that wellness promotion is a key characteristic of leisure activities which can increase the life satisfaction of elders. Activities that promote wellness, such as exercise, sports, and dance are therefore ideal activities to include in efforts to improve elders' life satisfaction. Also, activities that allow a person to display humor can promote wellness and thereby enhance life satisfaction. McGuire and Boyd (1993) report that in one study, a positive relationship was found between self-perceived health and the frequency with which a person displays humor in a variety of situations.

According to Netz (1989), congruence between actual and desired use of time, rather than amount of activity or selected leisure activities contributes to life satisfaction in later life. Similarly, Seleen (1982) found that the degree of congruence between actual and desired time utilization was significantly correlated with life satisfaction. Seleen's study found satisfaction with leisure to significantly contribute to life satisfaction. Studies by Graney (1975), Ray (1979), Knapp (1977), Edwards and Klemmack (1973), DeCarlo (1972), Adams and Groen (1975), Frekany and Leslie (1975), Emes (1977), and Owens (1982) have also found that leisure activity is significantly related to enhanced life satisfaction, psychological well-being, and various physical and social benefits. Positive leisure participation patterns enhance happiness, which in turn is related to greater longevity. Recent studies (Duenwald, 2002) have correlated longevity with positive thinking and optimism, traits that are enhanced by positive leisure behavior. Healthy lifestyles (including daily recreational exercise) and having strong relationships (that can be enhanced through social recreational activities) have a greater impact on how well people age than does heredity (Selland, 1999).

Research cited by Pollak (1999) also seems to indicate that higher levels of participation in recreational activities, even nonstrenuous ones such as playing cards, going to movies, or visiting friends, can help older adults to live longer. A study involving 2,761 older Americans over a twelve-year period found that those who participated in physical, social, and "productive" (cooking, shopping, gardening, and volunteering) leisure activities lived longer. In another study on the topic of longevity in which 4,000 North Carolina residents age sixty-four and older were studied over a six-year period, it was found that those who attended religious services regularly were 46 percent less likely to have died (Jackson, 1999). Another study ("Help others, for a longer life," 2002) found that helping others can enhance the longevity of older adults. Volunteering is a leisure activity that can provide the opportunity to help others. Of all leisure activities, regular exercise is the most important one of all for increasing longevity and promoting physical and psychological health (Brody, 2000).

As suggested by Adams (1988), the relationship between physiological and psychological well-being and participation in leisure activities may not necessarily be one-way. In particular, Adams studied friendship activity and found that greater psychological well-being can lead to greater involvement in friendship activity. In a related vein, McAuley (1993) states that self-efficacy (the belief in one's abilities to meet the demands of a situation) is related to exercise both ways: Greater self-efficacy is related to greater participation in physical activities; greater participation in physical activities is related to greater self-efficacy. Therefore, leisure activity participation can have a "snowball effect" in that participation can lead to enhanced psychological well-being and life satisfaction, which in turn can lead to greater involvement in other activities. Related to this concept is research indicating that the more people are socially engaged, the better off they are cognitively, and that in addition to social activities, recreational activities such as playing cards and checkers that were mentally stimulating could reduce the risk of Alzheimer's disease (Nagourney, 2002). Other recreational activities that are recommended for promoting mental sharpness in later life include taking courses, reading, hobbies, puzzles, regular exercise, traveling to new places, gardening, knitting or crocheting, and group activities (Brody, 2002). Another study involving 1,772 adults age sixty-five and over found that those with high levels of leisure activity had 38 percent less risk of developing dementia (American Academy of Neurology, 2001). Certainly, older adults who are not affected by Alzheimer's disease and are thinking more clearly are more capable of participating in a variety of leisure activities. As discussed in the next section, involvement in these other leisure activities can also have a variety of specific mental and physical benefits.

Specific Benefits of Recreation

The mental benefits of recreational activities have been widely documented. Some of the leisure-related factors that are related to good mental functioning in old age are having active involvements through life, continuing keen mental interests after retirement, liking to learn new things, enjoying to go new places, and getting regular physically strenuous activity (Goleman, 1994). One study found that retirees who remained active in pursuits such as walking, bicycling, or gardening maintained their mental functioning at a higher level than did inactive retirees (Kolata, 1991). In another study ("Shaping Up," 2000), participation in a regular walking program for six months was found to improve cognitive skills (including those essential to driving a car) of sedentary older adults. In one study (Jaret, 1996), physically fit older men were found to have surprisingly youthful-looking brain waves. According to Chase (1994), with training and exercise, people in their seventies and eighties can sharpen mental skills such as spatial orientation or inductive reasoning. Dembner (2002) reports that findings from national studies indicate that most mental decline is caused by disease and disuse, not advancing years, and that recreational activities that provide either aerobic exercise or mental exercise can help the brain acquire new cells and add new connections among brain cells in order to overcome other deficits.

Bridge is apparently one example of an active involvement/mental interest that can help maintain optimal mental functioning. Schafer (1991) cites a study in which elderly bridge players were found to have better memory and reasoning abilities than nonplayers. According to Schafer (1991), activities such as crossword puzzles, classes, stimulating conversations, and challenging hobbies probably have the same effects as bridge has.

Memory loss is one of the aspects of declining mental abilities commonly associated with advanced age. A research study of nursing home residents indicates that some types of memory loss in old age can actually be reversed by giving elders more *reason* to remember things (Schafer, 1992). In the study, two groups in the nursing home were compared on tests of short-term memory and ratings of overall mental alertness. One group was given tokens redeemable for gifts when they answered questions testing their memory correctly. The other group was given tokens only as mementos when they answered questions correctly. At the end of the study, the group that received gifts performed much better than the other group on tests of short-term memory and overall mental alertness, and were also found to be physically healthier. Follow-up studies two years later found that only 7 percent of the group receiving gifts had died, compared with 30 percent of the other group. In conclusion, this study shows that when there is more meaning, more motivation to remember things, elders' mental and physical health can be affected positively. The important point for recreation programs is not that gifts need to be given to program participants but that, in a variety of ways, elders need to be made to feel that the programs are meaningful and important. Motivating elders is no small challenge, and not only in the United States. As Simons (1992) reports, French retirement home administrators state that their most difficult task is to keep people busy and motivated, because by age seventy-five (the age when most people come to live in a retirement home), they have been feeling useless for a long time and have given up.

In a related vein, the problems of loneliness and depression (discussed earlier in the chapter) can be alleviated through specific recreational activities. Pennix et al. (2002) found that aerobic exercise significantly lowered depressive symptoms in adults age sixty and over. Riddick and Keller (1992) report that several studies have shown that participation in a bibliotherapy program can lead to a significant reduction in depression. Riddick and Keller (1992) state that dance/movement has been found effective in reducing loneliness, and that activities such as music programs, video game play, and pet therapy are effective in improving social interaction (and thereby help to reduce loneliness). Creecy, Wright, and Berg (1982) found that social and community activities relieve feelings of loneliness, whereas watching television reinforces feelings of loneliness.

Physically active recreational activities, such as exercise, sports, and dance, are beneficial for elders in a variety of ways. Research (Winslow, 2002) indicates that older adults can reverse the effects of aging by decades by starting a moderate but consistent exercise program in later life. Weight-bearing and resistive exercise can reduce bone loss with aging and increase bone density, thereby reducing the risk of osteoporotic fractures (Lindsey, 2002). Endurance, strength, and balance training can also improve mobility and reduce the risk of falling (Lindsey, 2002). Tai chi is an activity that is particularly effective for older adults in reducing the risk of falling. In one study (Lindsey, 2002), participation in a tai chi program reduced multiple-fall risk in older adult fallers by 47.5 percent over a period of a few months. Other research (Li et al., 2002) found that a six-month tai chi program led to improvements in global self-esteem, domain-specific physical self-worth, and physical strength and condition. McAuley and Rudolph (1995) conducted a literature review of thirty-eight studies on elders and found the majority of the studies reporting a positive relationship between physical activity and psychological well-being. The longer the program, the more positive the results tended to be. A great deal of research has been completed that further documents the benefits of physical activity for elders, as discussed in the chapters on exercise and dance that appear later in this book. The following list is presented as a summary of the benefits of desirable leisure activities such as exercise, sports, dance, music, art, social activity, traveling, and education.

Physiological Benefits	Social/Psychological/Emotional Benefits
Improved circulation	Greater psychological well-being
Improved respiration	Higher quality of life
Greater flexibility	Higher morale and life satisfaction
Greater strength	Higher self-esteem, self-concept, and self-efficacy
Greater endurance	
More energy	Keener mental abilities
Lower blood pressure	Feelings of achievement and accomplishment
Lower cholesterol	
Improved mobility	Greater optimism
Greater physical independence	Greater levels of social interaction
Greater longevity	Laughter
Improved general health	Lower anxiety and hostility
Reduced risk of osteoporotic fractures	Lower incidence of loneliness and depression
Reduced risk of falls	Improved perceived health
	Reduced fear of falling

Clearly, the benefits elders can derive from the more desirable leisure pursuits are impressive. Unfortunately, as discussed in the next section of the chapter, the current rates of participation by elders in the more desirable leisure pursuits, such as physical activities, are abysmal.

CURRENT STATUS OF LEISURE SERVICES FOR ELDERS

Elders, and American adults in general, engage in sedentary recreation such as watching television and reading newspapers much more than they participate in active forms of recreation. However, as reported by Fisher, Pickering, and Li (2002), older adults are even less active than younger adults (e.g., the incidence of sedentary lifestyles is almost twice as great among women seventy-five and over as compared to women ages thirty to forty-four). Almost 40 percent of men and over 50 percent of women age seventy-five and over are inactive, meaning that they do not participate in at least thirty minutes of moderate physical activity on all or most days of the week. Walking is the most popular physical activity of older adults (more than 50 percent participation), whereas participation rates for team sports, racquet sports, cycling, aerobics, gym, and jogging are each less than 10 percent (Fisher, Pickering, and Li, 2002). However, there is no need to give up physically active leisure pursuits because of age. A study that compared physiological measurements of younger and older scuba divers found that, physiologically, there is no reason why older adults cannot continue to scuba dive ("Scuba Diving Forever. Almost," 2003). Yet many older adults cease participating in a variety of leisure pursuits, even ones that are not physically demanding. A longitudinal study of older adults in Canada (Strain et al., 2002) found that theater, movies, spectator sports, and travel were leisure activities which were least likely to be continued, whereas watching television and reading were leisure activities most likely to be continued. The researchers concluded that leisure education could enhance elders' participation in the more desirable, beneficial leisure activities.

A study that compared the involvement of older adults in leisure activities before and after retirement found that time spent watching television, doing hobbies, reading, seeing relatives, seeing friends, participating in religious activities, and traveling within a 100-mile radius increased after retirement. There was no change in the amount of time spent in physical exercise and social activities, but there was less time spent seeing former co-workers, drinking alcohol, and engaging in sexual relations (Rosenkoetter, Garris, and Engdahl, 2001). A study comparing the leisure activities of adults with disabilities and without disabilities, ages eighty to eighty-five, found that those with disabilities had a lower but undiminished commitment in overall activity. Overall, the preferred activities of both groups were in the emotional, spiritual, and social categories, and engagement in valued activities did not change significantly over a one-year period (Lefrancois et al., 2001).

According to MacNeil et al. (1987), the research literature on leisure patterns of elders indicates that:

1. the most popular activities are sedentary-isolate (e.g., watching television) and sedentary-social (e.g., visiting friends);
2. most leisure activities occur at home or close to home;
3. participation in active-social (e.g., sports) and active-isolate (e.g., fishing) activities is infrequent; and
4. more meaningful leisure activities are needed that place increased emphasis on cognitive and physical abilities (e.g., active-social and active-isolate activities).

A study on time use by frail older adults in nursing homes, in assisted living facilities, and in the community with home health services (Pruchno and Rose, 2002) found that in all three settings, most of the day is spent alone and at home. There is an underutilized potential for improving the lives of these older adults through leisure activities, given the fact that nearly 60 percent of their time in a typical day is unobligated. Earlier studies also found that the leisure activities of elders are sedentary, the most popular ones being watching television, reading, gardening, and indoor hobbies (Leitner and Leitner, 1996). Brody (1998) reports that approximately 60 percent of older adults engage in virtually no leisure time physical activity, and McAuley (1993) reports that less than 10 percent regularly participate in vigorous activity. Thus, approximately 60 percent of elders lead sedentary lifestyles, and 90 percent are underactive.

Despite the low rates of participation by elders in physical activities, there are numerous examples of elders participating and excelling in a variety of sports and other leisure pursuits. For example, McClurg (1990) discusses "late bloomers," people in their sixties and seventies who enter into competitive sports after retirement. McClurg (1990) cites a sixty-seven-year-old woman who is winning medals in cross-country skiing events and in cycling competitions as one example of how elders can excel in sports. Another example is seventy-two-year-old Hugh Anglin, who cycles 150 miles a week and engages in long-distance treks such as a 920-mile ride from Yellowstone to Sante Fe ("Wheeling by in the Fast Lane," 1992). Albert Hanna, at age seventy-two, set out to be the oldest person to reach the top (29,035 feet) of Mt. Everest (Henning, 2002). Then there is Norman Vaughan, who at age eighty-eight (just three days before his eighty-ninth birthday!) climbed the 10,302-foot summit in the South Pole named after him, "Mt. Vaughan" (Mifflin, 1995). His message: "Young and old: Dream big, and dare to fail." Duane (2001) presents an upbeat image of leisure in later life in his article about older adults who still enjoy the sport of surfing, including a man named John Ball, who at age ninety-four is America's oldest living surfer.

Older adults can also enjoy a variety of volunteering opportunities as a leisure experience while helping others. A relatively new form of volunteering for elders is police work. Zaslow (2003) reports that older adults are volunteering for police forces in record numbers. They enjoy their work, are proud of it, and have become indispensable in some counties in Florida.

Statistics lend some hope that elders of the future will be more active. McClurg (1990) reports that 4.3 percent of all downhill skier visits to Colorado were by people ages fifty-five to sixty-four; 1.2 percent were by skiers sixty-five and older. Canadian senior center users provide concrete evidence of the possibilities for changing patterns of leisure behavior and the ability to become more active. According to Pageot (1986), in 1973 and in 1977 the most popular leisure activities of the senior center users were watching television, listening to the radio, and reading, but in 1985, the most popular activities were adapted aquatics, lawn bowling, bowling, fitness courses, and folk dance; the top three activities of 1973 and 1977 did not even make the top ten list in 1985.

Musicians and artists can continue to excel in later life. Schonberg (1990) writes of the pianist Mieczyslaw Horszowski who, at age ninety-seven, gave a piano recital at Carnegie Hall and accepted invitations to play a dozen or so concerts around the world.

In summary, a number of elders are actively engaged in beneficial leisure pursuits such as sports, dance, exercise, drama, music, art, social activity, traveling, and education. Unfortunately, the majority of elders are presently spending most of their free time in less beneficial leisure activities, such as watching television, reading newspapers, and relaxation. How different is the current status of leisure for elders as compared with that of younger adults?

Exercise 1.2 is presented to provide an opportunity to compare the leisure activities of elders and college students, and to gain insight into the reasons for the differences that exist. After you have completed Exercise 1.2, please consider the following questions: What are the reasons for the differences in the activities listed in the three columns? What are the reasons for the differences in the activities cited by the three elders you interviewed?

Perhaps some of the elders you interviewed are active, and some are sedentary. Being seventy or eighty years old is certainly a more pleasant prospect if your body and mind are in good shape and you are able to enjoy most of the recreational activities that you currently enjoy. Doctors suggest the following lifestyle guidelines (many of them are leisure related) for people in their twenties to slow down the aging process and facilitate a happier and healthier later life (Shanahan, 1999):

1. Exercise regularly.
2. Do not drink alcohol excessively.
3. Limit sun exposure.
4. Build up bone density (through exercise and diet).
5. Don't smoke, or quit if you do.
6. Eat foods that are rich in vitamin E.
7. Take a positive attitude.

These suggestions should prove to be beneficial in promoting maximal leisure well-being in later life. However, as discussed in the next section of the chapter, a variety of factors affect the leisure behavior of older adults.

EXERCISE 1.2. Leisure Activities of Elders and College Students

Instructions

1. In the first column, list the most common leisure activities of your classmates, based on brief interviews of at least three of your classmates.
2. In the second column, list the most common leisure activities of elders, based on brief interviews with at least three elders.
3. In the third column, list the most common leisure activities of the elders you interviewed, when they were young adults.
4. After completing this exercise, answer the following questions:
   a. How do the leisure activities of the elders you interviewed compare with the leisure activities of elders as reported in the literature?
   b. Are the leisure activities of the elders when they were young adults more similar to their current activities, or to the activities of your classmates?
   c. How similar are the current leisure activities of the elders you interviewed to those when they were young adults?
   d. Based on this exercise and your answers to the previous questions, would you predict your leisure activities in later life to be more similar to your present activities or to those of today's elders?

Classmates' Activities	Elders' Activities	Elders' Past Activities

FACTORS AFFECTING RECREATION
PARTICIPATION PATTERNS

The factors affecting leisure activity participation patterns of elders are numerous and complex. According to research by Searle and Iso-Ahola (1988) on the determinants of leisure behavior of elders, leisure attitude is the most important factor influencing leisure behavior. Those with more positive attitudes toward leisure were more likely to participate in leisure activities. However, the Protestant work ethic is a strongly valued belief for many elders, which can create negative attitudes toward leisure and inhibit participation in recreational activities. Leisure activities that are perceived as being fun but without purpose would be scorned by elders who hold the work ethic dear. Meanwhile, elders living in retirement communities such as Leisure World (see Chapter 4) and enthusiastically participating in a variety of leisure activities such as golf, swimming, tennis, and dancing, are obviously more comfortable with the concept of leisure and are not adversely affected by negative attitudes toward leisure and a strong work ethic. Although elders with a strong work ethic might be difficult to coax onto the golf course, leisure pursuits with a productive component (e.g., hobbies that result in the production of marketable goods) can be very successful with this population. In fact, Beck and Page (1988) report that for men, solitary activities have almost as strong a positive impact on happiness as social activities. They hypothesize that solitary activities such as hobbies can promote psychological well-being in some cases more effectively than social/recreational activities because feeling productive is important to many retired men. Because women were not as prominent in the workplace years ago, the work ethic is probably not as great an obstacle to leisure for older women as it is for older men. A greater work ethic among older men than among older women can probably account for, in part, the greater participation by women than men in various recreational activity programs for elders in retirement homes, nursing homes, senior centers, day care centers, and the community.

Another leisure-related advantage that older women have compared to older men is that since women tend to be more responsible for management of kin and other social relationships, in later life women may find it easier than do men to solidify and expand informal social relationships after retirement (Szinovacz, 1992). However, older women also have leisure-related disadvantages compared to older men. As discussed by Szinovacz (1992), older women tend to be at a disadvantage economically, and also tend to have more household and family obligations that can cause them to have less free time than older men have. For example, women, more often than men, find themselves in a caregiver role for their spouse in later life. Caregivers to elders often reduce or cease leisure activities due to lack of time, feeling too tired, or having too much stress in their lives (Dunn and Strain, 2001).

Attitudes toward old age and aging have a similar effect on the leisure activity participation patterns of both older men and women. Elders that view aging and old age negatively are less inclined to be involved in leisure activity programs for senior citizens. Thus, an eighty-five-year-old, when asked why he won't go to the local senior center, might reply: "I don't like being with those old people." The same person might also shy away from involvement in more youthful leisure pursuits with the attitude that "People my age don't do things like that anymore." On the other hand, the older adult who views old age and aging positively will have no qualms about participating in activity programs for elders and will also feel comfortable engaging in youthful leisure pursuits such as skiing, skating, and even white-water rafting!

The effects of positive attitudes toward aging on the physical and mental well-being of older adults were demonstrated in a study conducted at Harvard Medical School (Cromie, 1999). In this study, there were two groups of seniors—one that was exposed to positive words about aging on a computer screen, and another group that was exposed to negative words. The walking gait of those exposed to the positive words improved by almost 10 percent, whereas the gait of those exposed to negative words did not change. The researchers concluded that improved self-image can partly reverse negative physical changes of older adults. Furthermore, the researchers concluded that stereotypes of aging have a powerful impact and possibly play a role in reduction in walking speed and lower levels of activity among older adults.

Falling is a significant health-related problem for older adults that should be a factor considered in contemplating involvement in leisure activities, but fear of falling can at times be an attitudinal barrier preventing participation in potentially beneficial leisure activities. Yardley and Smith (2002) found that beliefs about the consequences of falling motivates avoidance of leisure activities among adults ages seventy-five and over. The commonly feared consequences of falling are loss of functional independence and damage to identity. Studies indicate that 30 to 50 percent of older adults fear falling, with one of the major fears being that if they fall, their doctors or children will want to put them in a nursing home (Kleinfeld, 2003). The fear of falling can be so strong for some older adults that it prevents them from participating in almost any activity.

Another attitudinal factor related to leisure activity choices is personal leisure interests. One's interests may be influenced by spouse's activities and interests; parents' and peers' activities and interests; educational experiences and other social learning factors; the media; physical and mental abilities; activity skills; and knowledge of available leisure services. Some of these factors are beyond the control of the leisure services provider, but knowledge of available leisure services and the media are two factors over which there is some control. The media should be utilized to its greatest advantage to ensure that a maximum number of elders are aware of the full range of leisure services available to them.

A factor influencing elders' leisure interests which is beyond the control of leisure services providers is the older adult's past involvement in leisure activities. Searle and Iso-Ahola (1988) found that people who were active during their early and middle adult years were more likely to be active in later life. Iso-Ahola, Jackson, and Dunn (1994) found a great deal of stability to exist in activities across the life span, and that elders are less likely than younger adults to start new activities, replace old activities with new ones, or cease participating in current activities. Iso-Ahola, Jackson, and Dunn (1994) conclude that older persons desire more stability in their activities in order to maintain a continuation of a perceived optimal level of arousal. However, despite the apparent desire of elders to maintain stability in their activities, recreation specialists should present and encourage participation in new activities. Variety is important for people of all ages; too much stability can lead to boredom, lack of motivation, and eventually depression.

Demographic variables such as age, sex, education, socioeconomic status, health, race, and cultural and religious background also affect the recreation participation patterns of elders. Suggestions for planning activities to meet the needs of groups who vary greatly in these demographic characteristics are offered in Chapter 7, on program planning. Health status is a particularly influential variable. Health status influences the type of activities participated in, and the goals and objectives of the activities. Health problems are often cited as a factor restricting the leisure activities of elders. Searle and Iso-Ahola (1988) found present health status to be an important determinant of leisure behavior. Those in better health were more likely to participate in leisure activities. Similarly, Young, King, and Oka (1995) found that for women, poor health was a predictor of a completely sedentary lifestyle. Their study also found unmarried men and smokers to be likely candidates for being completely sedentary.

Specific health problems constrain participation in particular leisure activities. For example, poor vision was found to be the most serious problem inhibiting participation in continuing education programs (MacNeil et al., 1987). As discussed in many chapters of this book, in particular the ones on leadership, program planning, exercise, and dance, the recreation specialist can adapt activities to ensure maximal involvement and success by elders with a variety of health problems and impairments.

Other variables, such as climate, availability of transportation services, mass media services, proximity to family and friends, technological advances, and the quality, quantity, and type of recreational facilities available, influence the recreation participation patterns of elders. Fisher, Pickering, and Li (2002) state that barriers to participation of older adults in physical activities include lack of social support, insufficient disposable income, low levels of perceived self-efficacy, and fears and concerns related to safety and the environment. A study in Chicago found fear of crime to be a major deterrent to recreation behavior (MacNeil et al., 1987). Meanwhile, security/protection from crime is often cited as a desirable feature of retirement communities that encourages greater participation in activities, particularly nighttime activities.

Another major influence on the leisure activities of elders is the amount of free time available. According to MacNeil et al. (1987), lack of free time is consistently identified in the research as a major reason for reduced participation in recreational activities. However, as discussed by Leitner, Leitner, and Associates (2004), there appears to be a gap between perceived leisure and actual free time available. Although people may claim that they do not have enough time to participate in physical activities, they somehow do have enough time to watch television! Being too busy can be used as an excuse to avoid participation in activities.

However, some elders truly do have a lack of free time. First of all, not all elders are retired. For economic and other reasons, some elders continue to work well past age sixty-five. Another factor affecting free time is time spent performing household and personal care functions. Having to care for a family member who is ill can severely restrict the quantity and quality of free time available. Therefore, even though as an age group those sixty-five and over have more free time than other adults, it is inaccurate to say that all elders have a great deal of free time.

As stated, the factors affecting the leisure behavior of elders are numerous and complex. The following list summarizes these factors.

Factors Related to Greater Activity Involvement	Factors Inhibiting Activity Involvement
Positive leisure attitudes	Strong work ethic
Positive attitudes toward aging	Negative attitudes toward aging
Greater free time available	Lack of free time due to needing to care for an ill family member, or needing to work long hours for economic reasons
Feelings of safety and security	Crime/fear of crime
Good health	Poor health

Good transportation services available	Poor transportation
Higher levels of education and socio-economic status	Poverty, lower educational levels
Good facilities and programs available	Lack of available programs and facilities
Awareness of leisure opportunities	Lack of awareness of available opportunities
High level of activity involvement earlier in one's life	Low level of activity involvement earlier in one's life

SUMMARY

The older population is growing, and leisure services for elders are expanding to meet increased demand. This book is intended to provide useful information for leisure services providers, students, and volunteers of all ages working with elders of all functioning levels, in all settings. However, because the eighty-five and over population is the fastest growing segment of the older population and the number of impaired elders is steadily increasing, special emphasis is devoted in this book to the provision of leisure services for elders who are moderately impaired or low functioning. As discussed in the final chapter, career prospects for work with this segment of the older population are especially bright.

However, you need not contemplate a career in recreation and aging in order to find the information presented in the ensuing chapters useful or relevant. We are all aging, and we all need to be prepared to meet the challenges of later life. It should be clear from the information presented in this chapter that leisure is a key factor in ensuring a high quality of life in old age.

Even though you will be reading a great deal about adapting activities for moderately impaired and low-functioning elders, you should remain optimistic about your later life. Keep in mind that activities in earlier adulthood are a key determinant of activities in the third age. Your activities in later life might be nothing at all like those of elders today, if your activities today are nothing like the activities of elders when they were your age. So, keep those Rollerblades, skateboards, skis, and surfboards in good shape; you might be needing them for many years to come!

REFERENCES

Adams, M. and Groen, R. (1975). Media habits and preferences of the elderly. *Leisurability*, 2(2), 25-30.
Adams, R. G. (1988). Which comes first: Poor psychological well-being or decreased friendship activity? *Activities, Adaptation, and Aging*, 12(1/2), 27-42.

Administration on Aging (2003). Profile of older Americans: 2002. <www. seniorjournal.com>.

Allison, M. and Smith, S. (1990). Leisure and the quality of life: Issues facing racial and ethnic minority elderly. *Therapeutic Recreation Journal,* 24, 50-61.

American Academy of Neurology (2001). Leisure activity decreases risk of Alzheimer's disease. <www.sciencedaily.com/releases/2001/12/011225093636.htm>.

Associated Press (1998). Healthy living may reduce illness at end of life, study finds. *The Boston Globe,* April 9, p. A17.

Bandon, A. (1997). Aging by the numbers: Longer, healthier, better. *The New York Times Magazine,* March 9, pp. 44-45.

Barringer, F. (1993). Disability rates of elderly drop, study finds, challenging theory. *The New York Times,* April 6, pp. A1, A13.

Barrow, G. M. (1989). *Aging, the individual, and society* (Fourth edition). St. Paul, MN: West Publishing Co.

Beck, S. H. and Page, J. W. (1988). Involvement in activities and the psychological well-being of retired men. *Activities, Adaptation, and Aging,* 11(1), 31-47.

Bizjak, T. (1993). New boom generation—85 and up. *The Sacramento Bee,* January 25, pp. A1, A5.

Brody, J. E. (1998). Adding years to life and life to years. *The New York Times,* June 2, p. C7.

Brody, J. E. (2000). Adding zest to the golden years, simply. *The New York Times,* January 18, p. D8.

Brody, J. E. (2002). Better memory: It doesn't come in a pill. *The New York Times,* January 8, p. D8.

Chase, M. (1994). Feed your brain, and it may thrive in old age. *The Wall Street Journal,* November 21, p. B1.

Creecy, R. F., Wright, R., and Berg, W. E. (1982). Correlates of loneliness among the black elderly. *Activities, Adaptation, and Aging,* 3(2), 9-16.

Cromie, W. J. (1999). Exposure to positive stereotypes improves elders' health, research finds. *Harvard University Gazette,* November 4, p. 5.

DeCarlo, T. J. (1972). Recreation participation patterns and successful aging: A twin study. Unpublished doctoral dissertation, Columbia University.

Dembner, A. (2002a). Mind games: Can brain exercises help you stay sharp? *The Boston Globe,* December 10, pp. B7, B10.

Dembner, A. (2002b). Over-50 women say aging's not so bad. *The Boston Globe,* November 19, p. C4.

Dembner, A. (2003). Gender gap narrows among older adults. *The Boston Globe,* February 14, pp. A1, A10.

Duane, D. (2001). Silver surfers. *The New York Times Magazine,* April 15, pp. 38-39.

Duenwald, M. (2002). Power of positive thinking extends, it seems, to aging. *The New York Times,* November 19, pp. D1, D6.

Duenwald, M. (2003). "Oldest old" still show alertness. *The New York Times,* March 18, p. D5.

Dunn, N. J. and Strain, L. A. (2001). Caregivers at risk? Changes in leisure participation. *Journal of Leisure Research,* 33(1), 32-55.

Dychtwald, K. (1997). Gerontocracy, gerassic park, and other possible consequences of an aging society. *Innovations in Aging,* 26(2), 16-18.

Edwards, J. N. and Klemmack, D. L. (1973). Correlates of life satisfaction: A reexamination. *Journal of Gerontology,* 28(4), 497-502.

Emes, C. G. (1977). The aging process and its effects on activity selections for the elderly. *Leisurability,* 4(1), 14-17.

Ferguson, C. (1998). Fountain of youth bubbles in brains of oldest old. *Harvard University Gazette,* March 5, pp. 1, 4.

Fisher, K. J., Pickering, M. A., and Li, F. (2002). Healthy aging through active leisure: Design and methods of SHAPE—A randomized controlled trial of a neighborhood-based walking project. *World Leisure,* 44(1), 19-28.

Frekany, G. A. and Leslie, D. K. (1975). Effects of an exercise program on selected flexibility measurements of senior citizens. *Gerontologist,* 15(2), 182-183.

Goldberg, C. (2002a). Even elders reflect broad bias against the old, study finds. *The Boston Globe,* October, 28, pp. A1, A5.

Goldberg, C. (2002b). Study sees emotions deepening with age. *The Boston Globe,* November 6, p. A32.

Goleman, D. (1994). Mental decline in aging need not be inevitable. *The New York Times,* April 26, pp. B5, B7.

Graney, M. J. (1975). Happiness and social participation in aging. *Journal of Gerontology,* 30, 701-706.

"Help others, for a longer life" (2002). *The New York Times,* November 12, p. D6.

Henning, J. (2002). The old man and the peak. *The Wall Street Journal,* April 3, p. A20.

Hilts, P. J. (1999). Life at age 100 is surprisingly healthy. *The New York Times,* June 1, p. D7.

Hudson, S. D. and Rich, S. M. (1993). Group travel programs: A creative way to meet the leisure needs of older adults. *Journal of Physical Education, Recreation, and Dance,* 64(4), 38-40.

Iso-Ahola, S. E., Jackson, E. L., and Dunn, E. (1994). Starting, ceasing, and replacing leisure activities over the human life span. *Journal of Leisure Research,* 26(3), 227-249.

Jackson, N. B. (1999). Paths to a higher plane and longer life. *The New York Times,* August 17, p. D9.

Jaret, P. (1996). Think fast. *Health,* March/April, pp. 44, 46.

Kaufman, J. E. (1988). Leisure and anxiety: A study of retirees. *Activities, Adaptation, and Aging,* 11(1), 1-10.

Kim, M. S. (2000). Life satisfaction, acculturation, and leisure participation among older urban Korean immigrants. *World Leisure,* 42(2), 28-40.

Kleinfeld, N. R. (2003). For elderly, fear of falling is a risk in itself. *The New York Times,* March 5, pp. A1, A25.

Knapp, M. R. J. (1977). The activity theory of aging: An examination in the English context. *Gerontologist,* 17(6), 553-559.

Knox, R. A. (1999). Living longer is the best revenge. *The Boston Globe Magazine,* May 23, pp. 24, 35-42.

Kolata, G. (1991). Mental gymnastics. *The New York Times Magazine,* October 6, pp. 15-17, 42.

Kolata, G. (1992). New views on life spans alter forecasts on elderly. *The New York Times,* November 16, pp. A1, A11.

Kolata, G. (1996). New era of robust elderly belies the fears of scientists. *The New York Times,* February 27, pp. A1, B12.

Kolata, G. (2002). Is frailty inevitable? Some experts say no. *The New York Times,* November 19, p. D5.

Kunstler, R. (2001). New options for therapeutic recreation in the naturally occurring retirement community. *Parks and Recreation,* 36(5), 74-81.

Lawton, M. P. (1994). Personality and affective correlates of leisure activity participation by older people. *Journal of Leisure Research,* 26(2), 138-157.

Lefrancois, R., Leclerc, G., Dube, M., Hamel, S., and Gaukun, P. (2001). Valued activities of everyday life among the very old: A one year trend. *Activities, Adaptation, and Aging,* 25(3/4), 18-25.

Leitner, M. J. and Leitner, S. F. (1996). *Leisure in later life* (Second edition). Binghamton, NY: The Haworth Press.

Leitner, M. J., Leitner, S. F., and Associates (2004). *Leisure enhancement* (Third edition). Binghamton, NY: The Haworth Press.

Li, F., Hormer, P., Chaumeton, N. R., Duncan, T. E., and Duncan, S. C. (2002). Tai chi as a means to enhance self-esteem: A randomized controlled trial. *Journal of Applied Gerontology,* 21(1), 70-89.

Lindsey, C. (2002). Fighting frailty in the elderly. *Biomechanics,* 9(7), 20-30.

MacNeil, R., Teague, M., McGuire, F., and O'Leary, J. T. (1987). Older Americans and outdoor recreation: A literature synthesis. *Therapeutic Recreation Journal,* 21, 18-25.

Mannell, R. C. (1993). High investment activity and life satisfaction among older adults. In Kelly, J. R. (ed.), *Activity and aging: Staying involved in later life* (pp. 125-145). Newbury Park, CA: Sage.

McAuley, E. (1993). Self-efficacy, physical activity, and aging. In Kelly, J. R. (ed.), *Activity and aging: Staying involved in later life* (pp. 187-205). Newbury Park, CA: Sage.

McAuley, E. and Rudolph, D. (1995). Physical activity, aging, and psychological well-being. *Journal of Physical Activity and Aging,* 3(1), 67-96.

McClurg, K. (1990). Blood, sweat, and years. *Summit Magazine,* Spring, pp. 21-23.

McContha, J. T. and McContha, P. D. (1989). The study of the relationship between wellness and life satisfaction of older adults. *Activities, Adaptation, and Aging,* 13(1/2), 129-139.

McCormick, S. (1991). The greying of parks and recreation. *Parks and Recreation,* March, pp. 60-64.

McGuire, F. A. and Boyd, R. K. (1993). The role of humor in enhancing the quality of later life. In Kelly, J. R. (ed.), *Activity and aging: Staying involved in later life* (pp. 164-173). Newbury Park, CA: Sage.

McPherson, B. D. (1999). Population aging and leisure in a global context: Factors influencing inclusion and exclusion within and across culture. *World Leisure and Recreation,* 41(3), 5-10.

Mifflin, L. (1995). 3 explorers of a certain age, scaling mountains and more. *The New York Times,* April 2, p. 37 (Arts and Leisure section).

Nagourney, E. (2002). Social whirl may help keep the mind dancing. *The New York Times,* October 29, p. D7.

Netz, Y. (1989). The congruence between actual and desired use of time by individuals pre- and post-retirement: A predictor of life satisfaction in old age? *World Leisure and Recreation,* 31(1), 12-15.

Owens, D. J. (1982). The relationship of frequency and types of activity to life satisfaction in elderly deaf people. *Dissertation Abstracts International,* 42, p. 3110A.

Pageot, J. C. (1986). The leisure patterns of the aged Canadians. *World Leisure and Recreation Association Journal,* 28(2), 26-27.

Pennix, B. W. J. H., Rejeski, W. J., Pandya, J., Miller, M. E., DiBari, M., Applegate, W. B., and Pahor, M. (2002). Exercise and depressive symptoms: A comparison of aerobic and resistance exercise effects on emotional and physical function in older persons with high and low depressive symptomology. *Journal of Gerontology,* 57B(2), 124-132.

Pollak, M. (1999). Stay busy, live longer, experts suggest. *The New York Times,* August 24, p. D8.

Pruchno, R. A. and Rose, M. S. (2002). Time use by frail older people in different care settings. *Journal of Applied Gerontology,* 21(1), 5-23.

Purcell, R. Z. and Keller, M. J. (1989). Characteristics of leisure activities which may lead to leisure satisfaction among older adults. *Activities, Adaptation, and Aging,* 13(4), 17-27.

Ray, R. O. (1979). Life satisfaction and activity involvement: Implications for leisure service. *Journal of Leisure Research,* 11(2), 112-119.

Recer, P. (2001). Elders keeping vigor longer, study finds. *The Boston Globe,* May 8, p. A10.

Riddick, C. (1993). Older women's leisure activity and quality of life. In Kelly, J. R. (ed.), *Activity and aging: Staying involved in later life* (pp. 86-98). Newbury Park, CA: Sage.

Riddick, C. C. and Keller, M. J. (1992). Efficacy of recreation on influencing the social psychological health of elders. *Parks and Recreation,* March, pp. 20-24, 161.

Rimer, S. (1998). As centenarians thrive, "old" is redefined. *The New York Times,* June 22, p. A1.

Rimer, S. (1999). Older people want to work in retirement, survey finds. *The New York Times,* September 2, p. A10.

Rodriguez, C. (2001). Widowers peak. *The Boston Globe,* September 10, pp. A1, A10.

Rosenkoetter, M., Garris, J., and Engdahl, R. (2001). Postretirement use of time: Implications for postretirement planning and postretirement management. *Activities, Adaptation, and Aging,* 25(3/4), 11-17.

Russell, R. V. (1990). Recreation and quality of life in old age: A causal analysis. *The Journal of Applied Gerontology,* 9(1), 77-90.

Schafer, W. (1991). Use it or lose it. *Stress and Health Report.* July/August, Chico, CA: Enloe Hospital Stress and Health Center, p. 1.

Schafer, W. (1992). When the light's on and nobody's home. *Stress and Health Report.* September/October, Chico, CA: Stress and Health Center, pp. 1-2.

Schonberg, H. C. (1990). A pianist who makes longevity an art. *The New York Times,* April 22, pp. 23, 27.

"Scuba diving forever. Almost" (2003). *The New York Times,* February 11, p. D6.

Shanahan, M. (1999). When you're young, prepare for growing old. *The Jerusalem Post,* July 18, p. 9.

"Shaping up" (2000). *Consumer Reports on Health,* February, p. 6.

Searle, M. and Iso-Ahola, S. E. (1988). Determinants of leisure behavior among retired adults. *Therapeutic Recreation Journal,* 22, 38-45.

Selcen, D. (1982). The congruence between actual and desired use of time by older adults: A predictor of life satisfaction. *Gerontologist,* 22(1), 95-99.

Selland, K. (1999). In aging, author says, genes aren't everything. *The Boston Globe,* April 10, p. A12.

Simons, M. (1992). As French get older, social security gets wobbly. *The New York Times International,* August 28, p. 4.

Strain, L. A., Grabusic, C. C., Searle, M. S., and Dunn, N. J. (2002). Continuing and ceasing leisure activities in later life: A longitudinal study. *Gerontologist,* 42(2), 217-223.

Szinovacz, M. (1992). Leisure in retirement: Gender differences in limitations and opportunities. *World Leisure and Recreation,* 34(1), 14-17.

Tye, L. (1999). Report cites rate, risks of binge drinking among the elderly. *The Boston Globe,* April 6, p. A17.

Wengler, K. G. (1992). Retirement communities in Canada: Toward a leisurely model. *World Leisure and Recreation,* 34(1), 23-24.

"Wheeling in the fast lane" (1992). *The Sacramento Bee,* February 27, p. E6.

Winslow, R. (2002). Yes, you can turn back the clock. *The Wall Street Journal,* May 8, pp. D1, D3.

Yardley, L. and Smith, H. (2002). A prospective study of the relationship between feared consequences of falling and avoidance of activity in community-living older people. *Gerontologist,* 42(1), 17-23.

"You may be younger than you think" (2000). *UC Berkeley Wellness Letter,* January, p. 5.

Young, D. R., King, A. C., and Oka, R. K. (1995). Determinants of exercise level in the sedentary versus underactive older adult: Implications for physical activity program development. *Journal of Aging and Physical Activity,* 3(1), 4-25.

Zaslow, J. (2003). The granny patrol: Florida cops recruit elderly volunteers. *The Wall Street Journal,* February 3, p. A1.

PART I:
SETTINGS

Chapter 2

Senior Centers and Clubs

INTRODUCTION

The purpose of this chapter is to provide information on senior centers and clubs, more specifically, the role of recreation in senior centers and clubs. Topics discussed in this chapter include the history and background of senior centers and clubs; goals and objectives of senior centers; a rationale for recreation as a component of senior center programs; the population served; description of the senior center setting; considerations in recreation program planning in senior centers; and funding sources for senior centers.

LEARNING OBJECTIVES

The learning objectives of this chapter are to be able to

1. cite statistics on the growth of senior centers and clubs in the United States,
2. identify the appropriate target population for senior centers,
3. identify appropriate programs to be offered at senior centers,
4. identify program goals for senior centers,
5. describe the senior center facility (setting), and
6. identify the steps involved in program planning in senior centers.

HISTORY AND BACKGROUND

The National Institute of Senior Centers (NCOA, 2002) defines a senior center as a place where "older adults come together for services and activities that reflect their experiences and skills, respond to their diverse needs and interests, enhance their dignity, support their independence, and encourage their involvement in and with the center and community." Senior centers are a relatively new concept in the United States, with the greatest growth occurring since 1965. The first senior club was established in

Boston in 1870, and more than seventy years later the first senior center was established in New York City in 1943. Since that time there has been tremendous growth in the number of senior centers: In 1966 there were 340 senior centers; by 1970, there were 1,200 senior centers; by 1978, approximately 6,000 centers were in operation (Gelfand, 1984); by 2002, there were approximately 15,000 centers in operation serving 10 million elders (NCOA, 2002).

A distinction needs to be made between senior centers and senior clubs. A senior center operates in a permanent facility and provides a central location for services, whereas a senior club may have no regular meeting place (Ralston, 1983). A senior center is usually more available to elders than clubs and may be open three or more days per week, whereas a senior club may be open only one day per week or less; depending on the individual club, it may stay open five days per week. The personnel working in a senior center and club usually differ: Senior centers commonly employ a full-time administrator, full- and part-time activity leaders, volunteers, and a secretary. On the other hand, many senior clubs have no paid staff. In addition, according to Ralston (1983), senior centers have diverse funding sources and implement a variety of activities. Senior clubs typically are supported by dues and contributions, and programming usually emphasizes social and recreational activities. In general, senior centers are more concerned with serving as a bridge to the community and as a focal point for common interests and concerns than are senior clubs (Gelfand, 1984).

Senior centers are the primary concern of the next section; their goals and objectives are described in detail.

GOALS AND OBJECTIVES

Senior centers offer a variety of services for older adults. They are designated as community focal points through the Older Americans Act (NCOA, 2002). According to the National Institute of Senior Centers (NISC, 1988), a multipurpose senior center is a place where older adults can congregate to fulfill many of their social, physical, emotional, and intellectual needs. Center programs enhance elders' dignity, independence, and involvement in the community. Activities and services offered through multipurpose senior centers include the following (Administration on Aging, 2003):

1. recreation;
2. health promotion (including wellness and fitness activities);
3. meals;
4. education;

5. arts programs;
6. leisure travel/trips;
7. transportation;
8. center volunteering;
9. community volunteering;
10. employment assistance;
11. financial assistance;
12. information, referral, and counseling;
13. Internet training;
14. social/community action;
15. intergenerational programs; and
16. community outreach.

Clearly, most of the services offered at senior centers are leisure related. A major goal of programs at senior centers is to provide meaningful leisure experiences that can enhance the well-being of older adults in the community.

Generally, senior centers provide an informal support system (Ralston, 1983) and should try to meet the needs of the older adults in the communities they serve. In addition, senior centers serve as resources for information on community affairs and senior citizens' services, as well as training centers. An important objective of a senior center is to encourage input from the elders it serves and maintain their support (Gelfand, 1984).

According to Gelfand (1984), another important objective is to provide activities that are relevant to the target population. The elders' needs should be assessed then, subsequently, programs should be planned according to their needs, interests, and abilities. Hawkins and McLean (1993) state that it is important for senior centers to offer a wide variety of services and programs to meet the diverse needs of the older population.

Recreation is an important service offered by senior centers and contributes greatly to the effectiveness of senior centers in enhancing the well-being of attendees. In a study of senior centers (Gelfand, 1984), the data indicated that senior center users viewed themselves as being more healthy than elders who do not attend senior centers. In addition, attendees had higher life satisfaction than nonattendees.

TARGET POPULATION

Krout (1993) estimates that between 10 and 20 percent of elders in the United States attend senior centers at least once a year. Approximately 10 million elders attend senior centers in the United States annually (NCOA, 2002). The characteristics of the attendees are changing. In the 1970s, surveys showed that senior center attendees were relatively young (between the ages of sixty and seventy-four) and healthy, but in the twenty-first century, it seems that the trend is toward serving an older and less healthy population. Approximately 60 percent of senior centers in the United States reported an increase in the number of frail older adults attending their centers, and 10 percent of attendees are over age eighty-five (NCOA, 2002). Stable characteristics of the population of senior center attendees are that the majority are women and white (NCOA, 2002). Many senior center attendees live alone, as reflected in statistics for the older population in general. Therefore a major function of senior center programs is to combat loneliness.

Recreation programs in senior centers will be influenced by trends in the population of senior center attendees. The statistics cited in the previous paragraph seem to indicate that more activities which address the needs of the more frail, older (eighty-five and over) segment of the older population will be needed. On the other hand, the Administration on Aging (2003) predicts that by 2010, baby boomers will constitute more than two-thirds of the fifty and over population, pointing to a need for senior centers to modify their programming to reflect the needs and interests of baby boomers (e.g., rock and roll music at senior centers?). Will baby boomers choose to attend senior centers, or will senior centers continue to be increasingly attended by the eighty-five and over segment of the older population? The characteristics of the attendees will largely determine the direction that recreation programs in senior centers take in the future. What do you think senior centers will be like fifty years from now (when a twenty-year-old college student today will be seventy years old), compared to the senior centers of today? Exercise 2.1 addresses this question.

Looking at your answers to Exercise 2.1, how similar do you think senior centers fifty years from now will be to senior centers today? What changes do you predict? How did you feel about the recreational activities offered at the senior center you visited? How interested would you be in participating in activities like these when you are age seventy or eighty or ninety?

THE SETTING

A senior center should be located in an area in the community that is attractive and where elders feel comfortable. The area should be convenient and accessible to the target population. The facility itself should be accessible to people with disabilities, contain a variety of rooms of different sizes, and provide private areas for counseling (Gelfand, 1999).

EXERCISE 2.1. Senior Centers Today Versus Fifty Years from Now

Instructions

1. Visit a local senior center (it will also help you to complete Exercise 2.2).
2. Take notes on the characteristics listed in the first columns and write your answers in the second column.
3. Project fifty years into the future and comment on the same characteristics, writing your answers in the third column.

Characteristic	Senior Center Visited	Senior Centers Fifty Years from Now
Age of attendees		
Health of attendees		
List of services and activities offered		
Types of recreational activities/description (e.g., type of music, dance, etc. offered)		

More than 6,000 senior centers receive funding from the Older Americans Act. They can be run by a variety of organizations, such as the following (Administration on Aging, 2003):

1. local nonprofit organizations;
2. state and local governments;
3. national charitable organizations; and
4. voluntary and religious organizations.

Ideally, a large multipurpose senior center with an attendance of over 200 older adults should be spacious and provide a variety of rooms. According to Murrin and Bilezikjian (1975), a large multipurpose senior center should be based on the following model:

Spaces Offered	Square Feet Recommended
1. *Outdoor space:* parking lot, patio, game courts, landscaped areas, pickup and drop-off zone	
2. *Indoor space:*	
a. Administration area/office space	250
b. Conference space	200
c. Classroom and crafts room	650 and 250
d. Arts and crafts room	1,000
e. Library/quiet lounge	500
f. Game room/noisy lounge	800
g. Kitchen	500
h. Rest rooms	400
i. Coatroom	50
j. Janitor/custodial space	50
k. Storage	225
l. Large assembly room	5,000
m. Circulation space	475
Total square footage	10,500

The large assembly room should be the focal point of the facility. This can be established by allowing the assembly room to be in the middle of the center with all adjoining rooms leading to the assembly room forming a circle around it. As a general guideline, there should be thirty square feet of space per person (Murrin and Bilezikjian, 1975).

Some senior centers own their building; some meet in a church; others meet in a recreation center, a local government facility, a community center of a voluntary organization, or a housing authority building. Other possible locations for programs are libraries, universities, and apartment house recreation rooms.

Exercise 2.2 asks you to compare the guidelines for senior center facilities to the characteristics of the senior center facility that you visited for Exercise 2.1.

Looking at your answers to Exercise 2.2, how adequate is the senior facility you visited? How would you improve the facility? More specifically, what facilities would you add to enhance the provision of recreational activities?

RECREATION PROGRAM PLANNING IN SENIOR CENTERS

Senior centers offer a wide range of challenging and diverse activities to accommodate the needs of the older adults they serve. Senior centers attendees are higher functioning than the older adults that attend senior day care centers or reside in assited living facilities or nursing homes. One way to take this factor into account is to include senior center attendees in the program planning process.

Exercise 2.3 is presented in order to provide insight into recreation program planning in senior centers. This exercise asks you first to contemplate how your present recreational needs and interests would be most effectively met by a recreation center.

After you have completed Exercise 2.3, compare your answers in the second and third columns. What are the similarities and differences? How similar are the two columns? What are the reasons for the differences that appear? Based on the results of this exercise, what have you learned about recreation program planning for senior centers of today and in the future?

Presently, a consideration in recreation program planning in senior centers is the high elder/staff ratio. Activities with a very high attendance (e.g., 50 to 100 attendees) can occur with only one or two staff members available to oversee the activity. Because of the great number of participants for every staff member, the type of recreational services provided tend to be more diversionary or educational in nature, as opposed to programming in senior day care centers, where therapeutic activities are more appropriate. Thus, in senior centers, recreational programming often does not include individual goal setting and charting of progress, which is significantly different from the therapeutic recreation services of senior day care centers.

According to Gelfand (1984), programming should be under the direction and support of the elders it serves. In this way, senior center attendees

EXERCISE 2.2. Senior Center Facility Characteristics

Instructions

1. Visit a local senior center and bring with you a list of the facility recommendations/guidelines from this chapter. Estimate how the facility compares to these guidelines.
2. Write your answers in the spaces below.

Facility Characteristics	Facility Characteristics of the Senior Center Visited
Outdoor space	_____ _____
Office space	_____ _____
Conference space	_____ _____
Crafts room/classroom	_____ _____
Arts and crafts room	_____ _____
Library/quiet lounge	_____ _____
Game room/noisy lounge	_____ _____
Kitchen	_____ _____
Rest rooms	_____ _____
Coatroom	_____ _____
Custodial space	_____ _____
Storage	_____ _____
Large assembly room	_____ _____
Circulation space	_____ _____

EXERCISE 2.3. My Ideal Recreation Center/Senior Center

Instructions

1. In the recreation center column describe, for each characteristic, what would best suit your present needs and interests. Let your imagination go, be idealistic. Under attendees, describe them in terms of demographics such as age, sex, socioeconomic status, etc.
2. Now, imagine yourself at age eighty. In the senior center column describe, for each characteristic, what you imagine would best suit your needs and interests at age eighty.

Characteristics	Recreation Center	Senior Center
1. Activities offered	_____	_____
	_____	_____
	_____	_____
	_____	_____
2. Classes offered	_____	_____
	_____	_____
	_____	_____
	_____	_____
3. Trips, other programs offered	_____	_____
	_____	_____
	_____	_____
	_____	_____
4. Facilities	_____	_____
	_____	_____
	_____	_____
5. Staff	_____	_____
	_____	_____
	_____	_____
	_____	_____
6. Attendees	_____	_____
	_____	_____
	_____	_____
	_____	_____

have direct input into programming activities related to their specific interests, abilities, and needs.

Recreational activities that incorporate work or productivity (e.g., produce handmade crafts for sale) can be a positive feature of a recreation program in a senior center. The provision of worklike roles in a senior center program can be especially beneficial for individuals who have a strong work ethic. The idea of going to a center to engage in leisure activities might be repulsive to some people. However, these individuals might be attracted to attending a senior center if worklike experiences were offered that made them feel productive. The work experience can help make leisure time purposeful, create a sales outlet for crafts, yet still preserve the retirement lifestyle (Schreter and Hudson, 1981).

The National Council on Aging (NCOA, 1975) developed a philosophy of the senior center movement that is still relevant in the twenty-first century as a philosophical basis for program planning:

1. Aging should be viewed as a normal developmental process.
2. People need peers for interaction, encouragement, and support.
3. Adults have the right to have input in matters affecting them.
4. Elders have ambitions, capabilities, and creative capacities.
5. Elders have basic needs.
6. Elders are capable of continued growth and development.
7. Elders need access to information to solve problems.
8. Elders need a climate of trust and support.

If the philosophical principles listed are incorporated into the program planning process, recreational activities and services will enhance attendees' morale.

According to the National Council on Aging (NCOA, 1975), program planning should follow these steps:

1. Assess individual needs.
2. Identify criteria and indicators of need fulfillment.
3. Identify barriers to need fulfillment.
4. State objectives and action steps to attain these needs.
5. Monitor and assess the objectives.
6. Examine the impact, measure the data, and evaluate the program.

Recreation programs in senior centers should cover a very wide range of activities since the high-functioning population usually attending senior centers allows limitless possibilities. New technology is creating new activity possibilities. Examples of some innovative senior center programs are described by Mattimore (1993):

1. *Teleconferencing program for homebound elders:* Called the "party line," teleconference equipment is installed at the center, enabling up to nine people to converse with one another and the party line operator. The operator welcomes everyone and gives all a chance to talk. The neediest, loneliest elders can be reached by this service.

2. *Computer classes:* There is an international computer network for elders called Senior Net, which links elders via computer across the United States.

3. *Interactive television programs:* The cable station has a phone number on the screen. Dial the number and a menu will appear on the screen. The caller then presses numbers as instructed on the phone for further information.

Sincere attempts to understand elders' needs and allowing senior center attendees the opportunity to have input in program planning will greatly enhance the effectiveness of the recreation program.

SUMMARY

In summary, senior centers serve as a community focal point; a resource center for information and health services; and a center for recreational, social, and educational activities. More senior centers are needed today and even more will be needed in the future to meet the needs of an expanding older population.

REFERENCES

Administration on Aging (2003). Senior centers. <www.aoa.gov/factsheets/ seniorcenters.html>; <www.aoa.gov/naf/notes/seniorcenters.html>.

Gelfand, D.E. (1984). *The aging network: Programs and services* (Second edition). New York: Springer Publishing.

Gelfand, D.E. (1999). *The aging network: Programs and services* (Fifth edition). New York: Springer Publishing.

Hawkins, B.A. and McLean, D. (1993). Delivering services to a diverse aging population: Challenges for the future. *Journal of Physical Education, Recreation & Dance,* 64(4), 31-34.

Krout, J.A. (1993). Do senior centers serve 7 million elders? *Perspective on Aging,* 22(2), 8-9.

Mattimore, H. (1993). Seniors and computers. *California Parks & Recreation Magazine,* 49(2), 24-25.

Murrin, R. and Bilezikjian, E. (1975). *Architectural programming for a senior center: Spatial allocation, organization, and recommendations.* Washington, DC: NCOA.

National Council on Aging (NCOA) (1975). *Senior group programs in America.* Washington, DC: NCOA.

National Council on Aging (NCOA) (2002). Senior centers. <www.ncoa.org/content.cfm?sectionID=107>.

National Institute of Senior Centers (NISC) (1988). *What is a multipurpose senior center?* Washington, DC: NCOA.

Ralston, P.A. (1983). Levels of senior centers: A broadened view of group-based programs for the elderly. *Activities, Adaptation, and Aging,* 3(2), 79-92.

Schreter, C.A. and Hudson, N. (1981). Investing in elder craftsmen. *Gerontologist,* 21(6), 655-661.

Chapter 3

Senior Day Care Centers

INTRODUCTION

The purpose of this chapter is to provide the reader with an understanding of senior day care services. More specifically, this chapter focuses on the role of recreational services in senior day care. Topics covered include history and background of senior day care; goals and objectives of senior day care programs; a rationale for recreation as a component of senior day care services; research in senior day care; population served; description of the setting for day care programs; considerations in provision of services; and funding sources.

LEARNING OBJECTIVES

Upon completion of this chapter, the student will be able to

1. cite statistics on the growth of senior day care centers in the United States,
2. identify the appropriate target population for senior day care centers,
3. identify the appropriate recreational programs to be offered at senior day care centers,
4. identify program goals for senior day care centers,
5. describe the senior day care facility (setting),
6. identify considerations in planning and leading recreational activities in senior day care centers, and
7. contrast recreational programs in senior day care centers with those in senior centers.

HISTORY AND BACKGROUND

Senior day care is fairly new in the United States, although it is a well-established program in many European countries. Padula (1983) traces the beginning of senior day care programs to the establishment of the first psychiatric day hospital for the emotionally disturbed in 1942. England initiated day hospitals for physically impaired adults; by 1969 there were ninety geriatric day hospitals in Great Britain (Matlack, 1975).

On the other hand, senior day care services did not really become widespread in the United States until the 1970s. According to Whirrett (2002) there were nearly 300 adult day care programs in the United States in 1978; by the 1980s, there were 2,100 centers in operation; and by 2002, there were 4,000 centers nationwide. However, according to Rogers (1999), approximately 10,000 centers are needed to meet the needs of the expanding older population. According to the Administration on Aging (2003), a national study indicates that 56 percent of U.S. counties did not have enough adult day care centers to meet the needs of its older population.

A distinction needs to be made between geriatric day hospitals and senior day care. According to Matlack (1975) geriatric day hospitals are hospital-based health-related programs that serve ill and impaired older persons. Emphasis is placed on remedial services such as physical therapy, occupational therapy, and psychotherapy, although social and recreational activity are components of such programs. Some of the purposes of geriatric day hospitals are to help maintain frail elderly persons in the community, to discharge patients into the community earlier than would otherwise be possible, and to reduce recidivism of clients discharged into the community.

In a different light, Padula (1983) defines senior day care as a primarily social program for frail elders and older adults with disabilities. According to Matlack (1975), senior day care programs place more emphasis on providing physical and mental stimulation for patients and respite for their families, whereas geriatric day hospitals focus more on remedial services. Many senior day care centers offer occupational therapy, physical therapy, therapeutic recreation, transportation, meals, educational programs, crafts, and counseling (Gelfand, 1999).

According to the National Institute on Adult Day Care (1991), adult day care is a community-based program designed to help elders with functional impairments through an individualized care plan. It provides health, social, and related support services in a protective setting during any part of a day, but does not provide twenty-four-hour care. It is a structured and comprehensive program.

Senior day care is the primary concern of this chapter; its goals and objectives are described in detail in the following section.

GOALS AND OBJECTIVES OF DAY CARE

Senior day care promotes the social, psychological, emotional, and physical well-being of frail elders and older adults with disabilities. A goal of senior day care is to restore and/or maintain individuals at their optimal functioning level. Activity programs afford participants the opportunity to become motivated to increase their competence in the skills of daily living (e.g., grooming and eating). Senior day care assists individuals in dealing with the environment.

Another important objective of senior day care is to provide respite for families. Day care affords families the opportunity to continue in their day-to-day lives and yet feel comfort in knowing that their elderly family member is spending the day in a caring environment.

In addition, day care attempts to increase physical independence. Through a program of exercise and physically active activities, program attendees are able to strengthen or relearn skills and gain confidence in their own mobility.

An additional objective of day care is to maintain elders in the community who are at risk of institutionalization. Senior day care serves as an alternative to nursing home care, and without day care services many elders would have no choice but to enter a nursing home.

Social interaction is another goal of senior day care services. Programming attempts to foster socialization among the participants through a variety of activities. Many older adults enter the program due to social isolation.

Day care programs also offer diversion for older adults. Activities attempt to alleviate boredom and help participants make better use of leisure time.

RECREATION IN SENIOR DAY CARE: A RATIONALE

Based on the aforementioned goals and objectives of senior day care programs, it is apparent that recreation services should be a major component of such programs. In particular, some of the goals of therapeutic recreation that coincide with those of senior day care programs are provision of enjoyable leisure activities; promotion of individual growth on a continuum of dependence-independence; provision of opportunities for social contact and formation of friendships; and maintenance and/or improvement of physical and/or mental capabilities. The provision of social contact opportunities is especially important in light of statistics which indicate that approximately 30 percent of senior day care participants live alone (Gelfand, 1999).

Indeed, recreation activity in senior day care programs play a major role in facilitating the happiness and well-being of its participants. As described later in the chapter, participants of senior day care centers are retired and usually do not have major household responsibilities; senior day care attempts to help older persons with disabilities make beneficial use of their vast amount of leisure time. The research studies cited in the next section further illustrate the value of recreation programs in senior day care centers and the value of senior day care centers in general.

RESEARCH IN SENIOR DAY CARE

Several articles support the notion that senior day care services are beneficial for older adults (Gustafson, 1974; Kistin and Morris, 1972; Koff, 1974; Kostich, 1972, 1974; Lurie and Kalish, 1976; Rathbone-McCuan, 1976; Rathbone-McCuan and Levinson, 1975; Smyer, 1980; Turbow, 1975; and Wan, Weissart, and Livieratos, 1980). Many of these articles describe successful senior day care programs and explain the benefits of day care services for impaired older persons. Turbow's (1975) study on the effects of senior day care services on forty-five older adults over a six-month period indicated that program attendees experienced reduced anxiety, improvement of interpersonal relationships, and maintenance of independent living.

The study by Wan, Weissart, and Livieratos (1980) is of particular interest because of the large sample size and sophisticated research methodology used. The researchers examined the physical, psychological, and social functioning of more than 1,000 older persons receiving day care and/or homemaker services (experimental group) and of a control group of more than 1,000 older adults. Subjects in this study were randomly assigned to control and experimental groups, thus establishing initial equivalency of the two groups.

The results of this study indicated that persons receiving day care and homemaker services were significantly better off in terms of physical, psychological, and social functioning than the control group. This study provides scientific evidence that day care services can help make significant improvements in the lives of elders. Naturally, it is not always feasible to study problems in a controlled, experimental fashion similar to the Wan, Weissart, and Livieratos (1980) study (comparison groups, random assignment of subjects to control and experimental groups, and control of variables). However, similar types of research efforts on the effects of different kinds of recreation services in senior day care settings will yield further insight on how to improve recreation opportunities for senior day care participants, as well as provide information that can help justify the existence of recreation programs in senior day care settings.

TARGET POPULATION

Senior day care centers serve adults with disabilities ages sixty and older. Most day care participants are at risk of institutionalization, and day care plays a major role in allowing these individuals to remain in the community. Participants with a broad range of disabilities are represented in the day care population. All of the persons enrolled in a senior day care program are in some way mentally and/or physically impaired. Mental impairments include depression, dementia, and emotional disturbances. Physical impairments include stroke disabilities, vision impairment, arthritis, Parkinson's disease, loss of limb, developmental disabilities, heart disease, and pulmonary disease. The severity of the disability differs with each person, but all are given individualized and meaningful activity to assist in adjusting to disabling conditions.

Senior day care centers serve people of a wide age range; participant ages usually range from 60 to more than 100. Actually, the age range can be even greater. Many centers are called adult day care centers, not senior day care centers, and are open to adults with disabilities of all ages. Some centers, although most of the attendees are eighty or older, might have several attendees in their fifties, and even some that are younger. Thus, it is possible for three generations or more to exist at an adult day care center. This is a major consideration in programming in that people of different age groups may have different activity interests.

According to the National Institute on Adult Day Care (1991), the average age of adult day care center attendees is seventy-six, and two-thirds of all participants are women. Many are widowed. A common complaint for many of the elders is the feeling of loneliness. Some of the participants live with a family member (children or other relative), some live either alone or with a spouse, and others live in personal care or foster homes. Family tension often exists for those seniors living with families. The causes of family tension are usually twofold: threat of loss of independence on the part of the elder, and resentment on the part of the caretaker because of the added responsibilities in caring for an older family member.

Some other characteristics that generally apply to day care attendees are as follows:

1. They are not engaged in gainful employment or in child-rearing responsibilities, and thus have a good deal of leisure.
2. They have limited means of transportation resulting in isolation from most community resources. For many persons, the day care center provides the only social contacts in their lives.
3. Many people initially feel threatened by the concept of day care. For the majority, it is their first exposure to such a facility and the idea of a leisure-oriented program is unfamiliar. Many are committed to the work ethic and view any recreational programs as a waste of time. Also, some elders feel threatened by exposure to other older adults with disabilities and many deny any identification with this group.

Although most day care participants reside in the community, many are not eligible to attend a senior center, because senior center participation would require a higher functioning level than they possess. Day care offers a structured program of activities, whereas senior centers offer a more elective program of activities. Day care participants would not be capable of attending a senior center on their own initiative.

A difficult issue to address is when a senior center attendee's physical and/or mental functioning deteriorates to the point of which he or she is no longer appropriate for senior center participation and is referred to a senior day care center. Imagine the emotional trauma of being told that you can no longer go to a place where you have friends, enjoy activities, and have been attending for many years. Then, imagine going for the first time to a senior day care center, not knowing anyone there, and seeing that most of the program participants have obvious physical and/or mental disabilities!

One trend in the delivery of services that can help with this adjustment is the housing of senior center and senior day care center programs in the same building or adjoining buildings. This arrangement would enable the older adult being "demoted" to senior day care to continue attending some of the activities at the senior center during the transition period. Also, if the older adult has a spouse or close friend at the senior center, that person could join the older adult in transition for lunch and other activities. If the senior center and senior day care center are not in the same or adjoining buildings, then a way to ease the transition can be to have the older adult continue attending the senior center while he or she begins attending the senior day care center two or three days a week. Eventually, the senior center can be phased out and attendance at the senior day care center can be increased.

Although some program participants actually improve their physical and/or mental functioning as a result of the services provided to them, the reality is that many older adults experience a natural decline. Not only do senior center attendees sometimes have to be "demoted" to senior day care, but sometimes senior day care attendees reach a level of functioning at which they are told that they can no longer attend the center because of the burden they place on staff. For example, there are not enough staff at senior day care centers to be able to deal with elders who are incontinent. It is especially difficult for staff to inform someone who enjoys attending the center that he or she can no longer come to the center. In some cases, a lower-functioning older adult can continue participating in a senior day care center with the help of a spouse or a personal assistant so that center staff are not overburdened with caring for that person.

Another source of participants are nursing home residents. Some institutionalized persons may attend day care in preparation for reentry to the community. Other nursing home residents attend day care as an off-premises activity several days per week, but continue to reside in the nursing home. As with populations found in other activity settings for elders, the main characteristic of the participant population in day care centers is great diversity in terms of needs, interests, and abilities.

THE SETTING

One important characteristic of senior day care centers is that they must be accessible to persons with disabilities. There should be as few steps as possible. A chairlift should be present at staircases because many participants are unable to negotiate steps. Rest rooms should be nearby and also be accessible for persons with disabilities. The rest rooms should have grab bars and high toilet seats, and be large enough for wheelchairs. Doors should be easy to open, not pressurized. There should be ramps and railings at all stairways. A safety hazard to be avoided is scatter rugs. There should be curtains on the windows in order to minimize glare. Centers should provide good lighting, good ventilation, and proper temperature maintenance. (Older persons usually prefer warm room temperatures.) Low lounge chairs or sofas should be avoided as this type of furniture may be difficult for elders to get in and out of. All centers should comply with fire and health regulations. There should always be at least two exits. Telephones should be readily available. Another desirable feature is a canopy at the entrance in the event of inclement weather.

The interior of the center usually reflects four major themes: comfort and enjoyment, maximal mobility, facilitation of social interaction, and orientation to time and place. Comfortable chairs (all chairs should have arms), music, and aesthetically pleasing decoration help to maximize the comfort and enjoyment of the participant. Arrangement of furniture and equipment is usually such that the participant can move about freely and safely with minimal chance of accident. A large clock and posters and signs in large print should be present to help orient the participant to time and place. The daily schedule and a calendar should be within easy view for all to see. A bulletin board where participant artwork can be displayed and/or announcements can be posted is highly recommended for the benefit of the more confused participants. The reality orientation board can be made out of a large piece of tagboard. In large print it lists the date, weather, upcoming holidays, and the name of the facility.

The arrangement and complexity of the facility varies greatly from center to center. Most centers have a dining room where meals and snacks are served daily. It is desirable to have a designated "quiet" room for rest and/or solitude. There is also usually a separate office area for staff. In addition, it is advantageous to utilize more than one partitioned or separate activity room so that more than one activity may occur simultaneously without interference. Some centers have separate rooms for crafts, exercise, games, discussions, and media (books, magazines, talking books for the blind, etc.), as well as sitting rooms (for small group discussions and impromptu conversations), whereas other centers simply have one large room where all activities take place. In addition, an area for smoking should be provided. Storage areas and an area for participant personal belongings are also desirable.

CONSIDERATIONS IN THE PROVISION OF SERVICES

Leading Activities

In this section, leadership skills that are different from those needed by workers in other settings for recreation for older adults are highlighted.

Safety and health considerations must be taken into account when leading activities at a senior day care center. Because many of the attendees are taking some kind of medication, the activity leader must be aware of the effects of drug use on program involvement and interaction (for example, if a person is administered a medication that causes a side effect of drowsiness, allow that person to engage in a passive activity, or provide an opportunity to just sit and rest).

Not all senior day care centers have medical staff; therefore, it is desirable that the activity leader be able to respond effectively to medical emergencies (for example, administer aid to a person who is choking). It is advantageous to have training in both first aid and cardiopulmonary resuscitation.

In senior day care centers, the staff may find themselves assuming various roles while carrying out different responsibilities. The participant may see the staff in varying positions, changing with each activity. It is not uncommon for participants to view staff as teachers, counselors, nurses, doctors, secretaries, or personal confidants. Although the roles may shift, the relationship between staff and participant should always remain professional. Participants' responses to activity leaders may be influenced by their perceptions of the leader's role at that moment.

In general, the leader of recreational activities in a senior day care center needs to be more autocratic in leadership style than a recreation leader working with higher-functioning populations. For example, in senior centers, the participants are more capable of being involved in program planning. On the other hand, the staff at senior day care centers are responsible for more of the planning. The participants enrolled in a day care center tend to be not as mentally competent as attendees of senior centers and clubs. Thus, day care personnel should be more autocratic in both leading and planning activities. However, senior day care staff should attempt to solicit input from program participants regardless of what level it is.

Senior centers and day care differ in another aspect of leadership. There is a greater staff/participant ratio in day care, thus affording more individualized programming. Also, participant evaluation is more of an objective in day care than in senior centers; consequently, there is a greater extent of individualized goal setting.

In a related vein, the format of activities may differ in a senior center as opposed to in a day care center. Because of the large population with disabilities that exists at a day care center, leadership techniques will vary accordingly. Modification of activities is an important component in day care. Activities must be adjusted to suit each individual's abilities. For example, activities should be slow paced, simple, and contain few steps. In contrast, there would be less structure and modification of activities needed to accommodate the more healthy and vital population attending senior centers.

Senior day care centers also differ from nursing homes with regard to leadership style. Most day care centers operate five days per week and, within this framework, all participants have their own individual attendance schedule. Some attend two days per week whereas others attend four days per week. This is unlike nursing homes, which operate seven days per week. This has two implications for program planning: (1) senior day care cannot take advantage of community resources that are available only evenings and weekends, whereas nursing homes can, and (2) not all participants are present on any specified day of the week to attend a particular activity. Thus, a program planning consideration is to afford participants scheduled for all days of the week the opportunity to participate in special events. For example, Tuesday participants might become disturbed if all field trips were scheduled for Wednesdays. This would not be a concern for nursing homes but it would be for day care programs.

Senior day care center attendees tend to be less independent than those attending senior centers. One objective of senior day care is to foster independence and, to attain this, activities tend to be more therapeutic in nature. On the other hand, senior centers incorporate more purely diversionary activities rather than therapeutic recreation activities.

Field trips may entail more planning, coordination, and supervision for senior day care centers than senior centers. Because of the frailer population that attends senior day care centers, more special provisions for field trips are needed than would be required for a senior center population.

Exercise 3.1 is presented as a means of summarizing the major differences between senior centers and senior day care centers with regard to planning and leading recreational activities.

After you have completed Exercise 3.1, please answer the following question: What are the main differences in planning and leading recreational activities at the two facilities? An alternative way to complete this exercise is to actually observe the same activity being conducted at a nearby senior center and at a senior day care center, and then write your observations on the similarities and differences in the activity at the two facilities.

Attracting Participants

Several techniques are involved in the process of attracting participants. One publicity technique is to issue brochures in the mail and in person to the general public. Eligibility criteria and vital information about the program should be included in these brochures. Also, an article should appear in each issue of the local senior citizens' newspaper (if one exists). Special events can be publicized through the mass media (television, radio, newspaper). In addition, municipal, county, state, and voluntary social service agencies (including senior centers) should be well informed of the program so they can refer potential applicants to the program. Naturally, each participant has the potential to attract other seniors by word of mouth.

Community involvement in various activities can be an effective tool in letting people know about the program. As an example, bazaars and pot luck dinners keep the community aware of the program and help senior day care centers to keep in touch with potential enrollees. It is also helpful to display a large sign outside of the facility so that the community is aware of its existence.

EXERCISE 3.1. Planning and Leading Recreational Activities
at Senior Centers versus Senior Day Care Centers

Instructions

1. Select a recreational activity that could be led at a senior center or senior day care center. Some examples would be an exercise class, musical activity, or arts and crafts.
2. For each aspect of planning and leading recreational activities, compare how you would approach the activity differently at each facility.
3. As an example, presented below are some ideas regarding differences in planning and leading a dance activity at the two facilities.

Senior Center

Senior Day Care Center

Example: Dance Activity

Senior Center	Senior Day Care Center
Form a dance committee among the center attendees. Have them plan the dance and present their plans to the staff.	Solicit input from attendees regarding favorite music for dancing. Have the staff plan an adapted dance activity.
Have a large space available as a dance floor, with chairs off to the side for people to rest.	Arrange chairs in a circle or semi-circle for an adapted (seated) dance session.
Arrange for live or recorded music to be played for the dancers continuously, one song after the next.	Teach an adapted dance without the music, then perform it several times with the music. The extent of repetition/number of new dances presented depends on the functioning level of the participants.
Allow two hours or more for this event.	Session length should be about forty-five minutes.

Now, present your activity idea, showing how you would plan and lead the activity differently at each facility:

Senior Center

Senior Day Care Center

Referrals should be kept up to date. Any applicant who has not yet committed to the program should be contacted periodically. Letters and/or phone calls should be made to these applicants to determine their eligibility.

Once a prospective participant is identified, a home visit should be made by a staff member to assess eligibility status. Information about the program is disseminated to the applicant at this time. Bringing photographs of activities that occur at the center to the home visit can give the applicant a better idea of what the program offers. Also, it may be beneficial for another participant to accompany the staff member on the home visit. The participant who has been enrolled in the program for a good length of time may be able to offer insight into the program and relate well to the potential enrollee's apprehensions about joining the program.

Transportation

Another vital concern for day care centers is getting the participants to and from the center each day. For most older adults with disabilities, transportation is a serious problem; most are unable to provide their own transportation. In order to have high attendance, most senior day care centers will find it necessary to provide their own transportation. Money should be allotted in the budget to purchase and maintain a transportation vehicle. This vehicle must be designed for use by persons with disabilities.

The center's staff should establish a transportation area within which they can transport people to and from the center. Anyone living within this radius (for example, five miles) will have transportation provided. Those living outside the boundary will have to provide their own transportation (usually a family member or some other community resource). In addition, carpools should be encouraged. In this way, the bus routes can be held to a minimum and restricted to a reasonable time frame. (It would be inconvenient if the bus route was so long that people had to ride for excessive amounts of time.) It should be remembered that the upkeep of a vehicle can be quite costly; therefore, sufficient funds should be allocated for vehicle maintenance.

Assessment

A thorough assessment of needs, interests, and abilities should be conducted before a participant is involved in a program of activities. Needs, interests, and abilities may change once a person has been enrolled in the program for a period of time, in that old skills are relearned, new skills may be acquired, and interests may expand. During the initial home visit, a basic overview of the applicant is obtained. A mental status questionnaire is administered to the prospective participant and the physician is asked to complete a medical form that lists any physical limitations, medications, physical and psychological ailments, and any other comments or recommendations. An environmental assessment can also be completed during the home visit to better understand the person's living environment.

The following are some questions that could be asked during a home visit:

1. What do you do?
2. What are you interested in?
3. Who are your main social contacts? How often do you talk on the phone, and to whom?
4. What are your hobbies and interests?
5. Why would you like to come to the day care center?
6. What, if any, health problems do you have?
7. What (if any) medications do you take?
8. Do you have any health insurance coverage?
9. Who would we contact in case of an emergency?
10. What special considerations (medical, meals, or religious) should we know about?
11. Have you had any recent hospitalizations?
12. Are you involved with any other social service agency?
13. Are you able to take care of your own personal care needs (bathing, eating, grooming)? If not, who does these things for you?
14. Do you do the housekeeping, laundry, and meal preparation?
15. When is your birthday?
16. What is your total income?
17. What was your previous career?
18. What is your marital status?
19. Do you need transportation to the center?
20. Which days would you like to attend the center each week?

Appropriate Activities

Leitner and Merenbloom (1979) discuss a variety of recreational activities that are successfully implemented at senior day care centers, such as lectures, classes, expressive activities, drama, theater programs, concerts, games, parties and other social events, intergenerational activities, companion animals, computer games, bingo, therapeutic dance movement, music therapy, art therapy, and crafts. Exercise is, of course, an essential daily activity.

Because one-half of adult day care participants are cognitively impaired (National Institute on Adult Day Care, 1991), it is essential to incorporate into the center's activity program special activities for elders who are disoriented to varying degrees. According to Feil (1982), the disoriented are not demented; they can't cope with reality and survive by restoring the past. Field (1990) discusses the success of life history activity with Alzheimer patients in adult day care settings. In the "Living History" activity, a particular time, place, or person is re-created through costume "dress up," light historical research, and theater workshop style improvisation. Field (1990) states that an ideal time for these experiences are holidays. Noting that long-term memory is more intact in the early to mid stages of Alzheimer's, the re-creation of holiday traditions from years past can be very successful and a self-esteem booster for participants with Alzheimer's or who suffer some degree of disorientation. The "Living History" activity can be a special event in itself, or part of a larger celebration of a holiday or event.

Special Events

Special events are very important because they give the seniors a special activity to look forward to and involve the efforts of many people (staff and participants) in planning the event. Special events usually generate a great deal of enthusiasm and involve the coordination of the entire staff. Outstanding events are usually talked about among members for weeks after. Participants frequently suggest engagements for future events as a result of involvement in a stimulating special event.

The following are some interesting examples of special events that senior day care attendees can enjoy:

1. A picnic at a nearby park
2. A trip to a local racetrack
3. Trips to various cultural sites (museums, theater)
4. Attending the circus
5. Dining out (allow the participants to choose the restaurant)

Stimulating activities that can take place right at the center are

1. Las Vegas Day
2. Theme days (such as Mardi Gras or International Day)
3. Musical performances

4. Talent shows
5. Parties
6. Senior Olympics
7. Holiday celebrations

Family Contact

For a more effective program, staff should maintain close contact with participants' families. Phone calls should be made periodically to assess how the person is doing at home and discuss any problems the staff should be made aware of. Families should be encouraged to contact the center to ask questions or make suggestions. Families should be mailed copies of monthly schedules, announcements, and any other relevant information, and they should be invited to special events. Family dinners can be held periodically at the center so that family involvement can be maintained and encouraged.

Another function of family contact is to involve family members in the assessment of participant programs. One way this can be achieved is through a conference with family members and staff. Equally beneficial are support groups formed for families so that people with similar concerns can get together and discuss their older family members.

FUNDING

One of the biggest advantages of adult day care is its cost. According to the National Institute on Adult Day Care (1991), the average cost of a day at a center is less than half the cost of nursing home care, and much less than a visit from a home health nurse. According to Whirrett (2002), senior day care costs $25 to $70 per day ($50 per day is the average), with participant payments usually based on a sliding fee scale according to income.

Funding for adult day care center comes from many different sources. Direct payment by participants is but one source of funding. Public funding and donations by philanthropic organizations are other sources of funds. Religious organizations are a frequent source of support (both financially and in terms of providing space for facilities). According to Whirrett (2002), 80 percent of centers are nonprofit, 10 percent are for profit, and 10 percent receive public funding only. Although Medicare does not cover the costs of senior day care, some Medicaid waiver programs support alternatives to institutionalization such as senior day care. Research cited earlier in the chapter documenting the value of senior day care services lends support to increased funding for these programs.

SUMMARY

In summary, senior day care is a rapidly growing form of service that serves the social and recreational needs of noninstitutionalized older adults with disabilities. Senior day care is a critical service in enabling frail elders to maintain an independent, noninstitutional lifestyle. Recreation is a vital component of senior day care services.

REFERENCES

Administration on Aging (2003). *Profile of Older Americans: 2002.* <www. seniorjournal.com>.

Feil, N. (1982). *V/F Validation: The Feil Method—How to help the disoriented old-old.* Cleveland, OH: Feil Productions.

Field, D. (1990). T. R. /Life history with Alzheimer's patients in an adult day care setting. *California Parks and Recreation Society Magazine,* summer, pp. 17-18.

Gelfand, D. E. (1999). *The aging network: Programs and services* (Fifth edition). New York: Springer Publishing.

Gustafson, E. (1974). Day care for the elderly. *Gerontologist, 14*(1), 46-49.

Kistin, H. and Morris, R. (1972). Alternatives to institutional care for the elderly and disabled. *Gerontologist, 12*(2), 139-142.

Koff, T. H. (1974). Rationale for services: Day care and coordination. *Gerontologist, 14*(1), 26-29.

Kostich, A. (1972). A day care program for the physically and emotionally disabled. *Gerontologist, 12*(2), 134-138.

Kostich, A. (1974). A day care program for the physically and emotionally disabled. *Gerontologist, 14*(1), 31-32.

Leitner, M. J. and Merenbloom, S. (1979). Senior day care centers ensure fun for the elderly. *Parks and Recreation Magazine, 14*(11), 58-61; 84-89.

Lurie, E. and Kalish, R. (1976). On Lok senior day health center. *Gerontologist, 16*(1), 39-46.

Matlack, D. R. (1975). The case for geriatric day hospitals. *Gerontologist, 15*(2), 109-113.

National Institute on Adult Day Care (1991). Adult day care fact sheet. Washington, DC: National Council on Aging.

Padula, H. (1983). *Developing adult day care: An approach to maintaining independence for older persons.* Washington, DC: National Institute on Adult Day Care.

Rathbone-McCuan, E. (1976). Geriatric drug cure: A family perspective. *Gerontologist,* 16(6), 517-521.

Rathbone-McCuan, E. and Levinson, J. (1975). Impact of socialization therapy in a geriatric day care setting. *Gerontologist, 15*(4), 338-342.

Rogers, N. (1999). Caring for those who care: Achieving family caregiver wellness through social support programs. *Activities, Adaptation, and Aging,* 24(4), 27-40.

Smyer, M. A. (1980). The differential usage of services by impaired elderly. *Journal of Gerontology, 35*(2), 249-255.

Turbow, S. R. (1975). Geriatric group day care and its effects on independent living. *Gerontologist, 15*(6), 508-510.

Wan, T. H., Weissart, W. G., and Livieratos, B. B. (1980). Geriatric day care and homemaker services: An experimental study. *Journal of Gerontology, 35*(2), 256-274.

Whirrett, T. (2002). Adult day care: One form of respite for older adults. *ARCH fact sheet #54.* National Respite Network and Research Center, <www.archrespite.org/archfs54.htm>.

Chapter 4

Recreation in Residential Communities for Older Adults

Michael J. Leitner
Sara F. Leitner
Philip D. Shapiro
Nancy A. Shapiro

INTRODUCTION

The purposes of this chapter are to explore the status and desirability of age-segregated living arrangements, in particular, the desirability of age segregation in terms of the provision of leisure services to elders. Many different types of age-segregated living arrangements are discussed in this chapter.

In the first section of this chapter, the current status of age-segregated housing for older adults in the United States is described, including information on retirement communities and assisted living facilities. In the second section, research on elders' preferences for age segregation is presented. In the third section, the desirability of age-segregated living arrangements for older adults, especially with respect to leisure, is examined. The last two sections, written by retirement housing experts Phil Shapiro and Nancy Shapiro, present an overview of trends in recreation in retirement housing, and an in-depth case study of an independent living facility. Issues and questions for discussion are raised throughout this chapter.

LEARNING OBJECTIVES

Upon completion of this chapter, the student will be able to

1. cite statistics on the growth of retirement communities and other age-segregated housing in the United States,
2. compare facility characteristics of different types of age-segregated housing,

3. compare population characteristics of different types of age-segregated housing,
4. identify at least five recreational advantages of retirement communities,
5. identify appropriate leisure programs, facilities, and activities to be offered at age-segregated housing and retirement communities, and
6. identify considerations in planning and leading recreational activities in retirement communities and other age-segregated housing.

GROWTH OF AGE SEGREGATION

The trend toward increasing age segregation of society is caused by several factors: the growth of planned retirement communities; the growth of other retirement housing, such as independent living and assisted living facilities; and the migration of middle-class families to the suburbs, leaving areas within metropolitan areas with a significant increase in the proportion of noninstitutionalized elders living alone. The degree of age segregation in the United States has increased over the past few decades and is projected to continue to increase, even though 90 percent of elders live in conventional housing and only 10 percent live in age-restricted communities (Joint Center for Housing Studies of Harvard University, 2000).

Growth in the Senior Housing Market

According to Raymond (2000), the senior housing market will more than triple, growing from an estimated $126 billion in 2005 to $490 billion by the year 2030. Statistics cited by Raymond (2000) indicate that the senior housing market is divided as follows:

- 40 percent are assisted living facilities (23,114); by 2001, an estimated 33,000 assisted living facilities with 800,000 residents were operating in the United States (NCAL, 2001);
- 29 percent are nursing homes and nursing with assisted living arrangements (17,053);
- 21 percent are senior apartments/active adult/lifestyle communities (12,426);
- 7 percent are congregate housing facilities (4,064); and
- 3 percent are continuing care retirement communities (1,900).

More Elders Living Alone

A significant factor contributing to the increasing age segregation of U.S. society is the increase in the proportion of noninstitutionalized elders living alone, as cited in Chapter 1. The percentage of elders living in the household of an adult child has dropped, thus, there are fewer intergenerational households. There are also fewer intergenerational areas within metropolitan areas.

Age Segregation Within Metropolitan Areas

Cowgill's (1978) study shows how much age segregation in the United States increased from 1940 to 1970. He measured the extent of dissimilarity of residential distribution between the population of persons over age sixty-five, and persons under age sixty-five for 241 Standard Metropolitan Statistical Areas (SMSAs) in 1970. Cowgill also computed the extent of age segregation in those 241 SMSAs for the years 1940, 1950, and 1960. Cowgill found that a high degree of age segregation existed in 1970, and that the extent of age segregation had greatly increased since 1940. The greatest amount of age segregation was found to exist in the more rapidly growing SMSAs (especially in the West and South) and in areas with major military or educational institutions (such institutions create age-homogeneous population clusters within an area). According to Cowgill, the main factor related to age segregation is the growth and differentiation of the SMSA (the faster the SMSA is growing, the greater the extent of its age segregation).

Another factor related to increasing age segregation in the United States is the desire of older adults to stay where they are as they grow older. According to statistics cited by Kunstler (2001),

1. 86 percent of elders want to stay where they are as they grow older;
2. 70 percent of elders spend the rest of their lives where they were living at age sixty-five; and
3. 27 percent of elders live in "naturally occurring retirement communities" (NORCs). A NORC is defined as a building or neighborhood not originally designed for elders, but in which 50 percent or more of its residents are age sixty or older.

Regarding NORCs, Florida is an example of a state that is trying to deal with the challenge of making communities more suitable for older adults. Canedy (2002) describes efforts in Florida cities such as Dunedin (40 percent of its residents are age sixty-five or over) to be certified as "elder ready," a statewide program that attempts to encourage independent living by older adults through the creation of an infrastructure that makes everyday life easier for older people.

In summary, a high level of age segregation exists within the United States. According to research on this topic, the degree of age segregation in the United States seems to be increasing. As discussed in the next section, a variety of housing options are available for older adults who desire age segregation.

TYPES OF RETIREMENT HOUSING

Retirement Communities

The first planned retirement community in the United States was established in 1954 in Youngstown, Arizona (Gelfand, 1984). Many elders have moved to retirement communities in Arizona, Florida, California, and other Sunbelt areas. Planned retirement communities in the fringes of urban areas in the eastern and midwestern states have also experienced growth. Thus, planned retirement communities in most areas of the country seem to have experienced significant growth. Approximately 5 percent of Americans sixty-five and over live in retirement communities (Kuhn, 1995).

For the purposes of this chapter, a *retirement community* is defined as a community that is relatively independent, age segregated, and non-institutionalized, in which residents all meet a minimum age requirement and are separated from their career occupation in paid or nonpaid employment (Magnum, 1973). The minimum age requirement can be as low as fifty or as high as sixty-five. Some retirement communities are small and some are large, with 20,000 residents or more. When many of the large retirement communities were built in the 1970s, a large percentage of the first residents were younger retirees, in their late fifties or early sixties. Thirty years later, many of these original residents have passed away and their units purchased by younger retirees. However, many of the original residents are still residing in the retirement communities, and these people are in their late eighties and early nineties. One of the challenges facing retirement communities today is how to meet the diverse needs of a resident population with such a wide age range.

Continuing Care Retirement Communities

Continuing care retirement communities (CCRCs) are essentially retirement communities with multiple levels of care, including independent living, assisted living/personal care, and nursing care. CCRCs grew by 179 percent during the 1960s, 53 percent in the 1970s, and 50 percent in the 1980s. The average number of residents in a CCRC is 340, with most (average of 224) residents in independent living units (AAHSA, 1993). Most residents are female (75 percent) and single (70 percent), with the average age being approximately eighty-one (AAHSA, 1993). A study of adults ages sixty-five to ninety-five who moved to a CCRC indicated that the main reasons for moving to a CCRC were anticipating future needs, freedom from upkeep and home maintenance, desire for continued care, and a desire not to be dependent or a burden to anyone (Krout et al., 2002).

Other Retirement Housing

In addition to planned retirement communities, other prominent types of age-segregated housing are public housing for senior citizens, sheltered and congregate housing, foster care, retirement hotels, and mobile home parks. Public housing for senior citizens has increased significantly, with elders occupying nearly 50 percent of the more than 1 million units of public housing that had been constructed by 1980 (Gelfand, 1984).

Sheltered and congregate housing are designed to meet the needs of elders not able to maintain full independent living and yet are not in need of institutional care. According to Gelfand (1984), congregate housing provides housekeeping, dining, emergency, health, and recreational services, whereas sheltered housing offers more extensive services with an emphasis placed on meals and personal care.

A specialized form of sheltered housing is foster care, in which elders not able to maintain full independence are placed in a setting with a family support system. Foster care first became available to elders in the 1970s, and although foster care's effectiveness with older mental patients has been documented, it remains an underutilized resource (Gelfand, 1984).

Another type of age-segregated living arrangement is the single-room occupancy hotel, where elders live in hotels and rooming houses, most of which are located in commercial areas adjacent to downtown business districts. According to Gelfand (1984) these residents tend to live in isolation and deep friendships rarely develop.

In contrast to the single-room occupancy hotels are mobile home parks. Mobile home parks are more similar to retirement communities than the previously discussed types of housing, but differ from retirement communities in that the developments tend to be smaller, recreational facilities are not as extensive, and housing costs are lower. However, it can sometimes be difficult to distinguish between a retirement community and a mobile home park for elders, especially some of the larger mobile home parks.

In summary, a variety of housing options exist for older adults. Where would you like to live when you are an older adult? Exercise 4.1 is designed to stimulate thought on this topic.

ELDERS' PREFERENCES

The growth of age-segregated housing for elders has been well documented, but is the trend toward age-segregated housing desirable? Specifically, do elders prefer age-segregated housing or intergenerational living arrangements?

Swartout conducted an interesting study on this topic with residents of a Leisure World retirement community (Magnum, 1973). Thirty intensive and thirty casual interviews were conducted, in which none of the interviewees cited age segregation as a motive for residency in the community, nor as a desirable quality. However, community residents almost unanimously disapproved a proposed lowering of the minimum residency age from fifty-two to forty-two. This behavior somewhat contradicts their expressed attitudes regarding age segregation. The residents stated that they opposed the proposed lowered minimum age because they did not want children in the community; also, they felt that the younger people would have different interests than the older residents, which might cause conflicts (e.g., loud parties). Swartout concluded that the sample population actually viewed age segregation as being desirable, and was a motive for their moving to the community. Similarly, 83 percent of the subjects in Teaff et al.'s (1978) study of 1,875 aged persons stated a preference for age-segregated, as opposed to age-integrated, housing.

A difficult issue that now seems to be arising in retirement communities is that of desired age segregation within the community. Garcia (1993) discusses the clearly defined age divisions that exist at the famous Leisure World retirement community. A new social group was formed there, called the Nifty '50s-'60s Club. It has 550 members with a waiting list of 120. The club checks identification at their socials, so that seventy-year-olds can't "sneak in"!

Exercise 4.2 is presented to provide further insight into how to resolve this seemingly ridiculous, yet very real, problem.

EXERCISE 4.1. Personal Living Arrangement Preferences

Instructions

As a college student, rate the desirability of the following living arrangement factors (use a ten-point scale, ten being most desirable, one being least desirable):

1. Having ample recreational facilities at your disposal   _____
2. Living among age peers   _____
3. Living among other college students   _____
4. Ample security, especially at night   _____
5. Planned recreational activities for residents   _____

Now, answer these questions again, this time imagining yourself as a senior citizen (change the second question from "college students" to "retirees"). How does your second set of ratings compare with the first? What insights do you gain from this exercise regarding your personal preferences for retirement community living in later life? What insights do you gain from this exercise regarding elders' preferences for retirement community and other age-segregated living?

_____

_____

_____

_____

_____

_____

_____

_____

_____

_____

EXERCISE 4.2.
Solutions to the Retirement Community Generation Gap

Instructions

1. Imagine yourself as a healthy sixty-year-old resident of a retirement community. You know other young retirees in the community, also in good health. You have become fed up with most of the social activities of the retirement community because of the preponderance of "old-old" residents at the events. For example, you find that it is difficult to dance because of all the slow-moving dancers in their seventies, eighties, and nineties on the dance floor. In the first column, list your suggested solutions to this problem.
2. Imagine yourself as a fairly healthy seventy-five-year-old resident of a retirement community. You are a good dancer and feel outraged that anyone would want to exclude you from a dance or any other activity because you are too old. In the second column, list your suggested solutions to this problem.
3. After examining your answers in the two columns, what is your suggested "compromise" solution to this problem?

Solutions to Meet Fifties-Sixties Needs _____

Solutions to Meet Seventies-Plus Needs _____

_____   _____

_____   _____

_____   _____

_____   _____

_____   _____

_____   _____

_____   _____

_____   _____

_____   _____

_____   _____

_____   _____

_____   _____

_____   _____

DESIRABILITY OF AGE-SEGREGATED
LIVING ARRANGEMENTS

One area of emphasis in examining the desirability of age segregation is that of life satisfaction and morale. Several studies on this topic are described in this section of the chapter.

Poulin (1984) examined the relationships of age segregation, interpersonal involvement, morale, and life satisfaction of 232 elders. Data collected from seventy-eight residents of senior citizens housing were compared to that of 154 residents of natural community housing. Poulin found that the senior housing residents had slightly larger and more supportive interpersonal networks, but had less contact with their friends than the community residents. No significant differences were found in the life satisfaction of the two groups. Similarly, Deimling, Noelker, and Beckman (1979) and Gubrium (1970) found no significant relationship between residential age concentration and life satisfaction.

Atchley (1975) cited a study conducted by Rosow involving 1,200 aged residents of age-dense (comprised of 50 percent or more elders), aged-concentrated (33 to 49 percent), and normal aged-density (1 to 15 percent) housing. Subjects were screened for occupational status and whether they were residing in public housing, in order to have a range of social classes represented in the sample.

Three successive interviews (25 percent dropout rate) were conducted with the subjects. Rosow found that the greater the aged density of the housing, the greater the morale of its socially unstable aged residents; the lower the morale of its socially isolated aged residents; and that the morale of the sociable aged residents remained the same. Rosow concluded that high age density is more conducive to the development of friendships among older persons, these friendships coming disproportionately from among their aged neighbors. Rosow concluded that this increased opportunity for social contact improved the social life for the socially unstable aged (and improved their morale), had little effect on the highly sociable aged (they already had many friends), but made the socially isolated aged more depressed due to their continued inability to acquire friendships, even in the face of an increased opportunity to do so. Rosow concluded that the results of this study should not be interpreted to mean that age segregation is a cure-all; some elders simply do not care to socialize.

Messer (1967) studied the activity levels and life satisfaction of aged residents of age-homogeneous (N = 88) and age-integrated (N = 155) public housing in Chicago. In this study, the problem of subject self-selection was minimized, in that residents of the age-homogeneous housing were not there by choice; in Chicago, aged persons who apply for public housing are not asked whether they would prefer to live in age-segregated or age-integrated housing. Messer concluded that the age-segregated environment helped to ease the transition of its residents to the leisure-oriented role of later life. He also concluded that successful adjustment to old age is facilitated by the maintenance of high activity levels.

Hampe and Blevins (1975) examined the interaction patterns and life satisfaction of aged residents (N = 63) of a retirement hotel. Hampe's sample consisted of mostly female (75 percent), single, Caucasian, and low-income persons. Hampe and Blevins found that a high level of housing satisfaction existed among the residents. They concluded that the age-segregated environment provided a greater opportunity to create friendships and to interact with others. However, it was also concluded that age segregation can contribute to feelings of uselessness—that one is no longer part of the mainstream of society.

Teaff et al. (1978) also examined the impact of age segregation on the well-being of the older adults. The researchers conducted interviews with older persons (N = 1,875) in 753 public housing sites, based on a national probability sample. The authors found that age segregation was significantly related to greater activity participation, morale, and general well-being. Teaff et al. attempted to explain this finding in terms of reduced crime, and a more relaxed, less competitive atmosphere that existed in the age-segregated environments. Similarly, Carp's (1972) study of aged residents of San Antonio, Texas, also demonstrated the positive aspects of age-segregated living.

Poorkaj (1972) also studied the relationship of age segregation to life satisfaction. Poorkaj interviewed fifty-two elders with regard to life satisfaction, leisure activities, and health status. Three groups of subjects were studied: (1) residents of an age-integrated community and participants at a senior center; (2) residents of an age-integrated community and nonparticipants in social activities; and (3) residents of a planned age-segregated retirement community. The three groups of subjects were matched for age, sex, marital status, and religion. The researchers found that the morale of groups one and two were not significantly different, but that the morale of group three was significantly lower. Poorkaj concluded that possibly age segregation is not really as beneficial as we might be led to believe.

In summary, it is difficult to draw clear-cut conclusions as to the relationship of age segregation to life satisfaction. Sherman appropriately sums up this issue: Both age segregation and age integration can be satisfactory, if the older adult has made the choice based on personal needs and preferences (Gelfand, 1984).

Recreational Advantages of Retirement Communities

Although it is not clear whether age segregation has a positive effect on life satisfaction, it is clear that there are great advantages to retirement communities with respect to recreation, in particular, the availability of recreational facilities. According to Gelfand (1984), the retirement community in Youngstown, Arizona, has $2 million in recreation facilities, whereas nearby in Sun City, a retirement community has $12 million in recreation facilities. Gelfand (1984) also describes the impressive recreational facilities of Leisure World in Laguna Hills, California. Their facilities include five clubhouses, swimming pools, a golf course, horseback riding, and theaters. More than 150 clubs and organizations serve the leisure needs of Leisure World's approximately 19,000 residents.

Similarly, Osgood (1982) describes the extensive recreational facilities and programs of Hidden Valley, a retirement community in Arizona with approximately 6,000 residents. Recreational facilities at Hidden Valley include theaters, golf courses, tennis courts, numerous swimming pools, meeting areas, arts and crafts facilities, shuffleboard courts, Jacuzzis, and card and game rooms. According to Osgood (1982), residents are very active, and the extensive facilities receive a great deal of use. Nearly 80 percent of the community residents are involved in one or more clubs or organizations. Some of the more notable groups are the Aquabelles, a women's water ballet and water show team; the Garden Club, which directs an annual community-wide clean-up and beautification project; and the Community Choir, which gives two concerts a year for fellow residents. According to Osgood (1982), most Hidden Valley residents value leisure and enjoy participating in a great variety of recreational activities.

Aside from extensive recreational facilities and programs, retirement communities offer numerous other recreation-related advantages. One advantage of retirement community life is that it validates the retirement role. The "guilt" of not working is eliminated in a retirement community, because residents are surrounded by peers at play (Kaplan, 1979). Thus, retirement community life can have a positive effect on leisure attitudes, enabling greater participation in recreation, without feelings of guilt. Furthermore, the retirement community promotes and creates a leisurely atmosphere, conducive to recreation (Bultena and Wood, 1969).

Another recreation-related advantage of retirement communities is the clustering of age peers with similar interests. This clustering makes the provision of extensive recreation facilities and programs economically feasible (Sherman, 1975). In addition, the clustering of age peers with similar interests promotes higher levels of social interaction and the formation of friendships, as documented by numerous case studies of various retirement communities (Osgood, 1982). The concentration of older people in retirement communities is claimed to help maintain and in some cases enhance social, mental, and physical well-being in later life (Biggs et al., 2000).

Yet another recreational advantage of retirement communities is the easier lifestyle because of the services usually provided (e.g., building and grounds maintenance and transportation). The provision of these services enables residents to have more leisure time, time that can be used for recreational pursuits. Also, the easier lifestyle promotes greater independence and a feeling of freedom, which is a very desirable component of the recreation experience.

Also related to feelings of freedom, retirement community residents tend to be less restricted by crime and the fear of crime, due to the extensive security arrangements offered by many retirement communities. The reduced crime and fear of crime enables residents to feel free to enjoy a greater range of nighttime recreational activities.

In order to gain more insight into trends in retirement housing and the role of recreation in retirement housing, two experts in the field, Philip D. Shapiro and Nancy A. Shapiro, have written the remaining sections of the chapter. Mr. Shapiro has participated in the development, marketing, management, and consulting on more than 2,000 units of senior housing and skilled nursing communities. He has been affiliated with the American Senior Housing Association, National Association of Home Builders-Senior Housing Council, and the American Association of Homes and Services for the Aging. He is the developer of the Promenade on the River. Ms. Shapiro is the director of the Lifestyles Department of the Promenade on the River independent congregate living community for active seniors in Reno, Nevada.

TRENDS IN RETIREMENT HOUSING

Health care and housing experts who have had a keen eye on the "graying of America" have conceptualized and created unique and supportive housing arrangements that integrate various levels of ambulatory health care services, social services, recreational activities, and skilled nursing/long-term care services, to meet the challenging needs of today's older adults. These products are diverse within the setting of the continuum of senior housing and long-term care, including, but not limited to

- independent housing,
- active adult housing,

- independent congregate living (IL),
- assisted living (AL),
- residentially oriented dementia and Alzheimer's facilities (ALZ),
- residentially oriented skilled nursing facilities (SNF), and
- continuing care retirement communities (CCRC), which integrate all of the six products previously listed.

Independent housing is detached and attached housing structures that typically provide only shelter and, therefore, no services. They range from affordable housing financed through such organizations as the U.S. Department of Housing and Urban Development (HUD), Fannie Mae (FNMAE), and state housing authorities, to luxury apartments developed for upper-income clientele. They may offer recreational amenities, but they are à la carte. They can be purchased or leased. They may have a deed restriction for a fifty-five-plus or sixty-two-plus minimum entry age resident. To maintain competitiveness, many of these communities are now incorporating recreation and other amenities.

Active adult housing communities gained notoriety in the Sunbelt and now have sprouted up all over the United States. They typically are for-sale housing products that range from single-family to patio homes to condominiums. Developers add such features as exterior maintenance, athletic complexes, golf courses, swimming pools, social clubs, and security gatehouses to provide an organized social and recreational life, supported by the simplicity of homeowner maintenance features.

The housing boom for elders of the 1980s and 1990s, in which a dominant number of *"congregate" housing communities* (which include IL and AL) were financed and developed, was living testimony to another phenomenon referred to as "aging in place." Independent congregate living communities "bundle" apartment-style units with services such as dining/meals, recreational activities, transportation, emergency call systems, and other various social services. The typical entry age range, nationally, has been seventy-five to eighty years old. Developers/operators of these communities saw favorable acceptance and high absorption rates leading to initially fully occupied communities. Inevitably, the senior tenants, over time, developed acute and/or chronic conditions that ultimately led to their displacement from the community. In other terms, these residents "aged in place" to the extent that the congregate housing environment could no longer provide for new needs.

High turnover rates and poorly planned communities resulted in many failures, nationally, in which some sponsors, investors, and operators experienced substantial depreciation in their assets, while others experienced foreclosures by lenders.

The advent of *assisted living* facilities (AL), loosely defined as a housing environment that integrates IL-type services such as social, recreational, and hospitality services with additional personal care (assistance in bathing, dressing, grooming, eating, ambulation) and health care monitoring services (such as medication reminders) to accommodate for the needs of physically and cognitively frail elderly (typically with an entry age of eighty-five plus), filled a niche that was lacking between independent congregate living and skilled nursing settings. Many IL communities retrofitted living units to incorporate a contingent of AL units, to minimize turnover rates, and strengthen their position in the market by becoming a more diverse product. The AL products are now offered in a variety of models that provide for either dominant physically frail or dominant cognitive-impaired traits, or both of these models in one integrated setting.

Although the independent congregate/assisted living community provides more comprehensive services than its predecessor, it nevertheless still has shortcomings. Aging in place is a dynamic process. Whereas some residents at the assisted level may require acute health care services, and some may even decease in the AL setting, many others will continue to age and inevitably require skilled nursing care, on an around-the-clock basis. For family members and close friends of these elders, the decision to relocate them to a skilled nursing facility is emotionally and physically straining.

A continuum of residential communities for older adults is presented in Figure 4.1 as a way of visualizing the relationship of the different types of housing to one another and the population of older adults that each one serves.

Each of the product lines within the continuum in Figure 4.1 incorporates activity-amenity spaces to effectively serve the senior resident base that resides within the product. It is commonplace for independent housing developers to build parks, walking trails, tennis courts, basketball courts, swimming pool complexes, and other outdoor amenities within a master-planned subdivision design. Such benefits surely enhance the marketability of selling homes. Furthermore, municipal planners and zoning specialists are now demanding that housing developers incorporate green-scape and recreational programming into the site plans and establish permit approval conditions within their planning codes.

Active adult developments, similar to single family housing communities, are known for their programming of golf courses, tennis "clubs," walking and biking trails, aquatic complexes, and country club facilities. These communities typically have a fifty-five-plus age deed restriction to ensure that families and children do not penetrate their intended use of early-retiree

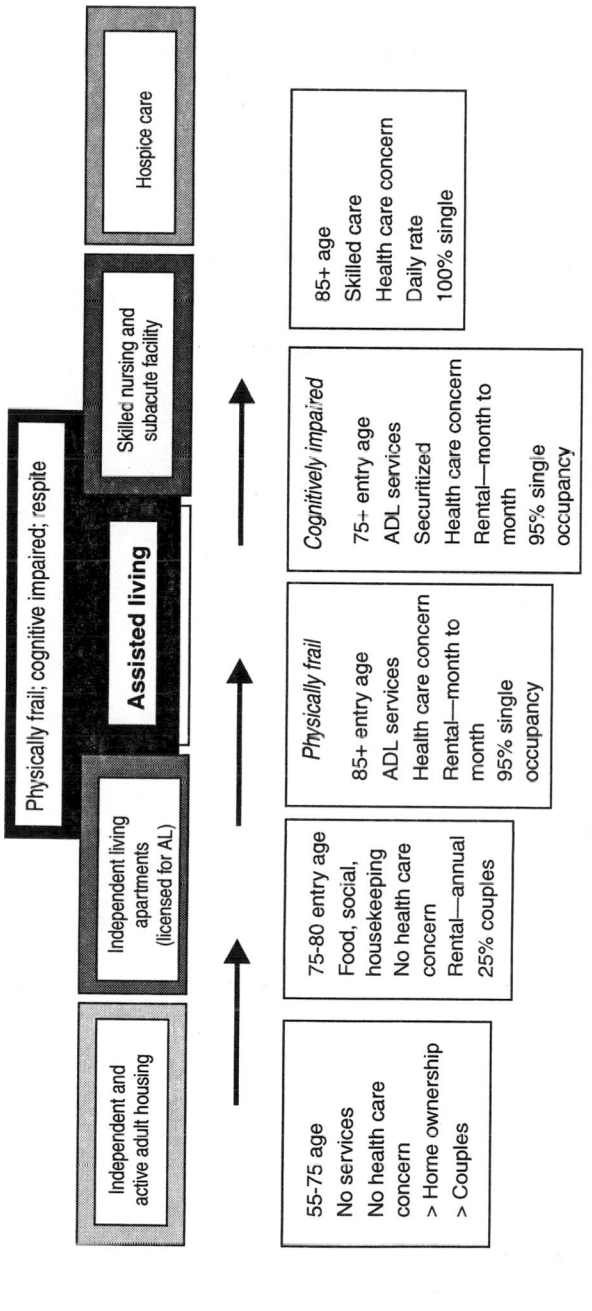

FIGURE 4.1. Types of Residential Communities for Older Adults

seniors. The country club staffs an activity specialist to coordinate daily activities that encourage socialization of residents. It usually programs a full-service restaurant for regular, holiday, and event-purpose dining.

Trends and Perspectives Relating to Activity Programming

Independent congregate living communities in the late 1980s were moving residents in with an average entry age of approximately seventy-five. Today's communities, however, are witnessing a trend of increasing entry age. As reported recently by the American Association of Homes and Services for the Aging, a trade association based in Washington, DC (that represents not-for-profit senior living and long-term care organizations), the average entry age into IL communities in 2001 is now eighty years old. The five-year spread poses a unique challenge for developers and operators as the correlate to an increase in entry age is usually a change in morbidity patterns of senior entrants. Changes in the health status of entrant seniors affects what activity spaces are programmed and the services that surround them. A word of caution, however, is that occasionally age and associated health condition may not be aligned. An eighty-five-year-old resident could look and actually be healthier than a seventy-eight-year-old resident. Genetic predisposition as well as the manner in which people have taken care of themselves over the years surely affect aging. Therefore, it is important that an activities specialist achieve a reasonable understanding of the physical, cognitive, and emotional health status of each of the residents and *tailor* activity programs around "real" people and their capabilities and interests.

There is a dilemma to cope with, as the design of a particular IL community will most likely be accomplished prior to knowing whom the residents will be. Furthermore, the initial core of residents upon opening a new community will not be the last core. In fact, over a five- to seven-year period from opening a community, current resident turnover statistics suggest that 100 percent of the initial resident base will have either relocated to another facility along the continuum (that offers a greater level of personal care and/or skilled nursing) or have become deceased. This turnover is known as *attrition*. The American Seniors Housing Association's report "The State of Seniors Housing 2003" depicts an annual IL resident attrition of about 20 percent.

In recognizing the dynamic of an ever-changing resident base, market researchers, developers, architects, interior designers, and operators need to be able to predict with reasonable accuracy the type of activity amenity spaces that they program into IL communities which will be accepted, appreciated, and utilized by senior residents. It is also advantageous to consider the era in which prospective residents spent their childhoods, family rearing, and working life in. In the early 1990s, the average entrant senior into an IL community would have been characterized as someone who would have spent a good portion of his or her childhood during the Great Depression. Many of today's senior entrants may have missed that historical period in our society. The next generation of senior entrants that are beginning to need IL communities were children during World War II and may have fought in the Korean War. These people are currently in their late sixties and early seventies. Recognition of where one "came from" may have a profound effect on the considerations for activity programming.

The *geographic location* of IL communities also plays a significant role in the ultimate programming of activity amenity spaces. Consider the distinction of an IL community situated in Minneapolis, Minnesota, versus a community located in Miami, Florida. Minneapolis may have a summer-like condition for sixty to ninety days a year, whereas Miami will be just the opposite with over 300 days of warm climate annually. There is a good reason why the majority of office buildings and malls in downtown Minneapolis are connected by climatized "skywalks." Weather has a great effect on the expectation of the type of activities that are indoors and outdoors.

From a *marketing perspective,* a developer/operator will study the competition to derive a comparative analysis of how other existing IL communities have programmed activity amenity spaces. Since we live in a free economy in which consumers have choice, economic competition is responsible for creating differentiated products. Everyone's looking to be the best to attract business. If five existing competitors in a given market area neglected to program a swimming pool and the market research determined that such an amenity would be attractive to new residents, a developer of a new IL community would have a great advantage.

The mission of the sponsor/owner of an IL community (examples of sponsors are not-for-profit religious and health care organizations, private families, public corporations) also has a direct effect on the type of activity amenity spaces to be programmed. Typically, not-for-profit organizations are more interested in covering their operating costs and being economically self-sufficient and less interested in generating large profits, versus a proprietary organization that is very economically motivated. This implies that extra net revenue earned by the not-for-profit organization may be reinvested into the IL community to enhance services whereas that same extra profit in a proprietary company may be earmarked for its investor-shareholders in the form of dividends. However, there are surely exceptions to this commentary.

The next list is of typical activity program spaces found in IL communities and a generalized description of each space and associated functions.

- *Exercise room:* This area may be stocked with free weights (light-weight dumbbells, mats, aerobic machines, and weight-resistance machine) for improvement in aerobic conditioning/circulatory system benefits and muscle mass (to avert the detrimental effects of falling).
- *Arts and crafts:* A variety of programs can occur in this space such as painting, decorating, drawing, pottery, horticulture, etc. It is a multi-purpose space.
- *Multipurpose room:* As its name implies, this space has many functions such as for movies, resident meetings, lectures, group exercising (e.g., stretching class), puzzle building.
- *Mail room:* This is a "gathering" space that surely has activity implications and should be designed to accommodate multiple residents.
- *Swimming pool (indoors in cold-weather climates, outdoors in warm-weather climates):* This is another "gathering" space that has social and exercise benefits, designed with lower water level heights than a typical pool (three to four feet height). The lower water level is good for water aerobics and water walking classes that tend to be popular with residents.
- *Spa/sauna:* This treatment is good for therapeutic and recreational use.
- *Outdoor activity areas:* In many instances this is a "forgotten" activity consideration—gardens, walking areas, gathering areas, with sun and shade considerations.
- *Library:* This area is usually started with resident book donations, a place for research and leisure reading.
- *Main lobby/reception:* This gathering space is situated by the reception/concierge staff and can be an inviting socializing area.
- *Dining room:* This is the "key" predictable activity amenity space in any senior living community (as residents eat daily two to three times each day dependent upon the community's service package).
- *Country kitchen:* There is a small, self-contained kitchen with seating for resident use to bake cookies, prepare soups, where chefs will display a new recipe, etc.
- *Private dining room:* This usually accommodates up to fifteen people; is separate from the main dining room to provide a private environment where family gathers for the celebration of a resident's birthday, an anniversary, a special event.
- *Coffee/snack shop:* This area may be programmed in the form of a "bistro" or as an alternative eating environment.
- *Beauty salon:* This area is a unisex salon for hair cutting, nail work, and foot work.

The number of activity amenity spaces, their corresponding sizes (in terms of total square feet), their configuration, the location of these spaces within an IL building structure, and the associated capital cost are all considered within a *functional program analysis*. Typically, the total square footage that will be allocated to a specific IL community is determined as a factor of the total building square footage. In real estate development (whether it be senior communities, department stores, office buildings, etc.) one key consideration is the percentage of "leasable" or "sales" space against the total square footage. In other words, a developer (owner) does not earn money on space that is allocated to nonrentable or nonsales activity. This space also includes *circulation* such as hallways, elevators, and lobbies.

If there were no economic consideration for the amount of space that could be allocated for activities, an activities specialist would seek unlimited amenities, as more variety is better than less. As a general rule of thumb in the development of IL communities, architects tend to allocate upward of 35 to 40 percent of the total square footage of a typical 125 apartment unit community to activity amenity spaces. Market feasibility analysis will define the ultimate apartment unit demand in a given market area, as well as the mix of units (studio, one bedroom, two bedroom, etc.) and their corresponding layouts and square footage sizes. The case study later in this chapter will take the reader through the activity programming decision-making process of a real-life IL community.

Location of activity amenity spaces is typically a function of the configuration limitations of the vacant land, prior to development. In dense, urban areas, it may be necessary to build multistory buildings due to the scarcity and cost of vacant land, whereas in suburban locales, plentiful land provides an opportunity to limit height (number of stories) and achieve a greater spread of spatial requirements.

For many years, architects have promoted the idea of establishing the main dining room of an IL community as the focal point of the activities, and have programmed other activity spaces around the perimeter of the dining room. One benefit of centralizing activity spaces is to limit horizontal walking distances of senior residents (to make it easy to maneuver through a building). Many residents will be challenged by walking distances of more than 120 lineal feet from their apartments to amenity spaces. A negative consideration of congregating all activity spaces on one floor, however, is the queuing effect it creates. Consider having to move 150 senior residents from three stories of apartments with two wings on each story to a centrally located activity floor. Alternatives to this approach are explored in the accompanying case study.

CASE STUDY:
PROMENADE ON THE RIVER, RENO, NEVADA

Promenade on the River (Promenade) is a picturesque eighty-four-unit independent congregate living (IL) community established in 2001, situated in a historic downtown Reno neighborhood and on the bank of the Truckee River flowing from Lake Tahoe through Reno. This community was conceived by Phil Shapiro and Nancy Shapiro, who also have served as the inaugural executive director and lifestyles director at Promenade, and played key roles in the initial market research and program development of activities within the community as well as ones integrated from the greater Reno market.

The first task in developing the community was to assess the desires and needs of its potential residents. The three most plausible approaches in assessing demographics and morbidities of a potential older adult housing market include (1) study of available statistics on a given geographic market area combined with (2) study of elders currently residing in similar or competitive living environments (in this case study that means an assessment of existing IL communities in the greater Reno, Nevada, geographic market area) and (3) a review of regional and national data on the profiles of seniors living in similar communities.

At a more intimate level of research, many sponsors of senior communities conduct a series of "focus group" interviews. Focus group research provides in-depth information regarding a particular problem or issue using group dynamics. In focus group research, a small group of people (usually eight to ten), guided by a moderator, openly discusses attitudes and ideas about a particular issue. Focus groups can be applied to business or consumer research, and participants can include customers, potential customers, employees, or general consumers.

Last, and possibly the most crucial factor in matching activities with residents, is the reliance on the senior community sponsor's mission on how it intends to service its residents. In other words, one sponsor may have a greater interest in providing optimal hospitality services such as housekeeping and food, whereas another is more apt to focus on security and building maintenance, both electing to place activities in a secondary role. The following is Promenade's mission statement, which is visibly framed on a wall upon entering the community:

> We, the owners and management of Promenade on the River, are Reno residents with a depth of professional experience in hotel, senior housing, and health care operations.
>
> Our *mission* encompasses our understanding that our residents have chosen a lifestyle that both respects their individuality and fos-

ters a sense of community. Our programs support our residents' aspiration to maintain active and independent lives, while encouraging social activity and interaction. Our goal is to promote the welfare of our residents and enrich their lives.

Our *belief* is that the primary responsibility of our staff is to meet the daily needs of our residents and make their Promenade experience a fulfilling one. We encourage staff teamwork and reward excellence, thus fostering efforts to provide the greatest degree of resident satisfaction. We strive to provide our residents with the highest level of service, exercise financial responsibility in controlling operating expenses, and offer excellent value.

Our *vision* is to affirm our commitment to create a "community" nurtured by purposeful and broad-based activities that stretch beyond the bounds of Promenade's amenities. Our programs are augmented by the art, culture, and educational opportunities available in the greater Reno area. We continuously interact with our residents to obtain their suggestions for improving their quality of life at Promenade, and we respond to ensure their well-being and satisfaction.

We chose to take a very *comprehensive research* approach toward producing an optimal and award-winning combination of activity amenity spaces and corresponding programs. Activities at Promenade are one of the key elements in maximizing independent living. During the planning phase of the project (which lasted thirteen months) we conducted a formal analysis of demographics and morbidities of seniors residing in other Reno-area IL communities. We produced matrices of these communities that also compared amenity spaces and programs. Over a three-month period, we conducted a series of focus group luncheons. We invited adults ages sixty-five to eighty-five years old to participate in an hour-long lunch combined with questions we asked about their current interests and hobbies. We focused on four distinct areas:

1. education,
2. recreation,
3. culture, and
4. food.

We also promoted that the participants talk about interests they had not yet pursued in their later lives. A very broad range of interests transcended across all the activity categories. Art, however, appeared to be of the greatest interest. A desire to participate in community-based cultural events such as attending the Nevada Opera, the Reno Philharmonic, theater, and the Nevada Ballet also provided us with a glimpse of the cultural interests that we have not seen in other communities across the country.

You can refer to Promenade's Web site at <www.promenadereno.com> to view a directory of amenities and programs that are offered. They include the typical programming stated earlier in this chapter. However, based upon our research findings and mission, we significantly augmented these activities with an *enriched* amenity space and activity programming. The Lifestyles department (known at most facilities as the activities department) adopted a policy of constantly surveying residents to gauge their attitudes about the programs being offered. The employees view the department as a continuous work in progress, allowing for flexibility in evolving current programs and adapting new ones. For example, out of stretching class evolved tai chi and yoga classes. Another example was the residents' complaint that the monthly printed calendar of activities and events was not detailed enough and that they were missing some of them. This led to the creation of an in-house, closed-circuit television channel that the Lifestyles department employees created with the support of the local cable television provider. Now, daily, the department creates a slide show from a Microsoft Power-Point software package that is viewed on channel 21 by all residents. They simply wake up, have a relaxing cup of coffee or tea, and flip to channel 21 and visually learn about all the day's events. This has resulted in an increase in resident participation.

One of the most important activities, and the most naturally occurring one, is the interaction between senior residents and their family members. Although the staff of seniors communities tend, over time, to become a surrogate family for many residents, we strongly believe that nothing replaces family relationships and interaction.

Another vital component of activity programming at Promenade that is specific to the goal of encouraging social interaction between our residents and their local and distant families is numerous intergenerational events such as parties, lectures, theme-based dinners (e.g., a luau party), and other creative events.

An innovative feature of each resident apartment (we call them "villas") is that they are equipped with separate modem lines as well as the ability to connect to high-speed cable. We created a *computer training center* in which to teach our residents how to use e-mail and basic Web-browsing capabilities. We are working with local volunteer high school students who have computer skills that are shared with our residents (so we have actually added an intergenerational aspect to this). We are witnessing a joy to learn supported by a new way to communicate between our senior residents and their families (adult children, grandchildren, and great-grandchildren). It is a fascinating experience for most involved.

Our focus group research also showed a strong interest in continuing education. To that end, we approached the University of Nevada, Reno, which is located within a few miles from Promenade, about creating a linkage with our senior residents. To our excitement, we were apprised of a program already in existence called Elder College. Courses are taught regularly by university professors for older adults on a broad range of subject matter. We were so enthused that we chose to pay the annual tuition for any Promenade resident that has interest in attending Elder College courses. We also provide the transportation to and from the university to make it that much more convenient to participate (the more convenient, the greater likelihood of participation).

Inherent in the Lifestyle department's mission is its interest in proliferating activity programming internally and externally that is both enjoyable and purposeful. Hopefully, these goals will correlate to the happiness and well-being of the residents and enhance their independent lives. However, in spite of national studies substantiating this correlation, the Lifestyles department employees also recognize the importance of maintaining a respect for an individual resident's privacy. In other words, sometimes residents have no interest in participating in activities. This can be a result of many things including underlying depression, being tired, not feeling well, or simply periods when a resident just wants a break from congregate living (associating with others). An aware activities specialist and staff always walk a fine line of knowing when to promote their mission and when to give it a break.

SUMMARY

In summary, the Promenade on the River is an example of an independent congregate living community for active seniors that has incorporated a concern for the quality leisure experiences of its residents. The design of the community, the recreational facilities provided for the residents, and the offering of innovative leisure-related programs all contribute to maximizing the quality of life for its residents.

Retirement communities and other living arrangements for elders seem likely to continue to grow in the near future. As these housing developments continue to grow, they will take on increasing importance as focal points for the delivery of leisure services to elders. Although research cited earlier in the chapter indicates some debate as to whether age segregation is desirable, well-planned communities for older adults have many advantages over unplanned, naturally occurring retirement communities. As discussed earlier in the chapter, many older adults live in NORCs, and the number is likely to rise. Obviously, living in a residence that is developed with the needs of older adults in mind is better than being stuck in a situation where you feel that you are too old to move, yet the residence where you live no longer meets your needs. Perhaps the debate over whether age segregation is desirable is irrelevant, as age segregation occurs naturally anyway. Perhaps the focus should be on enabling as many older adults as possible to live in planned, quality communities. Similar to Promenade on the River, these communities provide the best opportunity for the provision of quality leisure services for older adults.

REFERENCES

American Association of Homes and Services for the Aging (AAHSA) (1993). *Continuing care, retirement communities: An industry in action.* Washington, DC: AAHSA/Ernst and Young.

American Seniors Housing Association (2003). *The state of seniors housing, 2003.* Washington, DC: ASHA.

Atchley, R. (1975). *The sociology of retirement.* New York: Schenkman.

Biggs, S., Bernard, M., Kingston, P., and Nettleton, C. (2000). Lifestyles of belief: Narrative culture in a retirement community. *Aging and Society, 20*(6), 649-672.

Bultena, G.L. and Wood, V. (1969). The American retirement community: Bane or blessing? *Journal of Gerontology, 24*(2), 209-217.

Canedy, D. (2002). Florida redoubles efforts for the elderly. *The New York Times,* May 5, p. A21.

Carp, F.M. (1972). Mobility among members of an established retirement community. *Gerontologist, 12*(1), 48-56.

Cowgill, D.O. (1978). Residential segregation by age in American metropolitan areas. *Journal of Gerontology, 33*(3), 446-453.

Deimling, G.T., Noelker, L.S., and Beckman, A.C. (1979). The impact of race on the resources and well-being of aged public housing residents. Paper presented at Thirty-Second Annual Scientific Meeting of the Gerontological Society, Washington, DC, November.

Garcia, K.J. (1993). Generation gap at seniors' mecca. *San Francisco Chronicle,* February 15, pp. A1, A6.

Gelfand, D.E. (1984). *The aging network: Programs and services* (Second edition). New York: Springer Publishing.

Gubrium, J.P. (1970). Environmental effects on morale in old age and the resources of health and solvency. *Gerontologist, 10,* 294-297.

Hampe, G.D. and Blevins, A.L. (1975). Primary group interaction of residents in a retirement hotel. *International Journal of Aging and Human Development, 6*(4), 309-320.

Joint Center for Housing Studies of Harvard University (2000). Just the facts. *Interiors, 159*(12), 22.

Kaplan, M. (1979). *Leisure: Lifestyle and lifespan.* Philadelphia: W.B. Saunders.

Krout, J.A., Moen, P., Holmes, H.H., Oggins, J., and Bowen, N. (2002). Reasons for relocation to a continuing care retirement community. *Journal of Applied Gerontology, 21*(2), 236-256.

Kuhn, S.E. (1995). Where to move when you're ready to kick back. *Fortune,* April 24, pp. 86-90.

Kunstler, R. (2001). New options for therapeutic recreation in the naturally occurring retirement community. *Parks and Recreation, 36*(5), 74-81.

Magnum, W.P. (1973). Retirement villages. In R.R. Boyd and C.G. Oakes (eds.), *Foundations of practical gerontology* (Second edition) (pp. 237-250). Columbia, SC: University of South Carolina Press.

Messer, M. (1967). The possibility of an age-concentrated environment becoming a normative system. *Gerontologist, 7,* 247-251.

The National Center for Assisted Living (NCAL) (2001). About assisted living. <www.ncal.org/about/facility.htm>.

Osgood, N.J. (1982). *Senior settlers, social integration in retirement communities.* New York: Praeger Publishing.

Poorkaj, H. (1972), Sociological-psychological factors and successful aging. *Sociology and Social Research, 56,* 289-300.

Poulin, J.E. (1984). Age segregation and interpersonal involvement and morale of the aged. *Gerontologist, 24*(3), 266-269.

Raymond, J. (2000). Senior living: Beyond the nursing home. *American Demographics, 22*(11), 58-64.

Sherman, S.R. (1975). Mutual assistance and support in retirement housing. *Journal of Gerontology, 30,* 479-83.

Teaff, J.D., Lawton, M.P., Nahemon, L., and Carlson, D. (1978). Impact of age-integration on the well-being of elderly tenants in public housing. *Journal of Gerontology, 33*(1), 126-133.

Chapter 5

Nursing Homes

INTRODUCTION

The purposes of this chapter are to present general information on nursing homes, discuss the role of recreation in nursing homes, and examine special considerations in the provision of recreation in nursing homes. Topics discussed in this chapter include background information on recreation in nursing homes; an overview of resident characteristics and their implications for providing recreational services; other considerations in providing activities programs in nursing homes, including suggestions on how to work with Alzheimer's patients; an overview of activity ideas and innovative programs; and a humanistic perspective of recreation in nursing homes. Most of the discussion on considerations in providing activity programs and suggestions for innovative activities is also relevant to assisted living communities.

LEARNING OBJECTIVES

Upon completion of this chapter, the student will be able to

1. cite statistics on nursing homes in the United States,
2. describe the nursing home population,
3. identify appropriate activities for a recreation program in a nursing home,
4. identify considerations in planning and leading recreational activities in nursing homes, and
5. describe the nursing home facility (setting).

NURSING HOMES IN THE UNITED STATES

There are approximately 17,000 nursing homes in the United States (Lachs, 2001). The number of nursing homes in this country has declined because of the growth in the number of assisted living communities. Approximately 1 million older adults reside in assisted living (Shapiro, 2003), many of whom would be living in a nursing home if assisted living communities had not become so popular. Overall, 20 to 50 percent of the older population can be expected to live in long-term care facilities (including nursing homes and assisted living) at some time before death (Rehfeldt, Steele, and Dixon, 1999). According to Raymond (2000),

1. There is zero growth in the nursing home industry, and expansion in the assisted living sector is expected to continue.
2. Industry experts predict the end of nursing homes as we now know them. They will be replaced by a variety of new options that will enable older adults to live out their lives in homelike environments.
3. Whereas assisted living costs about $25,000 to $35,000 a year, nursing homes cost an average of $55,000 a year (Hoffman, 2000).

Nursing home care is expensive. Estimates are that if the date at which severe disability forces older Americans into nursing homes could be postponed by one month, the annual savings would be $3 billion ("More Research into Aging Urged," 1991). A government study found that nearly 50 percent of nursing home residents did not need the intensive medical care the home provided and that many residents could likely maintain their independence if they received adequate long-term care services in the home (Stucki and Mulvey, 2000).

RECREATION IN NURSING HOMES

Even though only 3.4 percent of the older population lives in nursing homes, these facilities are a major source of employment for recreation specialists working with elders. Voelkl (1993) reports that for every 100 beds, 1.2 activity directors are employed in nursing homes nationwide. Unfortunately, in the past, many of the nursing home activity coordinators were probably not fully trained, resulting in activity programs that were viewed negatively as being mindless or purposeless (Wilhite and Teaff, 1986). Despite the well-documented value of leisure activity for elders (see Chapter 1), budget restraints have caused some states to reduce funding for recreation programs in nursing homes (Johnson, 1991).

Researchers investigating the recreation participation patterns of nursing home residents indicate a need for increased resident involvement. Voelkl (1993) reports that 39 percent of resident time is spent in null activity and another 17 percent is spent in passive activity; 62.8 percent of the time is spent alone. The highest level of affect was reported to be experienced when engaged in independent leisure activities (e.g., hobbies, crafts, and socializing). Especially troubling is the great amount of time spent in "null" or no activity—just sitting, looking into space, with nothing to do. According to the U.S. Department of Health, Education, and Welfare (1979), for activities occurring inside the facility, 65 percent of all residents nationwide attend at least one activity per month and 35 percent do not attend. Activities outside the facility were not as well attended; only 31 percent of all residents nation-wide attended one activity outside of the facility during the course of a month. Of this total, 20 percent visited with family and friends, 10 percent went on shopping trips, and 8 percent participated in a group walk. There were additional small figures for attending movies, libraries, parks, etc. Of the nearly 70 percent that did not attend programs outside of the institution, 36 percent of the residents indicated that they did not attend the activities due to illness. The reasons the remaining 32 percent (who were physically able to but did not attend activities) gave were confusion, fright, or a refusal to attend (U.S. Department of Health, Education, and Welfare, 1979). Imagine—nearly 70 percent of nursing home residents do not leave the home even once a month! How would you feel if you did not leave your home, apartment, or dorm even once in an entire month?

The statistics cited in the previous paragraphs are from older studies. Exercise 5.1 is designed to examine the accuracy of these statistics for nursing homes today. Please complete Exercise 5.1 before moving on.

Looking at your answers in Exercise 5.1, how accurate do the statistics from the older studies on null activity and resident participation rates seem to be? How did you feel about what you observed in the nursing home? In particular, what were your feelings about the activities offered? How did the resident characteristics listed in the next section seem to match with the residents in the home you visited?

CHARACTERISTICS OF NURSING HOME RESIDENTS AND THEIR IMPLICATIONS FOR RECREATION SERVICES

According to Voelkl (1993), the following is true of nursing home residents:

1. Most are female (75 percent).
2. Most are white (93 percent).
3. Most are age 75 and over (84 percent).
4. Almost half are 85 and over (45 percent).
5. Most have memory impairment or disorientation (62 percent).
6. About half have Alzheimer's disease or a related dementia (Katsinas, 2000) (50 percent).

EXERCISE 5.1. Examining "Null Activity" and Recreation Programs
in a Local Nursing Home

Instructions

1. Arrange with a local nursing home to visit the home, observe some activities, obtain a copy of the activity schedule, and meet with the activity director or assistant activity director.
2. Try to spend at least two or three hours at the home.
3. As you walk through the home, pay special attention to the number of residents you observe in null activity. Try to estimate what percentage of the residents seem to be in null activity at any given point in time.
4. Ask the activity director or assistant activity director for their estimates on the percentage of residents who attend at least one activity inside the home each month, and the percentage who attend at least one activity outside the facility each month.
5. Write your answers in the spaces below.

Observations and Information from Activity Personnel

1. Percentage of residents who seem to be in null activity: _____

   _____

   _____

   _____

2. Percentage of residents participating in at least one activity per month:

   _____

   _____

   _____

3. Percentage of residents going outside the facility at least once per month:

   _____

   _____

   _____

   _____

4. Other observations: _____

   _____

   _____

   _____

Similar to other settings for recreation services for elders, the preponderance of females necessitates programming activities geared toward more feminine needs and interests, while also offering activities especially for males in order to help them overcome their reservations about participating in female-dominated activities. Unlike the other settings, nursing home residents are older and more impaired. Although the residents of assisted living are also mostly female, in their eighties, and may have memory impairment or disorientation, the functioning level of nursing home residents tends to be even lower. Depression is more of a problem, with 20 to 40 percent of nursing home residents estimated to be very depressed, as opposed to 3 percent of Americans over sixty-five being clinically depressed and 7 to 12 percent suffering milder forms of depression (Brody, 1994). Although someone in a depressed state does not feel like participating in activities and would be difficult to motivate, activities can cause an upward mood swing, which can create the momentum to lift someone from a depressed state.

Another important resident characteristic is that many are not ambulatory. Therefore, most activities need to be adapted to enable participation by elders in wheelchairs. In some nursing homes, even elders who can walk are in wheelchairs to reduce the risk of injury and allow for the limited number of staff to care for everyone.

Activities need to be simple and not put much demand on short-term memory. Day care centers might have one recreation therapist for approximately every ten elders, making it feasible to implement a therapeutic recreation program. Nursing homes have only 1.2 activity directors per 100 residents (on average), so the implementation of a therapeutic recreation program is more difficult. Activities often need to be more diversionary in nature, enabling one or two staff to work with groups of twenty to fifty residents at one time. To implement more therapeutic activities, the activity director needs to be resourceful at recruiting volunteers to assist with activities. Many more activities are possible when there are six or eight pairs of helping hands! Because so many residents have mental impairments or hearing loss, just introducing and explaining an activity to a large group can require having several helpers to reexplain the activity to everyone and demonstrate it if necessary.

A great deal of adaptation of activity should be implemented into the program to facilitate successful resident participation. Activity modification can include a large degree of repetition, reducing the number of steps required to accomplish specific tasks or goals, a great deal of demonstration, and activities that utilize long-term memory skills rather than short-term memory.

There is a relatively high turnover rate among nursing home residents. Approximately 50 percent of older adults who spend some time in a nursing home stay less than six months, and about 20 percent spend five years there (Hoffman, 2000). According to Gelfand (1984), the high turnover rate is due to: (1) residents returning home after a temporary stay (20 percent); (2) residents transferring to other nursing homes (13 percent); and (3) residents dying (e.g., in Alabama, 44 percent of patient deaths occurred within a few months of admission).

According to Gelfand (1984), most nursing home residents have no family support system to encourage their staying in the community. Only 10 percent of the residents have a living spouse, with 63 percent widowed and 22 percent never married. Many of the residents are socially isolated and more than 50 percent have no close living relative. In addition, at least 60 percent have no visitors at all. However, even though visits by family members are desirable, they can sometimes cause the family members to experience stress. Under extreme circumstances, they may become aggressive toward nursing home staff (Mazza and Vinton, 1999).

These statistics shed light on some of the difficulties activity directors face and why some "burn out" on their job. The activity directors infrequently get to see progress in their clients. Just the opposite, over time, many of the residents (some of whom have formed close relationships with the director) die. The activity director somehow needs to have the ability to be warm, caring, and open to forming fairly close relationships with clients, yet be able to cope with the prospect of their dying. The activity director is, for many residents, the one person who brings joy into their lives, and is sometimes also looked upon as a surrogate family member. At any time, many residents want and need the activity director's personal attention. Unfortunately, record-keeping responsibilities infringe on the amount of time the activity director can devote to face-to-face work with the residents.

The institutional nature of the nursing home also has several implications for recreation. Since the facility is open twenty-four hours per day, seven days per week, activities can be scheduled for evenings and weekends, unlike most senior centers and senior day care centers. This is helpful, in that it enables the scheduling of performers and speakers who are available only during evening hours or weekends.

Due to the typically small number of activity staff, activity programs in nursing homes commonly are able to offer only one activity at a time. However, the scheduled activities can and should be supplemented by opportunities for spontaneous activity, such as music listening, board games, gardening, etc. Having these opportunities available is especially important during the evenings and weekends when activity personnel might not be on duty. Refer to the chapter on program planning for more ideas for spontaneous activity opportunity ideas.

OTHER CONSIDERATIONS IN PROVIDING
RECREATIONAL SERVICES

The needs and desires of residents must be considered in program planning. In one nationwide survey of 150 residents and 150 nursing aides at forty-five nursing homes in five states ("Nursing Home Residents Stun Ethicists," 1989), residents rated being able to go out and leave the home for short periods of time to go for a walk or to do an errand as being of greatest importance. Considering the statistics cited previously in the chapter that nearly 70 percent of residents do not leave the home even once a month and that there are high rates of depression and disorientation among residents, it seems wise to try to provide more activities that occur outside of the home. Perhaps rates of depression and disorientation could be reduced if residents were able to go out more often. In this study, the nursing aides rated activities as being the most important aspect of nursing home life. One message from this finding is that activities are important not only for the residents but for the staff as well, because activities can create a happier atmosphere that makes life for the residents and work for the staff more pleasant. Certainly, if the residents are happier, the staff will find them more pleasant to work with.

Again, it might be interesting to examine the relevance of statistics from an older research study to nursing homes today. Exercise 5.2 asks you to compare the priorities of residents of a local nursing home to the priorities cited in the previous paragraph. This exercise can be completed in conjunction with the nursing home visit conducted to complete Exercise 5.1.

After you have completed Exercise 5.2, consider the following questions: How do your answers to Exercise 5.2 compare to the research cited in this section of the chapter? How do your interviews correspond with observations and suggestions of others cited in the following paragraphs?

Robertson (1988) discusses the importance of giving residents the freedom to choose their level of involvement in activities. Although this might not be possible with lower-functioning elders, it should be a goal as a person's level of functioning improves. Robertson (1988) recognizes that at the lowest levels of functional ability, coercion might be more appropriate than freedom to choose. However, greater freedom is the eventual goal.

In a related vein, a study on the effects of giving nursing home residents greater control over their activities found that residents enjoyed the opportunity to lead or assist in leading activities, as long as they did not have to take on more responsibility or control than they wished (Shary and Iso-Ahola, 1989). Previous studies cited by the researchers indicated that having greater personal control, choice, and responsibility improved nursing home

EXERCISE 5.2. Priorities of Residents of a Local Nursing Home

Instructions

1. During the nursing home visit conducted for Exercise 5.1, interview as many residents as you can.
2. Ask them what their priorities are regarding life in the nursing home. There might be some difficulty in accomplishing this task, as many of the residents might be unable to read a questionnaire or list of options. Another problem is that a simple open-ended question such as "What are your priorities?" might be too vague. Try the following approach:
    a. Be sure to personally introduce yourself and get acquainted before asking any questions.
    b. Perhaps begin by asking what are some of the favorite things about the nursing home.
    c. Try asking what are some things that would make life better in the home.
    d. Try to follow up on the previous question by asking what aspects of life in the nursing home or issues are most important to them. If needed, provide some choices, such as being able to go out of the home, quality of the food, visits from family members, activities, etc.
3. Write your answers below.

Favorite Things	Suggestions	Resident Priorities
_____	_____	_____
_____	_____	_____
_____	_____	_____
_____	_____	_____
_____	_____	_____
_____	_____	_____
_____	_____	_____
_____	_____	_____
_____	_____	_____
_____	_____	_____
_____	_____	_____
_____	_____	_____
_____	_____	_____
_____	_____	_____

residents' psychological and physical health, and lowered their mortality rate.

Another study on this topic reached similar conclusions. According to Green and Cooper (2000), four key factors related to residents being involved in activities are

1. residents' control over the activity,
2. residents' choice of activity,
3. level of motivation, and
4. ability level.

According to the Alzheimer's Disease and Related Disorders Association, Inc. (ADRDA, 1987), it is desirable to give even the confused, irrational residents as much control as possible (while being sure to never place a confused resident in a position of responsibility). Other suggestions for working with confused, irrational residents include avoiding negative, stressful feedback; offering reassurance; trying to distract rather than coerce or argue with a resident; and to break down an activity into its most simple steps when asking a confused resident to do something (ADRDA, 1987).

Another concern in working with Alzheimer's patients is agitation and aggressive behavior. Research (Flansberry et al., 1999) on this topic found that there was a link between the occurrences of agitation and

1. time of the day (risk of agitation increased after lunch time),
2. the activity pursued,
3. overstimulation,
4. the physical environmental cues, and
5. miscommunication or lack of communication.

Some of the modifications in physical and social environment that seemed to reduce agitation in this study included

1. eliminating coat racks and boot trays from view, as they seemed to be constant cues that it is "time to go";
2. closing curtains in the late afternoon as darkness set in;
3. more reminiscing exercises in the afternoon, such as singing old songs and talking about the past;
4. stimulating the senses through activities such as food preparation and baking; and
5. providing more socially oriented activities.

An in-depth analysis of interaction between therapeutic recreation professionals and Alzheimer's patients (Doyle and Singleton, 2000) provides a number of helpful insights into how to maximize the benefits of recreational activities for this population:

1. Focus activities on client strengths and preserved skills.
2. Be sensitive to communication strengths and weaknesses of the client and offer physical gestures and prompts when needed to enable the client to understand and find meaning in the experience.
3. Be familiar with the client's leisure history and try to make activities meaningful by connecting them to past experiences.
4. Repeat instructions for the activity at various points of the activity, as needed.
5. Perform the activity alongside the client and provide hand-over-hand assistance to stimulate the client to participate.
6. Structure environmental stimuli so as to reduce confusion and increase the chance of appropriate behavior.

Valenti (in Steffl, 1994) emphasizes the value of humor, singing, dancing, and clapping in working with elders with Alzheimer's. Humor can help to free the spirit, while singing and clapping provide an opportunity to make noise and can be good outlets for releasing frustration. Vecchione (1994) also states that elders with dementia respond well to music and movement. Other suggestions for working with elders with dementia include

1. physically helping clients get started with activities, as they often have difficulty initiating a task;
2. using activities that are repetitive in nature;
3. avoiding overstimulation; and
4. trying to utilize clients' past histories and build upon past interests and overlearned behaviors, such as playing the piano.

The importance of breaking down an activity into its most simple steps is further reinforced by research indicating that elders in nursing homes have the most positive subjective experience when they perceive that their skill levels are higher than the challenges of the activity (Voelkl, 1990). However, research also indicates that in independent activities such as reading and hobbies, residents may feel more comfortable being challenged and actually report a high frequency of high challenge/high skill experiences (Voelkl, 1990). Therefore, an activity program should provide opportunities for involvement in higher challenge/higher skill activities, especially on an independent basis. However, as shown in a study by Kolanowski et al. (2001), it is important to match skill and interest level in choosing activities. In this study, conducted with dementia patients in two nursing homes, residents exposed to matched skill level and interest activities displayed more positive affect compared to those exposed to skill match only activities. During the course of the activities program, the participants had fewer days when any dementia behavior was exhibited.

In Exercise 5.3, the suggestions from this section on working with nursing home residents with dementia are summarized in the first column. In the exercise, you are asked to go to a nursing home and observe some of the activities conducted with Alzheimer's patients. Have this exercise ready and available to you during your visit. Critique the activity observed in terms of the incorporation of the suggestions for working with Alzheimer's patients. If you observed the technique used during the activity, describe how it was used. If it was not used, indicate how the technique could have been incorporated into the activity to make it better.

In summary, there are many considerations in leading and planning recreational activities for residents with Alzheimer's disease. Incorporating the suggestions in this chapter can make activities with Alzheimer's patients more successful. In addition, new and different activities, as described in the next section, can benefit nursing home residents, including those with dementia, more than traditional activities that have been common to nursing home activity programs for many years.

ACTIVITY PROGRAMS IN NURSING HOMES

Activity programs in nursing homes have changed since the 1980s. In 2004, some nursing home activity programs offer adapted dance (see Chapter 13), yoga, weight lifting, aromatherapy, massage therapy, shiatsu, and reflexology to residents. Meanwhile, according to Wilhite and Teaff (1986), the most common activities offered in nursing homes in the 1980s were television (99 percent); reading books and papers (97 percent); cards, bingo, and games (94 percent); parties (89 percent); religious activities (89 percent); and arts and crafts (70 percent). In 1987, the Omnibus Budget Reconciliation Act was passed, which mandated that every nursing home that gets Medicare and/or Medicaid funds must have an activity program directed by a qualified individual (NAAP, 2003). In contrast, assisted living communities are not as closely regulated as nursing homes and there are concerns about inconsistencies in quality of services (including recreation) in assisted living facilities (Shapiro, 2003). As indicated by research cited on the effects of various recreational activity programs on nursing home residents,

EXERCISE 5.3. Recreational Work with Alzheimer's Patients

<u>Suggested Techniques</u>	<u>Observations from the Activity</u>
Giving residents control over the activity	_____
	_____
	_____
	_____
Breaking down a task into simple steps	_____
	_____
	_____
	_____
Distracting rather than coercing a resident	_____
	_____
	_____
	_____
Use of reminiscing	_____
	_____
	_____
	_____
Socialization opportunities provided	_____
	_____
	_____
	_____
Stimulating various senses	_____
	_____
	_____
	_____
Focus on client strengths and skills	_____
	_____
	_____
	_____

Use of physical gestures and prompts

_____

_____

_____

_____

Connecting the activity to client's history

_____

_____

_____

_____

Repeating instructions

_____

_____

_____

_____

Providing hand-over-hand assistance

_____

_____

_____

_____

Use of humor, singing, dancing, or clapping

_____

_____

_____

_____

Physically helping a client get started with a task

_____

_____

_____

_____

Using activities that are repetitive in nature

_____

_____

_____

_____

progress has been made since 1987 in documenting the positive effects of a variety of innovative recreational activities in nursing homes.

For example, one way to provide high-functioning residents with greater challenge is to have them perform "patient aide work," serving almost in the role of volunteer in bringing activities to residents who are in bed (Forsythe, 1989). However, commingling elders who are cognitively impaired with those who are not can have a negative effect. Teresi, Holmes, and Monaco (1993) report that commingling caused the high-functioning elders to have periods of demoralization or depression, and they expressed dissatisfaction with their quality of life. Thus, it appears that for commingling to be successful, the high-functioning elders should be given a role with status (e.g., patient aide).

A challenging activity that gives residents roles with status is the production of a residents' newsletter. According to Shour (1989), it is a vehicle for residents to express ideas, fears, and hopes, and provides an opportunity to work as a group. Hillebrand (1989) discusses how the artwork of residents and life reviews can be included in a residents' newsletter. Poetry by residents can also be included in a newsletter.

Peck (1989) discusses the special challenges in offering poetry workshops in nursing homes: unpredictable class size, insecurities (unsure of self), disruptive participants, nontalkers, speech difficulties, and straying from the topic. Some successful poetry projects include the use of sensory imagery; discussing what we have loved, what we have known; and using metaphors to describe yourself (e.g., What animal or flower describes you?).

Another example of a successful program possible with nursing home residents is a mapping project to facilitate reminiscence. Weiss and Thurn (1987) found that a mapping project attempted with nursing home residents with mild to moderate disorientation yielded positive results and stimulated reminiscence. As part of the mapping project, residents drew their childhood homes, drew a map of places they had lived and traveled to, and even made a map of things they had done (e.g., flowers they planted in their yards).

Weiss (1989) emphasizes the value of reminiscence, particularly when it is done on a one-to-one basis, for elders with some degree of disorientation. Weiss (1989) urges therapeutic recreation specialists to facilitate reminiscing for this population. One activity that can facilitate reminiscence is storytelling/story writing. John (1991) explains that by telling stories of events that happened in their youth, residents can enhance their storytelling abilities. The activity is mentally stimulating and offers the opportunity for volunteers and youth to learn from the residents. Art can also facilitate reminiscence and provide mental stimulation. Mooney (1992) describes art workshops for nursing home residents in Vermont that have produced critically acclaimed works of art which have been exhibited nationally and internationally. Music therapy can also help with memory as well as alleviate depression. Research (Mathews and Clair, 2000) indicates that music therapy can improve emotional well-being and increase feelings of happiness among nursing home residents with Alzheimer's disease and Parkinson's disease. Therapeutic play activities are also beneficial in several ways for nursing home residents. One study found that therapeutic play activities increased cohesion, creativity, self-exploration, and socialization and improved cognitive, physical, and memory functions of participants (Trzinski and Higgins, 2001).

Amid all of these innovative activities is the old standby: bingo. Parker and Wagner (1988) undertook an activity analysis of bingo and concluded that it is one of the most underrated recreational pursuits of elders. Bingo was found to have the following benefits: improvement of cognitive skills such as memory, ability to follow directions, and decision making; expression of feelings of joy and excitement; social interaction and cooperation in a group; improvement of fine motor coordination, hand/eye coordination, and sensory awareness. So, no more making fun of bingo in the nursing home!

A HUMANISTIC PERSPECTIVE (FROM THE FIRST EDITION)

This last section of the chapter is intended to be a humanistic perspective of recreational work in nursing homes. I (MJL) performed volunteer work in a nursing home, and would like to share some insights gained through this experience.

I have had many years of experience as a professor of recreation with a specialization in gerontology, and I have extensive experience as a recreation specialist in nursing homes, day care centers, senior centers, and community/private enterprise recreation programs for elders. Nevertheless, my volunteer work reinforced my feelings of how rewarding it is to be involved in the provision of recreation services for nursing home residents. Residents are exceptionally expressive of their gratitude for efforts to provide them with recreational experiences. Elders in general are great to work with because they tend to appreciate services provided to them; in particular, elders in nursing homes tend to be very appreciative.

At first, working in a nursing home might seem to be an unenjoyable, dreaded job. Quite honestly, I was unenthusiastic during the first few days of my latest volunteer stint in a nursing home. The environment seemed unpleasant, and many of the residents appeared to have severe mental disabilities.

However, after the first few days, my attitude changed. After working several weeks, I developed enjoyable, meaningful relationships with many of the residents. These relationships as well as the successes I enjoyed in planning and leading well-received recreational activities were instrumental in changing my attitude. I honestly *enjoyed* the time I spent in the nursing home, looked forward to going there every day, and had pleasant experiences to think about when I finished my work for the day. Thus, my advice is: If you don't enjoy working in a nursing home initially, stick with it for a while! Your attitude will probably change.

As a staff member or volunteer, your perception of residents changes drastically over time. Initially, you might perceive the residents as a mass of very old people, impaired both mentally and physically. However, that perception is almost totally destroyed after a while. You begin to relate to the residents as people—unique individuals with their own special personalities and characteristics. You realize what a mistake it is to lump all nursing home residents into the category of very old and impaired. Nursing home residents are as far from being a homogeneous population as a crowd at a baseball game. You must take the time to carefully listen to them in order to find this out.

However, one statement applies to almost all nursing home residents: The provision of recreational services is absolutely vital to their well-being. Recreation can help to compensate for some of the negative aspects of the nursing home environment. It can take peoples' minds off their troubles or illnesses and cheer them up for a while. Recreational activities give residents something to look forward to and something to discuss besides illnesses and complaints. Recreational activities not only make the residents happy but also brighten the atmosphere of the entire nursing home and have a positive effect on staff as well. Recreational activities can give staff an opportunity to see residents in new roles, possibly helping nonrecreation staff to gain insight into their work with the residents.

In particular, recreational activities involving volunteer groups or presentations by individuals or organizations in the community are exceptionally well received. Guest presentors often generate special excitement. New experiences are important for all people; nursing home residents are no exception.

Another basic need of human beings that applies to nursing home residents as well is the need to experience new environments and places. Field trips are excellent recreational activities for this reason. In addition to being enjoyable, field trips give residents a much-needed opportunity to be outside of the nursing home environment for a while.

However, it is wrong to assume that all residents necessarily dislike being in the nursing home. One high-functioning woman mentioned to me that she had been living in the nursing home for twelve years. I expected her to continue the conversation by complaining about her long stay in the home, and hoping she could live at home or with her children. Instead, she said, "This is really like home. When I stay with my children for a weekend, I can't wait to get back here." Although this woman did not claim the home to be a utopian environment, she is clearly content with her living situation in the home. Nursing homes are not necessarily desperately depressing places. Activity directors can make sure that the environment is not depressing by planning and effectively leading an extensive and varied recreation program.

Do not permit stereotypes of nursing homes to prevent you from working in a nursing home. Nursing homes will continue to be a major employer of geriatric recreation specialists. If you do become an activity director in a nursing home, do *not* limit the recreation program to what has been done in the past. Recreation for nursing home residents is a relatively new field, in terms of both research and practice. There are new developments constantly in the field. An activity director needs to keep abreast of these developments, try new programs, use imagination, and continuously try to improve and expand the recreation program to make it better than ever.

Try to think what it would be like to live in a nursing home, and how much effort you would desire the nursing home staff to put into recreational programs. Keep this thought in mind, and try to contribute all you can to the provision of recreation services—display the effort you would desire as a resident. Elders in nursing homes are more in need of recreation than any other segment of the older population. Let's provide them with the enjoyable, meaningful recreational experiences that they so desperately need and can benefit from.

A HUMANISTIC PERSPECTIVE
(PART TWO)

Twenty years later, I still feel the same way about working in nursing homes. The time I spend in nursing homes with my classes, trying the various activities described in this book, are my peak teaching experiences. Nothing makes me feel better than to see the joy that activities bring to residents who might otherwise be in null activity, and also to see students' fear of nursing homes and low-functioning elders be overcome.

Some residents are unpleasant to work with and will act hostile toward you when you're just trying to help them. Do not be upset; just look around the room and you will probably see some residents sitting quietly, hoping you will direct your attention their way. With sincerity and enthusiasm, you will be amazed at how much you can inspire the residents!

SUMMARY

Although only a small percentage of elders reside in nursing homes, it is an important area of concern because nursing home residents are in the greatest need of recreational activities. It is also perhaps the most challenging setting in which to provide leisure services for elders because of the mental and physical disabilities that require activities to be adapted in a variety of ways.

Nursing homes are also a major area of employment for recreation specialists working with elders. Despite the challenges inherent in working in a nursing home, it can be one of the most rewarding places to work. Where else can a person make such a significant impact on the quality of life of so many people?

REFERENCES

Alzheimer's Disease and Related Disorders Association, Inc. (ADRDA) (1987). *Fact Sheet on Alzheimer's Disease.* March. Chicago: ADRDA.

Brody, J. E. (1994). Personal health: Old notions about depression in the elderly are hindering efforts to provide treatment. *The New York Times,* February 9, p. B6.

Doyle, J. and Singleton, J. (2000). Leisure behaviour process and institutionalized persons with organic dementia. *World Leisure and Recreation,* 42(1), 18-24.

Flansberry, L., Dawson, D., Gravelle, F., and Singleton, J. (1999). Agitation of persons with Alzheimer's disease during respite recreational programming: Issues for enhancing service. *World Leisure and Recreation,* 41(2), 35-39.

Forsythe, E. (1989). One-to-one therapeutic recreation activities for the bed and/or room bound. *Activities, Adaptation, and Aging,* 13(1/2), 63-76.

Gelfand, D. E. (1984). *The aging network: Programs and services* (Second edition). New York: Springer Publishing.

Green, S. and Cooper, B. A. (2000). Occupation as a quality of life constituent: A nursing home perspective. *British Journal of Occupational Therapy,* 63(1), 17-24.

Hillebrand, W. V. (1989). Residents' newsletter as a therapeutic tool. *Activities, Adaptation, and Aging,* 13(1/2), 51-61.

Hoffman, E. (2000). Nursing homes don't have to break you. *Business Week,* 3708, p. 169.

John, M. T. (1991). *Story writing in a nursing home: A patchwork of memories.* Binghamton, NY: The Haworth Press.

Johnson, K. (1991). "Nursing homes drain Connecticut budget." *The New York Times,* May 14, pp. B1-B2.

Katsinas, R. (2000). The use and implications of a canine companion in a therapeutic day program for nursing home residents with dementia. *Activities, Adaptation, and Aging,* 25(1), 13-30.

Kolanowski, A., Buettner, L., Losta Jr., P., and Litaker, M. (2001). Capturing interests: Therapeutic recreation activities for persons with dementia. *Therapeutic Recreation Journal,* 35(3), 19-25.

Lachs, M. (2001). Choosing a nursing home. *Prevention,* 53, 181.

Mathews, R. and Clair, A. (2000). Brief in-service training in music therapy for activity aides. *Activities, Adaptation, and Aging,* 24(4), 17-29.

Mazza, N. and Vinton, L. (1999). A nationwide study of group work in nursing homes. *Activities, Adaptation, and Aging,* 24(1), 61-73.

Mooney, G. (1992). An arts program in Vermont that draws people out. *Smithsonian,* 23(8), 76 86.

"More research into aging urged" (1991). *The Sacramento Bee,* June 13, p. A2.

National Association of Activity Professionals (NAAP) (2003). "About NAAP." <www.thenaap.com>.

"Nursing home residents stun ethicists" (1989). *The San Francisco Chronicle,* January 19, p. B4.

Parker, S. D. and Wagner, C. E. (1988). The most underrated activity in nursing homes. *Activities, Adaptation, and Aging,* 12(1/2), 87-90.

Peck, C. F. (1989). From deep within: Poetry workshops in nursing homes. *Activities, Adaptation, and Aging,* 13(3), 1-153.

Raymond, J. (2000). Senior living: Beyond the nursing home. *American Demographics,* 22(11), 58-64.

Rehfeldt, R., Steele, A., and Dixon, M. (1999). Transitioning the elderly into long-term care facilities: A search for solutions. *Activities, Adaptation, and Aging,* 24(4), 27-40.

Robertson, R. D. (1988). Recreation and the institutionalized elderly: Conceptualization of the free choice and intervention continuums. *Activities, Adaptation, and Aging,* 11(1), 61-73.

Shapiro, J. (2003). Report calls for tighter rules on care for the elderly. Available at <www.npr.org/features/feature.php?wfId=1247333>.

Shary, J. and Iso-Ahola, S. (1989). Effects of a control-relevant intervention on nursing home residents' perceived competence and self-esteem. *Therapeutic Recreation Journal,* 20(1), 6-15.

Shour, A. (1989). A residents' newsletter: Social action and power. *Activities, Adaptation, and Aging,* 13(1/2), 43-49.

Steffl, B. M. (1994). Group work and professional programs. In Burnside, I. and Schmidt, M. G. (eds.), *Working with older adults: Group process and techniques* (Third edition) (pp. 352-362). Boston: Jones and Bartlett Publishers.

Stucki, B. and Mulvey, J. (2000). Can aging "boomers" avoid nursing homes? *Consumers Research Magazine,* 83(8), p. 20.

Teresi, J. A., Holmes, D., and Monaco, C. (1993). An evaluation of the effects of comingling cognitively and noncognitively impaired individuals in long-term care facilities. *Gerontologist,* 33(3), 350-359.

Trzinski, A. and Higgins, J. (2001). Therapeutic play activities: Building cohesion and socialization among nursing home residents. *Activities, Adaptation, and Aging,* 25(3/4), 24-32.

U.S. Department of Health, Education, and Welfare (1979). *The National Nursing Home Survey.* Washington, DC: U.S. DHEW. Publication No. 79-1794.

Vecchione, K. M. (1994). A recreational therapist's perspective. In Burnside, I. and Schmidt, M. G. (eds.), *Working with older adults: Group process and techniques* (Third edition) (pp. 318-332). Boston: Jones and Bartlett Publishers.

Voelkl, J. E. (1990). The challenge skill ratio of daily experiences among older adults residing in nursing homes. *Therapeutic Recreation Journal,* 24(1), 7-17.

Voelkl, J. E. (1993). Activity involvement among older adults in institutional settings. In Kelly, J.R. (ed.), *Activity and aging: Staying involved in later life* (pp. 231-245). Newbury Park, CA: Sage Publications.

Weiss, C. (1989). TR and reminiscing: The pursuit of elusive memory and the art of remembering. *Therapeutic Recreation Journal,* 23(1), 7-17.

Weiss, C. and Thurn, J. (1987). A mapping project to facilitate reminiscence in a long-term care facility. *Therapeutic Recreation Journal,* 21(1), 46-53.

Wilhite, B. and Teaff, J. D. (1986). Nursing home recreation: An unchanging diet of bingo, birthdays, and Bible? *Parks and Recreation Magazine,* August, 38-42, 63.

FOR FURTHER INFORMATION, CONTACT:

National Association of Activity Professionals
P.O. Box 5530
Seviereville, TN 37864
Telephone: 865-429-0717
Fax: 865-453-9914
www.thenaap.com

PART II:
FOUNDATIONS

Chapter 6

Recreation Leadership Principles

INTRODUCTION

The leadership and program planning competencies discussed in the next two chapters were identified through an exhaustive review of literature on the topic of leisure and aging, consultation with experts in the field, and a survey of providers of leisure services for older adults. Therefore, the competencies presented in these chapters reflect the concerns of practitioners as well as those of educators and researchers.

Leadership and program planning competencies specific to particular settings are discussed in the chapters on senior day care centers, nursing homes, retirement housing, and senior centers and clubs. The next two chapters focus on skills germane to work in most settings for recreational programs for elders.

This chapter focuses on the acquisition of competencies or skills needed in order to effectively lead recreational activities with elders. Most of the leadership skills discussed in this chapter are presented in the following format: (1) a statement of the skill or competency; (2) a problem situation related to the skill; and (3) examples of solutions to the problem, incorporating knowledge related to the skill or competency. This problem-solving approach is utilized in order to facilitate skill acquisition.

LEARNING OBJECTIVES

The following is a list of learning objectives for this chapter:

1. Understand the basic principles of group work with elders.
   * Plan, construct, and maintain activity groups.
   * Demonstrate the ability to communicate accurately, effectively, and concisely, both orally and in writing, to program participants and staff.
   * Provide the opportunity for social development among program participants.

- Modify activities appropriately to facilitate the involvement of participants with a wide range of physical and mental abilities.
2. Effectively motivate older adults to participate in program activities.
    - Use touch and other nonverbal communication techniques to motivate the participants.
    - Use verbal communication techniques to motivate the participants.
    - Foster a positive self-image within the older adult.
    - Use the remotivation technique.
3. Effectively implement the daily program or schedule.
    - Assist in daily activities, such as lunch and transportation.
    - Perform effectively in leading various activities.
    - Perform effectively in teaching activity skills.

COMPETENCIES

Understand the Basic Principles of Group Work with Elders

Plan, Construct, and Maintain Activity Groups

In most settings for recreation services for elders, many activities are conducted on a group basis. Therefore, the recreation leader must know how to effectively initiate new activity groups and foster the success and continuation of a group over a period of time.

Situation. The supervisor has suggested a new activity to be initiated at the center, a singing group. A group must be initiated that will meet and rehearse at least once a week for twelve weeks. The objectives of the group are enjoyment and improved performance in singing. Describe how to approach planning, developing, and maintaining this singing group.

Solution. In planning the group, the concept or theme of the group should appeal to the needs and interests of the group. For instance, at a veterans' home or hospital where patriotic feelings are more prevalent, the group could be called "Singing Patriots." The group could concentrate on singing patriotic standards such as "God Bless America." On the other hand, if the participant population is primarily Jewish then the group should focus on singing Yiddish or Hebrew songs. The key factor in initiating the group is to attract participants to the group by centering the group's activities to the needs and interests of the target population.

In developing the group, it is essential to have a leader of the group, someone who will see that cohesiveness in the group is maintained and progress in goal attainment (i.e., mastering songs) is achieved.

It is also important to consider the varying functioning or ability levels of group members. Slower learners should be offered extra assistance or opportunity to practice so that group progress is not inordinately slowed. Also, lower ability participants can be matched with the higher functioning participants in order to receive assistance and also enhance the higher functioning participants' self-esteem by giving them a special role as "assistant." However, if the varying ability levels of participants is seriously straining the group, then it might be appropriate to divide the group into "beginning level" and "intermediate or advanced" level. Perhaps the two different groups can eventually sing together, with the beginners singing an easier harmony part to accompany the advanced singers who perform the more difficult lead part. According to Burnside (1994b), alert elders should not be mixed with elders with dementia because it is more difficult to keep all group members interested, and alert elders may think they are really slipping.

Positive reinforcement is an important consideration in maintaining activity groups. Participants should be praised for their efforts and should be made aware of progress achieved in terms of goal attainment. Providing variety and challenge are also important considerations in ensuring that the group continues (e.g., new songs should frequently be presented, in addition to practicing and perfecting a small number of familiar songs).

In summary, some essential considerations in planning, developing, and maintaining activity groups are

1. gear the group toward the interests and needs of the target population;
2. compensate for the varying ability levels of participants by either forming subgroups or developing a buddy system;
3. provide positive reinforcement to motivate group members to continue in the group;
4. present new challenges (e.g., new songs) often enough to prevent boredom from setting in; and
5. schedule the group to meet one or two times per week, often enough to maintain familiarity and interest, but not too often so as to become tiresome.

Demonstrate the Ability to Communicate Accurately, Effectively, and Concisely, Both Orally and in Writing, to Program Participants and Staff

Effective communication skills are vital in performing recreational work with any population. However, effective communication is especially challenging in working with elders, due to the prevalence of sensory deficits among elders.

Situation. A college class is scheduled to come to the center to lead a massage activity. Some of the program participants have considerable vision and/or hearing deficits. What methods of communicating this announcement can be utilized to compensate for the sensory impairments of the participants?

Solution. All of the following techniques should be utilized, as it is imperative to use a combination of verbal and written communication methods in order to compensate for the variety of sensory impairments of group members: (1) verbal announcement of the upcoming activity during lunch or some other large group activity; (2) posters prominently placed throughout the center, or announcements on a blackboard or display board; (3) verbal reminders to individual participants; and (4) personalized written invitations to participants.

In summary, use both written and verbal communication techniques, so as to combine the strengths and counteract the weaknesses inherent in each type of communication. Some helpful techniques to enhance the effectiveness of communication in working with elders follow:

1. Whenever possible, determine if hearing is keener on one side than the other, and get as close to the better ear as possible when talking.
2. Maintain eye contact when talking and keep lips in plain view to facilitate lip reading. Also, men should keep mustaches trimmed, and women should wear bright lipstick to facilitate lip reading (Burnside, 1994a).
3. Speak clearly, slowly, and loudly.
4. Keep explanations short and simple; whenever possible, provide an easily understood example. For instance, if one is trying to communicate that a massage activity will take place next week, perhaps briefly massage the person's hands so that the person understands what the activity will entail.
5. Write messages in large print.
6. Repeat both written and verbal messages numerous times. It is especially important to repeat the message just before the activity.
7. Arrange the group in a circle to maximize hearing and vision (Burnside, 1994b).
8. Use names when addressing group members in order to grab their attention (Burnside, 1994b).
9. Remember to ask for feedback to ensure that the person really understood the message.

There are also some special considerations in communicating with aggressive older adults. The problem of inappropriate aggressive behavior is more common among low functioning elders than it is in work with other older adults. The following suggestions can be helpful in dealing with inappropriate aggressive behavior (American Psychiatric Nurses Association, 1998):

1. First, try to understand the causes of the aggressive behavior. Frustrations can develop from loss of abilities, unwanted dependence, illusions, and impaired hearing or vision. Low functioning older adults with limited verbal communication skills might only be able to express their feelings/frustrations through aggresive behavior.
2. After recognizing the factors causing the aggressive behavior, try to empathize with the needs and feelings of the person.
3. Try to communicate support to the older adult for his or her losses and needs.
4. Look for early warning signs of aggressive behavior and try to prevent escalation of these behaviors.
5. Try to enhance the involvement of the older adult in activities and help them to be able to do things for themselves.
6. Express caring for the older adult's needs and preferences.
7. Try to take the time to interact therapeutically and avoid rushing interactions, as it will add to feelings of frustration.

Provide the Opportunity for Social Development
Among Program Participants

A recreation program is often the only social outlet for an individual. Even nonverbal activities, such as dancing, can facilitate social development. Considerations such as the wearing of name tags and personal introductions of participants at the beginning of each activity can enhance the social aspects of activities.

Situation. Mr. X is one of the higher-functioning residents in his nursing home, yet he does not talk to other participants and tends to shy away from group activities, avoiding almost all social contact. How can this man's social interaction be improved?

Solution. First, it is important to understand the root causes of Mr. X's problem. Is he afraid of being embarrassed or looking foolish? Does he feel inadequate among others or, on the other hand, does he feel so superior to the others that he feels interacting with the other residents is "below his level"? Is it possible that none of the activities offered interest him? Action designed to foster Mr. X's social interaction should be based on the results of assessing the causes of the problem. This assessment can be accomplished by interviewing Mr. X and possibly also talking to his family. Nevertheless, some generally applicable techniques are worth trying, regardless of the causes of the problem:

1. Encourage Mr. X merely to "try" an activity, stressing that he has the opportunity to leave the activity whenever he so desires.
2. Offer Mr. X some status that gives him higher self-esteem and encourages others to seek interaction with him. For example, ask Mr. X to be the leader's assistant for a particular activity.
3. Try to involve Mr. X in nonverbal activities that interest him, activities in which social interaction is not the main focus, but would be an important by-product. An example of such an activity is an exercise session.

In summary, remember that social interaction is as important for elders as for people in any age group. Interaction should be encouraged in a gentle manner in order to avoid strong resistance by elders who tend to avoid social interaction.

Modify Activities Appropriately to Facilitate
the Involvement of Participants with a Wide Range
of Physical and Mental Abilities

In leading group activities, varying ability levels among participants can pose a special challenge.

Situation. A shuffleboard game is planned for ten participants. Four participants have no significant mental or physical impairments; two are blind; two are confused, but mobile; and two are wheelchair bound and frail. Describe how to modify and conduct this activity to facilitate the involvement and enjoyment of all participants.

Solution. In a competitive game such as shuffleboard, the activity is most exciting and interesting to the participants when the players are of equal ability. When modifying a game the objective is to make the competition as even as possible. The activity leader and/or higher-functioning participants should help the lower-functioning participants as needed. For example, the blind participants should be guided to the starting line and be given a great deal of verbal feedback, but should push the disc independently. Meanwhile, the frail people should receive physical assistance in pushing the disc, or be allowed to begin from a closer position. The confused participants should receive a great deal of orientation to the game through demonstration.

Imagination is an important asset in appropriately modifying activities. Rules can be modified in a variety of ways. Although it is desirable to make activities easier for lower-functioning participants, it is also important *not* to overly modify an activity, resulting in higher-functioning participants feeling frustrated.

Carter, Van Andel, and Robb (in Vecchione, 1994) identify several ways to adapt an activity:

1. Change the rules of the game.
2. Use lighter or softer equipment.
3. Decrease distances.
4. Modify equipment in order to make the activity easier to accomplish.
5. Provide more frequent rest periods.
6. Encourage participants to sit instead of stand.
7. Change the techniques used in the activity.
8. Change an activity to a partner or team activity if performing it individually might cause anxiety.

Exercise 6.1 is presented in order to test your imagination in attempting to modify an activity for a diverse group of elders.

Effectively Motivate Elders to Participate in Program Activities

Use of Touch and Other Nonverbal Communication Techniques to Motivate the Participants

Although nonverbal techniques can be as effective as verbal motivational techniques, nonverbal techniques are often overlooked. The squeeze of a hand, a hug, or a kiss can be a great stimulant or reinforcer for a particular behavior. Also, smiles and laughter can provide a great deal of motivation.

Sincerity is essential in utilizing nonverbal techniques to motivate elders to participate in activities. Especially in working with impaired elders, one might play "favorites"—some confused elders might seem especially affectionate. However, it is important not to play favorites—even higher-functioning people crave attention. Also, remember that elders of different cultural/ethnic backgrounds respond differently to nonverbal techniques. Nonverbal techniques might not be appropriate in working with elders of certain cultural backgrounds in which physical contact is less accepted.

EXERCISE 6.1. Modifying Activities for Diverse Groups

Activity: Beachball volleyball

Participants: Eight of the twelve elders in the group are in wheelchairs. The ambulatory elders are moderately disoriented. Two of the group members are blind, and one is deaf.

Instructions: Describe how you would introduce and lead the activity, special equipment you would use, how you would modify the rules of the game, how you would arrange the participants, and special assistance you would try to offer during the activity.

*Introduction:*_____

_____

_____

_____

_____

Adapted equipment: _____

_____

_____

_____

_____

Rule modifications: _____

_____

_____

_____

_____

Special assistance: _____

_____

_____

_____

_____

Use of Verbal Communication Techniques to Motivate the Participants

Elders who have experienced a loss of physical skills, the loss of a spouse, or have dealt with other difficult life changes can be especially difficult to motivate. These people can potentially benefit the most from participating in activities. Another challenge the recreation leader often faces in attempting to motivate elders to participate in activities is their belief in the work ethic. Many elders view work as the most important life activity, and view recreational activity as meaningless. Thus, many elders do not wish to participate in recreational activities.

Do not coax, beg, threaten, or force an elder to participate in an activity—treat elders with the respect they deserve. Even if the reasons given for not participating in an activity seem childish to you, avoid talking to elders in a condescending manner. *Never* treat elders as children! Emphasize the specific benefits of an activity related to the particular needs of an individual (e.g., in trying to convince an elder with back problems to participate in an exercise activity, emphasize the back flexibility improvements that can be gained from an exercise session). Personal invitations and providing leadership roles for people can help motivate them to participate in an activity. In addition, a brief demonstration of the activity or display of a finished product (e.g., for an art activity) can be a motivating factor. Another useful technique is to utilize peer influence to motivate participation. Determine who the "leaders" in a group are, and focus on obtaining their participation in the activity. Then, have the leaders attempt to motivate the others to join in.

Remember that lack of motivation is *not* the only reason for non-participation in an activity. Lack of interest can also be a major factor. It is important to distinguish between these two factors and determine the criteria necessary to induce participation for each individual. Other reasons for not wanting to participate in an activity can be fear of injury, unwillingness to try something new, or misunderstanding what the activity actually is.

Situation. Mrs. C is in good health, communicates well, and is fairly alert. She has come to a massage activity (hand massage and facials), but when she is approached to be given a massage, she says that she does not want one. As the activity leader, you are frustrated because you are certain that she would enjoy a hand massage immensely. However, you also know that Mrs. C can be pretty stubborn, and any attempts to try to convince her to participate will only make her more firm in her opposition to joining the activity. What can be done to get her involved?

Solution. Sit near Mrs. C while you massage someone else's hands, making sure that she can see exactly what you are doing, and can hear the massage recipient express his or her enjoyment of the massage. Ask Mrs. C if she has any questions about what you are doing. Doing so will not only arouse Mrs. C's interest in the activity but it should also help to eliminate any fears or misunderstandings she had about the activity. After watching the activity for a while, she will likely request a massage, without you even having to ask her to participate.

Ability to Foster a Positive Self-Image Within the Older Adult

One's self-image is an important factor in motivation to participate in recreational activities. A low or negative self-image can lead a person to feel incompetent to participate in activities that they could realistically participate in and enjoy.

Situation. Mr. C is in excellent health, loves sports, but refuses to be involved in sports-related activities, claiming, "I don't want to make a fool of myself." How should Mr. C be approached in attempting to get him involved in sports-related activities?

Solution.

1. Break down the activity into component parts and subtasks. Allow Mr. C the opportunity to master each subtask, and after feeling a sense of accomplishment in mastering the easier subtasks, encourage him to attempt the activity.
2. Involve Mr. C in the activity initially in a nonthreatening, nonactive role (e.g., scorekeeper) and focus on his expertise in the scorekeeper role.
3. Provide a great deal of sincere positive reinforcement for tasks performed well.
4. Allow Mr. C to reminisce about past sports accomplishments.
5. Try noncompetitive sports in which all participants are winners.
6. Modify activities to ensure success (and a positive self-image).
7. Perhaps make the activity especially challenging. Have Mr. C "challenge the champ"—in this situation, there's nothing to lose, and simply playing against the best, win or lose, will enhance one's self-image.

In summary, enhancing self-image is not only important in attempting to motivate one to become involved in an activity, but is also an important by-product of participation in activities.

Use of the Remotivation Technique (Kohut, Kohut, and Fleishman, 1979;
Moran, 1979; Teaff, 1985)

Remotivation is a motivational technique appropriate for use in work
with moderately disoriented elders. Remotivation would not work well with
severely disoriented elders; reality orientation is a more appropriate technique to use with that population. Elders without any cognitive impairment
would also not be good candidates for remotivation, as they are able to participate in more intellectually challenging discussion groups. The purposes
of remotivation are to remotivate old interests, draw people out, and bring
them closer in touch with reality. Remotivation helps to reduce feelings of
isolation by providing opportunities for interaction with others.

The leader of a remotivation session is called the remotivator. The
remotivator begins by choosing a topic to discuss. The range of topics is limitless (e.g., animals, seasons, baseball, desserts, flowers, dance, children,
etc.). However, topic areas should not be sensitive ones that might arouse
negative feelings (examples of inappropriate topics are politics, death, and
dying). The remotivator plays the role of the student by only asking questions concerning the topic and not supplying any answers to questions. The
participants become the experts, supplying all the information. There are no
right or wrong answers; all responses are accepted.

A remotivation session works well with a group of about eight persons. A
session consists of five steps, each step lasting approximately ten minutes.
Visual aids should be used whenever possible.

The five steps of a remotivation session are as follows:

1. *Climate of acceptance:* The remotivator personally greets each member of the group, making everyone feel welcome. A warm, supportive
   atmosphere is created.
2. *Bridge to reality:* The remotivator begins by asking questions about a
   broad topic, then through questions and answers, narrows it down to
   the topic at hand. Props are then passed around in order to orient group
   members to the topic by appealing to a range of their senses (touch,
   smell, sight, sound, even taste). The remotivator then reads a relevant
   poem to the group (the poem can be original, already published, or
   taken from a song). The purpose of the poem is to create imagery and
   stimulate thought about the topic. The remotivator then asks questions
   about how the participants fit into the topic.
3. *Sharing the world we live in:* A bounce question can be asked (a question with *no* logical answer) to stimulate thought. An example of a
   bounce question is: How many drops of rain have ever fallen? The

remotivator then asks the group members questions concerning personal experiences related to the topic.

4. *Appreciation of the world:* The remotivator asks questions regarding the pros and cons of the topic. The participants are asked to relate the topic to other things in the world.

5. *Climate of appreciation:* The remotivator briefly reviews what has been said during the session, then personally thanks each person for attending.

The following are two sample remotivation sessions:

Sample Session #1

I. *Topic:* Desserts
II. *Props:* A bag of cookies or candy to share. Photographs of desserts from magazines.
III. *Steps:*
  A. *Climate of acceptance:* Personally greet all members of the group. Shake hands and talk briefly to each individual.
  B. *Bridge to reality:*
     1. *Broad questions:*
        a. What is your favorite part of a meal?
        b. Do you ever eat less food and try to save room for dessert?
        c. Which meal do you end with dessert?
     2. Pass around props to stimulate interest in the topic.
     3. *Poem:* Excerpt from the song "Savoy Truffle" by George Harrison (1969) or "The Candyman."
     4. *More specific questions:*
        a. What are your favorite desserts?
        b. Are there particular times of the day when you like to eat sweets?
        c. What beverage do you like to drink with dessert?
        d. What are the different types of desserts?
  C. *Sharing the world we live in:*
     1. *Bounce question:* How many chocolate chips do you think you have ever eaten?
     2. *Personal experience questions:*
        a. Do you ever give sweets as a gift? What do you give?
        b. Did you ever bake a birthday cake for someone? When? What kind?
        c. What is the most delicious dessert you make?

      d. What is your favorite kind of candy?

      e. What is your favorite flavor of ice cream?

      f. Are there any desserts you do not like? Which ones?

D. *Appreciation of the world:*

  1. *Pros and cons:*

      a. How do you feel when you eat dessert?

      b. Do you ever eat dessert and wish you had not indulged?

      c. What are the good things about dessert?

      d. What are the bad things about dessert?

  2. *Relate the topic to other things in the world:*

      a. How do desserts affect your teeth?

      b. How do children feel when they eat desserts?

      c. How much money do you think is spent in the United States on sweets?

      d. How many people do you think are employed by companies and bakeries that make desserts?

E. *Climate of acceptance:* Review what has been said and thank each person for attending.

Sample Session #2

  I. *Topic:* Rain

 II. *Props:* A bucket of rain water. Umbrellas, rain jackets, and other rain apparel.

III. *Steps:*

  A. *Climate of acceptance:* Personally greet all members of the group, shake hands, and talk briefly to each individual.

  B. *Bridge to reality:*

    1. *Broad questions:*

      a. What is your favorite type of weather?

      b. What is your least favorite type of weather?

    2. Pass around the bucket of rain water, and let everyone wet their hands in the water in order to bring the participants closer in touch with the discussion topic. Also pass around the other props as visual aids.

    3. *Poem:* Excerpt from the song "Rain" by John Lennon and Paul McCartney (1966), "Singin' in the Rain," or "Rain, Rain Go Away."

    4. More specific questions:

      a. What other songs have been written about rain?

      b. What causes rain?

  c. Where are the rainiest places in the United States? In the world?

  d. What time of year does it rain the most?

C. *Sharing the world we live in:*

  1. *Bounce question:* How many drops of rain fall in five minutes in an area of one square mile?

  2. *Personal experience questions:*

   a. Has anyone ever had a flood in his or her house due to excessive rain? How bad was it?

   b. Do you enjoy going for a walk in the rain? Where do you like to go?

   c. Have you ever seen a rainbow? How did it make you feel?

   d. What was the worst rainstorm you were ever caught in?

   e. When you stay indoors when it rains, what do you like to do?

   f. Can you tell when it is going to rain? How?

D. *Appreciation of the world:*

  1. *Pros and cons:*

   a. What are some of the good things about rain?

   b. What are some of the bad things about rain?

   c. What activities are you prevented from doing when it rains?

   d. How can rain be used productively?

   e. How can rain be a destructive force?

  2. *Relating the topic to other things in the world:*

   a. How does the rain affect the traffic?

   b. How do people dress when it is raining?

   c. What happens to grassy fields when it does not rain for a long time?

   d. How does rain affect football games and other outdoor sports events?

   e. What happens to the reservoirs and dams when it rains a great deal?

E. *Climate of appreciation:* Review what has been said and thank each person for attending.

Exercise 6.2 is presented in order to test your understanding of the remotivation technique and ability to prepare a remotivation session plan on a given topic.

EXERCISE 6.2. Remotivation Plan

Instructions

Fill in your answers in the blank spaces below. Refer to the sample sessions for desserts and rain described in the text for examples of each category of questions.

1. Topic: Dance

2. Props: _____

_____

3. Two broad questions: _____

_____

4. Poem or song lyrics on the topic of dance: _____

_____

5. List four "more specific" questions about dance: _____

_____

6. Identify a "bounce question" on the topic of dance: _____

_____

7. List six personal experience questions on the topic of dance: _____

_____

8. List four pro and con questions on the topic of dance: _____

_____

9. List five questions that attempt to relate dance to other things in the world:

_____

_____

Effectively Implement the Daily Program or Schedule

Assistance in Daily Activities Such As Lunch and Transportation

Regardless of the setting, most recreation programs for elders include the provision of lunch and/or other meals. In addition, transportation is an important consideration in conducting field trips. Therefore, assistance skills related to transportation and the provision of meals are very important in performing recreational work with elders.

Situation one. A field trip has been planned to a museum that is located approximately thirty minutes away from the center. How can the travel time be utilized as "recreational" time?

Solution. Numerous activities are possible within the confines of a van. The following list identifies some feasible activities:

1. A sing-along, facilitated (if possible) by live musical accompaniment on a guitar or recorder flute, or taped music
2. A musical jamboree, in which the riders play along on small rhythm instruments and kazoos
3. A "name that tune" quiz game, which involves singing and guessing the names of songs
4. Any type of verbal game, such as "license plate bingo," "twenty questions," and trivia quizzes
5. A discussion on a selected topic, perhaps current events, or a review of the day's activities and discussion of upcoming activities
6. A remotivation session on a selected topic or a reality orientation activity, in which the riders are familiarized with their environment and oriented to time, place, and person
7. A tape recording can be produced by the participants for a former staff member and sent to that person. Each participant can take a turn recording a short message.
8. Movement to music, utilizing taped or live music, and incorporating exercise that requires very little space, such as finger, hand, ankle, head, and neck exercises
9. A music appreciation activity, requiring only taped music and closed windows

In summary, many activities are possible while traveling. However, the opportunity to recreate during transit is often not utilized. The ride can be just as enjoyable as the field trip itself. Without recreation or stimulation in general, the riders might become so drowsy during the ride that they continue to be in a low-energy state during the field trip.

Situation two. During the noontime meal, it is obvious that the program participants tend to eat quickly and do not interact. How can the mealtime be made more recreational?

Solution. Mealtime should be enjoyable. Some ideas for making meals more recreational follow:

1. Relaxing, pleasant music (live or recorded) will make the mealtime more enjoyable and relaxing.
2. A performance by staff, either dramatic or musical, can transform the noon meal into a dinner theater.
3. A theme created for mealtime can stimulate the atmosphere of eating in a specialty cuisine restaurant. For example, Italian, Mexican, or French days can be simulated, in which the menu items are identified in both English and the foreign language, appropriate music is playing in the background, and props and decorations are placed in the dining area to create the desired atmosphere.
4. Discussion topics can be suggested or announced for the entire group to encourage interaction among the "diners."
5. Assigned seating can be utilized as a mechanism for facilitating conversation, seating elders together who would be most likely to engage in conversation. How frustrating it is to sit too far away from a friend to be able to converse during the meal!
6. An activity that requires group input, such as discussing possible topics or scripts to be utilized in an upcoming drama activity, would not only be enjoyable but also encourage interaction among the diners.
7. To reduce the potential for feelings of frustration and aggressive behavior (especially with regard to low-functioning elders), try to keep the noise level down to avoid confusion, and serve food that is familiar (American Psychiatric Nurses Association, 1998).

Meals should be nutritious and enjoyable. As with transportation, mealtime is often not fully utilized as an opportunity for socialization and enjoyment, but it can be a very recreational experience.

Ability to Perform Effectively in Leading Various Activities

To effectively lead group activities, it is important to understand group dynamics and theories of leadership. These topics are described only briefly in this section; however, further reading on these topics is suggested

(Burnside, 1978; Deichman and O'Kane, 1975; Jacobs, 1976; Kubie and Landau, 1971; and Niepoth, 1983).

In terms of group dynamics and leadership theory, it is important to recognize the need for different leadership styles in different situations. For example, in leading a discussion group for high-functioning elders, the leader should be more laissez-faire, allowing the participants to control or lead the activity themselves as possible. At the other extreme, the leader of a field trip for mentally impaired elders would need to be quite autocratic to ensure the safety of the participants. Although you might desire to be a "democratic" leader, maintaining a balance between exerting authority and allowing freedom, some situations necessitate leadership that is either more laissez-faire or autocratic.

In general, six steps should be followed in leading group activities:

1. The leader introduces himself or herself and each person in the group.
2. Introduce the activity, using the introduction as an opportunity to arouse interest in the activity.
3. Explain the activity, providing clear step-by-step directions.
4. Demonstrate the activity with a few participants and ask for questions.
5. Conduct the activity.
6. End the activity before it becomes boring.

The introduction to an activity is critical because it can either arouse interest in the activity, or turn people off to it. A sense of group unity and promotion of social interaction can be facilitated by a good introduction. Also, the introduction gives the group an impression of the leader (Is the leader well-prepared? Is the leader sincere and enthusiastic?). Exercise 6.3 gives you an opportunity to prepare a motivational introduction for an activity.

One additional consideration in leading group activities is the position of the leader in the group. A mistake made by inexperienced recreation leaders is explaining an activity from the position of being in the center of a circle of participants. In this position, several participants will see only the leader's back. The activity leader should be a part of the circle, in a position that is facing all of the participants.

In summary, the quality of leadership in an activity is critical to the success of an activity. Personality traits that are difficult to teach, such as genuine enthusiasm for the activity and caring for group members, are also important for a recreation leader to consider when leading a group activity.

EXERCISE 6.3. Introducing an Activity

Instructions

In the space below, write a motivational introduction for a music sing-along activity that you are presenting to a group of high-functioning elders in a retirement home.

_____

_____

_____

_____

_____

_____

_____

_____

_____

_____

_____

_____

_____

_____

_____

_____

_____

_____

_____

_____

Ability to Perform Effectively in Teaching Activity Skills

In many settings, a recreation worker not only leads activities but also provides instruction in various recreational activity skills. In providing instruction, one must not lose sight of the "means" (the learning process) due to overly focusing on the end product (acquisition of activity skills). In other words, the method by which a person acquires skills can be just as enjoyable and rewarding as the actual acquisition of the skill(s) itself. Elders can and do learn new skills, although progress might sometimes be slower and more difficult to notice. Patience on the part of the recreation leader can greatly enhance the enjoyment of the learning process.

In order to enhance the learning process, the following considerations should be kept in mind:

1. Reassure participants who are having difficulty and give these people extra assistance.
2. Demonstrate techniques as much as possible, but try to keep explanations as brief as possible. Do not overload a person with verbal feedback.
3. Do not refer to written materials if possible; rather, try to focus attention on seeing how participants are progressing and assisting them as necessary.
4. If possible, post clearly visible directions or illustrations that are easy to refer to and can be helpful in trying to perfect a new skill.
5. Frequently ask for feedback and questions from participants.
6. Avoid frustration and fatigue from developing by taking periodic brief rest periods.
7. Discourage competitiveness; learning should be individualized. However, periodically observing other participants can be helpful in two ways and should be encouraged. First, observation of others also having difficulty learning the skill will prove reassuring to a struggling participant. Conversely, observing participants performing well can serve as motivation and an instructional aid for participants attempting to learn a new activity.
8. Volunteers can also be helpful in teaching activity skills, especially with a large group with diverse abilities. Volunteers can be used to provide individual assistance to group members who are having greater difficulty with skill acquisition.

In summary, remember that elders can acquire new skills, and the acquisition of new skills can be very enjoyable and rewarding. Individualized goal setting in teaching new skills is desirable and can help to compensate for variance in the ability levels of participants.

SUMMARY

A variety of skills relevant to leading recreational activities with elders were covered in this chapter. Effective leadership is the key to the success of recreational activities with elders. Good program planning and preparation (the topic of the next chapter) are also important, but without strong leadership, even a well-planned activity can be a disappointment.

REFERENCES

American Psychiatric Nurses Association (1998). *Caring for aggressive older adults across level of care* (videotape). Washington, DC: American Psychiatric Nurses Association.

Burnside, I.M. (1978). *Working with the elderly.* Belmont, CA: Wadsworth Publishing.

Burnside, I.M. (1994a). Group work with the cognitively impaired. In Burnside, I.M. and Schmidt, M.G. (Eds.), *Working with older adults: Group process and techniques* (Third edition) (pp. 109-129). Boston: Jones and Bartlett Publishers.

Burnside, I.M. (1994b). Leadership and co-leadership issues. In Burnside, I.M. and Schmidt, M.G. (Eds.), *Working with older adults: Group process and techniques* (Third edition) (pp. 92-105). Boston: Jones and Bartlett Publishers.

Deichman, E.S. and O'Kane, C.P. (eds.) (1975). *Working with the elderly: A training manual.* Buffalo, NY: D.O.K. Publishing.

Harrison, G. (1969). Savoy Truffle. In *George Harrison Anthology.* New York: Warner Bros. Publications.

Jacobs, B. (1976). *Working with the impaired elderly.* Washington, DC: National Council on Aging.

Kohut, S., Kohut, J.J., and Fleishman, J.J. (1979). *Reality orientation for the elderly.* Oradell, NJ: Medical Economics Company.

Kubie, S.H. and Landau, G. (1971). *Group work with the aged.* New York: Greenwood Press.

Lennon, J. and McCartney, P. (1966). Rain. In *The Compleat Beatles,* Volume 1. Greenwich, CT: Cherry Lane Music Co.

Moran, J.M. (1979). *Leisure activities for the mature adult.* Minneapolis, MN: Burgess.

Niepoth, E.W. (1983). *Leisure leadership: Working with people in recreation and park settings.* Englewood Cliffs, NJ: Prentice-Hall.

Teaff, J.D. (1985). *Leisure services with the elderly.* St. Louis, MO: C.V. Mosby.

Vecchione, K.M. (1994). A recreational therapist's perspective. In Burnside, I. and Schmidt, M.G. (eds.), *Working with older adults: Group process and techniques* (Third edition) (pp. 318-332). Boston: Jones and Bartlett Publishers.

OTHER SOURCES OF INFORMATION

National Remotivation Therapy Organization, Inc.
www.remotivation.com

Chapter 7

Program Planning Principles

INTRODUCTION

This chapter focuses on the acquisition of skills or competencies needed to effectively plan recreation programs for elders. The chapter begins with a list of competencies followed by a discussion of these competencies. Similar to the previous chapter, a problem-solving approach has been utilized in discussing many of the competencies.

LEARNING OBJECTIVES

1. Identify and understand the needs, abilities, and interests of program participants.
   - Develop an awareness of recreational activities that can meet the need for recognition, achievement, and intellectual stimulation.
   - Develop an awareness of the special needs and interests of various ethnic, racial, and religious groups.
   - Develop an awareness of the effects of variation in socioeconomic status on the needs and interests of program participants.
2. Effectively utilize resources that can enhance recreational activities and programs.
   - Solicit contributory services from appropriate agencies (awareness of community resources).
   - Solicit volunteer assistance for activities.
   - Effectively supervise and coordinate a volunteer program.
3. Plan an appropriate program of recreational activities.
   - Develop an awareness and understanding of program goals and objectives.
   - Solicit input from program participants in program planning.
   - Plan appropriate, stimulating field trips.
   - Devise daily, weekly, and/or monthly activity schedules.
   - Identify spontaneous/informal activity opportunities that can be offered to elders to supplement the planned program of activities.

COMPETENCIES

Identify and Understand the Needs, Abilities, and Interests of Program Participants

Develop an Awareness of Recreational Activities
That Can Meet the Need for Recognition,
Achievement, and Intellectual Stimulation

Recognition, achievement, and intellectual stimulation are important needs for most people, including elders. These needs are fulfilled through work activities for many people. Elders need the opportunity to meet these needs through recreational activities, because most participants in a recreation program for senior citizens are likely to be retired. Feelings of achievement, recognition, and intellectual stimulation are benefits of a variety of recreational activities.

Situation. Many of the program participants are recently retired from prestigious jobs, and in order to compensate for this role loss, activities that will give these people feelings of achievement, recognition, and intellectual stimulation need to be planned.

Solution. Some recreational activities that can generate feelings of *achievement* are

1. goal-oriented recreational activities, such as arts and crafts projects;
2. skill acquisition recreational activities, such as learning a new sport, craft, musical instrument, or dance; and
3. recreational activities with long-range goals, such as a twenty mile/month walking club or a weight reduction program.

The following are some recreational activities that can generate feelings of *recognition:*

1. Form a resident council or membership committee in which elected officers (president, vice president, etc.) receive recognition.
2. Produce a monthly newsletter in which achievements of participants and their family members are announced.
3. Celebrate milestones such as birthdays and anniversaries.
4. Host a monthly awards ceremony in which participants receive recognition for accomplishments such as charitable donations, assistance with activities, and progress made in weight reduction or exercise pro-

grams. Be sure to give recognition in a meaningful way to *every* participant.

Some examples of *intellectually stimulating* activities are

1. foreign language classes,
2. creative writing activities,
3. current events discussions,
4. intergenerational activities in which elders share knowledge with children or even tutor the children in subjects (e.g., history), and
5. creative drama activities.

In summary, achievement, recognition, and intellectual stimulation are important needs that can be met through recreational activities. The fulfillment of these needs will enhance the psychological well-being and overall life satisfaction of program participants.

Develop an Awareness of the Special Needs and Interests of Various Ethnic, Racial, and Religious Groups

Situation 1. The program participants are quite ethnically and racially diverse. Social interaction among all participants is desirable, but the problem of deep-rooted prejudices among the program participants exists.
Solution.

1. First, staff should not deny that the problem exists. Elders grew up in a different era in which prejudice was more prevalent and accepted, thus prejudice can often be more common among program participants than staff.
2. Coercion or forced attitude change is *not* a solution. Such an approach will most likely cause resentment.
3. Staff should encourage interaction among participants in an unobtrusive manner. Cooperative activities, such as a large-scale arts and crafts project, and group activities, such as singing or exercise, can often be so involving and stimulating that prejudices are temporarily forgotten, barriers are broken, and interaction occurs among all participants of the activity, regardless of race or ethnic background.
4. Prejudicial remarks should be confronted immediately in order to discourage this type of behavior or attitude.
5. Plan activities that give recognition to various racial and ethnic groups and also help to educate participants about positive contributions of

that group. For example, a discussion on famous black Americans, a Latin music appreciation session, or an entertainment/comedy half hour featuring famous Jewish comedians would not only be enjoyable but also make the participants appreciate the special contributions of these ethnic, racial, and religious groups.

In summary, attitude change in the area of prejudice can be quite difficult. The most effective approach for a recreation leader is to plan enjoyable activities that include nonthreatening interaction among all participants, and also to educate participants about different groups through recreational activities.

Situation 2. It is the winter holiday season, and most of your program participants are Christian and will be celebrating Christmas. A few Jewish participants do not observe Christmas but will be celebrating Chanukah. How should the holidays be celebrated so as not to offend anyone?

Solution. It is difficult not to offend anyone in this situation, since matters of religion are sensitive issues. First, it is important to understand why the "typical" way of handling the holiday season is wrong. The typical way is to make a very big deal about Christmas, with many decorations (well in advance of the day) and activities related to the holiday beginning a month or more in advance of the big day. The typical approach also involves having a Chanukah celebration, and some decorations, in the hopes that this will help the Jewish participants feel included.

This approach, though used by many activity directors, is wrong for several reasons. First and foremost is the issue of separation of church and state. If your program receives any government funding then it could be viewed as a violation of the law to celebrate a religious holiday in a public setting, using public funds.

The counterargument is that Christmas is not a religious holiday, that it is possible to celebrate just the secular aspects of the holiday. This argument is wrong because Christmas, though it is probably the most widely celebrated holiday in the United States, is a religious holiday, the most important holiday of the year for Christians. To secularize the holiday or to try to ignore its religious basis can be offensive to Christians.

Similarly, to try to equate Chanukah with Christmas (though it is commonly done) is a distortion of the Jewish religion. Relative to other Jewish holidays, Chanukah is a minor festival—Rosh Hashanah, Yom Kippur, and Passover are much more important holidays for Jews. Why make a big deal of Chanukah if the other holidays are ignored? It does not make sense.

Religion, though celebrated and observed with others in a congregation, is a personal matter. Why would a person need to celebrate a religious holiday at a senior center or day care center? Is it not preferable to celebrate religious holidays your own way, in your own home, at your own church or syn-agogue?

A different problem exists for nursing home and retirement home residents. Making a big fuss about Christmas can, for some residents, be depressing, because it is a family holiday, and it reminds them of the situation they are in and causes them to miss family and home that much more. Also, there is the danger of postholiday blues—so much build-up to Christmas, and then it is over.

Regardless of the setting, another consideration is that not all people are necessarily religious or care to observe religious customs. Even if the holiday is associated with a person's religion, there can be ill feelings about being forced to celebrate a religious holiday they do not care to observe.

Of course, the bigger problem is to be in the minority, to be reminded of your differences to the point of feeling left out, alienated, and different (in a negative way). Imagine, as a Christian, living in a retirement residence with mostly Jewish elders. It is December, and you notice that all the halls are decorated in blue and white, there are Chanukah menorahs and HAPPY CHANUKAH signs everywhere. At least ten times a day, staff wish you a "Happy Chanukah." There are Chanukah parties and traditional Chanukah foods that are unfamiliar to you are prepared and served. The "Chanukah hype" begins a month before the holiday and continues through the eight days of the holiday. During this "month of Chanukah," there is a small Christmas party for you and the other few Christians in the home. Can you imagine the alienation you would feel (for an entire month) if you were one of those Christians in the minority? Now, can you imagine the alienation that many Jews feel, being in the minority?

One other concern regarding religious holidays such as Christmas, Chanukah, and Easter is that the way they are celebrated with elders can be offensive if done in a childish way. Is it really appropriate to have a Santa Claus for residents of a nursing home, or to have them participate in an Easter egg hunt?

However, the childish character of some holiday celebrations can be one solution to the problem of celebrating religious holidays. An excellent Christmas-related activity for program participants wishing to celebrate Christmas would be a field trip to celebrate the holiday with children of a private religious school or from a church youth group or preschool. Another meaningful activity would be to collect money or toys or make gifts for needy children.

Other holiday activities that would be appropriate are educational classes or presentations to learn about the customs and traditions of different holidays, and optional field trips for program participants to attend holiday celebrations in the community. A special "songs of Christmas" activity is fine, as long as it is labeled as such. To name an activity "winter songfest" when it is essentially a Christmas sing-along with just a few non-Christmas songs mixed in is not appropriate (yet commonly done).

Another consideration is that many American, nonreligious holidays that can and should be celebrated/observed with elders are often overlooked. Some examples are Veterans Day, Memorial Day, and Flag Day. These holidays are especially meaningful for elders and celebrating them would not be construed as childish, nor would they arouse melancholic feelings of missing family and home.

In summary, holiday celebrations are a valuable part of a recreation program, and there are ample nonreligious holidays to celebrate. Religious holidays such as Christmas need not be totally ignored; educational activities, field trips, and special projects can give elders the opportunity to celebrate the holiday, yet not make those observing the holiday feel alienated. Although separation of church and state is not an issue in a private residential facility such as a "Christian retirement residence," the concerns of childish celebrations, missing family and home, and postholiday letdown would still need to be considered in deciding how to observe Christmas and other religious holidays.

Develop an Awareness of the Effects of Variation in Socioeconomic Status on the Needs and Interests of Program Participants

Variation in socioeconomic status is an important factor influencing recreational needs and interests. The participants of recreation programs in nursing homes, adult day care centers, and senior centers and clubs often vary greatly in terms of educational background and economic status.

Situation. Most of the program participants have never attended college; in fact, many never completed high school. One of the new participants is a retired lawyer. This new participant is *not* becoming involved in the activities offered or even socializing with other program participants because he feels "above" everyone else.

Solution.

1. Encourage the ex-lawyer to utilize his superior educational background constructively. This man could initiate and lead a new weekly or daily "legal advice" session, in which he would help participants with legal questions or problems. Alternatively, he could prepare presentations or discussions on selected legal topics. Such activities would give recognition to and utilize the ex-lawyer's superior educational background and also involve the man in interaction with other

participants. Hopefully, once the man has talked with other participants, barriers will be broken down, common interests will be discovered, and he will become more involved in program activities.
2. Provide other leadership roles for the ex-lawyer, such as involvement in planning program activities and assisting in leading discussion groups.

On the other hand, the special needs of participants with a very limited educational background must be considered. Confusion during activities due to an inability to understand written or verbal instructions should not be misinterpreted as disorientation or senility.

Similarly, variation in economic status of the participants needs to be considered, especially for field trip activities where there is a cost. A small amount of petty cash should be allocated in the budget to pay for field trips and other activities for which some participants would not be able to afford.

Effectively Utilize Resources That Can Enhance Recreational Activities and Programs

Solicit Contributory Services from Appropriate Agencies (Awareness of Community Resources)

Situation. The activity leader is trying to think of new activity ideas, but it seems as if all activity ideas have been exhausted. What community agencies or businesses could provide recreational activities for the program?

Solution. The following list identifies some community resources and ideas for recreational activities:

1. Local *florists* could present a flower show or provide an activity on flower arranging.
2. The local *police department* could send a representative to make a presentation on crime prevention; the local *fire department* could send a representative to discuss fire prevention.
3. The local *humane society, pet stores,* and *dog fanciers clubs* could provide puppies, birds, or other animals for a pet show or pet grooming activity.
4. *Ministers* from local *churches* could lead Bible reading or discussions on holidays and other topics.
5. *Arts and crafts* store employees could provide demonstrations.
6. Owners of local *dance studios* could schedule a performance (perhaps bring a children's class to perform).

7. Local *pharmacists* might be interested in leading discussions on drug use.
8. Managers of local *clothing stores* could plan a fashion show.
9. The local *public librarian* can provide large-print books for leisurely reading, films for free rental, and book discussions.
10. *Travel agents* are often willing to present slide shows on travel to foreign countries.
11. Local *restaurateurs or bakers* can present a cooking or baking demonstration or class.
12. Local *beauty supply store* employees or *cosmetologists* can present a display or demonstration of beauty products.
13. Local *hospital personnel, doctors, dentists,* and *nurses* can lead discussions on health-related topics.
14. Youth organizations such as *Boy Scouts* and *Campfire Girls* might be interested in joining with the program participants for special holiday celebrations and other intergenerational activities.
15. Local *universities and community colleges* can be helpful in many areas.
    a. *Professors* in fields such as *history, political science,* and *health education* can lead discussions on topics of interest to program participants.
    b. *Students* from the *recreation* or *community services* department can plan and lead a variety of activities.
    c. Students from the *music* department could be invited to perform.
    d. *Art* students could lead an art activity or demonstrate art techniques.
    e. *Students from clubs and organizations* might be interested in doing a presentation or demonstration. For example, a *folk dance club* might be interested in performing, or a *foreign students organization* might be interested in leading discussions on life in foreign countries.
16. A *horticulture group or club* could conduct a gardening class.
17. An *agricultural organization* could present an informational discussion on farming.
18. *Ecological or environmental groups* could lead discussions on the environment or perhaps lead a nature walk.
19. Local *historical societies* or *clubs* could make presentations on a variety of topics.
20. *Hobby clubs* could be called on to present fascinating displays. For example:
    a. An *antique collectors club* or *antique automobile collectors club* could bring a display of their collections.

b. A *stamp* or *coin collectors club* could bring a display and present information on collecting stamps and/or coins.

c. A *bridge club* might be interested in teaching a "bridge for beginners" class.

d. A *photography club* could present a lecture on the art of photography and display some outstanding photographs.

e. A *martial arts club* might be willing to schedule a demonstration.

21. The local *chamber of commerce* will be able to provide information on most of the aforementioned resources, as well as other potential program resources.

In summary, a large number of potential program resources are available in most communities. These resources should be utilized fully to provide as diverse a program as possible.

Solicit Volunteer Assistance for Activities

Volunteer assistance is essential in order to conduct activities such as field trips, which require a great deal of supervision. Solicitation of volunteers should be an ongoing process, as volunteers tend to have a high turnover rate. The following is a list of organizations to contact for volunteers:

1. Local universities and community colleges, in particular, departments of recreation and leisure studies, gerontology, community services, and physical education should be contacted. These departments might be able to offer volunteers through regular classes, students required to accumulate field work experience hours, or internship students who are required to work full-time for one semester.

2. Local high schools might be able to provide some motivated student volunteers.

3. The state or area agency on aging can often refer elders who wish to do volunteer work.

4. Fraternities and sororities often seek to provide voluntary assistance for worthy community causes.

5. Local churches often provide some volunteers for programs.

6. Service groups such as Lions or Eagles might be able to provide some volunteers for the program.

7. A notice in local newspapers along with a brief description of volunteer opportunities available can be very helpful in attempting to recruit volunteers.

Effectively Supervise and Coordinate a Volunteer Program

During the initial interview with a volunteer, administer a questionnaire to determine interests and abilities and then direct the volunteer toward those areas. Explain the goals and philosophy of the program and arrange a work schedule.

Expose the volunteer to all facets of the program, including field trips, staff meetings, program planning, and leading or coleading diverse activities. Also establish a one-on-one working relationship between the volunteer and one participant for the purpose of meeting on a regular basis.

To maintain continuity in the program, keep in close contact with the volunteer by meeting regularly to discuss concerns or problem areas. Another effective means of promoting a cohesive volunteer program is to organize meetings for all volunteers to meet as a group periodically (every two or three weeks) to share experiences. This group interchange can be both educational and motivational.

Volunteers should receive recognition for their work, both daily and also in special ways. For example, an annual or once a semester "awards banquet" for volunteers can be an excellent way to provide recognition to volunteers.

The volunteer coordinator should keep a record of each volunteer's time schedule for future reference. The coordinator should be cognizant of giving recognition and support to volunteers since they are working mainly for intrinsic purposes.

Situation. A volunteer, when not assigned to a specific activity, loafs around the center and does not get involved in activities.

Solution. First of all, volunteers should receive a written job description when they begin work in order to clarify exactly what is expected of them. However, some volunteers may have less initiative than others and require more direction from the staff. The volunteer coordinator should be prepared to direct the volunteer to specific tasks in the event that all activities are being led by other personnel.

Volunteers can experience a greater sense of commitment and responsibility if they have their own individual projects to work on during their free time at the center. Various projects assigned to each volunteer to be worked on during their unscheduled time can enhance the volunteers' feelings of achievement and creativity. Volunteer projects can include the following:

1. Planning a special field trip, including making phone calls, transportation arrangements, advertising, and visiting the site prior to the trip to ensure accessibility for the handicapped

2. Working one on one with a participant writing a biography, letter, journal, etc.
3. Researching a specific area of interest (e.g., art, music, dance therapy for the elderly) and presenting an in-service training session to the staff
4. Preparing a special event at the center and making the necessary arrangements (e.g., guest speakers, holiday celebrations, theme events such as a Mardi Gras or European Appreciation Day)
5. Creating a special bulletin board in honor of a particular participant and working with that individual and/or family members to gather memorabilia to present
6. Writing and/or collecting articles from staff and/or participants for a monthly newsletter

In summary, a volunteer program can be a great advantage to a facility. Keeping lines of communication open between coordinator and volunteer and allowing the volunteer a creative working environment can greatly enhance the volunteer's experience.

Plan an Appropriate Program of Recreational Activities

Develop an Awareness and Understanding of Program Goals and Objectives

It is important to understand the goals and objectives of the agency in general and the recreation program in particular in order to have a clear philosophy to guide program planning efforts. Careful attention should be paid to ensure that program activities are supportive of, and not in opposition to, program goals and objectives.

The following goals usually apply to most recreation programs for elders:

1. Activities should be enjoyable and emotionally satisfying.
2. Activities should be participated in by free choice.
3. A varied program of activities should be presented.
4. Social interaction among participants should be encouraged.
5. Physical, mental, and emotional benefits of activities should be maximized. Recreational activities should facilitate improvements in or maintenance of physical and mental functioning and/or promote developmental growth.

6. Maximal involvement in activities should be encouraged.
7. Maintenance of activities of daily living (e.g., dressing, eating) should be promoted through activities.

McGuire (1987) identified three goals specifically for recreation programs for frail elders:

1. Attempt to improve functioning.
2. Try to prevent further deterioration.
3. Make optimum use of existing functioning abilities.

In addition, McGuire (1987) identified dichotomies that are concerns for activity programs for frail elders and can be identified as program goals:

1. Greater humaneness (instead of depersonalization)
2. Greater control (instead of subservience)
3. Growth (instead of decline)
4. Stimulation (instead of boredom)
5. Increased knowledge (as opposed to ageism)
6. A prosthetic environment (instead of a penalizing one).

Solicit Input from Program Participants in Program Planning

Program participants can provide useful input in program planning. The following are some techniques that can be utilized for obtaining participants' input in program planning.

1. A resident council or participants executive committee can be formed. This body can meet on a regular basis, perhaps without the presence of staff to ensure the independence of this body. The president and vice president of this committee could then represent the participants at staff program planning meetings.
2. Ask participants for feedback on specific activities. For example, if a luncheon outing is being planned, ask for suggestions from all participants on what restaurant to patronize.
3. Hold a monthly or weekly activity in which past activities are reviewed and discussed, and participants have the opportunity to vote for their "favorite activities" in order to give staff feedback on participants' enjoyment of activities. Such an activity will aid staff in deciding which activities to repeat in the next program period.

4. Ask participants for feedback individually so that peer pressure does not influence their responses.
5. Written questionnaires could be administered to participants in order to obtain unbiased feedback. However, not all participants might be capable or inclined to complete a written questionnaire.

Regardless of the successfulness of efforts to solicit participant input in program planning, participants will appreciate the opportunity to provide input and will be likely to enjoy activities more, knowing that they were consulted in the program planning process. Therefore, efforts should be made to solicit participant input, even if these efforts seem frustrating at times.

Exercise 7.1 is presented in order to help gain insight into the difficulties of obtaining input from elders for program planning. Administer the following questionnaire to at least three different residents of a local retirement home or nursing home or attendees of a senior center or day care center. Then, answer the questions that follow.

Plan Appropriate, Stimulating Field Trips

Field trips are potentially the most enjoyable, memorable activities and yet can also be the most disastrous activities. Many elders (especially nursing home residents) rarely have the opportunity to travel to see new places or simply experience a change of environment, thus field trips can be especially rewarding. However, when working with more impaired elders, special precautions must be taken to avoid problems. The following are some suggested precautions:

1. Try to enlist enough staff and volunteers on the trip so that each wheelchair-bound, blind, and confused participant has his or her own individual assistant. If adequate staffing is not possible, but many of the participants are mobile and alert, pair those participants in need of assistance with a high-functioning participant. If either option is not possible, the number of participants who go on the trip should be limited in order to ensure the safety of all who do go.
2. Bring extra wheelchairs if the trip involves substantial walking and/or standing. Some of the mobile participants might become tired and prefer to be in a wheelchair for at least part of the time.
3. Be sure to make the ride to the destination recreational to avoid having a van full of drowsy people upon arrival at the destination.
4. Check in advance if the facility is accessible for the handicapped and if parking close to the facility is available. Also, ask about senior citizens' discounts.

5. Allow extra time at each end for loading and unloading the vehicle.
6. Encourage participants to wear identification/name plates. If confused participants stray from the group, they can be more readily identified and returned to the group. In addition, if all members of the group are wearing identification that includes the program name, people in the community will be made more aware of the program.

The following are some ideas for field trips:

1. A luncheon at a nearby restaurant
2. A dinner theater
3. A day at a race track
4. A tour of a museum
5. A tour of a local television station
6. A picnic and walk in a nearby park
7. A shopping trip to a nearby mall
8. A trip to a nearby beauty shop
9. A matinee at the movies
10. A visit to a local elementary school or preschool, either to observe a performance or to participate in a joint activity
11. A trip to a local festival or fair
12. An afternoon at the bowling alley
13. A trip to see a sporting event (professional or collegiate)
14. A home or hospital visit to an ill or recuperating program participant
15. A trip to another center or home for a joint activity
16. A trip to the library to borrow books for individuals and/or the center
17. A trip to the voting polls to give the participants the opportunity to vote in elections
18. A trip to a nearby historical site

Exercise 7.2 is presented in order to provide an opportunity to plan a field trip and gain insight into time considerations when going on a field trip with elders. In the left-hand column, identify the amount of time you think would be needed for each step of the field trip. Afterward, have an activity leader fill in the right-hand column, which is the actual amount of time needed for each step of the field trip. What insights did this exercise give you regarding the planning of field trips?

In summary, there are numerous appropriate, stimulating field trip options. If the necessary precautions are taken, field trips can be very rewarding activities.

EXERCISE 7.1. Soliciting Input for Program Planning Questionnaire

Instructions

Before doing this survey, obtain a list of activities offered at the facility and those activities that your respondents actually have attended.

1. Compare your survey responses to the information you obtained prior to the survey. How accurate are the survey responses?
2. Did the reasons for liking and disliking activities make sense (were they consistent)?
3. Were the new desired activities feasible ones to be offered by the facility?
4. How long did each interview take? Any difficulties encountered in trying to stay on the topic?

1. What activities are offered here? _____

_____

_____

2. Which ones do you attend? _____

_____

_____

3. Which ones are your favorites and why? _____

_____

_____

4. Which ones do you dislike and why? _____

_____

_____

5. Which activities do you not attend and why? _____

_____

_____

6. What new activities would you like to see offered? _____

_____

_____

EXERCISE 7.2. Planning a Field Trip

Field Trip Destination:

Estimate		Actual
_____	Time needed to prepare group to board the van	_____
_____	Boarding time	_____
_____	Driving time	_____
_____	Allowance for emergencies (e.g., bathroom)	_____
_____	Disembarking time	_____
_____	Duration of the field trip	_____
_____	Preparation for van reboarding	_____
_____	Reboarding time	_____
_____	Return trip driving time	_____
_____	Allowance for emergencies	_____
_____	Disembarking time	_____
_____	Total time for the field trip	_____

How close was your estimate to the actual time of the trip? _____

What insights did this exercise give you regarding the planning of field trips?

_____

_____

Devise Daily, Weekly, and/or Monthly Activity Schedules

Because of advance notice needed in order to arrange special events and field trips, it is advisable to plan activities on a monthly basis, with more detailed daily activity schedules (structured around the special events and field trips) printed either weekly or biweekly. Daily activity schedules should be posted throughout the center or nursing home, and a schedule of staff assignments should be posted prominently so that all staff and participants will know where to locate a particular staff member in case of emergency. The following are some guidelines to follow in devising daily activity schedules:

1. Always offer more than one activity simultaneously in order to provide a distinct choice for participants (e.g., if the main activity is physically or mentally demanding, then the alternate activity should be more passive).
2. Passive and active recreation should be interspersed. Do not plan more than two consecutive physically active or sedentary activities in order to prevent fatigue and drowsiness.
3. Physically active recreation should not immediately follow lunch.
4. Cognitively demanding activities should be scheduled in the morning because people tend to be most alert before lunch.
5. Exercise sessions for impaired elders should last only thirty minutes or less in duration and should be offered twice a day (once in the morning and once in the afternoon).
6. The schedule should allow for transition time for staff between activities to allow staff to adequately prepare for activities and clean up after activities.
7. In general, activities should last no longer than forty-five minutes, due to the limited attention span of most people.
8. Try to schedule at least one special or main activity each day, something for participants to look forward to and talk about afterward.
9. Most important, activities should be scheduled that meet specific goals and objectives of the program.

Exercise 7.3 is presented in order to provide an opportunity to apply the program planning principles presented in the chapter. A sample daily activity schedule follows. At least ten errors exist in this plan; identify them and explain how you would correct these errors. Mark your adjustments to the times and the activities, number your changes, and explain the rationale for each of your changes in the space following each time slot/activity.

EXERCISE 7.3. Daily Activity Schedule Troubleshooting

Instructions

List ten errors in this schedule and discuss how you would correct them:

Time	Activities
8:45	Orientation to activities of the day
9-10	Exercise
10-12	Art: Watercolor or charcoal sketching
12-12:30	Lunch
12:30-1	Games: Box hockey or ring toss
1-2:30	Dancing: Ballroom dance or adapted square dance
2:30-3	Storytelling
3-4:15	Current events discussion
4:15-5	Pictionary (game)

1. _____

2. _____

3. _____

4. _____

5. _____

6. _____

7. _____

8. _____

9. _____

10. _____

In summary, activity schedules should follow the aforementioned guidelines and be posted in numerous places in order to remind participants and staff of the day's activities. Although flexibility is sometimes desirable, the schedule provides structure, which facilitates the smooth operation of the program each day.

Identify Spontaneous/Informal Activity Opportunities
That Can Be Offered to Elders to Supplement
the Planned Program of Activities

Having opportunities available for elders to be able to spontaneously participate in informal activities is beneficial for several reasons:

1. It gives elders an alternative if they do not like the planned activity.
2. It gives elders freedom of choice and enhances feelings of control.
3. It allows elders to participate in activities when activity staff are not available to assist them.
4. It encourages greater independence.
5. It promotes socialization.

Halberg (1987) offers several examples of informal activities for long-term care facilities:

1. A garden—Residents can check on it any time.
2. Writing—Encourage residents to write letters or work on creative writing projects.
3. Assistance—Give higher-functioning residents the role of assistant for someone lower functioning; it is his or her responsibility to check on that person occasionally.

Many other spontaneous activity opportunities can be provided for elders in a variety of settings:

- Hobbies—Set up a knitting or crafts room.
- Music listening—Have records and tapes available.
- Reading—A small library and subscriptions to magazines should be provided.
- Exercise—Have exercise videos available to encourage exercising on their own.
- Games—Board games and cards should be readily accessible.

- Socializing—Encourage groups and clubs to form; members can decide to get together on their own.
- Movies—A video library could be provided.
- Table tennis, shuffleboard, and other active games—Make available a variety of games that do not require supervision or assistance.
- Swimming—A heated pool is a costly item, but it is very therapeutic!
- Piano—Encourage playing the piano, or perhaps have a player piano that can be easily operated.
- Ice cream parlor or popcorn machine—Natural meeting places that facilititate informal socializing are always popular.

Spontaneous activity participation should be encouraged. The more independence elders can have, the better. Brainstorm with your program participants for more ideas for spontaneous activity opportunities.

SUMMARY

This chapter presented an overview of program planning principles applicable to all of the major settings for recreational programs for elders. Some ideas for activities were also presented in this chapter, but many more program ideas are found in the chapters on exercise, adapted dance, recreational techniques, recreational programs, and intergenerational activities. The activity ideas found in these chapters should be incorporated into a comprehensive program of activities, following the principles discussed in this chapter.

REFERENCES

Halberg, K.J. (1987). Leisure programming in long-term care facilities: Far more than a monthly calendar of activities. In Keller, M.J. and Osgood, N.J. (eds.), *Dynamic leisure programming with older adults* (pp. 107-119). Alexandria, VA: NRPA.

McGuire, F.A. (1987). Recreation for the frail elderly. In Keller, M.J. and Osgood, N.J. (eds.), *Dynamic leisure programming with older adults* (pp. 99-106). Alexandria, VA: NRPA.

OTHER RESOURCES FOR PROGRAMMING

Barrett. S.L. (1980). *Parties with a purpose: A handbook for activity directors.* Springfield, IL: C.C. Thomas.

Fish, H.U. (1971). *Activities program for senior citizens.* West Nyack, NY: Parker Publishing Co.

Merril, T. (1967). *Activities for the aged and infirm.* Springfield, IL: C.C. Thomas.

National Council on Aging (NCOA) (1975). *Program planning: A guide to accountability, credibility, and trust.* Washington, DC: NCOA.

Shivers, J.S. and Fait, H.F. (1980). *Recreational service for the aging.* Philadelphia: Lea and Febiger.

Vickery, F.E. (1972). *Creative programming for older adults: A leadership training guide.* New York: Association Press.

Wapner, E.B. (1981). *Recreation for the elderly.* Great Neck, NY: Todd and Honeywell.

Chapter 8

Program Evaluation

INTRODUCTION

The purpose of this chapter is to provide information that can be utilized to enhance program evaluation efforts. The chapter begins with a discussion of the purposes of evaluation and an overview of evaluation methods. The chapter then focuses on considerations and procedures in two particular evaluation methods, interviewing and behavior observation.

LEARNING OBJECTIVES

Upon completion of this chapter, the student will be able to

1. understand the value of evaluation in providing recreational services for elders,
2. identify three benefits of strong program evaluation,
3. compare the strengths and weaknesses of at least four different methods of program evaluation,
4. identify three useful techniques in interviewing impaired elders, and
5. identify three considerations in conducting behavior observation.

PURPOSES OF EVALUATION

According to Edginton et al. (1998), evaluation of recreation programs is important for several reasons:

1. It provides information on how well the programs are meeting the needs of clients.
2. It helps assess changes in leisure behavior of clients.
3. It provides an opportunity for clients to provide input.
4. It encourages clients to be involved in supporting the work of your organization.

5. It provides feedback for recreation leaders and program planners on the effectiveness of their relationships with clients.
6. It promotes the development of sensitivity among service providers to their clients.
7. It facilitates the determination of program design effectiveness.
8. It indicates the need for program improvements.
9. It aids in attempts to link budget allocations to program performance.
10. It enables organizations to focus on tangible and specific objectives.
11. It facilitates the identification of program priorities.
12. It enables the identification of deviations from performance standards so that corrective action can be implemented quickly to ensure acceptable levels of performance.

EVALUATION METHODS

There are several different methods for collecting evaluation data:

1. Unobtrusive observation and notation of statistics, such as the number of participants in an activity; the percentage of residents or center attendees that choose to participate in an activity; the number of participants who arrive at an activity more than five minutes early or leave the activity more than five minutes early; and the time duration and frequency of the activity
2. Written questionnaires completed by program participants on their attitudes toward activities, as well as questionnaires to assess the impact of a program on variables such as life satisfaction and perceived health
3. Oral interviews with program participants in order to assess attitudes and the effects of a program on life satisfaction, perceived health, and other variables
4. Behavior observation by independent, unbiased observers in order to assess participants' enjoyment of activities or other variables
5. Importance-Performance Analysis (I-P), is a method in which data can be collected either through written questionnaires (with higher-functioning elders) or through oral interviews (with lower-functioning elders). As discussed by Gillespie, Kennedy, and Soble (1989), the I-P Scale assesses client expectations and satisfaction with program performance. For example, using a three-point scale, participants will rate the importance of program characteristics such as length of the session, staff enthusiasm, quality of the facilities, etc., and will also indicate their rating of the activity's actual performance on each of these

characteristics. Areas that rate high in importance but low in performance are ones that need to be improved. Areas rated low in importance and in performance do not require much attention, and those low in importance but high in performance can possibly receive less attention than they had been receiving. The areas rated high in importance and in performance indicate program strengths that should be maintained.

Each of the aforementioned techniques has particular advantages and disadvantages. The questionnaires and interviews have the advantage of directly assessing variables whereas observational methods are less direct and more prone to inaccurate interpretations. However, observational methods have the advantage of being less obtrusive and are less likely to generate biased responses from participants than interviews and questionnaires.

Written questionnaires have the advantage of being less costly, less time consuming, and therefore easier to administer to large numbers of people than the other methods. Unfortunately, when working with impaired elders, written questionnaires are often not feasible. Therefore, in order to evaluate recreation programs for impaired elders, interviews and behavior observation tend to be more effective. The remainder of this chapter will focus on considerations in interviewing impaired elders, and the use of behavior observation to assess elders' enjoyment of recreational activities.

Interviewing Impaired Elders

The JWK International Corporation (1978) discussed the problems of survey research methods with elders. One problem cited is the potential influence of others, particularly authority figures, on the results of a study.

Another problem cited by the JWK Corporation (1978) was short-term memory deficits commonly found among older adults. To compensate for this problem, the number of answer choices to questions should be limited, and an attempt should be made to ask questions that require recognition rather than recall. The authors also suggested that the use of technical language and elaborate scaling be avoided, and that although the interviewer should try to keep interviews on the topic of the questions, interviewees should *not* be interrupted excessively.

Faber and Leitner (1981) also discuss considerations in interviewing impaired elders, based on a study of the effects of an intergenerational music activities program on senior day care participants. The authors offer the following recommendations for interviewing impaired elders:

1. Questionnaires should be as short and simple as possible to compensate for deficiencies in cognitive functioning. A combination of close-ended and open-ended questions seems to be most effective in that close-ended questions are simple enough for most people to answer, while the open-ended questions allow more alert respondents an opportunity to fully express their feelings on a topic. Negative and positive statements should be interspersed in the close-ended questions, in order to deter interviewees from simply answering yes (or no) to every question without really considering or understanding the meaning of each question.

2. Prior to initiating data collection, the interviewer should develop a rapport with the interviewees by engaging the interviewee in a conversation on any topic the interviewee feels comfortable discussing. Also, the interviewer should familiarize oneself with the interviewees by unobtrusively observing them during activities.

3. The interviewer should be an "outsider," not a staff member, in order to ensure that the results of the study are unbiased.

4. Interviews should be conducted in a quiet, isolated area. The interview setting should be free of sensory distractions and should minimize the potential impact of peer influence on the interviewee's responses. As noted by Pastalan's Empathetic Model (Perlberg, 1978), older adults expressed a marked inability to hear clearly in crowded areas where there is background noise. In fact, locating the source of various sounds was proven difficult in that noise from across a room may seem to be coming from only a few feet away—the same distance from which the interviewer's voice originates. In addition, a secluded quiet area for interviews prevents peer pressure from affecting the interviewee's responses and also prevents interruptions from disturbing the interview.

5. The interviewer should have predetermined, standardized responses to requests for clarification of questions. Otherwise, variation in clarification of questions could cause the questions to be interpreted and answered in different ways. Thus, standardizing clarifications can further enhance the validity of the results.

6. The interviewer should introduce the purpose of the interview in vague terms, such as "we are seeking your input in attempting to improve the quality of recreation programs here" rather than specifically identifying what particular aspect of the program is being evaluated. If interviewees are informed of the specific objectives of the evaluation research, their responses might be biased in an attempt to provide the interviewer with information the interviewee thinks the interviewer is seeking.

7. Periodically reorient interviewees to the subject of concern but do allow the interviewees to engage in some seemingly unrelated rambling and reminiscing. Occasionally, elders with impaired mental functioning are actually organizing their thoughts while engaging in apparently irrelevant discussion. Moen (1978) also noted that the expressed needs of older adults are often elicited during the course of conversation rather than in direct response to questions.

8. Do not dwell on negative comments such as "I wish I was dead"; rather, acknowledge and gently accommodate such comments with a reassuring hand on the shoulder, sustained eye contact, and several concerned head nods. In order to renew interest in the topic of the interview, the interviewer might add: "I'm also interested to hear your responses to the questions on this survey. Would it be all right with you if we looked into some of these questions?" In this way, the needs of the interviewee are not ignored, but the interview is kept moving and eventually completed.

Although these suggestions will enhance data collection through interviewing, other data collection methods should be utilized in combination with interviews in order to obtain more valid data. The following section discusses the use of behavior observation in examining the effectiveness of recreation programs for elders.

Behavior Observation

There are several important considerations in using behavior observation in evaluating recreation programs for elders: the variable(s) to be examined; development of a behavior observation instrument; selection and training of behavior observers; establishment of inter-rater reliability among behavior observers; and procedures to follow in behavior observation.

Variable(s) to Be Examined

The variable(s) to be studied through behavior observation are determined by the criteria for evaluating the effectiveness of a program. For example, enjoyment of activities is typically an important criterion in evaluating a recreation program, in that enjoyment is a very essential goal of recreation. Therefore, observing and comparing enjoyment levels during different types of activities is one means of comparing the effectiveness of different types of recreation programs.

Instrument Development

Once the variable to be studied has been identified, behavioral indices for measuring the variable must be identified. The behavioral indices for a variable such as enjoyment will be different for different types of activities (e.g., musical activities versus art activities). A behavior rating form used in behavior observation should list the behavioral indices with space to note the frequency of occurrence of each behavior. Space should be left for comments and a numerical rating. Explicit instructions should be given for assigning numerical ratings based on the frequency of occurrence of the behavioral indices listed. Please refer to the behavior observation forms at the end of this chapter (Appendix A).

Selection and Training of Behavior Observers

As much as possible, behavior observers should have equal familiarity with the population to be observed before commencing data collection. Staff or others very familiar with the target population could use their knowledge to produce more accurate ratings, but are also prone to be more biased in their ratings than observers who are less familiar with the people to be observed. An effective alternative is to use observers who are unfamiliar with the population, because such observers will probably be less biased in their ratings. To compensate for their lack of familiarity with the people to be observed, the observers should undergo a thorough training period which not only involves practice behavior rating sessions, but also informal interaction with the population. This will familiarize the observers with the people to be observed and help make the people to be observed more at ease with the presence of the behavior observers. The training of the behavior observers should culminate in the establishment of a high rate (.75 or above) of inter-rater reliability before beginning data collection.

Inter-Rater Reliability

Inter-rater reliability refers to the percentage of agreement among behavior observers rating a particular individual or group (e.g., .75 reliability means that three of four raters obtained the same rating for a particular observation). During the training period for behavior observers, the trainees should observe the same individuals simultaneously, and then compare ratings. At least a .75 level of inter-rater reliability should be established before commencing data collection of an evaluation study.

Inter-rater reliability should be checked periodically throughout an evaluation study in order to ensure that the behavior observers are still consistent in their rating procedures and interpretation of the rating scale. If the behavior observers are observing different people during the observation sessions, then the raters should also assign a numerical rating for the entire group. The data on group ratings could then be compared in order to examine inter-rater reliability. If inter-rater reliability is lower than .75 on two consecutive trials, then data collection should be suspended until the raters receive additional training and a .75 level of inter-rater reliability is reestablished.

Behavior Observation Procedures

When working with elders with some short-term memory loss, it is advisable to periodically remind the group of the *general* purpose of the observers' presence in order to allay any fears or suspicions regarding them. However, the group being observed should *not* be informed of the specific hypotheses of the evaluation study in order to prevent the elders being observed from biasing the results by attempting to provide the observers with hypothesis-confirming (or hypothesis-disconfirming) results. For example, if behavior observation is being conducted in order to evaluate if intergenerational music activities are more enjoyable than musical activities without children, the group can simply be told that the observers are observing activities in order to examine ways to improve the recreational activities program.

Behavior observers should be seated as part of or slightly outside of the activity formation (e.g., a circle) and perform minor tasks to facilitate their acceptance as a natural part of the activity setting. The observers should be interspersed throughout the group and *not* confer with one another during the activities being observed. The observers should be inconspicuous and avoid peering at the elders being observed. Paraphernalia such as clipboards, which attract attention to the fact that observations are being conducted, should not be used.

A critical factor in maintaining unbiased ratings is to ensure the observers' status of nonparticipant in activities. In addition, it should be stressed that the observers' own enjoyment of an activity should *not* influence their ratings. The ratings should reflect the observer's perception of an individual's or group's reaction to an activity.

A Research Example

In order to further clarify the aforementioned behavior observation considerations, an example of the use of behavior observation in an evaluation study will be discussed in depth. Leitner (1981) utilized behavior observation in addition to interviewing in examining the effects of the presence of elementary schoolchildren on senior day care participants' enjoyment of musical activities. Thus, the variable examined in this study was enjoyment of activities. One group of senior day care participants were observed during activities with children for six weeks and during activities without children for six weeks. Another group was observed for twelve weeks during activities without children. The behavior ratings for activities with children were compared to those for activities without children in order to assess the effects of the presence of children on the participants' enjoyment of activities.

Leitner (1981) developed a behavior rating form to be used by the observers in this study through a multiphased process. First, a review of literature on behavior observation was conducted in order to gather information on behavioral indices of enjoyment. Senior day care personnel were also consulted in order to gain further insight into behavioral indices of enjoyment during musical activities. A draft version of the behavior rating form was then developed and sent to fifteen senior day care centers in Maryland for review by full-time personnel. Changes in the form were made based on the feedback from the senior day care personnel. Next, a panel of five researchers with expertise in behavior observation were consulted for further refinement of the form.

This particular study utilized four behavior observers, all of whom were students in either gerontology or recreation. The observers were oriented to methods and techniques of behavior observation, and to the physical, psychological, and social characteristics of senior day care participants.

A .75 level of inter-rater reliability was established on two consecutive practice trials before commencing data collection. Nine practice trials were conducted in which all four observers rated the same participant during an activity. Inter-rater reliability was checked throughout the study by noting the percentage of agreement on ratings of group enjoyment of activities. In this study, inter-rater reliability never fell below .75 on two consecutive trials.

Leitner (1981) noted that the involvement of observers in one of the activities biased the results of one session. The observers were unable to refuse participants' requests to dance with them during one activity, and the observers' participation in the activity appeared to affect the participants' enjoyment of the activity. The observation data for that particular session was not used in the data analysis because of this problem.

The behavior rating form and accompanying instructions used in this study are included at the end of this chapter in order to further clarify the development of behavior observation instruments (Appendix A). In addition, sample behavior observation forms for other types of activities are presented in order to illustrate how behavioral indices for a variable (enjoyment) should vary depending on the nature of the activity being observed (Appendixes B, C, and D). These additional behavior observation forms were developed by a graduate class in recreation for special populations at California State University, Chico. Exercise 8.1 is presented at the end of the chapter, after these sample behavior observation forms, in order to provide an opportunity for students to learn how to devise their own instruments for conducting evaluation research on recreational programs for elders.

SUMMARY

Evaluation of recreational programs for elders is important for a variety of reasons but can be difficult to accomplish because of the challenges in conducting research with elders, especially older, more frail elders. A variety of evaluation methods were discussed in the chapter. Greater emphasis was devoted to behavior observation methods, as it has perhaps the greatest potential for providing accurate information, especially on programs for elders with disabilities. Combining behavior observation with survey research methods can help provide a clearer picture of how to improve recreation programs for elders and also provide clearer evidence of the benefits of recreation programs, an especially important concern in times of budget cuts and the need to justify the existence of programs.

REFERENCES

Edginton, C.R., Hanson, C.J., Edginton, S.R., and Hudson, S.D. (1998). *Leisure programming: Service-centered and benefits approach.* Boston, MA: McGraw-Hill.

Faber, M. and Leitner, M.J. (1981). Considerations in interviewing the impaired elderly. Unpublished manuscript.

Gillespie, K.A., Kennedy, D.W., and Soble, K. (1989). Utilizing Importance-Performance Analysis in the evaluation and marketing of activity programs in geriatric settings. *Activities, Adaptation, and Aging,* 13(1/2), 77-87.

JWK International Corporation (1978). *Data collection problems and the elderly: Survey research methods.* Washington, DC: Administration on Aging.

Leitner, M.J. (1981). The effects of intergenerational music activities on senior day care participants and elementary school children. (Doctoral dissertation, University of Maryland, 1981). *Dissertation Abstracts International,* 42(08), 3752A.

Moen, E. (1978). The reluctance of the elderly to accept help. *Social Problems,* 25(3), 293-294.

Perlberg, M. (1978). The distorted world of old age. *Human Behavior,* 7(12), pp. 28-32.

APPENDIX A:
INSTRUCTION SHEET FOR BEHAVIOR RATING FORM

1. For all of the behaviors listed on the rating form, note the number of times each behavior is elicited by using slashes (e.g., 1/11). Comments may also be written in the space provided next to each item. If the participant exhibits a particular behavior throughout an activity session, write "present throughout" in the space next to that item.

2. Laughter includes a range of behavior, from loud outbursts of violent laughter to slight giggles.

3. Smiles includes a range of behavior, from wide, full smiles to slight half smiles.

4. Eyes closed—Note the number of times the participant's eyes close and remain closed for at least ten seconds. If the participant's eyes remain closed for more than one minute, note the length of time for which the participant's eyes were closed. If a participant's eyes are closed and he or she appears to be sleeping, it does not necessarily mean that this person is drowsy due to boredom with the activity. Senior day care participants have a wide range of ailments and impairments; many of the people are on medication that may cause drowsiness.

5. Unhappy facial expressions—This includes frowns, cry of sadness, pursed lips, and horizontal head shaking. Caution should be taken in noting the frequency of these behaviors, particularly frowns. Many of the older participants might appear to have drooping mouths due to sadness, but these drooping mouths may be due to facial muscles that have lost their tightness.

6. Affectionate touching behavior—This includes hugs, kisses, hand squeezes, hand pats on another person's head or back, a child sitting on a participant's lap, and other touching behavior as well.

7. Withdrawal behavior includes a wide range of behavior: nonparticipation in an activity, nonresponse to verbal and nonverbal cues, movement to sit farther away from coparticipants, and avoidance of contact with a coparticipant.

8. Rhythmic movements include swaying, dancing, foot stomping or tapping, head swaying or nodding, hand clapping, snapping of fingers, and other whole body and/or finer extremity rhythmical movements.

9. The items "Singing, humming, and/or whistling" and "Verbal requests for music selections" are self-explanatory.

10. Exclamations of annoyance or anger includes both verbal and nonverbal behaviors. Nonverbal behavior such as a wave of hand or the shake

of a head in disgust should be noted. Statements such as "Leave me alone" and "I don't like this" should also be noted.

11. Statements of affection or liking is focused on participant's verbal behavior toward coparticipants in the activity. Examples of such behavior would be: "I like you," "You're so cute," and "It's nice to see you here today."

12. Verbal exclamations of enjoyment and/or happiness is focused on participants' comments related to the activity. Comments such as "This is wonderful" and "Wasn't this fun" should be noted. In addition, statements of happiness such as "I feel great!" should be noted. Participants' requests for prolongation or repetition of the activity should also be noted (e.g., "Let's do this again!" or "I wish they didn't have to leave so soon!").

13. The following scale should be used in completing the ratings of activity enjoyment:

1	2	3	4	5
Very low, dislike	Low	Moderate	High	Very high

The following is an explanation of the ratings:

(1) Very low, dislike—This rating is to be used in instances in which the participant outwardly displays displeasure with the activity. The rater should be able to point out specific behaviors elicited during the activity that are indicative of the participant's dislike for the activity.

(2) Low—A rating of "2" indicates below average of enjoyment; a rating of "2" does not mean that the participant disliked the activity. A participant that displays a low or below average frequency of behaviors indicative of enjoyment would be rated a "2."

(3) Moderate—A rating of "3" is indicative of an average level of activity enjoyment. A participant rated "3" should be one that outwardly displays enjoyment, but only at a moderate (average) level.

(4) High—If a participant displays above average enjoyment of an activity, a "4" rating should be given. A "4" rating should be supported by notations of above average incidence of behavior indicative of enjoyment.

(5) Very high—When an activity appears to be truly special to a participant, a "5" rating should be given. A rating of "5" must be supported by observations that indicate a very high level of enjoyment. It is possible for a participant to obtain a "5" rating on numerous succes-

sive trials; however, the rater must indicate specific observations that support a rating of "5."

Before completing the rating of activity enjoyment for the participant observed, reflect on your observation, for this participant. Review the notes you took on the behavior of the participant during the activity session. Remember that the participant's overall enjoyment of the activity just observed takes into account both the participant's reaction to the activity itself, as well as the participant's interaction with other people involved in the activity.

14. The second rating is an estimation of the entire group's level of enjoyment of the activity.
15. Comments—Please include the following in your comments:
    a. Criteria for your rating of the participant's level of enjoyment; provide justification for the rating you gave
    b. Criteria for your rating of all participants' level of enjoyment
    c. Unusual circumstance that might have influenced participants' enjoyment of the activity (e.g., inclement weather, illnesses, background noise, etc.)
    d. Incidents that you felt were most significant or indicative of participants' level of enjoyment

APPENDIX B: BEHAVIOR RATING FORM—MUSIC ACTIVITY

Observer # _____ Participant # _____ Observation # _____

Activity observed _____ Date _____

Number of participants in the activity _____

Note the frequency of the following behaviors:

Laughter _____

_____

Smiles _____

_____

Eyes closed _____

Unhappy facial expressions _____

Affectionate touching behavior _____

Withdrawal behavior _____

Rhythmic movements _____

Singing, humming, and/or whistling _____

Verbal requests for music selections _____

Exclamations of annoyance or anger _____

Statements of affection or liking _____

Verbal exclamations of enjoyment and/or happiness _____

1	2	3	4	5
Very low, dislike	Low	Moderate	High	Very high

_____Rating of participants enjoyment of the activity

_____ Overall rating of all participants' enjoyment of the activity

Comments: _____

_____

_____

_____

_____

_____

_____

_____

_____

APPENDIX C: BEHAVIOR RATING FORM—ART ACTIVITY

Observer # _____ Participant # _____ Observation # _____
Activity observed _____ Date _____
Number of participants in the activity _____
Note the frequency of the following behaviors:
Withdrawal _____
Ignoring _____
Being sloppy _____
Frowning _____
Leaving early _____
Verbal expression _____
Yawning _____
Sighing _____
Talking to neighbor (unrelated) _____
Checking the clock/watch _____
Impatient _____
Talking to neighbor (related, e.g., asst.) _____
Helping others _____
Asking questions _____
Investigate _____
Creative _____
Looking at someone else's work _____
Smiling _____
Displaying work _____
Reminiscing (related to art) _____
Asking for repetition _____
Asking how to get more involved _____
High concentration _____
Verbal expression _____

1	2	3	4	5
Very low, dislike	Low	Moderate	High	Very high

_____ Overall rating of all participants' enjoyment of the activity

Comments: _____
_____
_____
_____

APPENDIX D: BEHAVIOR RATING FORM—
STRESS MANAGEMENT SESSION

Observer # _____ Participant # _____ Observation # _____

Activity observed _____ Date _____

Number of participants in the activity _____

Note the frequency of the following behaviors:

Withdrawal _____

Verbal expression _____

Leaving early _____

Disruptive noise: comments, laughing _____

Fidgety behavior _____

Unrelated talking _____

Checking the time _____

Missing an instruction/not following directions _____

Wandering eyes _____

Doing activity _____

Following instructions _____

Asking for clarification _____

Smiling _____

Asking for repetition _____

Reduced energy level _____

Flowing with music _____

1	2	3	4	5
Very low, dislike	Low	Moderate	High	Very high

Overall rating of all participants' enjoyment of the activity: _____

Comments: _____

_____

_____

_____

_____

_____

_____

_____

_____

_____

_____

EXERCISE 8.1. Exercise Session Behavior Observation Form and Questionnaire

Based on the examples provided in the appendixes, devise a behavior observation form for evaluating exercise sessions with impaired elders. In addition, write a questionnaire that could be administered orally, also to evaluate exercise sessions. Attempt to administer both the behavior observation form and the questionnaire with an elder you know fairly well, and compare the results obtained. How do the ratings on the two methods compare? (Administer them for the same exercise session.) Which rating do you think is more accurate? _____

_____

_____

_____

_____

_____

_____

_____

_____

_____

_____

_____

_____

_____

_____

_____

_____

_____

_____

_____

_____

_____

_____

Chapter 9

Leisure Counseling

INTRODUCTION

The main purposes of this chapter are to help the reader to understand leisure counseling and how to use it with elders. The chapter has been organized as follows: an explanation of key leisure counseling concepts and terminology; an overview of the history, background, and rationale for leisure counseling; a discussion of how to use leisure counseling with elders, including a detailed explanation of procedures to follow in conducting leisure counseling with elders; and a discussion of special considerations and concerns in counseling elders.

LEARNING OBJECTIVES

Upon completion of this chapter, the student will be able to

1. define leisure counseling,
2. describe the three major types of leisure counseling,
3. determine which types of leisure counseling are most appropriate for different categories of older adults,
4. identify at least five benefits of leisure counseling for elders,
5. identify and describe (in correct order) the eleven steps of the developmental-educational approach to leisure counseling, and
6. identify at least four special considerations in conducting leisure counseling sessions with elders.

CONCEPTS AND DEFINITIONS

For the purposes of this chapter, leisure counseling is defined as a helping process designed to facilitate maximal leisure well-being. Leisure education is also a process designed to facilitate maximal leisure well-being. However, leisure education is more of a self-help process, whereas leisure counseling is an individualized or small group helping process guided by a leisure counselor. This chapter focuses specifically on leisure counseling.

This chapter will examine *three* different types or approaches to leisure counseling discussed by McDowell (1976): (1) the leisure resource guidance approach; (2) the developmental-educational approach; and (3) the therapeutic-remedial approach. The step-by-step procedures of each of these different types of leisure counseling are discussed later in the chapter.

BACKGROUND AND RATIONALE

The first documented leisure counseling program was initiated at the Kansas City Veteran's Administration Hospital psychiatric ward in 1957 (Olson and McCormick, 1957). The rationale for the early leisure counseling programs was that leisure counseling could be used to help reduce recidivism by orienting patients to better use their leisure time after discharge from the institutional setting. It was hypothesized that a prominent cause of recidivism was the inability of patients to effectively deal with the vast increase in unstructured leisure time after discharge from the institution. Therefore, it was hoped that leisure counseling could help reduce recidivism by preparing patients to more effectively deal with the increased leisure time they would face after discharge.

Overs and his associates (Overs, Taylor, and Adkins, 1977) developed the first leisure counseling service for elders in the early 1970s. Overs' Milwaukee Avocational Guidance Leisure Counseling Model was not designed to be exclusively for elders, but rather sought to meet three human needs: (1) to help ease the transition from institution to community; (2) to facilitate developmental growth; and (3) to facilitate involvement in appropriate activity, especially for persons isolated from the mainstream of society. The Milwaukee Model was modeled after vocational counseling. Emphasis was placed on identification of recreational activity interests and awareness of available recreation resources. Attitudes and values related to leisure were not emphasized as strongly (Humphrey, Kelley, and Hamilton, 1980).

McDowell (1976) tested the effectiveness of a leisure counseling model in an experimental study that examined the effects of a leisure counseling program on the leisure attitudes, work attitudes, leisure self-concept, work self-concept, and leisure satisfaction of forty adult mental health outpatients. The forty subjects were randomly assigned to either control or experimental groups, and were studied over a nine-month period. The major findings of the study were that the leisure counseling program had a positive effect on leisure attitudes, leisure self-concept, and work self-concept.

McDowell's study is significant for several reasons. First, the study provides concrete evidence of the positive impact leisure counseling can have. It should be noted that McDowell used a powerful Solomon Four-Group design in this study, which lends even greater validity to the findings of the study. The study is also very significant in that it provides a clear rationale for leisure counseling services, especially if research on leisure and mental health is considered. As discussed in Chapter 1, leisure attitudes and self-concept are very important factors in determining psychological well-being. Keeping this statement in mind, and recognizing that McDowell's study indicated that leisure counseling had a positive effect on leisure attitudes and self-concept, leisure counseling apparently has great potential to positively impact mental health. The potential of leisure counseling to positively affect mental health provides a clear rationale for the existence and growth of leisure counseling programs for elders and other populations as well. Furthermore, recent study conducted in Canada (Nour et al., 2002) indicated that a leisure education program for older adults who have had a stroke positively affected their physical well-being and total quality of life.

Leisure counseling expanded rapidly through the 1970s and 1980s, as indicated by the extensive research and publications on this subject (see "Other Resources" at the end of the chapter). Leisure counseling can be especially beneficial for elders in several ways: (1) to help elders adjust to the increased leisure that retirement usually brings; (2) to help senior center or adult day care attendees to most effectively use their leisure time away from the center; (3) to help nursing home residents to most effectively utilize their unstructured leisure time in the institution, and also prepare residents about to be discharged to make the best use of their leisure after discharge (so as to reduce recidivism); and (4) to help elders adjust to the changes in their life (and leisure) caused by the death of a spouse.

Another benefit of leisure counseling is that it can help to increase positive attitudes toward leisure, thereby removing attitudinal barriers to participation in leisure activities. These attitudinal barriers include negative attitudes toward leisure, motives and needs, perceptions of personal freedom and control, lack of playfulness, and various personality traits (Backman and Mannell, 1986). A study conducted in a total-care facility for elders found that a leisure counseling program was more effective than a traditional leisure activities program in increasing positive attitudes toward leisure (Backman and Mannell, 1986).

Leisure counseling can also help elders to plan and organize their leisure, enabling them to create a desired sense of structure for their leisure which can help to maximize their enjoyment of it. According to Ginsberg (1988), elders can draw on the skills they used throughout their life in planning and organizing their work, school, and home life in structuring their retirement leisure time. However, Thompson and Cruise (1993) caution that elders should not wait until after retirement to learn about the role of leisure in later life.

Another benefit of leisure counseling and having elders actively participate in the planning of their leisure time is that it encourages elders to be proactive, to take control of their lives. Bolton (1985) discusses the importance of feeling in control in order for elders to take action to replace negative habits with more healthy alternatives and thereby improve their leisure well-being and overall wellness.

The current leisure participation patterns of elders lend further support to the need for leisure counseling to help elders plan their free time and make better use of it. According to Mahon and Searle (1994), elders prefer active pursuits but engage most in pursuits such as watching television. Consequently, elders who withdraw from their favorite activities show poorer health and lower life satisfaction. The following section describes three different approaches to leisure counseling for elders, all designed to help elders make better use of their leisure time.

USING LEISURE COUNSELING WITH ELDERS

The Leisure Resource Guidance Approach

The leisure resource guidance approach is most appropriate in working with healthy elders who have a variety of leisure interests and merely wish to learn of available programs related to their interests. The resource guidance approach is most appropriate for clients who do *not* seek to expand their leisure horizons, but rather are seeking information on recreational opportunities available to them. The procedures of the leisure resource guidance approach follow (based on McDowell, 1976):

1. Initial interview to get acquainted with the client
2. Administration of leisure-interest inventories and collection of demographic data. (Refer to the list of leisure interest inventories at the end of this chapter.)
3. Analysis of data collected (preferably computer assisted)
4. Matching of client's leisure interests and demographic characteristics with appropriate recreation programs
5. Discussion of the results of data analysis with the client, and referral to appropriate programs
6. A follow-up meeting with the client to examine the client's satisfaction with the programs to which the client was referred
7. Termination of counseling process once one has satisfactorily been matched with appropriate programs and is participating in one's desired recreational activities

In order to further clarify the leisure resource guidance approach to leisure counseling, a practical example is presented:

Example

Mrs. B has recently moved to Phoenix, Arizona, to retire. She is very satisfied with the variety of her recreational pursuits: tennis, swimming, square dancing, folk dancing, and theater going. However, being new to Phoenix, she is not aware of all of the recreational opportunities available to her related to her interests. Mrs. B wishes to facilitate her adjustment to life in Phoenix by becoming involved in her favorite activities as soon as possible. Therefore, she has sought out a professional leisure counselor to help her learn of and become involved in appropriate programs. Mrs. B does *not* wish to become involved in a long process to examine and expand her leisure interests but rather merely wishes to discover what programs are available to her in Phoenix.

The counselor meets with Mrs. B and explains the leisure counseling procedure to her. Mrs. B then completes several leisure interest inventories in order to clarify the nature and scope of her leisure pursuits. In addition, demographic data is collected such as income, transportation availability, residence location, educational background, marital status, religion, and ethnic background. This information, along with information gathered informally in the interview, is fed into a computer. The leisure counselor's computer has an up-to-date database of recreational programs in the Phoenix area (including tennis, swimming, folk dancing, square dancing, and theater programs). The demographic data and leisure interests of Mrs. B are matched against the database, and a referral of appropriate programs is produced. The referral includes a list of appropriate programs, including phone numbers, names, times available, cost, and accessibility. The referral is then presented to and discussed with Mrs. B. An appointment with Mrs. B is set for two weeks later, to discuss Mrs. B's satisfaction with her involvement in the programs to which she was referred. The counseling process is terminated once Mrs. B is satisfactorily involved in her desired recreational activities. However, the client is encouraged to periodically contact the counselor after terminating the process if the client has any questions or problems.

In summary, the leisure resource guidance approach to leisure counseling focuses on the dissemination of information on leisure resources. This approach is most appropriate for high-functioning elders with well-defined leisure interests. This type of counseling can be extremely helpful for elders who have recently moved to a big city, or have recently retired and have inadequate knowledge of leisure resources available.

The Developmental-Educational Approach

The developmental-educational approach to leisure counseling is also suitable for high-functioning elders, but it is a more involved process than leisure resource guidance counseling. In the developmental-educational approach, the counselor works closely with the client to discover new leisure interests and activities in an attempt to broaden the client's leisure horizons. An important objective of developmental-educational leisure counseling is to help the clients identify an "ideal" leisure lifestyle, and then assist them in bridging the gap between their real leisure lifestyle and their ideal leisure lifestyle through goal setting.

Two of the other objectives of developmental-educational leisure counseling are

1. to help one understand the importance of leisure in one's life.
2. to help one understand the effects of aging and social change on leisure; and
3. to help one identify one's attitudes and values toward leisure that serve as barriers to leisure fulfillment.

Developmental-educational leisure counseling efforts with elders should include the following steps (adapted from McDowell's [1976] suggested leisure counseling process).

Precounseling Assessment

In this step, the client completes leisure interest inventories and other relevant questionnaires, which can be analyzed by the counselor prior to the first counseling session in order to expedite understanding the client's leisure attitudes and behavior.

Establishing Rapport

In this step, the counselor should attempt to develop a warm trusting relationship with the client. In order for meaningful interaction to occur in which the client self-discloses a great deal, a trusting relationship is imperative. Thus, this stage of the counseling process should continue until the counselor feels assured that the client is comfortable confiding in the counselor. If the counseling process skips to the next step before rapport has adequately been established, discussions are likely to be shallow and not very beneficial for the client.

Defining Concepts

Some of the more important concepts to discuss and define in this step include leisure, recreation, work, and ideal leisure. Very often, counselors and clients define these terms differently. If these concepts are not defined and discussed at the beginning of the counseling process, discussions in the latter stages would be confusing. A counselor and client could talk about leisure and yet be talking about entirely different concepts (e.g., leisure as free time versus leisure as a state of mind). Therefore, it is important to reach mutual understanding of key concepts with the client before proceeding further.

Identifying Leisure Needs

In this step, the counselor helps the client identify the relationship of basic human needs (e.g., the need for physical activity, social interaction, new experiences, etc.) to leisure. First, the counselor must be assured that the client understands that the term *need* is being used to refer to a desirable component of one's life, *not* an urgent want or lack of something desired.

Next, the counselor should help the client to identify and understand basic human needs most relevant to his or her life. Recreational activities in which the client is currently involved that meet these needs should be identified. The counselor should also help the client explore "ideal" means of meeting these basic human needs, identifying desirable recreational activities the client is *not* currently engaged in (or is not performing as frequently as is desired) that would meet the needs identified.

It is useful for the counselor to chart notes related to this stage as follows:

Need and Description	How Met (Real)	How Met Ideally
Physical Activity (doing enjoyable activity that improves flexibility, strength, or endurance)	Walking (thirty min/day) Tennis (weekends only) Dancing (twice/year)	Walking (one hour/day) Tennis (ninety min/day) Swim (twenty min/day) Golf (three times weekly, four hours each time) Dancing (two times weekly, two hours each time)

Each need should be treated in depth, with real and ideal means of fulfilling the need listed in columns. Occasionally, clients claim that they are meeting their needs ideally and that they cannot think of any other ways to achieve their needs. In these situations, the counselor should use resource materials to stimulate the client's thought on the topic. For example, some resources for ideas on how to meet the physical activity need are the local college's physical education department course listings and descriptions in the college catalog, a sporting goods catalog, literature from the National Senior Sports Association, listing of clubs in the local phone directory, and listings of sporting events in the local newspaper.

Thus, this step helps the client to more fully understand the value and benefits of recreational activities. This step also prepares the client for the next step, goal setting. Once real and ideal means of satisfying needs have been identified, goals designed to bridge the gap between real and ideal leisure lifestyles are more apparent.

Identifying Leisure Goals

The purpose of the goal-setting phase is for the client to set realistic goals for improving one's leisure, both in the short-range (within the year), and long-term (beyond one year). Notes taken during the needs phase should be referred to in order to facilitate the goal-setting process. Goals should be set for each need identified, based on the discrepancies between the how met (real) versus how met ideally columns. Goals should focus on bringing one's real leisure lifestyle and fulfillment of needs closer to the ideal leisure lifestyle and ideal means of fulfilling needs. In order to encourage clients to set goals, emphasize that there are no risks in goal setting, that the goals are *not* set in concrete, and can be changed.

Obstacles to Goal Attainment

In this phase, the counselor helps the client to identify potential obstacles to attaining the goals identified in the previous phase. The counselor and client also discuss how the obstacles can be overcome.

The purpose of this phase is to ensure that goals set are realistic. If goals are not feasible or challenging enough, they should be revised. Discussion on obstacles should focus more on internal obstacles (e.g., guilt, procrastination, motivation, etc.), which the client can act on to overcome, as opposed to discussing external obstacles over which the client has little control (e.g., weather, cost, etc.).

Identifying Performance Criteria

In this stage, goals are further refined so that each goal has clearly identifiable behavioral indicators, which will serve as criteria for success in goal attainment. The key concern in this phase is to be sure that goals are stated in terms of observable, measurable behaviors and that the desired direction of change is stated.

For example, suppose a client identifies "to ski more" as a goal. After clarification of what is meant by "skiing more," a clearer way to state the goal might be: "to increase time spent skiing from ten hours per month to twenty hours per month." Similarly, performance criteria for the successful attainment of each goal should be identified, and each goal should be stated in measurable terms.

Leisure Alternatives and Consequences

In this step, alternative ways to approach meeting each goal are explored and evaluated. After examining the consequences of alternative means of meeting a goal, the most feasible alternative should be selected as an action plan for meeting the goal. For example, if the goal is to increase time spent skiing from ten hours per month to twenty hours per month, the alternative ways of accomplishing this objective should be examined. Some alternatives might be: (1) make one three-day skiing trip per month, and ski six to seven hours each day; (2) go on four weekend ski trips each month, and try to ski approximately five hours each weekend; (3) go on five one-day ski outings, attempting to ski approximately four hours each day. The feasibility of each alternative should be examined, considering cost, travel time, physical conditioning, and other factors. Finally, the best alternative for meeting the goal should be selected.

Disseminate Information

The purpose of this phase is for the counselor to provide the client with useful information on leisure resources, which will enable the client to enact his or her chosen alternatives for meeting his or her goals. The counselor should provide the client with agency names, phone numbers, program information, and other relevant information.

Participation and Evaluation

The purposes of this phase are to ensure that the client does become involved in the recreational programs and activities identified during the previous phases and to evaluate the client's progress in terms of goal attainment. As necessary, goals should be revised, or alternative means of meeting goals should be reexamined.

Termination and Follow-Up

Once satisfactory progress toward goal attainment has been achieved, the counseling process should be terminated. The last session should summarize the counseling process in a manner that leaves the client with a clear direction for continuing to work to improve his or her leisure. Follow-up contacts should be made with the client after terminating the process in order to check on the client's progress.

Thus, the developmental-educational approach to leisure counseling is an in-depth approach that attempts to help clients to expand their leisure horizons and improve their leisure well-being. This approach is most appropriate with high-functioning elders who do not have specific leisure-related problems but wish to enhance their leisure.

The Therapeutic-Remedial Approach

In contrast to the developmental-educational and leisure resource guidance approaches to leisure counseling, the therapeutic-remedial approach is most appropriate for lower-functioning elders or elders with specific leisure-related behavioral problems. Some examples of behavioral problems that can be related to misuse of leisure time are chronic television watching, social isolation, depression, and alcoholism. Therapeutic-remedial leisure counseling necessitates a close, empathetic relationship with the client. Topics such as leisure attitudes and self-concept, coping skills, behavioral problems and impairments, and support systems should be carefully examined. The therapeutic-remedial approach is similar to the developmental-educational approach in that it is an in-depth approach and should cover the eleven steps described in the previous section of this chapter. However, the therapeutic-remedial approach differs from the developmental-educational approach in that the counselor is more directive, and focuses more on the remediation of specific problems rather than the exploration of broadening leisure horizons.

Some important objectives of therapeutic-remedial leisure counseling are (McDowell, 1976)

1. identification of leisure-related behavioral problems and their causes,
2. identification of desired changes in leisure attitudes and behavior to alleviate the behavioral problems,
3. development of an individualized program of recreational activities that will facilitate integration into leisure living in the community,
4. initiation of involvement in activities with supervision,
5. development of a positive self-image and positive attitudes toward community living (if the client is being prepared for discharge from an institutional setting), and
6. development of community contacts that will enable the client to participate in community activities without supervision.

In summary, the therapeutic-remedial approach is a more direct approach that attempts to alleviate specific behavioral problems. Although it has several objectives that the developmental-educational approach does not, therapeutic-remedial leisure counseling would still follow the same eleven steps of the developmental-educational approach.

SPECIAL CONSIDERATIONS IN COUNSELING ELDERS

Leisure counseling with elders is different from leisure counseling with younger age groups in several respects. One consideration is the prevalence of the work ethic among elders. For some elders, the word leisure has a negative connotation. Strong negative attitudes toward leisure can sometimes be an obstacle to making progress. One approach to counteracting this problem is to give the client an exposure to the breadth and scope of recreation available to elders, possibly by showing slides, a videotape, or movie on this topic during one of the first few sessions. Doing so will give the client a more positive impression of leisure and recreation. Another suggestion is to strongly emphasize the specific benefits of various recreation activities in order to help the client understand the potential benefits of leisure activity.

Another common problem encountered is short-term memory deficits. One way to alleviate this problem is for the counselor and client to take notes during the session, and also tape-record the session. The notes and tapes can serve as useful reference materials for the counselor and client during each session, as well as between sessions.

Encouraging elders to participate in leisure counseling can be an especially perplexing problem. A helpful suggestion is to avoid labeling the process as leisure counseling, but rather name the program "leisure planning" or some other nonthreatening title. Another useful motivational technique is to play excerpts of a videotape or audiotape that demonstrates what leisure counseling is like, and how it can benefit people.

The first step in beginning a leisure counseling program with an individual is to collect background information and conduct an initial interview. Based on the interview and data collected, you must choose the most appropriate orientation (leisure resource guidance, developmental-educational, or therapeutic-remedial) to use. Although you would expect to utilize the therapeutic-remedial approach more in nursing homes and adult day care centers and the leisure resource guidance and developmental-educational approaches more with higher-functioning elders in the community, there will be situations in which a nursing home resident preparing for discharge needs nothing more than leisure resource guidance, whereas a healthy elder living in the community might need therapeutic-remedial leisure counseling.

The following is a list of suggested techniques and procedures to follow in counseling elders:

1. Plan sessions to last between thirty and forty-five minutes. Allow at least twenty minutes after the session for taking additional notes on the session.
2. Conduct sessions a minimum of once a week, hopefully two or three times a week.
3. Every session should have a clearly defined purpose, which is clearly stated at the beginning of the session in order to orient both the counselor and client to the topic at hand.
4. Note taking and tape recording are helpful sources of information and are encouraged.
5. Select a style of counseling most suitable to the situation. Be flexible enough to change styles (e.g., become more confrontational) if the original method chosen becomes ineffective.

It might be necessary and sometimes more desirable to conduct leisure counseling sessions in small groups instead of on an individual basis. As discussed in earlier chapters, the lack of recreation staff in some settings makes it almost impossible to devote time to one-on-one work with clients. Having to work in small groups can be a blessing if the clients feel more comfortable being in a group than being in a one-on-one counseling situation, and if the dynamics of the group are good, making the sessions more enjoyable and enlightening for all. The following is a list of suggested procedures and techniques for conducting leisure counseling sessions in small groups:

1. Ideal group size is six to eight persons.
2. Try forming groups based on similar needs/circumstances so that group members will have more in common and relate better (e.g., widowers' group, married couples' group, men's group).
3. Politely yet firmly avoid/cut off storytelling; make it a group "rule." If the sessions last only thirty to forty-five minutes and one person tells a twenty-minute story, not everyone in the group will have ample opportunity to express himself or herself.
4. Try to keep participants focused on the here and now, their present feelings, and how past events affect their present leisure.
5. Have group members sit close together in a circle in order to promote a feeling of psychological closeness and so participants can hear one another.
6. Begin the sessions with a task (e.g., a written exercise) that everyone can participate in or a question that everyone can answer.
7. Do not let one person dominate; redirect questions to other group members.
8. Basically follow the same steps and procedures when working in a group as you would in counseling an individual. For example, if developmental-educational leisure counseling is most appropriate with your group, follow the same eleven steps, in the same order, as you would follow in counseling an individual.

One final tip that applies both to group counseling and individual counseling is to make the sessions fun. The sessions do not need to be all talk; they can incorporate some activity. Having refreshments can also make the atmosphere more relaxed. Remember that the means are just as important as the end product. If the sessions are enjoyable, participants will want to continue coming to the sessions and will benefit more from the sessions. Also, even though it will take more time, if you as the counselor will let the clients help themselves and struggle a bit to find answers for themselves rather than you giving them the answers, the clients will benefit more in the long run and will develop greater independence. After all, promoting independence is a key goal of any recreation program.

The following exercises are presented in order to help gain additional insight into how to conduct leisure counseling sessions with elders. Exercise 9.1 focuses on the goal-setting phase of the counseling process; Exercise 9.2 concentrates on the obstacles phase; and Exercise 9.3 is related to leisure counseling for small groups.

Hopefully, Exercise 9.1 will make you excited about leisure in later life, as well as give you some insight into the goal-setting phase of the counseling process. The next exercise (9.2) is designed to help you with the next

EXERCISE 9.1. Personal Goals for Leisure in Later Life

Instructions

1. Under each category of benefits of leisure/leisure needs, list at least five leisure activities that you would like to participate in when you are sixty-five and older.
2. In the "Present" column, indicate current frequency of participation in each activity.
3. In the "Future" column, indicate your desired frequency of participation in each activity when you are sixty-five and older.

Leisure Activity   Present   Future

Fitness

1. _____ _____ _____
   _____ _____ _____
2. _____ _____ _____
   _____ _____ _____
3. _____ _____ _____
   _____ _____ _____
4. _____ _____ _____
   _____ _____ _____
5. _____ _____ _____
   _____ _____ _____

Socialization

1. _____ _____ _____
   _____ _____ _____
2. _____ _____ _____
   _____ _____ _____
3. _____ _____ _____
   _____ _____ _____
4. _____ _____ _____
   _____ _____ _____
5. _____ _____ _____
   _____ _____ _____

Relaxation

1. _____ _____ _____
   _____ _____ _____
2. _____ _____ _____
   _____ _____ _____
3. _____ _____ _____
   _____ _____ _____
4. _____ _____ _____
   _____ _____ _____
5. _____ _____ _____
   _____ _____ _____

Creativity

1. _____ _____ _____
   _____ _____ _____
2. _____ _____ _____
   _____ _____ _____
3. _____ _____ _____
   _____ _____ _____
4. _____ _____ _____
   _____ _____ _____
5. _____ _____ _____
   _____ _____ _____

Intellectual stimulation

1. _____ _____ _____
   _____ _____ _____
2. _____ _____ _____
   _____ _____ _____
3. _____ _____ _____
   _____ _____ _____
4. _____ _____ _____
   _____ _____ _____
5. _____ _____ _____
   _____ _____ _____

EXERCISE 9.2. Obstacles to Goal Attainment
and How to Overcome Them

Instructions

1. Select five goals from Exercise 9.1 for which you have at least a few *internal* obstacles.
2. For each goal, list the obstacles that might prevent goal attainment. Focus more on the internal obstacles, not the external ones.
3. For each obstacle, describe possible solutions/ways to overcome it.

Obstacles   Solutions/Ways to Overcome Obstacles

Goal #1

1. _____ _____
   _____ _____
   _____ _____

2. _____ _____
   _____ _____
   _____ _____

3. _____ _____
   _____ _____
   _____ _____

Goal #2

1. _____ _____
   _____ _____
   _____ _____

2. _____ _____
   _____ _____
   _____ _____

3. _____ _____
   _____ _____
   _____ _____

Goal #3

1. _____ _____
   _____ _____
   _____ _____

2. _____ _____
   _____ _____
   _____ _____

3. _____ _____
   _____ _____
   _____ _____

Goal #4

1. _____ _____
   _____ _____
   _____ _____

2. _____ _____
   _____ _____
   _____ _____

3. _____ _____
   _____ _____
   _____ _____

Goal #5

1. _____ _____
   _____ _____
   _____ _____

2. _____ _____
   _____ _____
   _____ _____

EXERCISE 9.3. Session Plans for a Leisure Counseling Group

Imagine that you are starting a new leisure counseling group in a retirement home. The group is high functioning and will be meeting for a series of ten forty-five-minute sessions. Prepare an outline for each of the first four sessions in this series. For each session, identify the purpose of the session, appropriate icebreakers/activities, written exercises to stimulate discussion, questions you could use, and anticipated problems and expected outcomes. Use a separate page for each session outline.

phase of the counseling process, the identification of obstacles to goal attainment, and how to overcome these obstacles.

Based on this exercise, how realistic do you think your leisure in later life goals are? Do any of them need to be revised in order to make them more feasible? Are they too easily attainable, and should you revise them to make them more challenging? If there were any obstacles for which you could not think of a solution, see if a friend or classmate can suggest some solutions.

The last exercise in this chapter (9.3) focuses on leisure counseling for small groups.

SUMMARY

The aims of this chapter were to help you to develop a greater understanding of leisure counseling and how to use leisure counseling with elders. Realistically, it is quite difficult to conduct leisure counseling with elders based solely on the information presented in this chapter. Attempt each of the three types of leisure counseling with fellow students, following the procedures and considerations discussed in this chapter. After some experience with fellow students, further training in counseling techniques, and using this chapter as a guide, you should well be able to conduct leisure counseling with elders.

Leisure counseling is a very important and useful skill in performing recreational work with elders. In almost all settings for recreational services for elders, leisure counseling has become a vital component of the program. Therefore, workers entering the field of recreational services for elders should be well-informed and well-trained in leisure counseling theory, procedures, and techniques. For further information on leisure counseling, refer to the "Other Resources" list at the end of this chapter.

REFERENCES

Backman, S. and Mannell, R. (1986). Removing attitudinal barriers to leisure behavior and satisfaction: A field experiment among the institutionalized elderly. *Therapeutic Recreation Journal,* 20(1), 47-53.

Bolton, C. (1985). Lifestyle management, proaction, and educational efficacy. *Educational Gerontology,* 11, 181-190.

Ginsberg, B.R. (1988). Structuring your retirement leisure time. *Parks and Recreation Magazine,* May, pp. 46-49, 59.

Humphrey, F., Kelley, I.D., and Hamilton, E.J. (eds.) (1980). *Facilitating leisure counseling for the disabled: A status report on leisure counseling.* College Park, MD: University of Maryland.

Mahon, M.J. and Searle, M.S. (1994). Leisure education: Its effect on older adults. *Journal of Physical Education, Recreation, and Dance,* 65(4), 36-41.

McDowell, C.F., Jr. (1976). *Leisure counseling: Selected lifestyle processes.* Center of Leisure Studies: University of Oregon.

Nour, K., Desrosiers, J., Gauthier, P., and Carbonneau, H. (2002). Impact of a home leisure educational program for older adults who have had a stroke. *Therapeutic Recreation Journal,* 36(1), 48-64.

Olson, W.E. and McCormick, J.B. (1957). Recreational counseling in the psychiatric service of a general hospital. *The Journal of Nervous and Mental Disease,* 25(2), 237-239.

Overs, R.P., Taylor, S., and Adkins, C. (1977). *Avocational counseling manual: A complete guide to leisure guidance.* Washington, DC: Hawkins and Associates.

Thompson, R. and Cruise, D. (1993). Leisure awareness and education: Preparing for retirement. *Journal of Physical Education, Recreation, and Dance,* 64(4), 35-37.

OTHER RESOURCES FOR LEISURE COUNSELING

Chase, D.R. (1977). Leisure counseling and leisure behavior research. *Therapeutic Recreation Journal,* 11(3), 94-101.

Dowd, T. (ed.) (1984). *Leisure counseling.* Springfield, IL: C.C. Thomas.

Edwards, P.B. (1977). Practice makes perfect. *Journal of Physical Education and Recreation,* 27(4), 40-42.

Edwards, P.B. (1980). *Leisure counseling techniques: Individual and group counseling, step by step* (Third edition). Los Angeles: Constructive Leisure.

Epperson, A. (1977). Educating recreators for leisure counseling. *Journal of Physical Education and Recreation,* 27(4), 39-40.

Epperson, A., Witt, P., and Hitzhusen, G. (1977). *Leisure counseling: An aspect of leisure education.* Springfield, IL: C.C. Thomas.

Fain, G.S. (1973). Leisure counseling: Translating needs into action. *Therapeutic Recreation Journal.* 7(2), 4-9.

Goldstein, I.E. and Compton, D.M. (eds.) (1977). *Perspectives of leisure counseling.* Arlington, VA: National Recreation and Parks Association.

Gunn, S.L. (1976). Leisure counseling using techniques of assertive training and values clarification. *Expanding Horizons in Therapeutic Recreation,* Volume 4. Champaign, IL: University of Illinois.

Gunn, S.L. (1977). A systems approach to leisure counseling. *Journal of Physical Education and Recreation,* 27(4), 32-35.

Gunn, S.L. and Peterson, C.A. (1977). Leisure counseling: An aspect of leisure education. *Journal of Physical Education and Recreation,* 27(4), 29-30.

Gunn, S.L. and Peterson, C.A. (1977). Therapy and leisure education. *Parks and Recreation,* 12(11), 22.

Hartlage, L. (1977). Leisure counseling from personality profiles. *Journal of Physical Education and Recreation,* 27(4), 43.

Hayes, G.A. (1977). Professional preparation and leisure counseling. *Journal of Physical Education and Recreation,* 27(4), 36-38.

Howe, C.Z. (1984). Leisure assessment instrumentation in therapeutic recreation. *Therapeutic Recreation Journal,* 18(2), 14-24.

Joswiak, K.F. (1979). *Leisure counseling program materials for the developmentally disabled.* Washington, DC: Hawkins and Associates.

Keller, J.F. and Hughston, G.A. (1981). *Counseling the elderly: A systems approach.* New York: Harper and Row.

Land, C. (1974). Recreation counseling for psychiatric patients in a day treatment setting. *Therapeutic Recreation Journal,* 8(4), 156-159.

Langford, N. (1980). Leisure counseling: Lessons my clients taught me. *Journal of Leisurability.* 5(3), 52-59.

Loersch, L.C. and Wheeler, P.T. (1982). *Principles of leisure counseling.* Minneapolis: Educational Media Corp.

Mazulski, M., Faull, V.H., and Ruthowski, B. (1977). The Milwaukee leisure counseling model. *Journal of Physical Education and Recreation,* 27(4), 49-50.

McDowell, C.F. Jr. (1974). Toward a healthy leisure mode: Leisure counseling. *Therapeutic Recreation Journal,* 8(3), 96-104.

McDowell, C.F. Jr. (1975). Emerging leisure counseling concepts and orientations. *Leisurability,* 2(4), 19-25.

McDowell, C.F. Jr. (1977). Integrating theory and practice in leisure counseling. *Journal of Physical Education and Recreation,* 27(4), 51-54.

McLaughlin, L.T. (1980). Leisure counseling with drug dependent individuals and alcoholics. *Leisurability,* 5(1), 9-16.

McLellan, R.W. (1977). Valuing: A necessary phase in leisure counseling. *Journal of Physical Education and Recreation,* 27(4), 31-32.

Mundy, I. and Odum, L. (1979). *Leisure education: Theory and practice.* New York: Wiley.

Neulinger, J. (1977). Leisure counseling: A plea for complexity. *Journal of Physical Education, and Recreation,* 2(4), 27-28.

Overs, R.P., Taylor, S., and Adkins, C. (1977). Avocation for the elderly. *Journal of Physical Education and Recreation,* 27(4), 44-45.

Rule, W.R. and Jarrell, G.R. (1980). Time dimensions in leisure counseling. *Leisurability,* 5(1), 3-8.

Smith, D.A. and Reynolds, R.P. (1980). Integrating leisure counseling and psychological services. *Therapeutic Recreation Journal,* 13(3), 25-30.

Veda, B., Brown, R., Mulvihill, S., and Rolf, C. (1980). A systematic approach to leisure education in community based recreation facilities. *Leisurability,* 5(1), 60-69.

Ward, V.E. (1981). Transition through leisure counseling. *Journal of Physical Education and Recreation,* 31(4), 36-37.

Weiner, A. and Gilley, W. (1978). The instructional status of leisure counseling within the community of higher education. *Therapeutic Recreation Journal,* 11(2), 148-155.

Weiss, C.R. (1980). Leisure education as an aspect of gerontological staff development. *Leisurability,* (1), 9-16.

LEISURE INTEREST INVENTORIES

Anastasi, A. (1976). *Psychological testing* (Fourth edition). New York: Macmillan.

McDowell, C.F. (1978). *Leisure well-being inventory.* Eugene, OR: Leisure Lifestyle Consultants.

McDowell, C.F. (1978). *So you think you know how to leisure? A guide to leisure well-being in your lifestyle.* Eugene, OR: Leisure Lifestyle Consultants.

McKechnie, G.B. (1974). *The leisure activities blank booklet.* Palo Alto, CA: Consulting Psychologists Press, Inc.

McKechnie, G.B. (1974). *The structure of leisure activities.* Berkeley, Institute of Personality Assessment and Research, University of California–Berkeley.

McKechnie, G.B. (1975). *Manual for the leisure activities blank.* Palo Alto, CA: Consulting Psychologists Press, Inc.

Mirenda, J. (1973). *Mirenda leisure interest finder.* Milwaukee, WI: Milwaukee Public Schools, Department of Municipal Recreation and Adult Education.

Overs, R.P. (1971). *Avocational Activities Inventory* (Revised). Milwaukee Media for Rehabilitation Research Reports No. 5A, Milwaukee Recreation and Adult Education Division, Milwaukee Public Schools.

Overs, R.P. and Page, C.M. (1974). *Avocational title card sort.* Milwaukee Media for Rehabilitation Research Reports No. 5F, Grand Forks, Vocational Adjustment Department, Medical Center Rehabilitation Hospital.

PART III:
RESOURCES FOR RECREATION PROGRAMS FOR ELDERS

Chapter 10

Intergenerational Activities

INTRODUCTION

Improved intergenerational relations has been a topic of increasing concern for several reasons: (1) growth in the population of adults over age sixty-five; (2) phenomena such as the growth of retirement communities increasing the degree of segregation of the older population from younger age groups in society; and (3) research findings and theoretical assumptions indicating that intergenerational relations can be improved through increased opportunities for intergenerational interaction. According to Fernandez-Pereiro and Sanchez-Ayendez (1992), research in the United States indicates that most children have negative attitudes toward aging and have a limited knowledge of older persons. Stock (1995) reports that a study of 400 children ages six to eleven conducted in December 1994 indicated that older children drew more negative pictures of elders and had more negative feelings about aging than the younger children did. The researchers concluded that children's attitudes toward elders develop at a very young age and grow increasingly negative, but that the more contact children have with elders, the more positive their views are.

The purpose of this chapter is to examine intergenerational recreational activity as a means of improving intergenerational relations. In this regard, the primary focus of the chapter is to provide practical information on how to plan and lead successful intergenerational recreation activities. The chapter begins with a presentation of literature and research findings related to intergenerational recreation, followed by an explanation of guidelines to follow in planning intergenerational recreational activity programs. Examples of successful intergenerational programs are also presented.

LEARNING OBJECTIVES

The learning objectives of this chapter are to be able to

1. describe the rationale/benefits of intergenerational activities,
2. identify at least five examples of successful intergenerational programs,
3. cite at least five examples of appropriate activities for intergenerational participation,
4. describe how to ensure intergenerational seating for an intergenerational activity,
5. identify at least ten guidelines to follow in planning and leading intergenerational activities, and
6. appropriately modify both active and sedentary games for intergenerational participation.

RESEARCH ON INTERGENERATIONAL RECREATION

Several statements in the literature on the topic of intergenerational activity express the value of such activity for elders, children, and society as a whole (Asadi, 1983; Bronfenbrenner, 1970; Powell and Arquitt, 1978; Leviton and Santa Maria, 1979; Seefeldt et al., 1979; Weinberger, 1979; and Fernandez-Pereiro and Sanchez-Ayendez, 1992).

The results of several research studies indicate that older persons desire intergenerational interaction. Daum and Getzel (1980) report that 74.3 percent of the respondents to the *Myth and Reality of Aging* survey (Harris et al., 1975) aged sixty-five and over expressed a preference for interaction with people of all ages as opposed to interaction with people their own age. Daum and Getzel recommend that greater opportunity for intergenerational interaction be provided; both young and old respondents to the Harris survey expressed a desire for interacting with people of all ages.

In a related vein, Seefeldt et al. (1979) examined the attitudes toward children of a nationwide sample of 542 persons aged fifty and over through the use of a self-report questionnaire. The results indicated that older persons feel that children are fun to be with, that children make good friends for the elderly, and that older persons prefer contact with children ages eight to twelve as opposed to children four to eight. The researchers also state the importance of intergenerational activity to children, as well as to elders.

Furthermore, Powell and Arquitt (1978) state that children's attitudes toward elders are a major influence on how older persons will be treated in the future society. Bronfenbrenner (1970) and Weinberger (1979) express the concern that future society will experience severe problems if intergenerational relations are not improved. According to Seefeldt et al. (1979), increased intergenerational contact can improve the attitudes of elders and children toward each other.

The assertation by Seefeldt et al. is supported by the success of an intergenerational interaction program involving older persons and Girl Scouts (Girl Scouts of the United States of America, n.d.). Other successful intergenerational interaction programs are described by Leviton and Santa Maria (1979), Meier (1980), Chowhary et al. (2000), Knapp and Stubblefield (2000), Pinquart, Wenzel, and Sorensen (2000), and Rothstein (2000). Keller (1992) states that the benefits of intergenerational recreation activity include the transfer of knowledge between the generations, enhanced community feelings, and an enhanced sense of worth for people of all ages.

However, if activities are poorly planned or led, intergenerational recreation can do more harm than good. Some of my students have said that their negative attitudes toward elders and visiting nursing homes and retirement homes stems from their negative experiences in childhood when they were forced to visit elders and participate in activities that they found to be depressing. The quality of the activities are crucial to the effects (positive, negative, or neutral) that an intergenerational program will have on those involved. The ideal scenario is when both young and old enjoy the activities they are participating in together, which in effect gives each group the message that "I really can enjoy being with them."

For my doctoral research I (MJL) sought to examine the effects of a six-week intergenerational music activities program on senior day care participants and twelve-year-old children. At first, the program bombed! In the first two weeks of the study, the activities without children were actually rated higher than the intergenerational ones. However, by the end of the study, the data collected indicated that the presence of children in the activity setting caused senior day care participants' enjoyment of musical activities to be significantly greater (Leitner, 1981). Another finding of the study was that the children's attitudes toward older persons became more positive after participation in the intergeneratonal music activities program. Many of the recommendations for program planning discussed in the next section of the chapter are based on the results of that study.

RECOMMENDATIONS FOR PROGRAM PLANNING

1. Eleven- and twelve-year-old children are excellent candidates for an intergenerational activities program because they are attentive and mature enough to enable participation in a wide range of activities with elders.

Older children and adolescents could also work well with elders, perhaps even doing service projects for impaired elders. Conversely, the range of activity possibilities with younger children would be more limited due to their shorter attention span and less developed oral and written communication skills. However, higher-functioning elders could work well as instructors for younger children in diverse areas such as crafts skills, spelling, and history. Even very young children (three- and four-year-olds) can provide enjoyment for elders on an occasional basis. For example, some nursing homes have had success with a once or twice a month "cuddling" hour, with young children providing a much-needed outlet for affectionate behavior.

There are advantages and disadvantages to both younger children and older children as participants in an intergenerational program. Older children sometimes have a "snotty" attitude, especially if their skills or knowledge in the activities are greater than the abilities of the elders. Thus, it is not only important to plan activities in which the elders can excel, but it is also important to emphasize to the children that one of the purposes of the program is for them to learn from elders, and that they are not doing elders or anyone else a favor by "showing up." Of course, with three- and four-year-olds, the word snotty takes on a whole different meaning! The main challenge with the younger age group is to plan simple activities for the two groups to enjoy together, and to arrange the activity setting in such a way as to foster interaction. A poor activity that I have observed is one in which nursing home residents are seated in a circle, and inside their circle, a group of preschoolers is playing and singing children's songs. The residents sit and watch, but after a while, they are bored. Some simple changes can make this activity more successful, such as having the children pair up with the residents, sit side by side with them, or face them. Simple partner exercises/movements to music can be attempted, with the aid of props such as scarves. Elders who are able can read large print, illustrated books to the children. Simple art activities, beach ball and balloon games, and storytelling are just a few of the many other activity possiblities with young children and elders.

2. A variety of musical activities can work well on an intergenerational basis. Elders and children often find that they can learn about different types of music from each other, and that they share a common knowledge of music such as patriotic songs and religious songs. Some examples of musical activities that can be successful on an intergenerational basis are a singalongs, talent show, musical jamboree (elders and children play instruments such as wood blocks, kazoos, etc.), musical charades game (elders and children work together to compose a song about a famous person *without* using the famous person's name in the song), and a variation of "Name that tune"

musical quiz game, where children and elders work in intergenerational teams to guess the names of songs.

3. An intergenerational music activities program conducted on a regular basis should involve activities twice a month. Twice-a-month activities would foster the formation of intergenerational friendships and yet would not be so frequent that such activities would become boring or tiring to the participants.

4. The number of children participating in an intergenerational activities program should be limited so that a one-to-one ratio of elders to children is maintained. A one-to-one ratio of elders to children can best facilitate inter-generational interaction and ensure that activities are adequately adapted for elders. If children outnumber elders, activities tend to become more child oriented and subsequently not as enjoyable for elders. In senior day care centers, assisted living facilities, and in other settings, absenteeism due to illness is a significant factor affecting participation in activities, whereas in retirement communities, attendance for activities can fluctuate depending on outside commitments of residents. Therefore, the number of children selected for an intergenerational recreation program should be less than the number of potential older adult participants in the program, due to factors that restrict elders' attendance in activities.

5. As a mechanism for facilitating the formation of intergenerational ties, a buddy system should be enacted for intergenerational programs whereby certain elders and children are assigned as partners or teammates for activities.

6. In a related vein, seating arrangements for activities should be such that elders and children are sitting next to one another, not clustered in an age-segregated arrangement. The seating arrangement for an activity is an important factor in determining the extent of intergenerational interaction during an activity. The clustering together of elders and children can severely restrict the amount of intergenerational contact that takes place during an activity. Unless seating arrangements are structured, elders will tend to cluster together, and children will also tend to cluster together. One idea for preventing this clustering is to place small chairs for children on both sides of the older adults participating in the activity, or having these small chairs placed directly across/facing each elder. Also, icebreaking activities that get children and elders to pair up (e.g., find someone born in the same month as you, but at least sixty years apart) can be participated in at the outset in order to get elders and children to sit together. The following procedure can also be effective in ensuring that an intergenerational seating pattern is formed:

   a. Have the residents or center attendees seated in an area *other* than
      the activity area where the activity is to be held before the chil-
      dren arrive.
   b. When the children arrive, they are asked to wait in the lobby rather
      than enter all at once.
   c. One or two children at a time are escorted in and introduced to their
      "host" or "hostess" for the activity.
   d. The elder/children pairs then escort each other to the activity area.
   e. One staff member remains in the lobby with the children until all
      children have entered.

7. Another means of facilitating interaction among activity participants is
to organize the larger group into several smaller groups of four or five persons each. Both the elders and the children feel less inhibited in a small
group than in a large group situation. Also, there is often more opportunity
for interaction in small group situations. In devising small groups, more
alert seniors should be paired with the more confused seniors so as to facilitate interaction in groups where confused seniors are members.

8. Before commencing activities, ample time should be allotted for elders
and children to get acquainted with one another. Tasks such as choosing a
group leader can be helpful in initiating communication among the activity
participants. Another aid in getting elders and children acquainted is wearing name tags. In fact, making name tags can be an appropriate icebreaker
activity.

9. Activities that require a high level of cognitive functioning, especially
fast thinking and quick responses, should be avoided. Many senior day care
participants and nursing home and assisted living residents are at least
slightly impaired with regard to cognitive functioning and are thus at a disadvantage in activities with children that require a high level of cognitive
functioning. It is difficult to lead activities involving mental abilities under
time pressure given the disparity in the abilities of the children and the elders. Furthermore, some elders might feel embarrassed about not being able
to "keep pace" with children. Therefore, conduct activities that do not rely
heavily on short-term memory or the ability to think of an answer to a question while under the constraint of time limits.

10. Conversely, activities that draw upon the past experiences of senior
citizens are recommended. Older persons can share a great deal of knowledge from their past with children, such as anecdotes about historical events
and living conditions of the past as compared to that of the present. In order
to ensure the success of such activities, staff should prepare seniors for the
activities so that each participant will be able to contribute to the activities.

11. Elders should be given specific roles in intergenerational activities
that can enhance their self-esteem and encourage the children to seek their

assistance in performing tasks related to the activity. For example, the role of host or hostess is one that many older persons probably enjoy but rarely are able to experience in their later years. In addition, roles such as team or group leader can help give elders greater status in the activities and encourage children to consult with them during activities.

12. Activities that involve some degree of competition excite and motivate children. However, competitiveness should be kept at a moderate level, otherwise the competitive aspect of the activity will dominate and hinder interaction among participants. For example, as mentioned earlier, "Name-That-Tune" can be a good game to play on an intergenerationaly basis. However, if the game is played with the same rules as the television version of the game (in which the first person or group to know the name of the song is the one to score a point), the spirit of competition and the rush to be the first one to give the correct answer would all but eliminate intergenerational interaction during the activity, even if the children and elders were paired together in small groups. Instead, if the rules were modified such that while each song was being played, each intergenerational group had two or three minutes to discuss and write down their answer, and that all groups answering correctly would get a point, then intergenerational interaction would be more likely because there would be less time pressure to give an answer. Of course, playing songs that elders are familiar with would also help, as it would encourage the children to consult with their elders for the correct answer.

13. Before commencing an intergenerational activities program, the children should be thoroughly oriented to the purpose of the program. Children should be made to understand that the primary focus of activities is to interact with the senior citizens and learn from each other, not to win whatever games are played.

14. It is desirable to conduct activities that enable the children to be active, expend excess energy, yet at the same time enable participation by elders without them having to move wheelchairs or perform any other maneuver that might lead to an accident. An example of such an activity is "People to People." In this game, the leader (odd person out) calls out various instructions to the players (who are all paired with a partner). Instructions such as "head to head," "nose to nose," "hand to elbow," etc. are followed by the players (they connect their body parts as directed) until the leader says "people to people," at which time there is a mad scramble and all players run around, trying to get a new partner and not be left as the odd person out. How to adapt this activity for a group of children and nursing home residents in wheelchairs? Simple! Only two changes are needed: all elders must have a child as a partner, and when it is time to get a new partner, the elders remain where they are, and only the children run around to find a new part-

ner. Similarly, other activities can be modified to allow for enjoyable participation by both age groups, enabling children to be physically active while minimizing safety risks for elders. Exercise 10.1 provides an opportunity to explore how to modify activities to be enjoyable for elders and children, enabling children to expend excess energy and elders to not feel at risk of bodily harm.

EXAMPLES OF SUCCESSFUL INTERGENERATIONAL ACTIVITY PROGRAMS

As discussed earlier in the chapter, music programs with children and elders have been successful. The award-winning film *Close Harmony* documents the success of an intergenerational singing group in Brooklyn, New York. Children and elders, strangers at the outset of the program, began by exchanging letters, eventually met one another, rehearsed, and performed together for a very enthusiastic audience.

The arts in general are good for intergenerational participation. Clark (1991) discusses the use of drama, writing, poetry, movement, dance, and music in nursing homes to bridge the gap between residents and youth. Similarly, Keller (1992) discusses an intergenerational program that matched elders as volunteer instructors and mentors to latchkey teenagers. The elders, who came from the local senior center, shared their craft skills (e.g., quilting) with the teens.

A related program, organized by RSVP volunteers, is the multicultural Folk Art Fair, designed to preserve cultural heritage through music, arts, and crafts skills of the past. The fairs are day-long events, usually held in school gymnasiums. Students are brought to the fair in groups and have time to talk with the elderly exhibitors about their work.

Gardening is another activity that can involve children and elders successfully. Brown et al. (1992) have authored an intergenerational garden curriculum titled *Roots and Shoots,* which explains how third graders and elders can work together on gardening projects, with elders teaching the children about gardening and gardening techniques. The National Gardening Association also sponsors an Intergenerational Gardens program in which elders share their gardening skills with youth at their own garden sites or at gardens that youth have through their school or special projects.

Another type of intergenerational gardening program is conducted through Butte College in California. Students at the college, in cooperation with elders in the area, have a garden in which they grow beans, corn, melons, and other fruits and vegetables. The students and elders share the harvest and give away the surplus to various community agencies.

EXERCISE 10.1. Activity Modification for Intergenerational Participation

Instructions

For each activity described below, explain how you would modify it to enable participation by a mixed group of elders in wheelchairs and children ages ten to twelve.

A. Activity: Touch Blue

How to play: Leader calls out instructions such as "touch something blue," "touch someone with blonde hair," "touch a pair of white socks." The players scamper about to touch these objects/people as quickly as possible.

Modification(s): _____

_____

_____

B. Activity: Elbow Tag

How to play: Players form a circle, each with a partner; there is some space between each pair, and partners' elbows are joined. There is one chaser and one runner. The chaser is trying to tag the runner. At any time, the runner can link elbows with one of the pairs in the circle. When that happens, the end person in the group of three becomes the new runner. If the runner is tagged, the chaser and the runner reverse roles. The circle/running area can be made bigger or smaller depending on how long chasers are running without having a break.

Modification(s): _____

_____

_____

C. Musical Chairs

How to play: Players are seated in chairs. When the music begins, players walk, run, or dance in a circle, around the chairs. The leader takes away one chair. When the music stops, everyone tries to find a chair in which to sit. The one left without a chair gets a letter; the game ends when someone has lost so many rounds of the game that he or she has accumulated all of the letters of the designated loser's word (e.g., pig, horse, etc.). Or, the game can be played until there is only one person left that has not become a "pig," "horse," or some other animal or thing.

Modification(s): _____

_____

_____

A very different "farm" program is The Grand-Time Striders, in which grandparents and grandchildren walk together at a fitness farm in Indiana. According to Harris (1992), walking helps to reduce tensions and makes the mind more alert.

Being physically active is a major component of the Week at Camp program, in which elders interact with 4-H members who serve as junior camp counselors and counselors. Activities include swimming, canoeing, square dancing, exercise, crafts, dinner theater, and a talent show.

Another 4-H intergenerational program involves members interviewing their older relatives, collecting old family photographs, and forming a family tree. The goals of the program are to gain a better appreciation of family heritage and to help elders in completing the process of life review.

Stamp collecting has also become an intergenerational affair, thanks to the Philatelic Project, in which stamps are brought to homebound elders, who then soak, dry, identify, and package the donated stamps. The stamp packages are shared with schoolchildren, Girl Scouts, Boy Scouts, and other elders. Elders in the program discuss the stamps on the phone and exchange stamps with one another.

As discussed in the chapter on programs, volunteering is a prominent leisure activity of elders, and numerous volunteering programs involve children and elders working together. For example, YES (Youth Exchanging with Seniors) has youth and elders working together on jointly selected projects of benefit to the community.

In Newton, Kansas, a preschool has been established in a retirement community. Residents volunteer their time with the children, helping with activities such as gardening, music therapy, and field trips.

Elders also volunteer their time with teenagers. Interages organized a program that brings elders and teens together for high school classroom discussions. Mentors, Inc., runs programs that match high school students with volunteer older adult mentors. The elders help the teens with a variety of problems.

A more intensive intergenerational experience designed to help young adults learn about older adults is the Nursing Home/Student Living Experience (Dickerson, 2001). In this program, graduate students received housing at an independent living retirement facility in exchange for meaningful interaction with the residents. The project required no budget and benefited both the students and the older adults.

Students in the Department of Recreation and Parks Management at California State University, Chico, have been conducting a variety of intergenerational recreational activities at various venues, with great success. The next section of the chapter explains some of these activity ideas.

OTHER INTERGENERATIONAL ACTIVITY IDEAS

Icebreakers should begin each intergenerational activity session in order to loosen people up, get reacquainted, and help everyone feel at ease with one another. An example of a good intergenerational icebreaker is People Bingo. Children are given "bingo sheets," each box having statements such as "I am over ninety years old," or "I have more than ten grandchildren," or "I or my spouse was in the armed forces." The children then go around to all the elders, asking them if any of these statements apply to them, and, if so, they fill in the name of the elder in the appropriate box. The children continue the activity until someone (the winner) has filled in all of the boxes on his or her sheet. This activity gets the children moving around, meeting many of the elders in a nonthreatening way, and also gives the elders a chance to meet the children.

Parachute activities are easily adaptable for mixed groups of children and elders in wheelchairs. The children and elders, interspersed in the circle, all hold on to the parachute. Everyone is actively involved in flipping whatever objects may be placed on the parachute, and the children enjoy running underneath, from one side to the other, etc. Parachute games provide laughter for all, good arm exercise for elders, and an opportunity for children to expend excess energy.

Relay races can also be adapted for intergenerational involvement. Lines of eight to ten players each are formed, with the children and elders interspersed. Elders can be seated or standing. The first team to pass the given object or action up their line and back wins a point. Objects such as balloons, balls, hats, etc., can be passed up and down the lines in different ways. Also, actions can be passed, for example, handshakes, smiles, pat on the back, wink, funny face, animal sound, a wave, hand squeeze, foot stomp, laugh, and hugs. Many possibilities exist, and the activity can work well even with frail, wheelchair-bound nursing home residents.

There are also sedentary games that the generations can enjoy playing together. The Match Game (based on the television game show) is an easy one to play. Divide the group into intergenerational teams of between three and ten per team. The leader gives the group a topic, for example, American presidents. Everyone then writes down the name of an American president that comes to their mind, keeping their answer secret from everyone else. After a minute or so, the leader has everyone hold up their answers. Each team gets one point for each matching answer on their team. The questions can be easy or difficult, depending on the functioning level of the group.

Password is another former television game show that can be played intergenerationally. It is a good activity for small groups (each team consisting of one elder and one child), but it can be adapted for larger groups, with five or six players on each team, and more than two teams. To begin, the leader gives the "clue giver" on each team the word that they are to try to get their team members to guess. The clue giver can give only one-word clues in trying to get team members to guess the word. The team that goes first gets ten points for guessing correctly; if they guess wrong, the next team tries and would get nine points for guessing correctly. Play alternates among teams (and the points awarded keeps dropping by one) until a team guesses the word. Give the elders ample time to think of answers; too much time pressure, especially for elders with some cognitive impairment, can be frustrating.

Another fun guessing game for intergenerational groups is Pictionary. The object of this game is for team members to correctly guess the name of an object, place, person, or action based on a picture drawn by their teammate. I have played this game with groups consisting of children and nursing home residents, and I have been impressed by the artistic ability of elders, as well as how much laughter this activity can generate. Again, the key is not to put the elders under a great deal of time pressure.

Charades also produce a great deal of laughter and can easily be played with children and elders. The key is to prepare a list of topics for the game that both generations will be familiar with, avoiding subjects such as current movies or current hit songs, which might be too difficult for elders.

There are also a variety of more physically active games that the generations can enjoy together, such as horseshoes, ring toss, shuffleboard or table shuffleboard, and lawn bowling. Along these lines, the CSU Chico Department of Recreation and Parks Management students conduct an ambitious event titled Intergenerational Games. The event involves children, college students, high-functioning elders from the community, and lower-functioning elders from nursing homes and retirement homes. Activities include tennis, walking, volleyball, golf putting, shuffleboard, softball, badminton, ping-pong, and even card games for those not willing or able to participate in the more physically demanding events.

An even more ambitious intergenerational recreational activities program was conducted in Israel in 1998 with Arab and Jewish elders, Arab children, and Jewish and Arab college students (see Photo 10.1) (Leitner, Scher, and Shuval, 1999). The purpose of this program was not so much to improve intergenerational relations as it was to use intergenerational recreational activities to try to induce positive changes in the attitudes of Arabs and Jews toward each other. Research findings indicated that the program was a resounding success in positively changing attitudes, and that the positive attitude changes remained even one year later (Leitner and Scher, 2000). The intergenerational recreational activities program involved a vari-

PHOTO 10.1. Intergenerational activities bring together Israeli Arabs and Jews.

ety of icebreakers and active games that have been described throughout this chapter. The extra challenge in this program was that the Jewish elders did not speak or understand Arabic, and the Arab elders did not speak or understand Hebrew. The Arab children and college students served as translators to facilitate communication between the Arab and Jewish elders. Thus, intergenerational recreation in this case was used as a peacemaking tool.

As discussed in the next chapter, other special events and programs that involve children and elders are also possible. Exercise 10.2 is presented to stimulate further thought on planning intergenerational activities.

SUMMARY

Intergenerational activities can be the most successful and enjoyable activities for elders and children if planned and led properly. However, intergenerational activities can be disastrous if *not* properly planned, given the great differences in needs, interests, and abilities of elders and children. The implementation of the recommendations discussed in this chapter can help to ensure the success of an intergenerational recreation program.

EXERCISE 10.2. A New Intergenerational Activity

Instructions

1. Create your own intergenerational activity, one not discussed in this chapter. It can be an entirely new activity or one that you are going to adapt for intergenerational participation.
2. Identify the name of the activity.
3. Specify the children (ages) and elders (functioning level) for which this activity is most appropriate.
4. List step-by-step directions for the activity.
5. Identify any concerns or special leadership considerations.
6. Identify facilities, equipment, and supplies needed for the activity.

Name of the activity: _____

_____

_____

Children: _____

_____

_____

Elders: _____

_____

_____

Step-by-step directions: _____

_____

_____

Concerns and special leadership considerations: _____

_____

_____

Facilities, equipment, and supplies needed: _____

_____

_____

REFERENCES

Asadi, L. (1983). The effects of instruction and recreation interaction on children's attitudes toward the elderly. Unpublished master's thesis, California State University, Chico.

Bronfenbrenner, U. (1970). *Two worlds of childhood: The U.S. and the U.S.S.R.* New York: Russell Sage Foundation.

Brown, M., Masatani, K., Daniels, J., and McCullough, M. (1992). *Roots and shoots: An intergenerational garden curriculum guide.* Palo Alto, CA: Elizabeth F. Gamble Garden Center.

Chowdhary, U., Schultz, C., Hasselriis, P., Kujath, H., Penn, P., and Henson, S. (2000). Intergenerating activities and aging appreciation of elementary school children. *Educational Gerontology,* 26(6), 541-549.

Clark, P. (1991). *Intergenerational arts in the nursing home: A handbook.* Westport, CT: Greenwood Press.

Daum, M. and Getzel, G. (1980). Preference for age-homogeneous versus age-heterogeneous social interaction. Paper presented at the Thirty-Third Annual Scientific Meeting of the Gerontological Society of America.

Dickerson, B. E. (2001). What's new: An update on the nursing home/student living experience. *Association for Gerontology in Higher Education Exchange,* 24(3), 14.

Fernandez-Pereiro, A. and Sanchez-Ayendez, M. (1992). Link ages: Building bridges between children and the elderly. *Ageing International,* 19(2), 10-14.

Girl Scouts of the United States of America (n.d.). *Hand-in-hand: Cross-age interactions* (Administration on Aging Grant 90-A-326). Washington, DC: Administration on Aging.

Harris, L. and Associates (1975). *The myth and reality of aging in America.* Washington, DC: National Council on Aging.

Harris, T. G. (1992). The grand-time striders. *Saturday Evening Post,* March/April, pp. 46-47.

Keller, M. J. (1992). Linking generations through recreation. *Parks and Recreation,* March, pp. 59-60.

Knapp, J. L. and Stubblefield, P. (2000). Changing students' perceptions of aging: The impact of an intergenerational service learning course. *Educational Gerontology,* 26(7), 611-622.

Leitner, M.J. (1981). The effects of intergenerational music activities on senior day care participants and elementary school children. *Dissertation Abstracts International,* 42(8), 3752A.

Leitner, M. J. and Scher, G. (2000). A follow-up study to peacemaking through recreation: The positive effects of intergenerational activities on the attitudes of Israeli Arabs and Jews. *World Leisure and Recreation,* 42(1), 33-36.

Leitner, M. J., Scher, G., and Shuval, K. (1999). Peace-making through recreation: The positive effects of intergenerational activities on the attitudes of Israeli Arabs and Jews toward each other. *World Leisure and Recreation,* 41(2), 25-29.

Leviton, D. and Santa Maria, L. (1979). The adults health and developmental program: Descriptive and evaluative data. *Gerontologist,* 19(6), 534-543.

Meier, P. (1980). Toddlers, elderly share quarters at day care center. *Senior Citizens Day Care News,* 1(1), 5.

Pinquart, M., Wenzel, S., and Sorensen, S. (2000). Changes in attitudes among children and elderly adults in intergenerational group work. *Educational Gerontology,* 26(6), 523-531.

Powell, I. A. and Arquitt, G. E. (1978). Getting the generations back together: A rationale for the development of community based intergenerational activity programs. *The Family Coordinator,* 3, 421-426.

Rothstein, R. (2000). What toddlers need: Graying boomers. *The New York Times,* March 1, p. A22.

Seefeldt, C., Jantz, R. D., Serock, K., and Bredekamp, S. (1979). *Elderly persons' attitudes toward children.* College Park, MD: University of Maryland.

Stock, R. S. (1995). Senior class: Some widely held misconceptions hamper understanding between the young and old. *The New York Times,* August 6, p. B5.

Weinberger, A. (1979). Stereotyping the elderly: Elementary school children's responses. *Research on Aging,* 1(1), 113-136.

Chapter 11

Recreational Programs and Special Events

INTRODUCTION

The purpose of this chapter is to describe several recreational program ideas appropriate for elders in a variety of settings and communities. The programs discussed in this chapter are travel programs, camping, Elderhostel and other educational programs, Adult's Health and Development Program; high-risk activities, Senior Olympics and other sports programs, Elderfest, volunteering, and programs for rural elders. Unlike most of the other chapters of the book that focus on activities primarily for adults age eighty and over, many of the programs described in this chapter are popular with younger retirees, and have minimum age requirements of fifty-five or even fifty.

LEARNING OBJECTIVES

The following are learning objectives of this chapter:

1. Identify at least three different types of travel programs for elders.
2. Identify three goals and objectives for senior adult camping programs.
3. Identify three practical considerations in providing camping programs for elders.
4. Identify three program ideas for senior adult camps.
5. Describe what an Elderhostel is.
6. Describe what the Adult's Health and Development Program is.
7. Identify at least three high-risk activity ideas appropriate for elders.
8. Identify the goals and objectives of the Senior Olympics.
9. Identify at least five practical considerations/procedures in organizing a Senior Olympics.
10. Describe at least three successful sports programs for elders.
11. Describe what an Elderfest is.

12. Identify at least three practical considerations/procedures in organizing an Elderfest.
13. Identify at least three different types of volunteering programs for elders.
14. Identify at least three successful recreation programs for rural elders.
15. Identify at least three special considerations in providing leisure services for rural elders.

TRAVEL PROGRAMS

Travel is a very popular leisure activity for older adults. Research (Patterson, 2002) indicates that travel is the number one leisure activity that people want to engage in when they retire. Travel is an important and meaningful leisure activity for older Americans, and they tend to travel more often, further, and stay for longer than do younger adults (Gibson, 2002). Other research findings regarding travel and older adults follow (Teaff and Turpin, 1996):

1. Among adults sixty-five and over, 52 percent plan to take three or four trips per year in retirement; only 6 percent planned to take less than one trip per year.
2. Adults over the age of fifty-five account for 80 percent of all vacation dollars spent in the United States. According to Hong, Kim, and Lee (1999), travel expenditure patterns of elderly households in the United States indicate that the most money is spent on transportation, followed by food, lodging, sightseeing, entertainment, and other travel expenses.
3. About 75 percent of retirees use some type of travel service.
4. Difficulties with airports and other personal problems cause many older adults to make changes in travel modes.
5. Older adults tend to prefer nonhectic, preplanned, group-based trips, although another study on this topic found that only 2.7 percent of adults ages fifty-five and over preferred to travel in groups.
6. The travel priorities for older adults are
   a. Visit new places (86.1 percent)
   b. Spend time with family (74.7 percent)
   c. Rest and relax (73.0 percent)
   d. Escape everyday routine (68 percent)
   e. Experience new things (67.8 percent)
   f. Spend time with friends (64.7 percent)

g. Visit museums and historical sites (62.6 percent)

h. Visit festivals and special events (58.4 percent)

7. In terms of lodging, the most important characteristics of accommodations for older adults were rated as

a. Cleanliness (99.4 percent)

b. Convenience or location (96.8 percent)

c. Room price (96.2 percent)

d. Easy access from main roads (94.2 percent)

e. Security systems (90.3 percent)

f. Parking lot lighting (90.1 percent)

8. A majority (55 percent) prefer to dine in the lodging site.

9. Other hotel amenities that older travelers tend to value are grab bars and supports in bathrooms; night-lights in bathrooms; legible and visible signs in hallways, public areas, and restaurants; extra blankets; and larger printing on schedules, information, and menus.

Penalta and Uysal (1992) discuss several factors influencing elders' travel patterns and potential obstacles to taking trips:

1. *Safety:* Safety has been identified as the greatest factor influencing the travel plans of elders. Elders desire to travel to places where they feel "safe and secure." Travel agents and tour promoters need to emphasize safety and security in their advertisements, and make necessary arrangements for older travelers to be in a safe and secure environment once their destination has been reached.

2. *Pets:* Having a pet can be a barrier to traveling and limits the number and frequency of trips made by elders. To alleviate this problem, some parks and resorts now offer kennel services for visitors at a minimal charge. Some hotels and motels allow pets in their rooms. For those edlers who do not wish to travel with their pet, pet-sitting services would be helpful.

3. *House-sitting services:* Similar to pet-sitting, house-sitting services would enable many elders to feel capable or more comfortable with the idea of traveling away from home.

4. *Accessibility:* Common physical limitations of elders should be considered in making travel services and destinations more comfortable for elders. For example, seats that are placed eighteen inches from the floor are more conducive for proper posture, and drawers, doorknobs,

and faucets that are easily opened with little use of wrist motion are helpful for elders.
5. *Intergenerational travel:* Elders seem to desire to travel with their grandchildren and are doing so in increasing numbers.

Another factor to consider in attempting to encourage more elders to travel is the large number of elders who have a chronically ill or impaired spouse. Physical assistance needs to be available while traveling, otherwise taking trips is impractical. For example, bathrooms that are big enough for an elder and a helping spouse to fit into are needed on planes, buses, and trains. At an airport or other transfer point, services need to be available to help elders in the bathroom (e.g., a man cannot easily enter the women's bathroom to assist his wife), to carry their luggage, and to get to their next destination. Such services would enable more elders to travel and help them to have peace of mind while they are en route to their destination. In addition, short-term nursing homes and senior day care centers in partnership with major resorts and hotels would be very attractive to older adults who have a low-functioning spouse (Leitner, 1999).

A popular way for elders to travel is in groups. According to Hudson and Rich (1993), some of the advantages of group travel for elders are

1. they meet others with similar interests,
2. they are able to enjoy worry-free travel (all arrangements are made for them), and
3. It is cost-effective due to group discounts that are widely offered.

Hudson and Rich (1993) also identified several benefits to be reaped by park and recreation departments that sponsor group trips:

1. It can be a source of revenue for the agency.
2. It helps to diversify their programs.
3. It makes the agency more visible.
4. It provides opportunities for intergenerational programming.
5. It increases and diversifies the agency's clientele.

Some guidelines for designing group tours for elders are offered by Gay (1999):

1. Ask potential customers if they require a special diet or have a medical condition requiring prescription medication, and inform tour leaders of these needs to ensure that they are met.
2. Try to schedule tours during off and shoulder seasons in order to take advantage of lower prices and smaller crowds.

3. Minimize the number of one-night stays in hotels, as the process of checking in and out and packing and unpacking is an unpleasant chore for many older adults.
4. Older adults tend to like tours that include all or most of the meals. Preferably, breakfast and lunch should be the big meals of the day and the evening meal should be a light one consisting of soup, salads, and fruits.
5. Try to schedule shorter and slower traveling periods for older adults.
6. Smaller buses and vans can travel down more narrow, interesting roads. Also, because of hearing problems that are so common among older adults, the tour guide has a better chance of being understood by everyone in a smaller vehicle than in a large tour bus, even with a microphone and good sound system.

According to Hudson and Rich (1993), especially popular destinations for elders are historical sites, natural wonders, seashores and beaches, and special events and festivals. Clements and Barret (1993) describe the special benefits of museum trips for elders, especially in fostering creativity. They describe a museum experience with three components:

1. A premuseum lesson to acquaint elders with the exhibitions they will be seeing, and hands-on experiences for those with developmental disabilities
2. The museum field trip
3. A postmuseum lesson in which elders actually work with the medium seen in the exhibition (e.g., clay), creativity and laughter being key elements

Trips can also be used as a means to facilitate therapeutic reminiscing. Elders can be encouraged to keep diaries, make scrapbooks, or draw pictures of situations or objects that evoke pleasant memories. The recreation therapist can then try to determine places to visit, such as historical sites, that would facilitate reminiscing and good feelings. Places that would stir unhappy recollections would be avoided.

Intergenerational travel is the business of Grandtravel, a travel agency that offers "very special vacations for grandparents and grandchildren." The advantages of Grandtravel are obvious; it not only gives grandparents and grandchildren time to enjoy each other's company and strengthen their ties, but it also provides a respite from child care for busy parents and enables children to take advantage of their school vacation time and see places that their working parents are unable to take them to. The Grandtravel journeys include opportunities for grandparents and grandchildren to relate to each other on an intergenerational level and connect with the family's past, private time alone together for grandparents and their grandchildren, and peer activities in which grandchildren enjoy activities with other grandchildren and grandparents are with the other grandparents. Grandtravel destinations include Washington, DC; Alaska; France; Holland; New England; England; and Scotland.

Intergenerational travel not only can be enjoyable for children and older adults but can also be used as a tool to promote peace. Research findings (Leitner, 1999) indicating that a program of intergenerational tourism caused the attitudes of Arab and Jewish elders to become more positive toward each other is an example of how such a program can help promote peaceful relations.

An innovative travel service for elders is the Senior Travel Exchange Program, designed to give elders the opportunity to travel overseas and meet seniors of other nations, develop friendships, and learn their customs. Older travelers from the United States stay in elders' homes in foreign countries to reduce hotel and meal costs. In return, the hosts travel to the United States at a later date, and the guests and hosts reverse roles. Trips are made in groups of twenty to twenty-five elders and the tours last twenty-five to twenty-eight days.

In a related vein, Mitric and Gibson (1988) report that elders are entering the bed-and-breakfast business for fun and profit. The head of the American Bed and Breakfast Association predicts tremendous growth in the homestay bed-and-breakfast market, particularly with elders. Half of the association's members are age fifty and over (Mitric and Gibson, 1988).

Backman, Backman, and Silverberg (1999) discuss the growing market for senior nature-based travel. Expenditures on nature-based tourism activities such as wildlife viewing and photography are greater than $14 billion worldwide, and older adults are a substantial portion of that market. Moisey and Bichis (1999) report that senior nature tourists are more likely to be motivated by activities that promote good health and physical fitness, their understanding of nature, and and their personal enrichment.

Similarly, Patterson (2002) suggests that adventure tourism for older adults is likely to become increasingly popular as more older adults seek physically challenging and "adrenalin-driven" activities such as whitewater rafting, horse riding, hiking, skiing, scuba diving, mountain biking, backpacking, and camping. An organization called Overseas Adventure Travel (OAT) has compiled a booklet titled "101 Tips from Adventure Travelers Over 50." To obtain a copy, contact OAT, 625 Mt. Auburn Street, Cambridge, MA 02138; telephone 800-493-6824.

As discussed in the next section, camping is already a popular adventure travel activity for older adults, and the extent of physical challenge and adrenalin rush derived from it varies greatly depending on the type of camping.

CAMPING

Senior adult camping has been successful throughout the country, from New York (Winfrey, 1977) to Oregon (Chenery, 1987). Topics discussed in this section include philosophy, practical considerations, and program ideas for senior adult camping.

Philosophy

As documented by research studies cited in Chapter 1, elders can and do enjoy outdoor recreation experiences. Even elders with disabilities can enjoy camping, as long as necessary adaptations are provided. Chenery (1987) reports that elders who were nearly blind, who used canes to walk, and had advanced heart problems were able to participate in and enjoy camping. According to Chenery (1987), the benefits of camping for elders include change of routine; refreshing of memories; gaining new perspectives; and renewal of the spirit and physical abilities. Some appropriate goals and objectives for a senior adult camp are (Armstrong, 1979)

1. to provide opportunities for social interaction,
2. to expose elders to new leisure activities in order to develop new activity interests and skills,
3. to learn about and gain a greater appreciation for nature,
4. to provide enjoyable activities which are physically and mentally stimulating, and
5. to provide the opportunity to experience an aesthetically pleasing environment (an important objective, especially for urban elders).

Winfrey's (1977) article on camps for elders in New York State illustrates the value of camping as a relief from the tensions of the city. Approximately 8,000 New Yorkers aged 60 to 104 visited nine camps in four states in 1977. The camps were supported by churches, community centers, and private individuals under the auspices of Vacations for Aging and Senior Citizens Association.

Practical Considerations

Armstrong (1979) identifies the following considerations in planning a successful camping experience for elders:

1. Involve the participants in the planning process.
2. Expose participants to new activities. Elders are as willing to learn as any other people.
3. Schedule religious activities, such as morning worship and quiet times before meals.
4. As much as possible, provide historical background information on the places to be visited.
5. Take photographs during the outing; many people enjoy seeing pictures of themselves at play after the experience is over.
6. Make provisions for those who have special dietary needs.
7. Schedule an orientation meeting for all staff and participants to be held approximately two weeks before the trip. The meeting gives participants a chance to meet staff and ask questions. Suggested topics for the orientation meeting are general camp policies, necessary items to bring to camp, health and safety considerations, emergency procedures, and a schedule of activities. Participants can be asked to complete a health questionnaire and a leisure interest inventory.
8. Determine methods of evaluating camp programs before the camp begins.

Hupp (1987) states that camps for third agers do not require a large number of staff and personnel because elders can be included in the staffing of such programs. Another advantage that older campers have is that they tend not to have the same time constraints that other camper populations have.

Program Ideas

Leisure interest inventories should be reviewed to obtain program ideas. Armstrong (1979) identifies the following sample program ideas:

1. Arts and crafts, such as sketching, oil painting, puppetry, and woodworking
2. Sports and games, such as volleyball, horseshoes, table games, canoeing, Frisbee, yoga, and swimming
3. Music and drama activities, such as singing, folk dancing, and short skits

4. Special events, such as a Cabaret night, travelogues, and an international dinner
5. Nature activities, such as birdwalks, all-day hikes, night hikes, and environmental education discussions and hikes
6. Sightseeing trips to points of interest

Another program idea is have an intergenerational camping experience. Hayden (1988) discusses the ECHO (Elder Campers Helping Others) model, in which elders share some time and life experiences with children in a variety of summer camp settings, ranging from environmental awareness camps for nine- to eleven-year-old 4-H members to developmental day camps for children ages six to fourteen to a special camp for children being treated for cancer and kidney disease. Similar to the Grandtravel concept, it would also be possible to have "grandcamps," where grandparents and grandchildren could enjoy a group intergenerational camping experience. To conclude this section of the chapter, Exercise 11.1 is presented to provide an opportunity to further develop the idea of grandcamps. Base your answers to the exercise on the information presented earlier in the chapter on camping for third agers and on Grandtravel, as well as the information on intergenerational programming presented in Chapter 10.

ELDERHOSTEL AND OTHER EDUCATIONAL PROGRAMS

Elderhostel, though vastly different from camping, does share a few similarities. Participants are exposed to new experiences and are provided with numerous opportunities for enjoyable, mentally and physically stimulating recreation activities. Also, Elderhostelers are provided with excellent opportunities for socialization. In addition, program participants must adapt to less-than-luxury living accommodations during their stay.

The Elderhostel program began at the University of New Hampshire in 1975 based on the idea of providing elders with a mentally and physically stimulating experience. Elderhostelers live on a college campus for a one-week period during which they attend educational classes and participate in a variety of recreational activities on campus. Thus, Elderhostel is a unique one-week college experience program designed especially for persons aged fifty-five and older. Research (Goggin, 1999) indicates that the motivation for learning for almost 80 percent of Elderhostelers is "the sheer joy of it."

Elderhostel has been a popular program. In 1978, 200 colleges and universities offered programs in thirty-eight states; by 1984, over 700 colleges and universities offered programs in the United States and overseas. According to Gurewitsch (1980), 13,000 elders enrolled in Elderhostel

EXERCISE 11.1. Planning a "Grandcamp"

Instructions

1. Assume that there are at least twenty grandparents and twenty grandchildren in your group.
2. In the first column, list an activity schedule (with approximate times) for the first day of the camp; in the second column, do the same for the second day of the camp.
3. Each day's plan should include at least one special event or main activity; describe this activity in detail, including staff and set-up considerations, time needed, detailed plans for the activity, and leadership considerations.

Day #1 Activities

_____

_____

_____

_____

_____

_____

_____

Day #2 Activities

_____

_____

_____

_____

_____

_____

*Details of the main
activity of the day*

_____

_____

_____

_____

_____

_____

_____

*Details of the main
activity of the day*

_____

_____

_____

_____

_____

_____

_____

programs in 1979 and approximately 20,000 were enrolled in 1980. Elderhostel has become much more popular, with approximately 200,000 program attendees in 2002 in thousands of different programs located in over ninety countries (Elderhostel, 2003).

Most programs are limited to thirty-five to forty participants. Most U.S. programs are one week in length and international programs are usually two to three weeks in duration (Goggin, 1999). Elderhostel is a nonprofit international organization and program costs are kept as low as possible. Program fees include registration costs, six nights of accommodation, all meals, five days of classes, and a variety of extracurricular activities. The Elderhostel office is responsible for coordinating all of the available programs, registering participants, disseminating information, and publishing catalogs. To obtain further information on Elderhostel and a copy of their latest catalog of programs, contact Elderhostel at 877-426-8056 or <www.elderhostel.org>.

It seems as if there is an ever-expanding need for new Elderhostel programs. If your college or university does not have an Elderhostel program, perhaps one can be started. Exercise 11.2 gives you an opportunity to generate ideas for a new Elderhostel program at your college or university.

Simons (1991) describes an interesting educational program for elders in France called "le brain jogging." The programs takes place in private clubs, clinics, homes, and hospitals for the aged. The largest network of courses is a program named Eureka, which has workshops in more than 120 towns and villages. The courses consist of fifteen weekly sessions of two hours each. Usually twenty to twenty-five elders are in a group. The sessions begin with a discussion of the week's news to stimulate curiosity and communication with others. Mental jogging exercises follow the discussion. The exercises involve perception, concentration, reasoning, speech, and imagination. Program counselors encourage participants to do homework such as going shopping without a list, or memorizing a train schedule or poem. They also encourage elders to play bridge, chess, and other mentally stimulating games.

In the United States, Beck et al. (1991) report that 320,000 Americans age fifty and over were enrolled in college courses, including 65,000 at the graduate and professional levels. Thousands more are attending lectures, auditing classes, and forming study groups. According to Beck et al. (1991), the vast majority are attracted back to school for the sheer joy of learning. Recognizing that elders are a growth market, universities are now designing whole divisions for adult learners. A fast-growing program is the "Learning in Retirement" study group that is designed specifically for elders. Members of the program pay an annual fee and design their own courses, recruiting teachers from among their peers. One of the larger programs is

EXERCISE 11.2. Designing an Elderhostel

Instructions

1. First, look through a recent Elderhostel catalog. Determine a program theme which is not currently being offered but which you feel would be popular with elders.
2. List the classes to be offered on your selected theme, and identify local people who could teach the classes.
3. Identify appropriate extracurricular activities to be offered and staff needed.
4. Make some phone calls to determine the approximate cost per person of housing and meals.

Program theme: _____

_____

_____

List of classes to be offered: _____

_____

_____

Personnel (describe) needed to teach the classes: _____

_____

_____

Extracurricular activities to be offered: _____

_____

_____

Staff needed for extracurricular activities: _____

_____

_____

Approximate cost per person of housing and meals: _____

_____

_____

Delaware's "Academy of Lifelong Learning," with an enrollment of 1,400 students age fifty-five and over participating in 110 courses. In Israel, Bar-Ilan University's program of courses for older adults was attracting approximately 2,000 enrollees in 1995. In China, The University for the Aged has a network of more than 800 institutions for elders. One of its star students was Qian Likun, age 102, who among other things was studying health care for the elderly, which helps him care for his eighty-one-year-old daughter. As described in the next section, universities have more to offer elders than just courses and workshops.

ADULTS' HEALTH AND DEVELOPMENTAL PROGRAM

Founded by Dr. Dan Leviton at the University of Maryland, the Adults' Health and Developmental Program (AHDP) is a nine-week, once-a-week clinic for adults ages fifty-five and over. The purpose of the program is to contribute to the health, life satisfaction, and morale of elders by providing opportunities to participate in enjoyable activities and form friendships with same-age peers and college students. Research on evaluating the effects of the program on its participants indicates that it has been successful in meeting its aims (Leviton and Santa Maria, 1979).

Program participants are matched with their own student staff member (usually in their late teens or early twenties) for weekly ninety-minute sessions of physical activities, such as creative dance, brisk walks, swimming, tricycling, trampolining, and bowling, followed by an hour of discussion on topics such as loneliness, communication, and sexuality in later life. Intergenerational friendships among participants and student staffers form easily. The program has had a positive impact not only on participants' health and morale but also the student staffers' attitudes toward aging.

The AHDP serves as many as 120 elders per semester, at a minimal cost per person. The program can be adopted by other colleges and universities, and a film is available that further explains how the program is run. For further information, contact Dr. Dan Leviton, Adults' Health and Developmental Program, PERH Building, University of Maryland, College Park, MD 20742.

HIGH-RISK ACTIVITIES

Dr. Leviton is also an advocate of high-risk activities for elders. Leviton (Alessio, Grier, and Leviton, 1989) believes that more older adults are willing to experience the thrills and adventures of activities that would be classified as high-risk, and that a great deal can be learned from participation in such activities because they involve tasks that are physically and/or mentally challenging. Activities can be perceived as high risk in nature and carry the benefits associated with high-risk activities yet be executed in such a way that safety is assured. Alessio, Grier, and Leviton (1989) state that the opportunity to participate in high-risk activities need not be limited to only the fittest elders, but they emphasize that simply avoiding injury is not enough, because a near-miss incident that causes anxiety could be harmful to someone with a heart condition. Therefore, extra precaution needs to be taken with elders who have heart conditions, respiratory ailments, osteoporosis, hypertension, and other health problems. Assistance should always be immediately available. Alessio, Grier, and Leviton (1989) discuss some examples of appropriate high-risk activities for elders:

1. *Ropes challenge and initiatives courses:* These facilities have been constructed at schools, camps, parks, and other recreational facilities across the United States. The courses have eight or ten events. Some are elaborate courses with dozens of cables, telephone poles, beams, and towers, up to seventy-five feet high and crossing deep ravines, and others are simply constructed of ropes and boards. The courses can be adapted to meet the needs of different age groups and levels of functioning.

   The course should begin with an orientation designed to allay fears regarding safety. Next, icebreaker activities should be led to encourage interaction among the group (usually ten to twelve in size). The icebreaking activities can also be helpful to the instructor/leader in identifying limitations of the group members. For example, an elder who obviously has weak upper body muscle tone should avoid activities in which arm strength is important. Special body support devices, use of large handles and straps to ensure proper grip, and brightly colored materials should be used in order to maximize the safety of the participants. With proper precaution, ropes challenge and initiatives courses can be safely participated in and enjoyed by elders.

2. *Waterfront activities:* Some of the possibilities in this category include a rope swing into a swimming lake, canoeing, rafting, kayaking, and sailboating. Although these activities are not necessarily dangerous, they do provide a sense of adventure and excitement.

3. *Dry land activities:* Not all elders like to be in the air, hanging on ropes, or in the water! Some dry land high-risk activity possibilities are mountain hiking, biking, caving, riflery, and archery. In addition, activities that are not high risk but are adventurous in nature, such as a treasure hunt or other group problem-solving task, can be exciting and

help build the confidence needed for participation in more challenging activities.

In summary, a variety of high-risk activities can be successful with elders. As discussed in the next section, some sports activities that might be classified as high risk, such as downhill skiing, are gaining increasing popularity with elders.

SPORTS PROGRAMS

In 1977, a ski school in Keystone, Colorado, started the first learn-to-ski program for adults age fifty and over ("Never too Late for Ski School," 1977). The learn-to-ski program package includes accommodations, lift tickets, lessons, a race, and a party. Every morning throughout the week, warm-up exercises followed by two-hour group ski lessons are scheduled. Afternoons are devoted to cross-country ski tours, mountain ecology sessions, videotaping sessions to improve skiing techniques, and opportunities for relaxation in the swimming pool or whirlpool. More recently, Breckenridge ski resort hosted the fourteenth annual senior winter games in February 1994 (Rosen, 1993). The "70+ Ski Club," is a group for skiers age seventy and over. Both "70+" and another organization called "Over The Hill Gang" sponsor ski trips throughout the world for their members. The "70+" club already has over 4,000 members and attracts several hundred older skiers to its annual convention in the Catskills in New York State. For further information on "70+," contact Richard Lambert at <RTL70plus@aol.com>.

Tennis is an increasingly popular sport with older adults. Participation in tennis by adults ages fifty and over doubled from 1988 to 1992; 1.1 million men and 713,000 women age fifty and over played tennis at least four times in 1992, compared with only 531,000 men and 440,000 women in 1988 ("Tennis Play up for Americans 50 and over," 1993). The Super Senior Tennis Inc. (SST) organization was formed to meet the needs of players over age sixty, and they sponsor tournaments throughout the United States in every age division from sixty to eighty, plus events for those eighty-five and over (Tullius, 1988). There are four annual national championships in each bracket, and four to six tournaments per month in Florida and Southern California. The United States Tennis Association (USTA) also sponsors tennis programs for older adults. For further information, contact the USTA chapter in your region.

The National Senior Games Association (NSGA) also offers tennis programs for older adults. Their tennis competitions for adults ages fifty-five to eighty promoted health and fitness for elders as well as the development of friendships ("Kretschmer Sponsors Seniors Tennis Classic," 1982). The NSGA is a nonprofit organization dedicated to helping people age fifty and over enjoy participating in recreational and competitive tournaments in golf, tennis, bowling, skiing, and other sports. Participation in their programs has been increasing: In 1987, there were 1,869 competitors ages sixty to seventy-nine and 102 over age eighty; in 1997, there were 6,828 competitors in the sixty to seventy-nine age group, and 559 in the over-eighty group (Noble, 1998). The NSGA also offers a Vacation Home Exchange program that allows members to enjoy a lodging-free vacation by exchanging homes with another member in a desired location. For further information on NSGA programs, see the National Senior Sports Association Web site, <www.nsga.com>.

Another increasingly popular sport with older adults is softball. The Senior Softball World Championship tournament, initiated in 1993, expanded to 100,000 participants in 1994 (Pesky, 1994) and has continued to grow.

All these sports competitions for elders creates a need for cheerleaders, and the Sun City Poms are right there to fill the void. Their average age is seventy-three, and they perform an energetic "pom-pom" routine, complete with back flips, cartwheels, and splits, wearing glittering costumes with silver sequins and red satin (Bishop, 1991). They made their debut in 1979 as cheerleaders for a women's softball team and performed throughout the United States, including at the International Cheerleaders' Convention.

There is also a need for sports programs for elders who are at a lower level of functioning. One example of a successful program is a home-delivered "bowling alley." The "alley" is a thirty-foot carpet with marked spaces on which to place the plastic pins. The rubber bowling ball weighs only three pounds. The beauty of the program is that elders can participate right in the retirement home or nursing home, and even those who are frail can succeed at it.

In summary, a variety of options are available for elders who enjoy sports. The following is a partial listing of organizations that sponsor sports programs for older adults:

- Men's Senior Baseball League <www.msblnational.com>
- Senior Softball World Championship <www.seniorssoftball.org>
- American Canoe Association <www.acanet.org>
- U.S. Cycling Federation <www.usacycling.org>
- U.S. Golf Association <www.usnseniorgolf.org>
- U.S. Handball Association <www.ushandball.org>
- U.S. Paddle Tennis Association <www.paddletennis.org>
- U.S. Squash Racquets Association <www.us-squash.org>

SENIOR OLYMPICS/SENIOR GAMES

Another interesting sports program is the Senior Olympics, founded in 1969 by Warren Blaney. The Senior Olympic movement is sponsored by Senior Sports International, a nonprofit corporation. The first Senior Olympics in 1969 involved 175 people participating in three events (marathon, swimming, and track and field) over a four-day period. By 1980, over 4,000 people participated in more than fifty athletic events and other recreational activities throughout the year (Provost, 1981). A National Senior Games–Senior Olympics event held in Orlando in 1999 attracted 12,000 participants (Villarosa, 1999). Another organization, the U.S. National Senior Sports Organization (USNSO) (now the National Senior Games Organization), organizes sports competitions for elders, similar to the Senior Olympics. Their U.S. National Senior Sports Classic III held in June 1991 in Syracuse, New York, attracted over 5,000 athletes ages fifty-five and over, including a ninety-nine-year-old swimmer ("Successful Aging," 1991). The seventeen sports categories in the event included archery, badminton, basketball, cycling, field events, softball, volleyball, and a ten-kilometer road race. In 1990, USNSO conducted sports competitions for approximately 100,000 adults ages fifty-five to ninety-nine in seventy cities. According to Wilson (1991), the typical older adult sports enthusiasts are not necessarily lifelong athletes, especially affluent, or well-educated, but basically tend to be energetic and willing to volunteer for anything.

The goals of the Senior Olympics (Provost, 1981, p. 174) are as follows:

1. "To encourage all adults to exercise regularly for better health, greater happiness, and higher productivity"
2. "To give recognition to all adult athletes in every sport, at every age level"
3. "To contribute to enhanced international relations through opportunities provided to form international friendships through the Tour of Champions and the attendance of athletes from foreign countries at the Senior Olympics in the United States"
4. "To bring adults and youth together in a positive environment"

The Senior Olympics are based on the belief that athletics are physically, mentally, and emotionally beneficial, and that participation in athletics throughout life can help to retard the aging process. The Senior Olympics aim to involve adults in athletics as early in their lives as possible so that participation in sports can continue throughout the lifespan and produce maximal benefits. The Senior Olympics are also based on the belief that competition can be enjoyable and healthy, that it can reinforce feelings of self-worth and dignity. Another benefit of competition is that it can motivate people to train and engage in physical conditioning during the year in preparation for the big event.

The Senior Olympics emphasizes that winning is not the only measure of success; all participants are recognized for their involvement. The event is an opportunity for people ages 20 to 120 to compete against same-age peers in a variety of sports. Provost (1981) presents guidelines for developing local Senior Olympics programs:

1. Establish an executive committee responsible for drafting policies and procedures, preparing a budget, and publicizing the event. A representative cross section of the community should be on the committee, including recreation and physical education students and faculty, members of service clubs and the chamber of commerce, media personnel, and representatives of senior citizens' clubs and organizations.
2. Expenditures should be minimal. Use of athletic facilities should be obtained at no cost. Volunteer staff should be able to plan and lead all activities. Donations of awards and prizes for the events should be solicited from local businesses. Any other expenses should be covered by entry fees. Entry fees should be set as low as possible to ensure maximal participation, yet be set high enough to ensure that all expenses are covered.
3. Select sports for the program that are most popular in the community. International rules for all sports should be used wherever possible and distances should be measured in meters.
4. Keep complete and accurate records of results in all events, and develop a record book that will give each year's participants goals to strive to attain.
5. Age classifications for events should begin with the age twenty to twenty-four category, and continue in five-year increments, *without* an upper limit. If there are a large number of entries in one age category, then divide the category on the basis of ability (e.g., A, B, C, and D levels). The winners of one ability level should compete in the next ability level in the next Olympics.
6. Modifications in rules and equipment (e.g., reducing heights, weights, game time, etc.) should be made as necessary.
7. All participants should be required to submit a medical release form from their physicians. A doctor and/or nurse should be available at most events.
8. Liability and accident insurance coverage should be obtained.

For further information on conducting a local Senior Olympics, consult the U.S. National Senior Games Association <www.nsga.com>.

ELDERFEST

Elders have many talents besides athletic prowess, and Elderfest is a festive community event designed to display some of these talents to the community in order to destroy myths and stereotypes of aging. An Elderfest can be a one-day, two-day, or even a weeklong event and involves the display of the arts and crafts, hobby, dance, and musical talents of local elders, for people of all ages in the community to view. In Chico, California, the event began in 1981 with 300 participants, but quickly grew to an annual one-day event involving over 1,000 people (see Photo 11.1). The following guidelines for coordinating a local Elderfest are based on the success of the Chico Elderfests (Leitner, 1983):

1. Organization of the event should be intergenerational in nature. In Chico, the event was coordinated by local elders; students from the CSU, Chico, Department of Recreation and Parks Management; the Chico Area Recreation District; and local businesses.
2. In addition to a general steering committee for the event, which is responsible for fund-raising, overseeing the budget, and determining the location, date(s), and time(s) for the event, several committees should be formed, each with a distinctive role in the event, such as a display/ exhibits committee, entertainment committee, refreshments committee, transportation committee, and a publicity committee.
3. Policies for the event must be predetermined, such as
   a. What is the minimum age requirement for exhibitors and performers?
   b. Can exhibitors sell merchandise?
   c. Can a local business be allowed to have a display table in return for a generous contribution?
   d. What are the geographical limitations on participation?
4. The participation of people of all age groups, especially of youth, is key to the success of the event in meeting its aim of dispelling myths and stereotypes of aging. Wherever possible, college students and children should be integrated into the event, performing tasks such as assisting with parking, setting up exhibits, and ushering for entertainment.

PHOTO 11.1. Two seniors perform at a Chico Elderfest.

The Chico Elderfest experienced difficulties in attracting young adults and children to attend the event. During the first several years of the event, it was held on a Saturday in order to facilitate maximal attendance. Despite massive publicity efforts, it was mainly older adults who attended the event. Even though the attendance was excellent (1,000), the population most in need of a positive experience to improve attitudes toward elders (young adults and children) was not attending the event in great enough numbers for the event to meet its aim of dispelling myths and stereotypes of aging. Therefore, the event was changed to a weekday, and local schools arranged to have classes attend throughout the day at specific times. College students were enlisted to guide the children through the exhibits, displays, and entertainment. Although the overall number in attendance declined slightly, the event became more intergenerational in nature and was able to better meet its goal of improving young people's attitudes toward elders and aging. For further information on how to conduct an Elderfest, consult Leitner's (1983) article.

VOLUNTEERING

Many elders are involved in volunteer work as a leisure activity. The benefits of volunteering include (Leitner and Leitner, 1994) a euphoric feeling called "helper's high": enhanced self-esteem from the feeling of helping others; feelings of achievement and recognition; learning new things; meeting people and making friends; the feeling of giving care and love to others and vice versa; and being able to participate in leisure activities that might otherwise be too costly (e.g., ushering at a theater and being able to see performances for free).

The different types of volunteering options available include (Leitner and Leitner, 1994) the following:

1. *Sports programs offered through municipalities:* Volunteers are usually needed for coaching, officiating, organizational help, and fundraising. Programs for youth, elders, and other special populations have a special need for volunteers.
2. *Hospitals and nursing homes:* Volunteers are needed for a variety of functions, including assistance with recreational activities programs.
3. *Cultural organizations and recreational/educational settings:* Organizations that promote art, music, theater, and dance, and museums, aquariums, and zoos need volunteer help with fund-raising, security, leading or assisting with group tours, especially from schools, and in organizing and leading special events and activities.
4. *Travel-related volunteering:* Many of these programs are environmentally related but there also programs, for example, for elders wishing to travel to Israel and engage in a program of volunteer work to help new immigrants or other people or organizations in need of helping hands.
5. *National and international organizations:* Endless possibilities exist in this category, ranging from sports organizations such as the National Senior Sports Association, to hobby clubs such as stamp collecting, to organizations for elders, such as the American Association for Retired Persons.
6. *Local causes and organizations:* The possibilities in this category include libraries, schools and after-school programs, the local humane society, churches and synagogues, and shelters for the homeless.
7. *Elders in need:* Many of the local area agencies on aging coordinate volunteer programs in which healthy elders lend assistance to frail and disabled elders. Assistance can involve home visits, telephone calls, going for walks, taking short trips, doing errands together such as shopping, and even providing professional help such as legal and tax preparation assistance.
8. *Performing groups:* Perhaps the most enjoyable and uplifting way for elders to help others is to be in a performing group, such as a drama group, band, or choir, and perform for residents of retirement and nursing homes, and attendees of senior day care and senior centers.

An example of a thriving performing group comprised of elders wishing to volunteer their time by uplifting elders through music and dance is ATTAD (Aid to the Aged in Institutions). The group, founded in 1984 by Naomi Sklar, is based in Netanya, Israel, and travels to hospitals and homes for elders throughout Israel. Their entertainment troupe, comprised mainly of English-speaking older adults, is able to communicate without any problems to elders whose primary language might be Russian, Yiddish, Hebrew, Spanish, Ahmaric, or Portuguese, through the language of music, dance, and touch. Their troupe travels in a group sometimes as large as forty volunteers, sometimes as small as four volunteers. Regardless of the troupe's size, they are able to transform a depressing institutional setting into an enthusiastic, jubilant group of elders with eyes wide open, hands clapping, and feet tapping. ATTAD also assists elders through fund-raising activities, recruiting volunteers, and acquiring amenities such as tape players, movie projectors, musical instruments, and art supplies for institutions. For further information on ATTAD, contact Naomi Sklar, President, ATTAD, P.O. Box 377, Netanya, Israel 42103.

In addition to recreation-related volunteering opportunities, there are work-related volunteer opportunities for elders. Hamilton (1991) reports that small business owners and communities are benefiting from the knowledge and experience of elders through organizations such as SCORE (Service Corps of Retired Executives), RSVP (Retired Senior Volunteer Program), and the International Executive Service Corps. SCORE provides small businesses with free advice; RSVP provides a means for elders to volunteer for community service; and the International Executive Service Corps gives managerial and technical advice to third-world countries that are making the transition to market economies.

Many of the programs discussed thus far in the chapter are more accessible to urban elders than they are to rural elders. As discussed in the next section, a number of programs have been developed specifically for this population.

PROGRAMS FOR RURAL ELDERS

Definition

For the purposes of this book,* the term *rural* refers to areas outside of standard metropolitan statistical areas (SMSAs), whether farms, open countryside, or villages, towns, or cities of up to 50,000 in population. In twenty-

---

*This section is based on Leitner, M.J., Shepherd, P.L., and Ansello, E.F. (1985). Recreation and the rural elderly, in *Leisure in Later Life* (First edition), pp. 291-324.

eight of the fifty states, 40 percent or more of the state's elders live in rural areas (Harbert and Wilkinson, 1979). Although recreational programs and services for rural elders are in need of improvement and expansion, some excellent programs are being offered.

Existing Programs

In Colorado, rural elders are able to enroll in outreach courses offered through community colleges (Blanding, Turner, and Gerbrandt, 1993). Courses include computer science, creative painting, musical expressions, mental jogging, and "senior shape-up." Some courses were renamed in order to sound more exciting/recreational in nature. For example, "Interpersonal Communication" was renamed as "How to Talk So People Will Listen," and "Prominent Women in History" was renamed as "Women Who Dared to Be Different."

In Nebraska, Project Rural ALIVE (Americans Living in Varied Environments) provides recreational activities such as bingo and watching movies to rural elders as part of a nutrition and social interaction program (Goldenrod Hills Community Action Council, n.d.). A similar program in Kentucky offers recreational activities that include listening to music, oral reading, discussions, live music by elders, poetry reading, art demonstrations, social events, hobbies, and holiday celebrations (Northeast Kentucky Area Development Council, Inc., 1971). Recreational activities are also offered as part of a meals program for rural elders in Idaho. According to Simonsen (n.d.), the meals not only promote proper nutrition but also provide a form of social recreation.

In Washoe County, Nevada, Native American elders began teaching Indian dances, songs, and rhythms to Native American children in the evenings at their senior center. The elders contribute valuable knowledge that helps to preserve their culture, while the children are able to increase their appreciation for their culture.

In northeast Kentucky, senior centers are partially heated by solar greenhouses. Elders grow vegetables and houseplants in these greenhouses, and the sale of these products helps to raise money for the senior centers. The program not only provides an enjoyable activity for rural elders but is also a productive activity that fosters feelings of pride and dignity.

Recreational programs for rural elders are also offered as part of community service programs. Success with such programs has been reported in areas of Arkansas; Florida; Franklin County, New York; and West Virginia. Dancing, cards, and other games are enjoyed by over 500 elders in rural Gadsden County, Florida (Ford, 1976), whereas in Idaho, dances, bus trips, picnics, parades, and potluck dinners are part of the activity program (Reed, 1970).

Stough (1974) discusses a church program labelled "adult education" in rural Oklahoma, with over 700 enrollees and thirty volunteer instructors participating in activities with a heavy emphasis in the arts. Beaver and Elias (1980) report that an experimental painting class helped to increase social interaction, feelings of self-worth, self-confidence, and independence among its participants. Hirzel (1977) describes a senior companion program in rural counties of Maryland, in which elderly volunteers work with frail and ill elders in order to stimulate interest in new activities and hobbies as well as to provide companionship.

In summary, there are many successful recreational programs for rural elders, despite the numerous obstacles to service provision. These obstacles, along with various solutions, are discussed in the next section.

Obstacles to Service Provision and Ways They Can Be Overcome

Transportation is a particularly significant barrier to recreation participation among rural elders because many rural elders do not own an automobile (Carter Administration, 1979), public transportation services are not as readily available as they are in urban areas, and greater distances need to be traveled due to the lower population density in rural areas. Research indicates that transportation is a barrier to use of human services in general (including recreational services) for approximately 50 percent of rural elders (Larson and Youmans, 1978; Means, Mann, and Van Dyk, 1978). According to Notess (1978), a factor that might compound the problem of lack of transportation is the desire of many rural elders to ride on vans or buses only with people that they know.

However, there are some solutions to problem of transportation. A free bus ride system can increase the number of trips made by rural elders for social and recreational purposes. Another possibility is the coordination of elders who own and drive cars with those who do not. School buses can be used to transport rural elders to and from senior centers. To reduce transportation needs, mobile centers can be used to provide recreational services to different areas within a region during different days of the week. For example, Murray (1979) recommends bookmobile visits to nursing homes in order to meet the recreational reading needs of rural institutionalized elders.

A parallel concept is that of roving activity specialists. Due to the geographic dispersion of the rural elderly, programs are often conducted on a small scale, i.e., a relatively low number of participants and staff. For programs to be conducted on a larger scale, they would often need to include a geographic area so large that transportation to and from the center would not be feasible for intended service recipients. A disadvantage of small scale programs is that they are only able to provide a limited range of activities, given the limitations of a small staff. A solution to this problem is to have activity specialists visit different centers within a region on different days of the week. In this way, centers might have a music specialist one day, an art specialist another day, and so on. Roving activity specialists could enrich the lives of rural elders by exposing them to a wider range of activities than would otherwise be possible.

According to Notess (1978), another obstacle to recreation services for rural elders is their tendency to reject anything considered to be charity, such as free rides and free meals. The National Association of Area Agencies on Aging (1978) also cites mistrust of federal programs as an obstacle to providing leisure services for rural elders. One approach to overcoming this obstacle is to elicit the cooperation of churches and religious organizations in providing leisure services to rural elders. Karcher and Karcher (1980) state that the church is the most trusted institution of rural elders and that outside programs need to tie in with the rural church. Many community activities are church related, and the church is the most widely participated in social organization for rural elders. Rural churches can stimulate the development of leisure activities for elders, assist in grant solicitation, and can even make contacts with nearby colleges and universities for student volunteers to assist with the provision of recreational activities.

Stough (1974) presents case studies of church-sponsored recreation programs for rural elders. These case studies indicate that religious institutions are a convenient meeting place, a location for social contacts and recreation, and are often a sponsor of senior citizen clubs. Murray (1979) recommends that with the help of churches, large print books of light spiritual reading be available to satisfy the reading interests of rural elders. Rural elders tend to congregate in churches, fire departments, grange halls, county fairgrounds, town commons, and community centers. These places are therefore natural focal points for the delivery of leisure services for rural elders, and are also good places to post flyers and posters publicizing programs.

Inadequate publicity and lack of awareness of existing programs can be an obstacle preventing rural elders from participating in recreational activities. The ability of service providers to locate elders in need of services can be difficult, given the resistance of rural elders to intervention programs, and the geographic dispersion of the rural population. Means, Mann, and VanDyk (1978) suggest reaching out to isolated rural elders in order to increase their awareness of recreational opportunities. Notess (1978) recommends that outreach programs are more effective when the service provider visits the client's home and wins the trust of clients and their families. According to Coward (1979), the inclusion of family members and close friends can increase the impact of services and make them more efficient. Family-oriented programming for rural elders is therefore desirable.

The Voice-a-Gram Program (Administration on Aging, 1976), a program in which isolated elders and their families exchange prepared messages on tape cassettes, is an example of an outreach service that can help reduce loneliness of isolated elders and increase their awareness of recreational opportunities. Other recommended publicity techniques are radio interviews, speeches, news articles, and regular columns in rural newspapers (Ambrosius, 1979).

Another way to make rural elders more aware of existing recreational opportunities is through the provision of pre- and postretirement leisure counseling services. Leisure counseling for rural elders can not only increase rural elders' awareness of existing programs, but can also assist elders in making appropriate choices in use of free time and can help to remove psychosocial barriers against engaging in leisure activities. For more details on leisure counseling, refer to Chapter 9.

SUMMARY

Many of the programs discussed in this chapter were initiated by one motivated individual with a good idea, who was able to inspire others and eventually create a program serving thousands of elders. There is always room for new programs; what new program ideas do you have? Exercise 11.3 is an opportunity to explore ideas for new programs that might be successful with elders and even be profitable.

We hope your program is a big success!

EXERCISE 11.3. A New Recreational Enterprise Especially for Elders

Instructions

1. Based on this chapter, decide on a recreational program for elders that is not yet being offered, but that you feel would be well-received by elders. Select a program idea that could be offered privately, on a profit-making basis.
2. Describe the idea and exactly what activities the program would involve. Your program can be a "spin-off" of an existing program.
3. Briefly but clearly identify the physical and psychosocial needs of elders that your program would fulfill. Try to support your statements with research cited in Chapter 1.
4. In the spaces provided, identify the specific target population for your program (the young-old? the old-old? healthy or impaired? urban or rural? etc.); geographic location; facilities, equipment, and supplies needed; staff needed; approximate program costs; fees to be charged; estimated number of participants; and expected profit margin.

My program idea: _____

_____

_____

_____

Specific activities in the program/program description: _____

_____

_____

_____

Physical and psychosocial needs of elders that the program would fulfill:

_____

_____

_____

_____

Target population: _____

_____

_____

_____

Geographic location: _____

_____

_____

_____

Facilities, equipment, and supplies needed: _____

_____

_____

_____

Staff needed: _____

_____

_____

_____

Cost estimate: _____

_____

_____

_____

Program fees: _____

_____

_____

_____

Projected number of participants: _____

_____

_____

_____

Expected profit margin: _____

_____

_____

_____

REFERENCES

Administration on Aging (1976). Voice-a-gram: Prescription for loneliness. *Aging Magazine,* 5, 261-262.

Alessio, H. M., Grier, L. J., and Leviton, D. (1989). Trailblazing recreational programming with the elderly: High-risk activities. *Activities, Adaptation, and Aging,* 13(4), 9-16.

Ambrosius, G. R. (1979). *A report on national rural strategy conference to improve service delivery to rural elderly.* Spencer, IA: Iowa Lakes Area Agency on Aging.

Armstrong, C. H. (1979). *Senior adult camping.* Martinsville, IN: American Camping Association.

Backman, K. F., Backman, S. J., and Silverberg, K. E. (1999). An investigation into the psychographics of senior nature-based travelers. *Tourism Recreation Research,* 24(1), 13-22.

Beaver, M. and Elias, B. (1980). Enhancing the well-being of the marginal elderly through art appreciation. *Gerontologist,* 20(5), 63 (Abstract).

Beck, M., Glick, D., Gordon, J., and Picker, L. (1991). School days for seniors. *Newsweek,* November 11, pp. 60-63.

Bishop, K. (1991). Smashing a cliché with sis, boom, bah. *New York Times,* February 27, pp. B1, B7.

Blanding, C. W., Turner, J., and Gerbrandt, M. (1993). Creating leisure opportunities for rural seniors: The community college outreach concept. *Journal of Physical Education, Recreation, and Dance,* 64(4), 52-54.

Carter Administration (1979). *Small community and rural development policy.* Washington, DC: The White House.

Chenery, M. F. (1987). Camping and senior adults. *Camping Magazine,* March, pp. 50-51, 62.

Clements, C. and Barret, D. B. (1993). The quality of life program: Fostering creativity in seniors through a museum experience. *Journal of Physical Education, Recreation, and Dance,* 64(4), 48-51.

Coward, R. T. (1979). Planning community services for the rural elderly: Implications from research. *Gerontologist,* 19, 275-282.

Elderhostel (2003). About elderhostel. <www.elderhostel.org>.

Ford, Q. E. (1976). *A model project for aging: Coordinated service program for senior citizens in a rural county.* Quincy, FL: Gadsen County Senior Citizens Council, Inc.

Gay, J. (1999). A guide to tour designing for seniors. *Tourism Recreation Research,* 24(1), 90-92.

Gibson, H. J. (2002). Busy travelers: Leisure-travel patterns and meanings in later life. *World Leisure,* 44(2), 11-20.

Goggin, J. M. (1999). Elderhostel meets the "silent revolution." *Tourism Recreation Research,* 24(1), 86-89.

Goldenrod Hills Community Action Council (n.d.). *Project Rural A.L.I.V.E. (Americans Living in Varied Environments): An evaluation.* Washington, DC:

National Clearinghouse on Aging, SCAN Social Practice Resource Center, #CF 000 387.

Gurewitsch, E. (1980). Elderhostel: A good idea is growing and growing. *Aging,* 303-304, 12-16.

Hamilton, P. W. (1991). Help wanted. *D and B Reports,* March/April, p. 28.

Harbert, A. S. and Wilkinson, C. W. (1979). Growing old in rural America. *Aging Magazine,* January, pp. 36-40.

Hayden, C. S. (1988). Elder campers helping others—The ECHO project: A unique intergenerational model. *Activities, Adaptation, and Aging,* 11(1), 11-19.

Hirzel, D. (1977). Elderly will help elderly. *Washington Star,* March 7, p. 19.

Hong, G. S., Kim, S. Y., and Lee, J. (1999). Travel expenditure patterns of elderly households in the United States. *Tourism Recreation Research,* 24(1), 43-52.

Hudson, S. D. and Rich, S. M. (1993). Group travel programs: A creative way to meet the leisure needs of older adults. *Journal of Physical Education, Recreation, and Dance,* 64(4), 38-40.

Hupp, S. (1987). Camping in the third age. *Camping Magazine,* January, 20-22.

Karcher, C. J. and Karcher, B. C. (1980). Higher education and religion: Potential partners in service to the rural elderly. *Educational Gerontology,* 5(4), 409-421.

Kretschmer sponsors seniors tennis classic (1982). *Parks and Recreation,* December, pp. 12-13, 52.

Larson, D. K. and Youmans, E. G. (1978). *Problems of rural elderly households in Powell County, Kentucky.* Washington, DC: U.S. Department of Agriculture.

Leitner, M. J. (1983). Elderfest: The experience of a lifetime! *Parks and Recreation,* 18(8), 56-58.

Leitner, M. J. (1999). Promoting peace through intergenerational tourism. *Tourism Recreation Research,* 24(1), 53-56.

Leitner, M. J. and Leitner, S. F. (1994). *How to improve your life through leisure.* Salt Lake City, UT: Northwest Publishing.

Leviton, D. and Santa Maria, L. (1979). The adults' health and developmental program: Descriptive and evaluative data. *Gerontologist,* 19(6), 534-543.

Means, G., Mann, J., and Van Dyk, D. (1978). Reaching out to the rural elderly: Services to rural America. *Human Services in the Rural Environment,* 3(2), 1-6.

Mitric, J. M. and Gibson, G. (1988). Seniors enter BandB business for fun, profit. *Chicago Tribune,* March 13, Section 12, p. 2.

Moisey, N. and Bichis, M. (1999). Psychographics of senior nature tourists: The Katy nature trail. *Tourism Recreation Research,* 24(1), 69-76.

Murray, M. S. (1979). Variables affecting the reading preferences of institutionalized versus non-institutionalized rural elder adults. *Dissertation Abstracts International,* 40, p. 1815A.

National Association of Area Agencies on Aging (1978). *Rural affairs committee report.* Washington, DC: Administration on Aging.

Never too late for ski school (1977). *New York Daily News,* November 13, travel section, p. 10.

Noble, H. B. (1998). A secret of health in old age: Muscles. *The New York Times,* October 20, p. D8.

Northeast Kentucky Area Development Council, Inc. (1971). *Country gathering: A nutrition demonstration project, final report.* Washington, DC: National Clearinghouse on Aging, SCAN Social Practice Resource Center, CF #000 351.

Notess, C. B. (1978). Rural elderly transit markets. *Journal of American Institute of Planners,* 44, 328-334.

Patterson, I. (2002). Baby boomers and adventure tourism: The importance of marketing the leisure experience. *World Leisure,* 44(2), 4-10.

Penalta, L. A. R. and Uysal, M. (1992). Aging and the future travel market. *Parks and Recreation,* September, pp. 96-99.

Pesky, G. (1994). Senior softball tourney expanding in '94. *Sporting Goods Business,* 27(2), 36.

Provost, C. A. (1981). *The Senior Olympics: Preventative medicine with findings pertaining to health and longevity.* Los Angeles: Warren W. Blaney.

Reed, G. R. (1970). *Survey of elderly participation in community activities for aged.* Washington, DC: National Clearinghouse on Aging, SCAN Social Practice Resource Center, #CF 000 233.

Rosen J. (1993). Breckenridge ski resort to host 14th Senior Winter Games. *Travel Weekly,* December 6, pp. 61-62.

Simons, M. (1991). Le brain jogging. *New York Times Magazine,* October 6, pp. 16, 44.

Simonsen, I. (n.d.). *Senior meals: Improved nutrition and social association in rural America.* Washington, DC: National Clearinghouse on Aging, SCAN Social Practice Resource Center, #CF 000 232.

Stough, A. D. (1974). *Brighter vistas: Church programs for older adults.* Washington, DC: Administration on Aging.

Successful aging. (1991). *University of California at Berkeley Wellness Letter,* August, p. 1.

Teaff, J. D. and Turpin, T. (1996). Travel and the elderly. *Parks and Recreation,* June, pp. 16-22.

Tennis play up for Americans 50 and over (1993). *Tennis Magazine,* August, p. 84.

Tullius, J. (1988). "Those guys can play!" *Tennis Magazine,* August, pp. 37-43.

Villarosa, L. (1999). More vie for slots on the senior varsity. *The New York Times,* November 30, p. D8.

Wilson, L. (1991). At the Senior Olympics. *American Demographics,* May, p. 37.

Winfrey, C. (1977). For the aged, camp life's slower, but much like that for young. *The New York Times,* July 16, pp. 23, 26.

Chapter 12

Exercise

INTRODUCTION

The aim of this chapter is to provide information on how to adapt appropriate exercises to specific older populations. For the purposes of this chapter, exercise is defined as movement that enhances flexibility, strength, endurance, as well as vents tension, and promotes feelings of well-being. Movement includes both total body involvement and manipulation of isolated body parts. Exercises are described in detail in this chapter in order to provide a basis for leading exercise sessions. In the first section, a review of literature on the physical and psychosocial benefits of exercise is presented. In the second section, the current level of physical activity among elders is discussed. Next, theory and techniques for effectively motivating elders to exercise and for leading exercise sessions with elders are examined. The remainder of the chapter deals with specific exercises designed for bedridden elders, elders with limited mobility, and high-functioning elders. Ideas for exercise-based games and activities are also presented.

LEARNING OBJECTIVES

The learning objectives of this chapter are to be able to

1. identify the physical benefits of exercise for elders,
2. identify the psychosocial benefits of exercise for elders,
3. identify techniques for effectively leading exercise sessions for elders,
4. identify factors and leadership techniques related to motivating elders to exercise,
5. describe the current status of exercise participation among elders, and
6. devise exercise session plans for high-functioning, impaired, or limited mobility elders, incorporating a variety of exercises and exercise-based games and activities.

BENEFITS OF EXERCISE

Physical Benefits

Elders who exercise regularly reap many physical benefits. Range of motion is enhanced, especially the motion of joints, which is a key factor in the prevention of arthritic deterioration and loss of function. Furthermore, flexibility and movement can be improved through exercise because the muscles and ligaments surrounding the joints are strenthened, thereby improving joint mobility. Exercise can also improve posture because the postural muscles are toned and strengthened (Weiss, 1990).

According to Flatten (1982), exercise in later life helps to maintain flexibility and strength, which are key components in performing activities of daily living (ADL) skills such as getting dressed, cooking, and bathing. Self-sufficiency and independence are fostered by the ability to perform ADL skills. A four-year study of almost 7,000 men and women over age sixty-five found that regular physical activity, in the form of walking, gardening, or vigorous exercise three times a week, was the health behavior most strongly associated with maintaining mobility (LaCroix et al., 1993). Other research ("Strength and Mobility Relationships in the Elderly," 1995) indicates that exercise which improves strength can increase functional mobility (ability to get out of bed or a chair, walk indoors and outdoors, and manage stairs) and independence. Strength training programs for elders have been shown effective in improving their strength. For example, a seven-week strength training program with three sessions per week with older women (average age of 71.1) was found to result in an average 44 percent gain in total body muscle strength (Sharon et al., 1993). According to Work (1989), the benefits of strength training for the elderly improved not only their ability to rise from a chair and climb steps but also walking speed, and decreased frequency of falls. Studies have shown that high-intensity strength training is safe for older adults even in their nineties, and that this training can lead to significant gains in muscle strength, size, and functional mobility. Brody (2002) reports studies have shown unequivocally that strength training is a fountain of youth, capable of turning back the clock for women in their seventies, eighties, and nineties. Research (Laditka and Laditka, 2001) shows that resistance training can improve strength, agility, balance, and bone mass, thereby promoting more active lifestyles and reducing the risk of injuries commonly associated with declining functional status.

Weiss (1990) states that exercise can help improve elders' coordination, reflexes, agility, body movement, and sense of balance. Unfortunately, although improved balance and decreased frequency of falls are benefits of exercise for elders, the fear of falling and being injured prevents many elders from exercising. Falling is a serious problem for elders: Approximately 30 percent of elders fall at least once a year, and 10 to 15 percent of these falls cause hip fractures or other bone injuries, which seriously impair health and hasten death ("Study Shows Exercise Reduces Falls by the Aged," 1995). Strength training increases physical strength, thereby decreasing the chances of falling, and it also increases bone mass so that if a fall should occur, the risk of fracture is reduced (Brody, 1999). A University of Oregon physical therapist has developed a training program for elders designed to make them steadier on their feet ("Elders: Ready, Steady, Go," 1993). The training course imitates real-life troublesome conditions, such as floors of thick foam that simulate uneven grass or sand, and goggles that block peripheral vision, in order to challenge declining eyesight and agility. After two months of practice, a group of older volunteers testing this course improved markedly, losing their balance approximately 40 percent less often. The volunteers also found that they were steadier at home, thereby enhancing their independence. Another study (Grahn-Kronhed et al., 2001) found that balance performance in healthy older adults could be improved by balance training including exercise that stimulates the visual, vestibular, and somatosensory systems.

Similarly, an Atlanta program using tai chi training for people ages seventy and over found that the tai chi group had a 25 percent reduction in falls when compared to a control group that did not exercise ("Study Shows Exercise Reduces Falls by the Aged," 1995). Another study, with over 2,000 people age sixty and over, found that regular exercise reduces the risk of falling by approximately 13 percent. The exercises in the study included stretching, weight training, endurance training, and balance training ("Study Shows Exercise Reduces Falls by the Aged," 1995). Walking can also improve balance, as evidenced by a study on the effects of a twelve-week walking program on nursing home residents (Asplund, Hester, and MacRae, 1993).

Cardiovascular endurance is another benefit of exercise. According to Weiss (1990), the body gains a greater ability to utilize adequate amounts of oxygen directed toward the working muscle. With improved breathing and cardiovascular efficiency comes a greater sense of endurance and increased energy. It is apparently never too late to start exercising and to reap its positive effects on cardiovascular fitness. A study in Michigan found that previously sedentary adults ages eighty to ninety-two who walked on a treadmill or rode an exercise bicycle for at least twenty minutes twice a week for six months significantly improved their cardiovascular endurance and lowered their blood pressure ("It's Never too Late to Start Exercising," 2003).

In addition, Weiss (1990) states that participation in regular exercise sessions induces a feeling of relaxation; consequently, muscular tension can be released and psychological and cognitive stress responses can be positively changed. Other physical benefits of exercise for elders discussed by Weiss (1990) include improved digestion, sleep patterns, circulation, and insulin efficiency (exercise increases the number of insulin receptors on muscle cells, an important benefit for diabetics).

With increased exercise and a more active lifestyle, elders have a decreased risk of osteoporosis and a lower rate of bone loss (Sherwood, 1991). The risks of diabetes, arthritis, and hypertension are also reduced (Frankel and Richard, 1980; Leaf, 1975). Schafer (1990b) reports that the blood pressure of a group of older men who continued to exercise remained constant at 120/80 over a twenty-three-year period, while the blood pressure of exercise dropouts increased from 135/85 to 150/90. Furthermore, Kaufman et al. (cited in Sherwood, 1991) suggest that for an elder who already has hypertension, a single bout of exercise can actually lower blood pressure.

Exercise also aids in weight control because it increases metabolism rates (Frankel and Richard, 1980). Research (Messier et al., 2000) on obese older adults with knee osteoarthritis found that weight loss could be achieved and sustained over a six-month period of time through a program of diet and exercise intervention. Schafer (1990b) reports that in a study comparing elders who had remained physically active with those who had become physically inactive, the exercisers had lost an average of 7.5 pounds over a twenty-three-year period, whereas the exercise dropouts had gained an average of seven pounds during the same time period. Another study (Hunter et al., 2000) found that a twenty-six-week resistance training program increased energy expenditure and oxidation rates in older adults, thereby improving their metabolism rates.

Elders who are physically active have a greater capacity to perform physical tasks along with an increased likelihood that physical activities will be successfully accomplished (Teague, 1989). Lack of exercise contributes to frailty. Research (Neergaard, 1999) indicates that about 70 percent of older women are too frail to lift ten pounds and 60 percent are unable to do household work such as vacuuming. Approximately 35 percent of men are equally frail. Performance standards for fitness for older adults were developed that incorporate routine tasks, such as

1. how many times in thirty seconds it is possible to rise from a straight-backed chair without using arms to push up (as a measure of lower body strength);

2. how many times in thirty seconds it is possible to lift a weight (five pounds for women and eight pounds for men) in a bicep curl (as a measure of upper body strength); and
3. how many yards it is possible to walk in six minutes (as a measure of aerobic fitness).

Research conducted in Holland with older adults (average age of nearly eighty) indicated that regular exercise can help elders ward off disease by strengthening their immune systems ("Work out at 80? Experts See the Gains," 2001). According to Karper and Goldfarb (1994), an exercise program for elders that included stretching, dumbell weight training, and walking, three days a week, fifty to sixty minutes per session resulted in a decrease in acute upper and lower respiratory tract infections, which in turn helps to reduce the incidence of colds, sore throats, and bronchitis. Blair et al. (cited in Sherwood, 1991) assert that physical fitness is associated with lower rates of all causes of death, including cardiovascular disease and cancer. A study on the effects of participation in a walking program for older adults found that walking two miles a day cut the risk of death almost in half for people in their sixties, seventies, and eighties ("Study Shows a Stroll by Elderly Adds Years," 1998). Brody (1994b) reports research indicates that among runners, both men and women have lower total cholesterol, lower body weight, and have less high blood pressure, all of which help to combat cardiovascular disease. Research by Pescatello, Murphy, and Costanzo (2000) indicates that low-intensity habitual exercise is sufficient to reduce cholesterol and help prevent heart disease. Similarly, Wannamethee, Sharper, and Walker (2000) found that light or moderate activity, such as regular walking and moderate or heavy gardening, can lower mortality rates for older men with established coronary heart disease.

Exercise also positively affects elders' psychomotor abilities. Spiriduso (1983) found that people who exercise tend to be faster than nonexercisers in performing psychomotor skills across all age groups. Similarly, Vercruyssen et al. (Sherwood, 1991) found that older physically fit individuals who exercise regularly have a faster reaction time than their sedentary counterparts. Surprisingly, these older physically fit adults are often as fast or faster in psychomotor skills than young sedentary individuals who have below-average fitness levels. Rikli and Busch (Sherwood, 1991) found similar results on physical fitness and age effects on reaction times: Active elders perform more like active young adults than do sedentary young adults.

In a related vein, Goggin and Keller (1993) found that reaction time (RT) and movement time (MT) losses among elders can be reduced and prevented through exercise and continued physical activity. Most elders who do not exercise will experience a decline in RT and MT, which in turn makes them feel incompetent and leads them to become more inactive.

Bortz (Sherwood, 1991) discusses a variety of detrimental effects of inadequate exercise:

1. The fat/lean body mass ratio favors fat.
2. Maximum oxygen consumption and cardiac output decreases.
3. Sense of balance is reduced.
4. The red blood cell count goes down and there is a greater risk of thrombotic disease (blood clots).
5. Total blood lipids increase (cholesterol and triglycerides increase).
6. Body water is lost and capacity to control the body's internal temperature is reduced.
7. Calcium from bones is lost.
8. An insensitivity to glucose can develop.
9. The senses of hearing and taste experience some loss.
10. The body has a diminished ability to assimilate drugs.

Jones (1993) adds that lack of physical activity increases feelings of fatigue, decreases physical work capacity, and increases blood pressure. Advanced age, along with inactivity, is associated with diminished aerobic capacity. However, Evans and Rosenberg (Sherwood, 1991) found that the decline in aerobic capacity is less severe among elders who exercise regularly. Schafer (1990b) also reports that in a research study comparing physically active and inactive elders, the exercisers lost only 13 percent of VO2 max (the rate at which the body depletes oxygen during exercise until exhaustion), whereas the exercise dropouts lost an average of 41 percent of their VO2 max over the twenty-three years of the study. VO2 max is an indicator of aerobic fitness level. In the same study, the exercisers reduced their resting heart rates from sixty-three to fifty-six, and the dropouts' resting heart rates remained constant. Another study on the topic of age-related declines in VO2 max indicated that for men the decline in physical activity with age, independent of body composition, was related to a decline in VO2 max (Toth et al., 1995).

Another important physical benefit of exercise for elders is the decreased risk of gastrointestinal hemorrhage. Exercise improves the flow of oxygen-rich blood to the gastrointestinal tract. Exercise also decreases the chances of developing intestinal disorders, including diverticulosis and ulcers (Brody, 1994a).

Berger and Hecht (1989) found that exercise can give an older adult a younger appearance, and that it can delay the onset of menopause in women and/or decrease the severity of its symptoms.

Even the very old can physically benefit from exercise. A study conducted with 100 men and women, average age of 87.1, on the effects of a high-intensity progressive resistance program for the hip and knee found that the program improved hip and knee extension strength, stair-climbing ability, and overall level of physical activity ("Frailty, Strength Training, and Nutritional Supplementation in the Very Old," 1995). A research study in Denmark with fifty-five women age eighty-five found that a regular exercise program reduced blood pressure and increased maximal oxygen uptake and maximal walking speed (Puggaard et al., 2000).

Schafer (1990b) reports that the loss of fitness generally associated with aging is actually caused more by a reduction in physical activity than it is by advanced age. In one research study, a group of men who continued to exercise for twenty-three years, up to age seventy, were found to be in far better physical condition than a group of men who were active at the beginning of the study but became physically inactive for at least eighteen years. Thus, aging does not necessarily induce lower fitness levels. A decline in physical activity is strongly correlated with a decline in fitness.

Exercise can extend the life span. Paffenbarger et al. (1993) cite data from a nine-year study of 10,000 male Harvard alumni which indicate that the most active men had half the risk of death as compared with the least active men. Similarly, Brody (1994b) cites a study which found that elders who participate in vigorous aerobic activity such as running are less likely to develop life-inhibiting diseases and have a lower death rate than those who do not run or engage in other vigorous aerobic activities.

However, there is some controversy over how strenuous exercise needs to be in order for it to have a life-extending effect. Brody (1995) states that a number of studies had indicated moderate exercise has life-saving benefits: men could gain an average of two years of life by participating in activities such as walking and stair climbing as long as they expended at least 2,000 calories a week. Dr. Steven Blair of the Cooper Institute in Dallas, in a five-year follow-up study of almost 10,000 men, found that moderately intense activities had mortality benefits. When men improved from being unfit to moderately fit, there was a 40 percent decline in death from all causes, whereas there was only a 15 percent decline in mortality when men improved from being moderately fit to being highly fit.

The findings of a study of 17,300 Harvard alumni led by Dr. I-Min Lee of Harvard (Brody, 1995) that life span is extended by vigorous, but not by nonvigorous, exercise has confused leading researchers in the field, even Dr. Ralph Paffenbarger of Stanford University, who co-authored the study with

Dr. Lee and had authored an earlier study of the Harvard men which had concluded that moderate physical exercise in adult life can significantly increase life expectancy. Gorman (1995) reports that the U.S. Centers for Disease Control and Prevention, in conjunction with the American College of Sports Medicine, had announced in January of 1995 that low-intensity activities such as gardening and walking the dog could be as beneficial as strenuous workouts. However, Dr. Lee found that only vigorous exercise such as jogging and fast walking significantly increased life expectancy (Brody, 1995). Yet another study on this topic (O'Neil, 2003) concludes that if exercise *feels* strenuous, it will help, even if the workout falls short of recommended guidelines.

What conclusions can be drawn? Dr. Paffenbarger (Brody, 1995, p. 49) states that "a little exercise is better than none, but more is better than a little." Moderate exercise, whether or not it extends the lifespan, does contribute to improved physical and mental health, such as improved mood, weight control, and strengthening bones (Brody, 1995). The more vigorous exercise seems to have a stronger positive effect on physical well-being and longevity, but elders who are completely inactive should not despair and think that, in light of the recent research studies, doing a little bit of exercise will do them no good. The Centers for Disease Control and Prevention calculated that if every sedentary American would at least walk, dance, or participate in similar activities for thirty minutes a day, there would be an annual decline in deaths of approximately 250,000 per year (Brody, 1995). In summary, even light exercise is healthy, but the more vigorous the exercise, the greater the benefits.

What is meant by the terms *light, moderate,* and *vigorous exercise?* The following list (Brody, 1995) presents activities in each category. Keep in mind that the activities in the light exercise column do yield health benefits, that ones in the moderate column have even greater health benefits and might even have life-extending benefits, and that the activities in the vigorous column yield the greatest health benefits and, according to the latest research, have the strongest life-prolonging value.

Light Exercise Activities	Moderate Exercise Activities	Vigorous Exercise Activities
Walking slowly	Walking at 3 to 4 mph	Walking at 4 to 5 mph, 45 minutes per day, 5 times week
Cycling slowly	Cycling at up to 10 mph	Fast cycling, at more than 10 mph, 1 hour, 4 times per week
Swimming slowly	Swimming with moderate effort	Swimming laps 3 hours per week

Fishing while sitting	Fishing (standing and casting)	Fishing (wading in a rushing stream)
Power boating	Canoeing, 2-3.9 mph	Canoeing, 4+ mph
	Racket sports (e.g., table tennis)	Racket sports (e.g., singles tennis), 1 hour, 3 times per week
	General calisthenics and conditioning exercises	Cardiovascular exercise (e.g., ski machine, aerobics), 2-3 hours per week

The lists are not exhaustive; they provide only examples of the types of activities that fit into each category.

Before moving on to a discussion of the psychosocial benefits of exercise, the following list summarizes the numerous physical benefits of exercise for elders that were discussed in this section.

<u>Exercise Improves or Increases</u>
Aerobic capacity
Cardiovascular endurance
Circulation
General health
Insulin efficiency
Digestion, weight control
Protective HDL cholesterol
Sleep
Relaxation
Joint mobility
Psychomotor abilities
Range of motion, movement
Functional mobility
Sense of balance
Walking speed
Posture
Youthful appearance
Flexibility
Strength
ADL skills
Independence, self-sufficiency
Ability to perform physical tasks
Energy level
Lifespan
General fitness

Exercise Lessens
<u>or Decreases the Risk of</u>
Loss of VO2 max
Heart disease
Heart rate at rest
All causes of mortality, including cancer
Diabetes
Body weight
Total cholesterol
Stress
Muscle tension
Arthritic deterioration
Reaction time and movement time losses
Osteoporosis, bone loss
Hypertension, blood pressure
Falling
Internal disorders
Gastrointestinal hemmorhages
Severity of menopausal symptoms
Acute upper and lower respiratory tract infections, incidence of colds, sore throats

Clearly, the physical benefits of exercise for elders are numerous and, as discussed earlier in this section, the negative implications of being sedentary are also great. The psychosocial benefits of exercise for elders are equally impressive, as discussed in the next section.

Psychosocial Benefits

Regular exercise leads to a general sense of well-being and accomplishment for elders (Weiss, 1990). Pate and Pierce (1993) add that exercise decreases tension, depression, and anger. O'Connor, Aenchloacher, and Dishman (1993) report that a survey found 85 percent of primary care physicians recommend aerobic exercise in treating depression. Depression is a major problem among older adults; 15 percent are above the symptom scale cutoffs for depression.

Berger and Hecht (1989) state that elders who exercise tend to be happier, feel higher self-esteem, and experience an improved quality of life as compared to their sedentary peers. Exercisers feel less anxiety, tension, and depression. A review of thirty-two studies on activity and mood among older adults found that regular exercise, particularly strength training, boosted moods (Khatri et al., 2001).

Physically active older adults have keener minds than those who are less active. Research (Schafer, 1990a) indicates that physically active elders outperform inactive elders on tests of memory, reaction time, and reasoning. These results may have been obtained because of a better oxygen supply to the brain occurring over the years due to exercise. Exercisers may also develop a quicker central nervous system.

Toole and Abourezk (1989) found that information processing speed increased for older adults who participated in an exercise program that included aerobic activity. Memory skills also improved. A study on the effects of a walking program on adults ages sixty to seventy-five found that memory and judgment improved as a result of the program (Associated Press, 1999).

In a study that tested the effects of aerobic conditioning on sedentary fifty-five to seventy-year-olds, Dustman et al. (1989) found improvements in neuropsychological tasks including enhanced measured response time, memory, mental flexibility, and visual organization. The researchers hypothesized that the exercise program induced enhanced cerebral metabolic activity.

In a related study, Abourezk (1989) found that active older adults remembered more information on memory capacity tests than did inactive persons.

This research lends additional support to the idea that regular participation in exercise improves cognitive functioning of elders.

Hird and Williams (1989) reviewed research on the relationships between exercise and its psychological benefits for elders and found a number of studies indicating that exercise can lead to improvements in elders' memory, body image, intelligence, self-efficacy, internal locus of control, and self-concept. Studies were also found that indicated exercise can lead to decreased anger, anxiety, and depression among elders.

Perri and Templer (1985) also suggest that regular exercise enables elders to have a greater perceived internal locus of control and an improved self-concept. Ross and Hayes (1988), based on the results of a study on adults ages eighteen to eighty-three, assert that regular participation in exercise is associated with enhanced psychological well-being, perhaps due to enhanced perceived physical health. Exercise increases the levels of endorphins (natural opiates) in the body, thereby increasing feelings of well-being. In addition, exercise can regulate norepinephrine release and consequently decrease depression.

A special benefit of *group* exercise programs for elders is that it promotes social growth and development (Arnold, 1977). Through interactions with others in an exercise program, elders enjoy companionship and feel part of a group. Chapter 1 discussed the benefits of leisure activity for elders in general, which included social interaction, decreased loneliness, enhanced life satisfaction, and improved quality of life. Regular enjoyable exercise, perhaps more so than any other form of leisure activity, can induce these positive changes.

The following lists are presented as a summary of the psychosocial benefits of exercise for elders. Exercise increases or enhances the following:

- Psychological well-being
- Feelings of accomplishment
- Self-esteem, self-concept
- Overall cognitive functioning
- Memory
- Reaction time
- Reasoning abilities
- Visual organization
- Self-efficacy
- Social growth and development
- Endorphin levels
- Happiness
- Quality of life, life satisfaction

- Intelligence
- Information processing speed
- Quickness of central nervous system
- Mental flexibility
- Body image
- Internal locus of control

Exercise helps to decrease, relieve, or prevent:

- Tension
- Anger
- Loneliness
- Anxiety
- Depression

The psychosocial and physical benefits of exercise for elders are impressive. Unfortunately, as discussed in the next section of the chapter, the current level of physical activity of elders in the United States is not impressive.

PHYSICAL ACTIVITY LEVELS OF ELDERS

Estimates of the level of physical activity (or inactivity) of elders vary but, overall, the estimates are low. According to Goggin and Morrow (2001), 69 percent of older adults are *not* participating in sufficient physical activity to obtain health benefits. Herbert and Teague (1989) state that a series of national health surveys indicated only 10 to 19 percent of elders in the United States participate in vigorous physical activity. Teague (1989) states that according to a 1985 survey, only 7.9 percent of elders were meeting the Public Health Service definition of appropriate physical activity. Berger and Hecht (1989) report that only 7 percent of Canadians ages sixty-five to sixty-nine participating in a national fitness survey demonstrated a recommended level of cardiovascular fitness. According to the "Surgeon General's Workshop on Health Promotion and Aging," (1989), only 7 to 8 percent of adults age sixty-five and over participated in any regular physical exercise at all.

There are various explanations for the low levels of physical activity of elders. Berger and Hecht (1989) discuss the negative effects of age-role stereotyping on exercising in later life. As early as preschool, children learn that exercise is less appropriate with advancing age, and the inappropriateness of different types of exercise for older adults tends to be learned by age twenty. Because of these age-role stereotypes learned early in life, many older adults view physical activity as increasingly inappropriate as a person ages.

Another factor that may be related to elders' inactivity is a lack of knowledge regarding exercise. According to Teague (1989), only 16 percent of survey respondents correctly identified needed exercise intensity.

The prevention of health problems is one important reason why elders should exercise more but, unfortunately, health problems inhibit many elders from exercising. According to Teague (1989), although most elders consider themselves to be in good health, 80 percent have at least one chronic illness, the common ones being arthritis (44 percent), hypertension (39 percent), hearing loss (29 percent), and heart problems (27 percent). Greater levels of physical activity can prevent or alleviate these problems; unfortunately, once these conditions exist, many elders believe that they must forsake exercise.

In a related vein, Herbert and Teague (1989) state that improvement in health is usually cited by elders as a reason for initiating an exercise program. However, the factors of choice of activities, previous program experience, and goal attainment appear to be more closely related to adherence to an exercise program.

Eggers (1988) conducted a study on healthy older women's entrance and adherence to structured exercise programs and concluded that: (1) a television fitness program directed toward elders would be well-received; (2) leaders of fitness programs for elders need to have proper training; and (3) publicity is needed to inform elders that quality exercise programs exist that can meet their biological, psychological, and social needs. A study on the use of a computerized exercise promotion interface with adults ages sixty to eighty-seven found that older adults were able and willing to accept computer-generated exercise recommendations (Kressig and Echt, 2002).

According to Shephard (1994), exercise programs should build on elders' previous habits and barriers to exercise such as absence of a companion, sight and hearing deficits, and cognitive and emotional problems. Also, with advanced age, feeling a lack of ability or ill at ease can be more of a problem. Shephard suggests using vigorous elders as role models. PIPERS (Peer Instructed Programs of Exercise and Relaxation for Seniors) in northern Virginia uses vigorous elders as role models, and actually trains senior volunteers to conduct exercise programs at thirty sites, for over 500 senior citizens in nursing homes, senior centers, adult day care centers, and churches (Thompson, 1993).

Quite a few vigorous elders can be used as role models. For example, Israeli marathon runner David Rimon was competing in marathons all over the world at age seventy-five (Kaufman, 1989). Mavis Lindgren, at age eighty-six, was preparing to run in her sixty-fifth marathon, all of them since she turned seventy (Friend, 1993)! Erwin Jaskulski, at age 100, who holds three world records in the 100- and 200-meter dashes in the ninety-five to ninety-nine age category, set a world record for his age category by running the 200-meter dash in just over two minutes (Hoover, 2002).

As discussed in the previous chapter, senior athletes are a great resource for vigorous older role models, and their numbers are growing. Knierim and Gandee (1993) report that from 1987 to 1991, there was a 105 percent growth in participation in the National Senior Olympics and that performances (e.g., race times, etc.) improved. Among women eighty and over, there was a 210 percent increase in participation.

In summary, it is possible to increase the level of physical activity of elders. The next section of the chapter discusses psychosocial factors, leadership techniques, and other considerations that are related to motivating elders to exercise.

LEADERSHIP AND MOTIVATION

The leader of an exercise program for older adults should portray constant optimism and cheerfulness (Harris and Frankel, 1977). A supportive, encouraging attitude can help to motivate and engage sedentary individuals in activity.

Weiss (1990) states that participants should be praised and given encouragement for their efforts and that the leader should provide unconditional acceptance for all ability levels. According to Clark (1994), a good exercise instructor working with elders should be caring, use good judgment, show respect for the elders, be open-minded, and exhibit a sense of humor.

Goggin and Keller (1993) discuss the importance of gearing activities for success since elders are often unwilling to participate in activities perceived as being too challenging or too difficult to complete successfully. Therefore, to ensure elders' success in exercise activities, adapt equipment as necessary; give elders the opportunity to have sufficient practice time to learn an activity properly; and be sure that you, as the leader, give clear directions.

Cosky (1993) states that the exercise leader should refrain from using directional commands (e.g., right and left) when teaching. Also, to make it easier for elders to follow along, mirroring should be encouraged. Mechanical, not human, assistance should be offered, so that elders can proceed at their own pace. Cosky also states that age-appropriate language and slogans should be used to title classes and attract participants.

The title of an exercise class can be critical in attempting to attract participants. Exercise 12.1 is presented to provide insight into what titles would most effectively attract elders to attend an exercise class.

EXERCISE 12.1. Best and Worst Titles for Exercise Classes for Elders

Instructions

1. Following is a list of ideas for titles for exercise classes for elders.
2. Select the three titles that you think are the best ones (most effectively attract participants).
3. Select the three titles that you think are the worst ones (ambiguous, condescending, etc.).
4. Explain your choices, indicating why you think some titles might seem offensive or intimidating to elders, why other titles might seem condescending or misleading, and why other titles would be attractive, appealing, or arouse interest.

Possible Exercise Class Names

Fitness for the Finer and Wiser
Golden Fitness
Fit with Fun
Lifetime Fitness
Senior Workout
Motion Motivation
Senior Synchronize
Chair Exercise
Grand People on the Move
Forever Young
Chair Dancing
Muscle Maintenance
Fit and Ready
Nonstrenuous Aerobics
Pound-a-Way

Senior Aerobics
Seniorcise
Sweating with the Oldies
Eldercise
Sitercise
Workout for Fun
Adapted Exercise
Elders in Action
Exercise for Elders
Aerobasit
Energy Boosters
Stretching to New Heights
Elder Aerobics
Getting in Shape Seniors
Movement to Music

Your three favorite titles (Write your own if you do not like any of the ones on the list): _____

_____

The three worst titles: _____

_____

Rationale for your answers: _____

_____

In selecting a title, the primary concern should be to attract participants. Perhaps if the title suggests that the activity will be strenuous, some elders will shy away from the activity. Others will be turned off if the title suggests that the activity is for people who are "over the hill." In completing this exercise, picture yourself as a resident of a retirement home and consider what might sound most appealing to you.

The leader should use touch (with discretion) when helping individuals or to gently arouse someone who is sleeping or daydreaming. Partner exercises are another means of providing physical contact (Weiss, 1990).

The use of touch is one example of a technique in which individual, cultural, and male/female differences need to be considered. Some elders love to be touched and are inspired by activities that involve physical contact, whereas others can become angry, even violent, if they are subjected to unwanted physical contact. Similarly, different people prefer different kinds of programs.

For example, a study of 549 men and 666 women over age sixty indicated that men preferred physical activities of an outdoor or competitive nature, whereas women preferred a music-accompanied or instructor-assisted activity (Iwaoka et al., 1993). Shephard (1994) also reports male/female differences in elders' motives to exercise, but states that these differences are smaller than they used to be; 58 percent of males and 55 percent of females identified feeling physically better as a motive for exercising. In the same study, 31 percent of females and 25 percent of males identified socialization as a motivation for exercise, and 44 percent of females but only 31 percent of males identified looking better and weight control as reasons for exercising.

In terms of cultural differences, a study of 1,351 elders in Japan produced interesting results related to motivating elders to exercise. Financial strain did not influence exercise habits, but higher levels of emotional support were associated with greater levels of physical activity. Higher levels of negative interaction were also associated with exercising more, the explanation being that, in Japan, the power of coercion and the desire to conform to the will of the group influences behavior. Thus, in Japan, criticism (negative interaction) can lead to positive health behaviors (exercise) ("Psychosocial Factors and Exercise in Japan," 1995)

For Americans, positive reinforcement seems to be the most effective means of motivating elders to exercise. According to Pepe (1993), family encouragement was most strongly correlated with involvement in the Senior Olympics, followed by availability of transportation and level of participation in sports as a youth.

In examining why some elders adhere to an exercise program and others drop out, Herbert and Teague (1989) discuss the applicability of several different psychological theories:

1. *The health belief model:* The key factors related to exercising in this model are perceived vulnerability to health problems and the belief that exercise will help prevent these problems, and stimulants to action that are either internal (e.g., pain) or external (e.g., reminders).

2. *Theory of reasoned action:* According to this theory, the combination of perceived social norms (how important others believe it is to exercise) and personal attitudes about a specific exercise prescription (e.g., a particular exercise class) will predict whether the older adult will sustain his or her involvement in an exercise program.

3. *Self-motivation and the psychobiologic model:* Studies indicate exercise adherers, compared to dropouts, are more self-motivated and tend to be slimmer.

Duida and Tappe (1989) examine motivation of elders to exercise using the Personal Investment Theory of motivation, which views the *meaning* of a situation as being the most influential factor in determining the extent of personal investment in an activity or a situation. The three main aspects of meaning are as follows:

1. *Personal incentives:*
   a. Task incentives—Older adults are more motivated to continue exercising if they see personal improvement in their ability to do the exercises or the activity.
   b. Ego incentives—Competition and being able to outperform others can be motivating.
   c. Social incentives—Some elders participate in physical activities because of the social contact they provide.
   d. Extrinsic rewards—Gaining social recognition or attention and approval from significant others can motivate elders to exercise.
   e. Health, stress coping, and fitness incentives—Elders desire to improve in these areas.
2. *Sense of self:*
   a. Sense of competence—Subjective judgment of ability to succeed
   b. Self-reliance—The amount of control the older adult has over personal fitness
   c. Goal directedness—The ability to set goals and meet them
   d. Sociability—More likely to exercise if a member of a group or belonging to a club that exercises regularly
3. *Perceived options:* Elders need to have appropriate facilities, programs, etc., available to them to be able to exercise.

Exercise 12.2 asks you to apply the Personal Investment Theory in attempting to motivate an elder to join and stay with an exercise program.

Related to the last factor, perceived options, good, adapted exercise equipment should be available so that elders of all functioning levels can use it easily. Blankfort-Doyle et al. (1989) describe an exercise program for nursing home residents that makes use of ergometer bicycles, a treadmill, and a two-person telemetric system. One bicycle was put on a table so that residents in wheelchairs could exercise their arms by turning the pedals of the bicycle with their hands. Pedal extension tubes were attached to the bicycle pedals to extend the pedals away from the bicycle, allowing elders with hip problems to ride. A small stool was placed next to the cycles to help patients get on, and fastening straps were used to secure residents' feet in the pedals. Residents and staff were enthusiastic about the program, participation was high, and there were no injuries during the fifteen months of the program. The adapted equipment enabled high-functioning elders to spontaneously engage in exercise, without the supervision of staff.

Also related to equipment and facilities is the general atmosphere in the exercise room. Weiss (1990) states that the exercise room should be well lit and airy. The room temperature should be comfortable, perhaps just slightly cooler than normal to prevent elders from overheating due to the activities and exercises being performed. Drinking water should be readily available as participants will likely get thirsty if they are exerting significant effort.

Exercise is too strenuous and should cease if any of the following symptoms are evident: shortness of breath, chest pain, lightheadedness or dizziness, prolonged fatigue, or a heart rate over 120 beats per minute (Harris and Frankel, 1977). The exercise leader should be cognizant of these overexertion signs and stop exercise immediately if they appear.

The exercise leader should involve the total person in an exercise program. Elders may feel more motivated to participate in a fitness program when physical, psychological, and social needs are being met (Whitehouse, 1977). Obtaining background information on each individual in an exercise program (e.g., habits, goals, etc.) will aid the leader in developing a more personal program. According to Whitehouse (1977), as individuals begin to improve their fitness levels, the leader will be more effective by specifically describing each person's progress rather than merely indicating general improvements.

Another important leadership principle is to recognize participants' problems, physical limitations, and fears. Sensitivity and compassion on the part of the leader can be a motivating factor. Fear of falling and of incurring an injury inhibits many elders from exercising. Therefore, chair exercising is appealing to many ambulatory elders because it seems safer. Weiss (1990)

EXERCISE 12.2. Motivating an Elder to Exercise

Instructions

1. Describe a sedentary older adult with whom you are familiar.
2. Describe the physical activity(ies) in which you would like this elder to participate.
3. For each aspect of personal investment meaning listed, explain how you would adapt or design the activity(ies) in order to maximize motivation to participate. For example, if the activity was weight lifting, for "task incentives" you could write that you would begin with easy (light) weights, at a low level of repetitions, from which it would be easy to quickly notice improvements in performance, such as increasing the number of repetitions or increasing the weights.

Description of the sedentary older adult: _____

_____

Physical activity(ies) targeted for participation: _____

_____

Task incentives: _____

_____

Ego incentives: _____

_____

Social incentives: _____

_____

Extrinsic rewards: _____

_____

Health, stress coping, and fitness incentives: _____

_____

Sense of competence: _____

_____

Self-reliance: _____

_____

Goal directedness: _____

_____

Social identity: _____

_____

Perceived options: _____

_____

states that chairs used for chair exercising should have straight backs, no arms, and nonskid feet (not on rollers).

According to Arnold (1977), the leader of an exercise program should relate exercise to the participants' total health to provide a rationale for the importance of exercise. The leader can motivate older adults by clearly defining the benefits of exercise for each individual. However, exaggerated predictions of success should be avoided. According to social cognitive theory as it applies to elders' motivation to exercise (Dzewaltowski, 1989), the key predictors of the desired behavior (exercising) are expected outcomes (will the program really improve my fitness?) and self-efficacy (having the confidence in abilities to succeed in the exercise program).

Goals can be set and a journal charting progress can be kept, thereby motivating elders to exercise in order to reach their goals. This journal can be a combined effort of both the exercise leader and the participants, and can be written in at the end of each session.

Creating a recreational atmosphere for the exercise session can foster a greater degree of motivation to participate. An effective motivational tool is to incorporate music into the exercise sessions. Ask the participants for a list of their favorite songs, then locate recordings of the songs and play them during the sessions. Just hearing the music could attract individuals to the activity who otherwise might decline from participating.

The exercise leader may occasionally need to physically assist the older adult in performing specific movements. Also, when possible, the leader should demonstrate and participate in the exercise along with the group. Experiencing a sense of joined effort in performing the exercises can be motivating.

Another effective tool of leadership is the use of colors. If the leader is wearing bright, intense colors (bright red, yellow, etc.), members of the group may actually be drawn to look at these colors and stay more focused on the leader and on the activity.

The leader should always be positioned where everyone in the group can easily see or hear him or her. The leader should be attentive to the body language of group members and check that everyone is breathing properly. If breathing is not smooth and steady, that person might be exercising too hard. Weiss (1990) states that the leader should periodically remind the participants *not* to hold their breath while exercising.

The exercise routine should involve all body parts. Sessions should progress in a relaxed manner, without undo exertion or fatigue. Furthermore, according to Arnold (1977), the degree of exercise intensity should be individually controlled by discouraging competition and encouraging individualized workouts.

Knowing about an activity in advance and having the opportunity to make decision to attend is an important concern. The leader should arrange for both oral and written announcements to occur just prior to the activity (e.g., at the meal just before your activity). You cannot assume that just because you have led an exercise class five times a week at the same time each day, the residents of the home at which you are working all remember when it is. Knocking on doors and personally inviting elders to attend the activity can bring several more participants.

Providing leadership roles to individuals in the group can promote a greater sense of involvement. Members should be given the opportunity to demonstrate and lead several exercises. Furthermore, participants should be asked for feedback on the effectiveness of the sessions.

Another motivating ingredient for older adults is the utilization of interesting props in the exercise session. The props can be items found at the center, projects created by participants during crafts activities, or objects brought from home to share with the group, (e.g., colorful scarves, funny hats, costume jewelry, etc.).

Relaxation techniques are an important aspect of an exercise session in that they can penetrate barriers for individuals who insist that exercise is too exerting. Relaxation techniques can act as motivating components of a session to which people look forward. Relaxation and massage (see Chapter 14) should be interspersed throughout the session.

The leader should begin each class with a five-minute warm-up period of gentle stretching, swinging, and bending to warm up the joints. A cool-down should occur at the end of each class to cool the muscles with gentle stretching and slow movements to bring the body back to a resting state (Weiss, 1990).

In summary, motivating older adults to participate in exercise can be a major challenge. The greater the sense of involvement the leader can generate in group members in the exercise session, the greater the attendance, hence, the greater the degree of benefits derived from exercise.

The following list summarizes the leadership and motivation theories, techniques, and factors discussed in this section of the chapter.

Initiating an exercise group
- Select an attractive title for the class.
- Publicize it well.
- Have good facilities and equipment available.
- Offer programs that appeal to both men and women.
- Enlist the help of peers and families to encourage elders to exercise.

Motivating elders to participate and adhere to the program
- The leader should understand theories of motivation and their applicability to elders exercising.
- Be knowledgeable about research on the benefits (physical and psychosocial) of exercise for older adults and relate the benefits to specific needs of the individual (e.g., to motivate an older adult with high cholesterol to exercise, you can actually point out research cited in this chapter on how exercise can lower cholesterol).
- Create a social atmosphere and commitment to the group.
- Offer praise, acceptance of all ability levels.
- Be aware of safety considerations, warning signs of exercise being too strenuous.
- Use appropriate chairs.
- Intersperse relaxation and massage in the sessions.
- Create a recreational atmosphere with props, music, and a sense of humor.
- Set goals; chart progress.
- Provide leadership opportunities for the participants.

Other leadership tips
- Participate with the group members.
- Position yourself where everyone can see you (the leader).
- Be encouraging, sensitive, optimistic.
- Provide physical assistance as needed.

EXERCISES FOR ELDERS

This section has been divided into three subsections: exercise for bedridden elders; exercise for elders with limited mobility; and exercise for high-functioning elders. Some of the exercises are based on ones in books by Anderson and Anderson (1980), Clark (1992), Corbin and Corbin (1983), Flatten, Willhite, and Reyes-Watson (1988), Frankel and Richard (1980), Jamieson (1982), Leslie (1989), McBride and Lefler (1986), Norton (1977), and Penner (1990). Consult these books for additional exercise ideas.

Exercises for Bedridden Elders

The following exercises are designed for elders restricted to bed. Bedridden elders will vary in ability. Higher-functioning elders will be able to complete more repetitions and will require shorter rests between exercises.

Lower-functioning elders may be able to accomplish fewer repetitions and may need more time to converse and rest in between exercises. The exercise leader would most likely lead the exercises for bedridden elders on an individual basis. Exercise sessions should last twenty to thirty minutes, allowing for periods of relaxation, being careful to avoid overexerting or fatiguing the patient.

The exercise leader should provide gentle physical assistance as necessary to help move body parts. Lower-functioning bedridden elders may need assistance raising their head or legs.

Exercises for the Neck

1. *Head raisers*
   a. Slowly raise the head as high as possible, bringing the chin toward the chest.
   b. Gently lower the head back to the pillow.
   c. Repeat two more times.
2. *Head turns*
   a. Keep the head on the pillow and slowly turn the head to the right. Be careful not to turn the head too much.
   b. Bring the head back to center position.
   c. Turn the head to the left.
   d. Bring the head back to center position.
   e. Repeat two more times.

Exercises for the Face

3. *Mouth openers*
   a. Open the mouth as wide as possible.
   b. Close the mouth.
   c. Repeat three more times.
4. *Tongue stretch*
   a. Stick the tongue out of the mouth.
   b. Return the tongue inside the mouth.
   c. Repeat three more times.
5. *Jaw rotation*
   a. Rotate the lower jaw from side to side.
   b. Repeat six times.
6. *Eye openers*
   a. Open the eyes wide.
   b. Close the eyes.
   c. Repeat three more times.

7. *Eye rotation*
   a. Rotate the eyeballs clockwise.
   b. Rotate the eyeballs counterclockwise.

Exercises for the Shoulders

8. *Arm raisers*
   a. Begin with the arms straight down by the sides.
   b. Lift the arms up toward the ceiling, then up overhead.
   c. Bring the arms back down to the sides.
   d. Repeat three more times.
9. *Overhead stretch*
   a. Begin with the arms straight down by the sides.
   b. Move the arms out to the sides, then overhead.
   c. Bring the arms back down to the sides, while keeping the arms in a parallel position to the bed.
   d. Repeat three more times.
10. *Elbow flexors*
    a. Begin with the elbows bent, hands pointing upward, palms facing the feet.
    b. Move the hands backward and try to touch the back of the hands to the bed.
    c. Bring the hands back to starting position.
    d. Move the hands toward the feet and place the palms on the bed while maintaining the arms in the same position.
    e. Move the hands back to starting position.
    f. Repeat three more times.

Exercises for the Arms

11. *Arm circles*
    a. Begin with the hands crossed on the abdomen.
    b. Raise the hands overhead keeping them crossed.
    c. Circle the arms in opposite directions back to starting position.
    d. Repeat three more times.
12. *Arm extensions*
    a. Begin with the upper arms on the bed, elbows bent, and hands facing upward.
    b. Straighten the arms and raise the hands toward the ceiling.
    c. Return the arms to starting position.
    d. Repeat three more times.

13. *Hands up*
    a. Begin with the arms at sides.
    b. Keeping the elbows on the bed, raise the hands upward with the palms facing upward.
    c. Return the hands to the bed.
    d. Raise the hands upward with the palms facing downward.
    e. Return the hands to the bed.
    f. Raise hands with the thumbs facing upward.
    g. Return hands to the bed.
14. *Hand circles*
    a. Begin with the elbows on the bed, hands held up.
    b. Turn the hands in a clockwise direction.
    c. Turn the hands counterclockwise.
    d. Repeat four more times.
15. *Wrist rotations*
    a. Begin with the arms placed next to the sides, palms down.
    b. Bend the wrists and bring the hands upward.
    c. Turn the hands so that the palms are facing upward.
    d. Bend the wrists so that the hands move toward the head.
    e. Return the hands to the bed.
    f. Repeat two more times.
16. *Wrist raisers*
    a. Begin with the arms at sides.
    b. Without moving the arms, move the hands and wrists to the right, then left.
    c. Repeat four more times.

Exercises for the Hands and Fingers

17. *Finger flex*
    a. Flex and extend the fingers.
    b. Repeat four more times.
18. *Finger spread*
    a. Spread the fingers as wide as possible.
    b. Repeat two more times.
19. *Thumb rotation*
    a. Rotate the thumbs clockwise, then counterclockwise.
20. *Finger stretch*
    a. Begin with the hands in a fist.
    b. Extend one finger at a time beginning with the thumb.
    c. After all fingers are extended, return one finger at a time back into a fist position beginning with the pinkie.

Exercises for the Chest

21. *The X*
    a. Begin with the arms straight out to the sides.
    b. Keep the arms straight, raise them upward in front of the chest to form an "X."
    c. Return the arms to starting position.
    d. Repeat three more times.
22. *Chest opener*
    a. Begin with the elbows on the bed, hands held upward.
    b. Keeping the elbows bent, cross the arms directly over the chest trying to touch the elbows together.
    c. Return the elbows out opening up the chest as much as possible.
    d. Repeat two more times.

Exercises for the Abdomen

23. *Abdomen contractions*
    a. Contract abdominal muscles for five counts, then release.
    b. Repeat four more times.
24. *Mini sit-up*
    a. Raise the head, shoulders, and legs as much as possible off the bed.
    b. Hold for three counts, then slowly lower back to the bed.
    c. Repeat two more times.

Exercises for the Lower Back

25. *Back press*
    a. Press the lower back to the bed while contracting the abdominal muscles, hold for three counts, and release.
    b. Repeat two more times.
26. *Knee to chest*
    a. Begin with legs extended straight out.
    b. Bend one leg and bring the knee toward the chest.
    c. Straighten the leg and return to starting position.
    d. Perform the same movement with the other leg.
    e. Repeat two more times with each leg.
27. *Double leg to chest*
    a. Begin with legs extended straight out.
    b. Bend both knees and bring both legs simultaneously to the chest (the hands can be used by placing them on the knees to help the momentum).

    c. Straighten the legs and return to starting position.

    d. Repeat one more time.

Exercises for the Legs

28. *Toe points*
    a. Begin with the legs together.
    b. Point the toes downward.
    c. Bring the toes upward and point the toes toward the head.
    d. Repeat three more times.
29. *Leg rotations*
    a. Begin with the legs slightly apart.
    b. Rotate the legs inward and point the toes toward each other.
    c. Rotate the legs outward and point the toes out to the sides.
    d. Repeat three more times.
30. *Feet circles*
    a. Begin with the legs together.
    b. Slightly lift the feet off the bed, then circle the feet clockwise three times.
    c. Circle the feet counterclockwise three times.
31. *The walk*
    a. Begin with the feet slightly apart.
    b. Alternate lifting one foot off the bed, then the other foot.
    c. Raise each foot four times.
32. *Leg pushes*
    a. Begin with the feet crossed at the ankles.
    b. Simultaneously try to push down with the top leg while trying to raise the bottom leg.
    c. Reverse the feet and repeat.
    d. Repeat one more time.

Towel Exercises for Bedridden Elders

A towel is an example of one readily available prop that can be utilized in assisting bedridden elders to move their body parts.

33. *The climb*
    a. The exercise assistant holds a towel vertically above the individual's head.
    b. The elder holds on to the towel and climbs upward using the hands.

34. *Pull-up*
    a. The exercise assistant holds the towel horizontally above the elder's head.
    b. The elder holds on to the towel and tries to pull the body weight up off the bed.
35. *Push-down*
    a. The exercise assistant places a towel beneath the lower calves of the elder and lifts the legs six to eight inches off the bed.
    b. The elder tries to push the legs downward toward the bed against the resistance of the towel.

Summary

Exercises for bedridden older adults include simple, nonstrenuous movements to stretch and strengthen muscle groups. Achieving movement of most body parts can be accomplished if the exercises are easy and performed in a slow, relaxed manner.

Exercises for Elders with Limited Mobility

In this section, the exercises described are intended to be performed from a seated position. All of the aforementioned exercises for bedridden elders can be adapted to be performed from a seated position for elders with limited mobility. The chairs should be arranged in a circle facilitating social interaction, group harmony, and visual contact among group members. Provide enough space between chairs to allow safe movement. Exercise sessions should last twenty-five to forty-five minutes, depending on the functioning level of the group. Ample time should be allowed for conversation and feedback from participants. Use a great deal of caution on all of these exercises.

Exercises for the Neck

36. *Head circles*
    a. Slowly rotate the head slightly in a clockwise direction. Be careful not to rotate it too much.
    b. Rotate the head counterclockwise.
37. *Chin to chest*
    a. Bring the chin down slowly and carefully toward the chest.
    b. Slowly roll the head back and look upward. Again, be very careful not to rotate the head too much.

38. *Head to side*
    a. Rotate the head toward one shoulder, but not all the way.
    b. Rotate the head toward the other shoulder.
    c. Repeat two more times. Be sure to do this one slowly and carefully.
39. *The "V"* (Modify this one by restricting the amount of rotation.)
    a. Roll the chin down slowly toward the chest.
    b. Rotate the head toward one shoulder, but not all the way, slanting the head.
    c. Roll the chin forward toward the chest.
    d. Rotate the head toward the other shoulder.
    e. Roll the chin back toward the chest.
40. *Inverted "V"* (Again, do this one slowly and restrict the rotation.)
    a. Roll the head backward so that the chin is pointed slightly upward.
    b. Rotate the head slightly toward one shoulder, slanting the head.
    c. Roll the head back, chin pointed upward.
    d. Rotate the head toward the other shoulder.
    e. Repeat one more time.

Exercises for the Shoulders

41. *Shoulder rotation*
    a. Rotate the shoulders forward, then backward.
42. *Shoulder rolls*
    a. Bring one shoulder as far forward as possible, while moving the other shoulder backward.
    b. Reverse shoulders.
    c. Repeat five more times with each shoulder.
43. *Shoulder lifts*
    a. Lift the shoulders up.
    b. Force the shoulders down.
    c. Repeat three more times.

Exercises for the Arms

44. *Arm rotations*
    a. Begin with arms extended out to the sides.
    b. Rotate arms in circles forward, then backward.
45. *Palms away*
    a. Begin with hands in lap.
    b. Reach out and upward, palms facing away from the body.

    c. Bring the hands downward, palms facing inward.

    d. Repeat three more times.

46. *The punch*
    a. Punch out alternating arms, one at a time.
    b. Punch forward, overhead, to the sides, downward.
    c. Punch four times in each direction.

47. *Forearm stretch*
    a. Place palms of hands on either side of body on the seat of the chair, thumb to the outside and fingers pointed backward.
    b. Slowly lean back in the chair and stretch the forearm. Hold for five counts.
    c. Repeat two more times.

48. *Elbow pull*
    a. Begin with the right arm overhead, bent at the elbow.
    b. Gently pull elbow behind the head with the other hand. Hold for five counts.
    c. Reverse arms.
    d. Repeat two more times on each side.

49. *Side stretch*
    a. Begin with arms extended.
    b. Hold the outside of the left hand with the right hand and pull to the left side. Hold for five counts.
    c. Reverse sides.
    d. Repeat two more times on each side.

50. *Arm stretch*
    a. Extend the arms upward.
    b. Bring the hands to the shoulders.
    c. Extend the arms forward.
    d. Bring the hands to the shoulders.
    e. Extend the arms to the sides.
    f. Bring the hands to the shoulders.
    g. Repeat one more time.

51. *Arm extensions*
    a. Reach up with one arm and simultaneously reach down toward the floor with the other arm.
    b. Switch arms and repeat.
    c. Repeat two more times.

52. *Arm lifts*
    a. Begin with both arms extended upward.
    b. Roll the lower back forward bringing the chin down toward the knees and simultaneously lower the arms then swing them backward.

   c. Roll the body upward and extend the arms back up.

   d. Repeat three more times.

53. *Forearm block*

   a. Begin with the arms in front of the chest, bent at the elbows.

   b. Keeping the arms bent, block with one forearm and then the other, involving the shoulders and upper back.

   c. Repeat five more times.

54. *Thumb points*

   a. Begin with the arms extended forward, hands in fists, thumbs pointed upward.

   b. Rotate the arms to point the thumbs downward.

   c. Repeat five more times.

55. *Reach-up*

   a. Begin with the arms extended upward, interlace fingers, turn palms upward.

   b. Reach up.

   c. Lower the hands.

   d. Repeat three more times.

56. *Arm swings*

   a. Begin with the arms in front of the chest, bent at the elbows, fingertips touching.

   b. Swing the arms downward and to the side, keeping the palms facing backward.

   c. Swing the arms back to the chest.

   d. Swing the arms to the other side.

   e. Repeat three more times.

Exercises for the Chest

57. *Elbow rolls*

   a. Begin with hands placed on shoulder, elbows extended outward.

   b. Rotate elbows forward, then backward.

58. *The opener*

   a. Begin with arms crossed in front of chest.

   b. Bring elbows backward as far as possible.

   c. Return arms to original position.

   d. Repeat four more times.

59. *Elbow turn*

   a. Begin with the arms in front of the chest, bent at the elbows.

   b. Rotate the arms around each other.

   c. Swing the arms to the sides and behind the back.

   d. Repeat four more times.

60. *Chest squeeze*

   a. Begin with the arms in front of the chest, hands clasped together. Keep the elbows up.

   b. Push the hands together for a count of five; relax.

   c. Repeat three more times.

61. *Chest strengthener*

   a. Begin with the arms bent at the elbows in front of the chest, hands in fists, and one fist on top of the other.

   b. Press down with the top fist while pushing up with the bottom fist. Hold for a count of five.

   c. Repeat four more times.

   d. Reverse and repeat.

62. *Finger grip*

   a. Begin with the arms in front of the chest, bent at the elbows, and the fingers of one hand gripped around the fingers of the other hand.

   b. Try to pull the fingers apart for the count of five.

   c. Repeat four more times.

Exercises for the Hands

63. *Hand spread*

   a. Separate and spread the fingers as much as possible.

   b. Repeat four more times.

64. *The squeeze*

   a. Squeeze a rubber ball (about 2½ inches in diameter) with all the fingers and thumb.

   b. Repeat four more times.

   c. Repeat with the other hand.

65. *Progressive squeeze*

   a. Squeeze the ball with one finger and thumb.

   b. Start with squeezing the ball between the pinkie and thumb, then ring finger and thumb, and so on.

   c. Repeat with the other hand.

66. *Wrist rotation*

   a. Turn the hands clockwise, counterclockwise.

   b. Repeat two more times.

67. *Finger-touch*

   a. Touch the thumb to the fingertips to each finger.

   b. Repeat one more time.

68. *Finger-stir*
    a. Grip each finger one at a time and circle clockwise, counter-clockwise.
    b. Repeat with the other hand.
69. *Palms-away*
    a. Extend the arms forward and interlace the fingers.
    b. Rotate the wrists and push the palms away.
    c. Repeat three more times.
70. *Wrist-turn*
    a. Extend the arms forward with the palms facing upward.
    b. Rotate the wrists so that the palms are facing downward.
    c. Repeat four more times.

Exercises for the Abdomen

71. *Tummy tighteners*
    a. Lift the feet about two inches off the floor and hold for a count of ten.
    b. Repeat three more times.
72. *Sit-ups*
    a. Slide forward in the chair, sitting straight.
    b. Hold arms in a comfortable position at shoulder level while rocking the body forward and then backward, but not allowing the back to touch the chair.
    c. Continue this motion for a count of ten.
73. *Tummy-hold*
    a. Pull in the abdominal muscles and hold for a count of six. Continue breathing evenly.
    b. Relax and repeat three more times.
74. *Tummy strengtheners*
    a. Cross one knee over the other.
    b. Lift both knees up lifting the bottom foot about one to two inches off the floor.
    c. Hold for a count of six. Continue to breathe evenly.
    d. Switch legs and repeat.
    e. Repeat two more times.

Exercises for the Sides

75. *Side twist*
    a. Extend both arms overhead; grasp the hands together.
    b. Turn the upper body to one side, then to the other side.
    c. Repeat four more times.

76. *The turn-around*
     a. Turn backward and place both hands on the top of the chairback.
     b. Pull the body around, look back, and hold for the count of six. Breathe evenly.
     c. Repeat on the other side.

77. *Side stretch*
     a. Place the hands on the lap.
     b. Extend both arms to one side.
     c. Return the hands to the lap.
     d. Extend both arms to the other side.
     e. Return the hands to the lap.
     f. Repeat three more times.

78. *Toner*
     a. Swing the arms from side to side, keeping the head stationary.
     b. Continue this movement for a count of six.

79. *Elbow turn*
     a. Place the hands on the shoulders, keeping the elbows pointed to the sides.
     b. Turn the upper body to the side, to the center, to the other side.
     c. Continue for a count of eight.

80. *Waist toner*
     a. Place the hands behind the head, interlace the fingers, and keep the elbows up.
     b. Bend the upper body to one side, straight, and then to the other side.
     c. Continue for six more counts.

Exercises for the Legs

81. *Under the chair point*
     a. Begin with the feet together.
     b. Lift the feet and move them beneath the chair as far back as possible, pointing the toes backward. Hold for five count.
     c. Repeat two more times.

82. *Knee to chest*
     a. Begin with the feet together.
     b. Place hands on one knee and lift the knee toward the chest.
     c. Lower the knee back down and repeat with the other leg.
     d. Repeat four more times with each leg.

83. *Leg stretch*
   a. Begin with the feet slightly apart.
   b. Lift the feet off the floor and extend both legs forward, keeping them straight.
   c. Return the feet to the floor.
   d. Repeat three more times.

84. *Leg push-out*
   a. Begin with the feet placed next to the inside of the legs of the chair.
   b. Try to push outward against the resistance of the chair. Hold for three counts.
   c. Repeat two more times.

85. *Leg push-in*
   a. Begin with the feet placed next to the outside of the legs of the chair.
   b. Try pushing inward. Hold for three counts.
   c. Repeat two more times.

86. *Knee lift*
   a. Lift the knees up toward the chest.
   b. Extend the legs forward.
   c. Bend the knees.
   d. Extend the legs forward.
   e. Repeat one more time.

87. *Leg cross*
   a. Extend the legs forward.
   b. Open the legs wide keeping them straight.
   c. Close the legs and cross the ankles.
   d. Repeat three more times.

88. *The bicycle*
   a. Move the legs in a bicycle-riding motion.
   b. Maintain this movement for a count of ten.

89. *Knee squeeze*
   a. Keeping the knees bent, lift the feet about one inch off the floor and squeeze the knees together for a count of five.
   b. Lower the knees and repeat two more times.

90. *Leg swings*
   a. Slide both feet to one side keeping both feet on the floor.
   b. Slide both feet to the other side.
   c. Repeat four more times.

91. *Ice skating*
    a. Point the toes on one foot and draw a large circle on the floor clockwise, then counterclockwise.
    b. Switch to the other foot and repeat.
    c. Repeat two more times.
92. *Scissors*
    a. Extend the legs forward.
    b. Lift one leg while lowering the other leg, then switch legs to create a scissorlike motion.
    c. Continue for a count of ten.
93. *The big "V"*
    a. Extend one leg to the side.
    b. Lower the foot to the floor.
    c. Extend the leg to the other side so that a large "V" has been drawn with the foot.
    d. Switch to the other leg and repeat.
    e. Repeat three more times.
94. *Leg circles*
    a. Extend one leg forward, point the toes, and circle the leg clockwise, counterclockwise.
    b. Switch legs and repeat.
    c. Repeat three more times.
95. *The bounce*
    a. Extend the legs forward.
    b. Keeping the legs together, bounce the legs up and down for a count of six.
96. *Skiing*
    a. Begin with one foot forward on the floor and the other foot extended back.
    b. Simultaneously slide the feet to the opposite directions in a skiing-type of motion and continue for a count of ten.

Exercises for the Feet

97. *Feet flexors*
    a. Begin with the feet slightly apart.
    b. Lift and arch the feet, point the toes downward.
    c. Flex the feet and point the toes upward.
    d. Repeat three more times.
98. *Toe spread*
    a. Separate and spread the toes as much as possible.
    b. Repeat two more times.
99. *Foot circles*
    a. Lift the feet and circle them clockwise, counterclockwise.
    b. Repeat four more times.

100. *Heel raisers*
   a. Place the feet flat on the floor.
   b. Raise and lower the heels, keeping the toes on the floor.
   c. Continue for eight counts.
101. *Toe raisers*
   a. Place the feet flat on the floor.
   b. Raise and lower the toes, keeping the heels on the floor.
   c. Continue for eight counts.
102. *Heel-slides*
   a. Place feet together flat on the floor.
   b. Slide heels from side to side, keeping the toes stationary.
   c. Continue for eight counts.
103. *Foot slants*
   a. Begin with the feet together flat on the floor.
   b. Move the heels, move the toes, move the heels, move the toes, until the legs are wide apart.
   c. Bring the feet back together in the same motion (heels, toes, heels, toes).
   d. Repeat one more time.
104. *Toe-walking*
   a. Arch the feet so only the toes are touching the floor.
   b. Walk on the toes.
   c. Continue for a count of ten.
105. *Heel-toe point*
   a. Place the toes of one foot on the floor; place the heel of the other foot on the floor.
   b. Switch foot positions over and over for a count of eight.
106. *The duck*
   a. Extend the legs forward keeping the feet together.
   b. Open the feet at the toes keeping the heels together.
   c. Close the feet.
   d. Open the feet at the heels keeping the toes together.
   e. Close the feet.
   f. Repeat four more times.
107. *Foot clap*
   a. Lift the feet and clap the soles of the feet together.
   b. Continue for eight counts.
108. *Foot movers*
   a. Place only the toes of each foot on the floor.
   b. Keeping only the toes on the floor, roll the feet in circles clockwise, then counterclockwise.

Summary

Exercises for older adults with limited mobility are designed to be performed from a seated position. If practiced regularly, the exercises can increase strength and flexibility, and allow for a greater range of movement.

Exercises for High-Functioning Elders

The exercises in the previous section can be performed from a standing position for high-functioning elders. In this section, yoga is discussed as an approach to achieve fitness for high-functioning elders. Although most yoga postures would be too difficult for lower-functioning elders, yoga can be a beneficial form of exercise for high-functioning elders.

Yoga can be practiced by elders to improve fitness levels. It can be especially appropriate for the older population in that the system of yoga postures focuses on every aspect of the individual through slow movement and rhythmic breathing. Exercise sessions should last approximately forty-five minutes. Participants should wear comfortable clothing and be encouraged to take off their shoes for the session.

The descriptions of each yoga exercise that follow include (1) a description of the benefits of the exercise; (2) a description of the starting position; (3) a step-by-step listing of movements involved in the exercise; and (4) an identification of special considerations for leading the exercise. The following exercises are based on Norton's (1977) book *Yoga for People Over Fifty.*

109. *Overhead stretch*
     Benefits: Stretches the muscles of the arms, feet, legs, and along the sides.
     Starting position: Stand erect, feet flat on the floor, arms at sides.
     Movements
     a. Raise the arms high overhead.
     b. Look up.
     c. Stretch through every part of the body.
     d. Rise up on the toes and continue reaching higher.
     e. Relax, lower the heels to the floor, and bring the arms back to the sides.
     f. Repeat two more times.
     Special considerations: In the event of balance problems, do not rise up on the toes. It may help to use the support of a chair and reach up with one arm at a time.

110. *Deep breathing bends*

   Benefits: Stretches lower back, hamstrings, and backs of knees.

   Starting position: Stand erect, arms at sides, and place feet shoulder-width apart.

   Movements

   a. Inhale and extend arms high overhead.
   b. Exhale and collapse the body into a slumped position bending from the waist and allow arms to dangle toward the floor.
   c. In this relaxed position, breathe slowly.
   d. Inhale and slowly return to the starting position keeping the chin tucked close to the chest.
   e. Repeat two times.

   Special considerations: If problems with balance occur, perform this exercise in a circle with everyone holding hands for added support.

111. *Upward stretch*

   Benefits: Stretches muscles in arms, hands, and sides.

   Starting position: Stand erect, arms at sides, and palms facing outward.

   Movements

   a. Inhale and slowly raise arms overhead.
   b. Exhale, interlock fingers, and turn palms upward.
   c. Take several breaths and reach up as high as possible.
   d. Slowly lower arms back to starting position.
   e. Repeat one more time.

112. *Side stretch*

   Benefits: Stretches arms, hands, wrists, and sides.

   Starting position: Stand erect, arms at sides, and palms facing outward.

   Movements

   a. Inhale and raise arms.
   b. Interlock fingers and turn palms upward.
   c. Exhale and slowly bend to one side as far as possible keeping the feet flat on the floor.
   d. Inhale and return to center position.
   e. Exhale and slowly move to the other side.
   f. Inhale and return to center position.
   g. Exhale and slowly lower arms.
   h. Repeat one more time.

   Special considerations: For added support, stand sideways, next to a wall and reach for the wall. Perform several repetitions on one side, then switch to the other side. This exercise can also be done in a doorway reaching from side to side.

113. *Pep up*

Benefits: Promotes circulation to the head, relaxes muscles in back and shoulders, and stretches the legs.

Starting position: Stand erect, feet twelve inches apart, hands clasped behind the back.

Movements

a. Inhale, lift clasped hands and arms while squeezing shoulder blades together.

b. Exhale, bend forward from the waist bringing clasped hands and arms up and away from back as high as possible.

c. Breathe deeply in this position while relaxing the head and neck.

d. Inhale and slowly return to starting position.

e. Repeat one more time.

Special considerations: Use a buddy system in which one person is performing the exercise and the other is spotting to avoid falls or accidents.

114. *Back stretch*

Benefits: Stretches the back and legs.

Starting position: Stand three to five feet from a wall; place feet shoulder-width apart. Place palms on the wall a little wider apart than the shoulders.

Movements

a. Move the buttocks and hips away from the wall and extend the spine.

b. Flatten the lower back keeping the head down, arms and legs straight, and palms kept firmly against the wall.

c. Take several deep breaths in this pose.

d. Slowly return to starting position.

Special consideration: This exercise can also be performed holding onto a window sill or sturdy chair.

115. *Child's pose*

Benefits: Relaxes the back and increases circulation to the head and face.

Starting position: Kneel on floor and sit back on the heels.

Movements

a. Place the head in front of the knees on the floor.

b. Move the arms in, back toward the toes, and rest them on the floor. Elbows should be relaxed.

c. Breathe and relax in this pose for a moment or two.

Special consideration: If it is uncomfortable placing the head on the floor, try using a pillow under the head.

116. *The tree*

Benefits: Strengthens the legs, ankles, feet, and improves balance.

Starting position: Stand sideways next to a wall.

Movements

a. Place one hand on the wall, raise one leg up and place the sole of the foot against the inside of the thigh of the other leg.
b. Concentrate on a spot about six feet away.
c. Slowly release the hand from the wall, then raise both arms overhead and bring the palms together.
d. Maintain this pose for several breaths.
e. Repeat the exercise on the other leg.

Special consideration: While trying to balance on one leg, concentrate on lifting and stretching the body upward. Try not to sink into the hip that is supporting the weight of the body.

117. *Triangle*

Benefits: Stretches and strengthens the legs and opens the hip/pelvic area.

Starting position: Stand erect, arms relaxed at sides, place feet three to four feet apart.

Movements

a. Extend arms out sideways at shoulder level, palms down.
b. Turn the right foot outward to ninety degrees.
c. Turn the left foot inward so that the heel of the right foot is in line with the arch of the left foot.
d. Bend to the right side without bending the knees.
e. Place the right hand on the right knee and extend the left arm upward. The extended arm should be in line with the lower arm.
f. Distribute the weight evenly between both feet.
g. Maintain this pose for several breaths.
h. Return to starting position.
i. Change position of feet and repeat the pose on the other side.

118. *Forward bend*

Benefits: Promotes circulation to the head, increases flexibility in legs and back.

Starting position: Stand erect, feet hip-width apart.

Movements

a. Bend forward bringing buttocks upward.
b. Extend and elongate the spine by flattening the back and reaching with the head as far as possible. Concentrate on moving the entire back as one unit from pelvis to neck.

    c. Bend forward keeping the back flat and place the hands on the knees. Keep the head down.

    d. Maintain this position for a moment and breathe evenly.

    e. To return to starting position, tuck the chin to the chest and uncurl up slowly with a rounded back.

Special consideration: In determining if the back is rounded or flat, try the following: Bend forward from the waist with a round back and straight legs. Reach back with one hand and place the fingers on the lower back and feel the vertebrae sticking out like small bumps on the spine. Straighten the back and feel how the vertebrae move in.

119. *Leg extensions*

    Benefits: Stretches the legs and feet.

    Starting position: Lie on back, knees bent, feet flat on the floor, and arms at sides.

    Movements

    a. Bring one knee to the chest.

    b. Straighten the leg upward.

    c. Stretch the foot and point the toes.

    d. Flex the foot so that the sole points upward.

    e. Return to starting position.

    f. Alternate legs and repeat.

    g. Repeat entire exercise two more times.

    Special consideration: This exercise is not recommended for people with sciatic pain.

120. *Leg lifts*

    Benefits: Strengthens back and abdominal muscles.

    Starting position: Lie on back, legs straight, arms at sides.

    Movements

    a. Raise the right leg while keeping the lower back on the floor.

    b. Slowly lower the leg.

    c. Repeat five times for each leg.

    Special considerations: Try inhaling while raising the leg and exhaling while lowering the leg. To protect the lower back, press the lower back to the floor. At the point where it is not possible to keep contact between the lower back and the floor, bend the knees or quickly lower the leg.

121. *Hand-foot extension*

    Benefits: Strengthens back and abdominal muscles.

    Starting position: Lie on back, knees bent, and arms relaxed at sides.

Movements

a. Bend legs and bring both knees to the chest.
b. Straighten legs upward.
c. Flex feet and stretch through the heels.
d. Lift arms and head as high as possible (arms are parallel, palms facing each other, fingers pointed upward).
e. Take several breaths in this pose.
f. Slowly lower head and arms.
g. Bend knees.
h. Lower legs to the floor.
i. Repeat one more time.

Special consideration: If holding the legs up is difficult, try practicing next to a wall so the feet and legs can rest momentarily against the wall, then lift again.

122. *Bridge*

Benefits: Strengthens back, thighs, hips, abdomen, and relaxes shoulders.

Starting position: Lie on back, knees bent, feet flat on the floor, arms at sides

Movements

a. Press lower back against the floor (pelvis will naturally rotate forward).
b. Tighten buttock muscles, inhale, and raise the body as high as possible (keep feet planted firmly on the floor).
c. Hold this pose two to three breaths.
d. Exhale and slowly lower body to floor.
e. Repeat one more time.

Special considerations: Keep the neck relaxed and slightly extended during the pose. Keep the feet about hip-width apart.

123. *Back twist*

Benefits: Aligns and relaxes the back.

Starting position: Lie on back, arms extended at shoulder level, palms down.

Movements

a. Inhale and slowly raise the knees to the chest.
b. Exhale and lower the knees to the floor to the right (keep knees together) and simultaneously move the head to the left.
c. Hold for several breaths and keep both shoulders flat on the floor.
d. Inhale and raise bent legs back to the chest.

e. Exhale and lower legs to the left as head moves simultaneously to the right.

f. Repeat two more times on each side.

Special consideration: Wrap both arms around the knees to make it easier to bring the knees close to the chest.

124. *Leg press*

Benefits: Strengthens legs and back; stretches hamstrings.

Starting position: Sit on the floor with legs extended straight out in front.

Movements

a. Place palms on the floor next to the hips, fingers pointing toward the feet (this helps to lift the back).

b. Keeping the legs together, press the backs of the knees to the floor. Keep the knees facing upward.

c. Flex the feet. Pressing the backs of the knees to the floor will cause the heels to rise off the floor.

d. Hold this pose for several breaths.

e. Repeat two more times.

Special considerations: If difficulty exists in keeping the back erect, perform the exercise next to a wall and momentarily rest the back against the wall. To maintain a straight back, concentrate on growing taller. Feel the spine to be sure no vertebrae are protruding.

125. *Forward bend*

Benefits: Stretches and extends entire body.

Starting position: Sit on the floor with legs extended straight out in front.

Movements

a. Keeping the back extended, reach with the hands toward the feet.

b. Reach as far as is comfortable while continuing to elongate the back.

c. Take several breaths in this position.

d. Repeat one more time.

Special considerations: For greater extension, stretch forward over the legs, bending from the hips and exhale. Try to bring the head to the ankles and navel to thighs closing the space between abdomen and thighs. Check the spine for protruding vertebrae and lift the sternum toward the chin for greater extension. The use of a towel may be helpful in this exercise. Wrap a towel around the balls of the feet and with straight arms, pull the towel to draw the shoulder blades back, expand the chest, and straighten the back. Remember to keep the knees facing upward.

126. *Head to knee*

Benefits: Stretches spine and hamstrings, and relieves tension in the back.

Starting position: Sit on floor with legs extended straight out in front.

Movements

   a. Bring the right foot to the upper left thigh, keeping the sole of the right foot as close to the body as possible. The left knee should stay flat on the floor.
   b. Inhale and bring arms overhead.
   c. Exhale and reach down the straight leg toward the toes and hold on to the leg at the farthest point that feels comfortable.
   d. Hold this pose for several breaths.
   e. Return to starting position.
   f. Reverse legs and repeat on the other side.
   g. Repeat entire exercise one time.

Special considerations: Keep the spine elongated with no vertebrae protruding. The back of the knee on the extended leg should remain flat on the floor, the knee facing upward. A towel can be wrapped around the foot of the extended leg to assist in stretching. For a greater stretch, exhale while descending down the extended leg.

127. *Frog*

Benefits: Stretches inner thighs; opens up pelvis and hip area.

Starting position: Sit with back against the wall, legs extended straight out in front.

Movements

   a. Bend the knees and bring the soles of the feet together as close to the body as possible.
   b. Keep the back straight and spine extended.
   c. Gently press the knees to the floor.
   d. Hold this pose for several breaths.
   e. Repeat two more times.

Special consideration: Avoid this exercise if severe knee problems exist.

128. *Meditation pose*

Benefits: Relieves stiffness in knees and ankles, increases blood supply in lumbar and abdominal areas.

Starting position: Sit on a folded blanket with legs extended straight out in front.

Movements
a. Bend the left knee.
b. Holding the left foot with the hands, place the sole of the foot against the right inner thigh.
c. Bend the right knee.
d. Place the right foot over the left ankle and against the left inner thigh.
e. Breathe evenly, and hold this position as long as possible.
f. Reverse and repeat.

Summary

This section presented a list of yoga exercises appropriate for high-functioning elders, but keep in mind the limitless possibilities for exercise classes for elders, such as aquatics, tai chi (Adler, 1983), aerobics, dance (see Chapter 13), team sports, weight training, and walking.

EXERCISE-BASED GAMES AND ACTIVITIES

Use discretion in terms of who you attempt these activities and games with. Higher-functioning groups might perceive some of these games and activities as being silly. Others, such as step aerobics, dowel, and scarf exercises, can be successful with both higher- and lower-functioning groups. Most of the games and activities in this section are recommended for use more with lower-functioning populations found in senior day care centers and nursing homes.

The games and activities described are an attempt to add variety to exercise sessions and inject some fun. However, they also have important benefits, just as the exercises do. In introducing these games and activities to elders, emphasize the benefits so that elders will perceive them correctly as worthwhile, fun activities, not as silly, meaningless, childish games. The benefits of the activities and games in this section include enhanced eye/hand coordination, improved flexibility and strength of arms and hands, and sharpening of concentration and short-term memory.

1. *Boccie*
   a. The group is situated into a square formation and divided into two teams.
   b. Each team has one set of three same-colored balls, but a different color from the other team.
   c. A larger ball is placed in the middle of the square.

d. Two persons from each team try to roll their balls to hit the larger ball.

e. These two players take turns rolling their balls.

f. Once rolled, the balls remain in place on the floor, undisturbed after each roll until all six balls have been rolled.

g. Each time the large ball is hit, that team receives two points. If neither team hits the ball, then the team whose ball comes closest to the large ball receives one point.

h. After the first two players roll their balls, then the next two players from each team take turns alternately rolling their three balls.

i. Continue until everyone has had two to three turns.

2. *Balloon volleyball*

a. A volleyball or badminton net is set up with one team on each side.

b. The players are seated in long rows facing the net, about one leg's distance away from the net.

c. A balloon is hit back and forth over the net with the objective being to keep the balloon in the air and not allow it to fall to the floor.

d. If the ballon does touch the floor, the team on the opposite side wins a point.

e. A game of fifteen or twenty-one points is played.

3. *Yarn exercise*

a. The group is seated in a large circle.

b. Several different colored balls of yarn are distributed to various people in the circle with the objective being to unravel the yarn by passing it around the circle.

c. Continue to pass the yarn around the circle until each person is holding so many different strings that a thick rope is formed.

d. Cut the balls of yarn off and tie knots to hold the rope together.

e. With each participant holding onto the rope, many group exercises can be performed (do each exercise approximately five times):

(1) Lift the rope overhead and back to the shoulders.

(2) Row the rope.

(3) Place the rope on the ankles and lift and lower the legs.

(4) Place the rope on the knees and lift and lower the knees.

(5) Make waves with the rope: half the group lifts the rope while the others lower it.

(6) Pass the rope to the right; to the left.

(7) Lift and lower the rope behind the head.

(8) Toss the rope in the air and catch it.

(9) Place the rope on top of the head and turn the head from side to side.

(10) Place the rope on the nose and lift the head upward.

(11) Place one arm above the rope and the other arm below the rope and switch.

(12) Hold the rope at knee level and step over the rope with each leg.

4. *Exercises with tennis balls*

    a. The group is arranged in a circle and each person is given two tennis balls: one to work with and one is used as a spare and kept in the lap.

    b. Numerous group exercises can be performed (attempt each exercise approximately five times):

        (1) Toss the ball up with one hand, then the other hand.

        (2) Toss the ball from one hand to the other hand.

        (3) Bounce the ball with one hand, then the other hand.

        (4) Squeeze the ball with each hand.

        (5) Place the ball between the feet; squeeze and lift the legs.

        (6) Place the ball on the floor and roll it side to side, from one foot to the other foot.

        (7) Pass the ball under the knee, from one hand to the other hand.

        (8) Pass the ball to the left; to the right.

        (9) Toss the ball up, catch it; bounce it, catch it.

       (10) Bounce and catch the ball on the side of the legs, in between the legs, on the other side of the legs.

5. *Exercise with dowels*

    a. The group is seated in a large circle and one dowel (approximately two to three feet in length and one to two inches in diameter) is distributed to each person.

    b. Perform each exercise approximately five times:

        (1) Lift the dowel overhead and back to the shoulder with one hand, then the other hand.

        (2) Lift the dowel overhead and back to the shoulders with two hands.

        (3) Extend the dowel forward and back to the chest with two hands.

        (4) Lower the dowel on the side toward the floor and up to the armpit with each hand.

        (5) Draw a circle in the air with the dowel with each hand.

        (6) Write your name in the air with the dowel.

        (7) Draw a figure eight with the dowel with each hand.

        (8) Extend the dowel forward, lower it to the knees, then raise it to chest level.

        (9) Extend the dowel forward with both hands, alternately lift one knee to touch the dowel then lower the knee.

(10) Extend the dowel overhead with two hands and reach toward the floor on each side.

(11) Extend the dowel overhead and twist the upper body from side to side.

(12) Place the dowel on the floor in front of the feet. Step over the dowel and back with each foot.

(13) Place the dowel on the floor in front of the feet and jump over the dowel and back with both feet.

(14) Place the dowel vertically on the floor in front of the feet. Step from side to side over the dowel with each foot. Jump side to side with both feet.

(15) Turn the dowel in a circle on the floor using the feet.

(16) Roll the dowel sideways from one foot to the other.

(17) Hold the bottom of the dowel and "walk" with the fingers to the top of the dowel. "Walk" with the fingers back to the bottom of the dowel. Switch to the other hand.

(18) Extend the dowel forward holding it at each end, and rotate it ninety degrees in each direction.

(19) Toss the dowel from one hand to the other hand.

(20) Hit the dowel on the floor on one side; switch hands; hit the floor on the other side.

6. *Exercise with scarves*
   a. Participants are seated in a large circle and a colorful scarf is given to each person.
   b. Many of the exercises using tennis balls and dowels can be adapted for this activity. Additional exercises using scarves are as follows (perform each exercise approximately five times):
      (1) Toss the scarf up and catch it.
      (2) Fling the scarf.
      (3) "Dry" your back with the scarf.
      (4) Tie the scarf on to different bodyparts.
      (5) Hold the scarf in front of the face and blow on it.
      (6) Circle each arm while holding onto the scarf.
      (7) Fold the scarf.
      (8) Roll the scarf.
      (9) Hold the scarf at each end and try to pull the scarf apart.

7. *Step aerobics*
   a. The group is seated in rows with each person able to see the leader.
   b. A book that is used as a step is placed on the floor in front of each person's feet, with the binder of the book facing the person.
   c. Use music with a distinct rhythm to accompany this activity.

    d. An almost infinite number of patterns can be performed in step aerobics. The following exercises are just a sample of the possibilities. ("Up" refers to stepping up on to the book.)

      (1) Right foot step up, step back down. Left foot step, step back down.

      (2) Right foot step up, left foot step up. Right foot step down, left foot step back.

      (3) Right foot step up, left foot step up. Right foot step side down, left foot step side down. Right foot step up, left foot step up. Right foot step back down, left foot step back down.

      (4) Left foot step up, right foot step up. Left foot step forward down, right foot step forward down. Left foot step up, right foot step up. Left foot step back down, right foot step back down.

      (5) Right foot step up, left foot step up. Jump twice. Right foot back down, left foot back down.

      (6) Both feet step up together, both feet step down side together. Step back up together, step back down together.

      (7) Right foot step up, right foot step forward, right foot step up, right foot step back down. Repeat with the left foot.

      (8) Both feet jump up together, jump to one side together, jump up together, jump to the other side together, jump up together.

8. *Parachute exercises*

    a. The group is seated in a circle with everyone holding on to a parachute. If a parachute is unavailable, obtain a large sheet and cut it into a circular shape.

    b. The following are some examples of parachute exercises (perform each exercise five times):

      (1) Lift and lower the parachute.

      (2) Pull the parachute toward the chest.

      (3) Make waves: Half of the group lifts the parachute while the other half lowers it.

      (4) Kick the parachute with one foot, then the other foot, then both feet simultaneously.

      (5) Place several balls on top of the parachute and lift the parachute up and down to make the balls jump around.

      (6) Try to make a ball fall through the hole in the center of the parachute.

      (7) Toss the parachute up and try to catch it.

      (8) Pass the parachute to the left; to the right.

      (9) Lift the parachute up high overhead so the participants can see one another's faces underneath it and shout "hello."

9. *Golf* (Flatten, Willhite, and Reyes-Watson, 1988):
   a. Collect four shoeboxes and remove one end of each box.
   b. Place the boxes side by side and upside on the floor.
   c. Attach tape to the sides of the boxes so they stay together.
   d. Write the number of points in large print on each box (i.e., 100, 50, 50, 100).
   e. Use three to five golf balls and a golf club or putter.
   f. Position the player about six feet from the boxes; player hits the balls in one at a time.
   g. Keep score and allow everyone two to three turns.
10. *Laundryball*
    a. The group is seated in a circle with a laundry basket in the middle.
    b. Toss balls into the laundry basket.
    c. Bounce balls to land in the basket.
    d. Pass the ball to another player who then tosses it into the basket.
    e. Throw many balls consecutively into the basket to see how many balls can be thrown in by one player before missing.
11. *Bowling*
    a. Collect ten large plastic soda bottles; place them on the floor in a tenpin bowling formation.
    b. The bowler is seated approximately six feet from the bottles and rolls three balls, one at a time, to try to knock down all the bottles.
    c. Scores can be kept as in regular bowling.
12. *Hockey*
    a. Players are seated in two lines facing each other, about three feet apart.
    b. Each player has a sponge bat. If sponge bats are not available, use homemade rackets (Corbin and Corbin, 1983). Use wire hangers, stockings or pantyhose, string or rubberbands, and plastic tape. Band the wire into a circular shape and insert it into the leg of a stocking. Pull the stocking tight around the top and bottom of the wire circle. Tightly tie or tape the stocking at the top and bottom. Cut off any excess material. Straighten the hanger hook and tape it so it forms a grip.
    c. Two large containers are placed at either end of the rows.
    d. One row of players tries to hit a sponge ball with their bat into one box while the other team uses the other box.
    e. Players try to defend their box as well by trying to keep the ball from going into their box. To help remember which box players are defending, tie yarn around the wrists of the players on one team, as well as on the containers. Each team has a different color.

13. *Exercise with bicycle inner tubes* (Corbin and Corbin, 1983).

Most bicycle shops will provide used bicycle inner tubes free of charge, since they are usually discarded. Ask employees at several bike shops to save them.

Cut the stems off the tubes and wash them, then tie the ends together. This offers a resistance exercise. For greater resistance, make the tube smaller, or larger for less resistance. For the following exercises, grip the tube at each end with both hands:

a. Hold one end against the chest and extend the other arm forward, then switch position of the arms.

b. Hold one end against the chest and extend the other arm upward. Switch.

c. Extend arms forward and open and close hands.

d. Extend arms overhead and open and close hands.

e. Bring arms behind the back and open and close hands.

f. Hook the tube under one foot and hold each end of the tube with one hand. Bend and pull, bending the elbows.

g. Place both feet on the tube and with both hands on the tube, curl hands upward toward shoulders, keeping the palms upward.

h. Continue the same motion with the palms facing downward.

i. Place the tube behind the back and hook thumbs at each end of the tube. Swing the arms forward and across the body in punching fashion.

j. Fold the tube into a ball and squeeze with the hands.

k. Loop one end of the tube around the foot and extend the leg. Hold the other end of the tube with both hands. Point and flex the foot.

l. Loop both feet together and repeat.

m. Hook both feet in the tube. Grasp the other end of the tube with both hands. Lift arms and pull the feet up.

n. Hook both feet in the tube and hold the other end with both hands and jog.

o. Hook both feet in the tube, extend legs, and open and close the feet.

p. Hook the tube around the ankles and then cross the ankles. Extend the legs and simultaneously lift one ankle and lower the other ankle. Reverse and repeat.

14. *Relay races*

Two teams are seated in two rows, facing each other. An action or movement is initiated at the beginning of each row and this action is passed one person at a time, down the row, to the end person and then back again. Movements can be physical and/or social in nature, and props can also be used. Some examples of relays follow:

    a. Pass a handshake.

    b. Pass a pat on the back.

    c. Pass a wink.

    d. Pass a smile.

    e. Pass a clap of the hands.

    f. Pass three stomps of the feet.

    g. Pass a ball to throw up in the air and catch.

    h. Pass a flower to smell.

    i. Pass a hat to be put on the head.

    j. Pass a scarf to tie around the neck.

    k. Pass a tambourine to shake.

    l. Pass the movement of riding a bicycle.

    m. Pass the movement of punching.

15. *Mock track meet* (Parker, Will, and Burke, 1989)

Elders are seated in a circle and they participate in each activity, one at a time. Scores are recorded for each individual and awards are distributed at the end of the activity for first, second, and third place winners of each event.

    a. 100-yard dash: Roll 100 inches of string into a ball as fast as possible.

    b. Discus: Throw a paper plate as far as possible.

    c. Javelin: Blow a wrapper off a straw.

    d. Shot put: Throw a nerf ball as far as possible.

    e. Broad jump: Measure each person's smile to find the biggest ones.

    f. Marathon: Jog in place (everyone at the same time, seated), and determine who can endure for the longest time.

16. *Others*

Horseshoes, ring toss, bean bag throw, croquet, and other games can be adapted for elders with limited mobility. Exercise 12.3 asks you to create your own exercise-based game or activity and to write an introduction to it that will help to motivate elders to participate and feel that the activity is meaningful.

SUMMARY

Many different exercises and activity ideas, for all levels of functioning, were presented in this chapter. The following written exercises (Exercises 12.4, 12.5, and 12.6) ask you to incorporate these ideas, as well as ideas from other sources (including your own imagination!) into cohesive session plans.

EXERCISE 12.3. An Original Exercise-Based Game or Activity

1. Introduction: _____

   _____

   _____

2. Arrangement of players: _____

   _____

   _____

3. Equipment, supplies needed: _____

   _____

   _____

4. Directions/instructions for the activity/game: _____

   _____

   _____

5. Possible variations/modifications: _____

   _____

   _____

EXERCISE 12.4. Session Plan for Bedridden Elders (Twenty Minutes)

1. Refer to the list of exercises for bedridden elders in this chapter.
2. Select exercises from this list that you would like to incorporate into a twenty-minute exercise session with a bedridden elder.
3. Decide how many repetitions of each exercise you would like to do, the sequence of the exercises, and time between each exercise for rest. In total, the session should last about twenty minutes.
4. Describe how you will make the session fun and interesting.

_____

_____

_____

_____

_____

_____

_____

_____

_____

_____

_____

_____

_____

_____

_____

_____

EXERCISE 12.5. Session Plan for Moderately Impaired Elders
(Thirty Minutes)

1. Refer to the list of exercises for elders with limited mobility in this chapter.
2. Select exercises from the list that you would like to incorporate into a thirty-minute session of chair exercises for moderately impaired elders.
3. Decide how many repetitions of each exercise you would like to do, the sequence of the exercises, and time between each exercise for rest. In total, the session should last about thirty minutes.
4. Describe how you will make the session fun and interesting.

_____

_____

_____

_____

_____

_____

_____

_____

_____

_____

_____

_____

_____

_____

EXERCISE 12.6. Session Plan for High Functioning Elders
(Forty-Five Minutes)

1. Refer to the list of exercises for high-functioning elders in this chapter, as well as the exercise-based games and activities. Some of the chair exercises for moderately impaired elders can also be adapted and conducted from a standing position.
2. Devise a forty-five minute exercise session plan that includes breaks for rest and deep breathing.
3. Be sure to include an adequate number of repetitions for each exercise.
4. Describe how you will make the session fun and interesting.

REFERENCES

Abourezk, T. (1989). The effects of regular aerobic exercise on short-term memory efficiency in the older adult. In Ostrow, A. C. (ed.), *Aging and motor behavior* (pp. 105-113). Indianapolis: Benchmark Press.

Adler, S. S. (1983). Seeking stillness in motion: An introduction to tai chi for seniors. *Activities, Adaptation, and Aging, 3*(4), 1-14.

Anderson, R. A. and Anderson, J. E. (1980). *Stretching.* Bolinas, CA: Shelter Publications.

Arnold, L. C. (1977). Organization of exercise programs. In R. Harris and L. J. Frankel (eds.), *Guide to fitness after fifty.* (pp. 233-236). NY: Plenum.

Asplund, L., Hester, M., and MacRae, P. G. (1993). The effects of a twelve-week prompted walking program on walking endurance, gait, and balance in frail nursing home residents. *Journal of Aging and Physical Activity, 1*(1), 91.

Associated Press (1999). Walking: A good workout for older minds. *The New York Times,* August 3, p. D10.

Berger, B. G. and Hecht, L. M. (1989). Exercise, aging, and psychological well-being: The mind-body question. In Ostrow, A. C. (ed.), *Aging and motor behavior* (pp. 117-157). Indianapolis: Benchmark Press.

Blankfort-Doyle, W., Waxman, H., Coughey, K., Naso, F., Carner, E. A., and Fox, E. (1989). An exercise program for nursing home residents. In Ostrow, A. C. (ed.), *Aging and motor behavior* (pp. 201-216). Indianapolis: Benchmark Press.

Brody, J. E. (1994a). New exercise benefits for the elderly. *The New York Times,* August 24, p. B8.

Brody, J. E. (1994b). Runners are ahead in aging healthfully. *The New York Times,* October 12, p. B9.

Brody, J. E. (1995). Trying to reconcile exercise findings. *The New York Times,* April 23, p. Y9.

Brody, J. E. (1999). Falls by elderly, a perilous yet preventable epidemic. *The New York Times,* June 8, p. D8.

Brody, J. E. (2002). Push up the weights, and roll back the years. *The New York Times,* June 4, p. D7.

Centers for Disease Control (1989). Surgeon general's workshop on health promotion and aging: Summary recommendations of physical fitness and exercise working group. *Journal of the American Medical Association, 262*(18), 2507-2508.

Clark, G. (1994). Water exercises for senior adults: Prescription for fun and fitness. *Journal of Physical Education, Recreation, and Dance, 65*(6), 18-21.

Clark, J. (1992). *Full life fitness: A complete exercise program for mature adults.* Champaign, IL: Human Kinetics Publishers.

Corbin, D. E. and Corbin, J. M. (1983). *Reach for it: A handbook of exercise and dance activities for older adults.* Dubuque, IA: Eddie Bowers Publishing.

Cosky, A. C. (1993). Fitness programming for the well elderly: Some practical pointers. *Journal of Physical Education, Recreation, and Dance, 64*(4), 58-59.

Duida, J. L. and Tappe, M. K. (1989). Personal investment in exercise among middle-aged and older adults. In Ostrow, A. C. (ed.), *Aging and motor behavior* (pp. 219-238). Indianapolis: Benchmark Press.

Dustman, R. E., Ruhling, R. O., Russell, E. M., Shearer, D. E., Bonekat, H. W., Shigeoka, J. W., Wood, J. S., and Bradford, D. C. (1989). Aerobic exercise training and improved neuropsychological function of older individuals. In Ostrow, A. C. (ed.), *Aging and motor behavior* (pp. 67-83). Indianapolis: Benchmark Press.

Dzewaltowski, D. A. (1989). A social cognitive theory of older adult exercise motivation. In Ostrow, A. C. (ed.), *Aging and motor behavior* (pp. 257-281). Indianapolis: Benchmark Press.

Eggers, J. L. (1988). Well-elderly women's entrance and adherence to structured physical fitness programs. *Activities, Adaptation, and Aging,* 11(1), 21-30.

"Elders: Ready, steady, go" (1993). *Health,* January/February, pp. 10-11.

Flatten, K. (1982). Physical fitness and self-sufficiency in persons over 60 years. *Activities, Adaptation, and Aging,* 3(2), 69-78.

Flatten, K., Wilhite, B., and Reyes-Watson, E. (1988). *Exercise activities for the elderly.* New York: Springer Publishing.

"Frailty, strength training, and nutritional supplementation in the very old" (1995). *Journal of Aging and Physical Activity,* 3(1), 108-109.

Frankel, L. J. and Richard, B. B. (1980). *Be alive as long as you live.* New York: Lippincott and Crowell.

Friend, T. (1993). Don't look back, father time, Mavis Lindgren, 86, is gaining on you. *The New York Times,* November 9, p. B13.

Goggin, N. L. and Keller, M. J. (1993). Movement is ageless: Enhancing leisure participation. *Journal of Physical Education, Recreation, and Dance,* 64(4), 55-57.

Goggin, N. L. and Morrow, J. R. (2001). Physical activity behaviors of older adults. *Journal of Aging and Physical Activity,* 9, 58-65.

Gorman, C. (1995). No sweat? Then no extra years. *Time,* May 1, p. 59.

Grahn-Kronhed, A. C., Möller, C., Olsson, B., and Möller, M. (2001). The effects of short-term balance training on community-dwelling older adults. *Journal of Aging and Physical Activity,* 9(1), 19-31.

Harris, R. and Frankel, L. J. (eds.) (1977). *Guide to fitness after fifty.* New York: Plenum.

Herbert, L. and Teague, M. L. (1989). Exercise adherence and older adults: A theoretical perspective. *Activities, Adaptation, and Aging,* 13(1/2), 91-104.

Hird, J. S. and Williams, J. M. (1989). The psychological effects of chronic exercise in the elderly. In Ostrow, A. C. (ed.), *Aging and motor behavior* (pp. 173-200). Indianapolis, IN: Benchmark Press.

Hoover, W. (2002). Erwin Jaskulski, 100, runs fast. *Island Weekly,* November 21-27, p. 16.

Hunter, G. R., Wetzstein, C. J., Fields, D. A., Brown, A., and Bamman, M. M. (2000). Resistance training increases total energy expenditure and free-living physical activity in older adults. *Journal of Applied Physiology,* 89(3), 977-984.

"It's never too late to start exercising" (2003). *University of California, Berkeley Wellness Letter,* 19(7), 1.

Iwaoka, K., Tanaka, N., Kagawa, M., Amano, T., and Kaneda, Y. (1993). Developing adapted physical activities based on the psychosocial and physiological characteristics of the elderly. *Journal of Aging and Physical Activity,* 1(1), 103.

Jamieson, R. H. (1982). *Exercises for the elderly.* Verplank, NY: Emerson.

Jones, J. (1993). *Strength conditioning: Vital to enhancing mobility throughout life.* Fullerton: California State University, Fullerton.

Karper, W. B. and Goldfarb, A. H. (1994). Effects of exercise on acute upper and lower respiratory tract infections in older adults. *Therapeutic Recreation Journal,* 27(1), 8-17.

Kaufman, T. (1989). Israeli marathoner runs for his life—around the world. *The Northern California Jewish Bulletin,* August 18, p. 17.

Khatri, P., Blumenthal, J. A., Bubyak, M. A., Craighead, W. E., Herman, S., Baldewicz, T., Madden, D. J., Doraiswamy, M., Waugh, R., and Krishnan, K. R. (2001). Effects of exercise training on cognitive functioning among depressed older men and women. *Journal of Aging and Physical Activity,* 9(1), 43-57.

Knierim, H. and Gandee, R. (1993). Participant and performance change in the National Senior Olympics. *Journal of Aging and Physical Activity,* 1(1), 64.

Kressig, R. W. and Echt, K. V. (2002). Exercise prescribing: Computer application in older adults. *Gerontologist,* 42(2), 273-277.

LaCroix, A. Z., Guralnik, J. M., Berkman, L. F., Wallace, R. B., and Satterfield, S. (1993). Maintaining mobility in later life: Smoking, alcohol consumption, physical activity, and body mass index. *American Journal of Epidemiology,* 137, 858-869.

Laditka, S. B. and Laditka, J. N. (2001). Effects of improved morbidity rates on active life expectancy and eligibility for long-term care services. *Journal of Applied Gerontology,* 20(1), 39-56.

Leaf, A. (1975). *Youth in old age.* New York: McGraw-Hill.

Leslie, D. K. (1989). *Mature stuff: Physical activity for the older adult.* Reston, VA: American Alliance for Health, Physical Education, Recreation, and Dance.

McBride, C. and Lefler, K. (1986). *Senior shape-up: An exercise guide for the very active to the physically restricted.* Tallahassee, FL: Loiry Publishing House.

Messier, S. P., Loeser, R. F., Mitchell, M. N., Valle, G., Morgan, T. P., Rejeski, W. J., and Ettinger, W. H. (2000). Exercise and weight loss in obese older adults with knee osteoarthritis: A preliminary study. *Journal of the American Geriatrics Society,* 48(9), 1062-1072.

Neergaard, L. (1999). Researchers design fitness performance standards for the elderly. *The Boston Globe,* June 5, p. A5.

Norton, S. (1977). *Yoga for people over fifty.* Old Greenwich, CT: Devin-Adair.

O'Connor, P. J., Aenchbacher, L. E., and Dishman, R. K. (1993). Physical activity and depression in the elderly. *Journal of Aging and Physical Activity,* 1(1), 34-58.

O'Neil, J. (2003). Exercising to your own rules. *The New York Times,* February 18, p. D6.

Paffenbarger, R. S. Jr., Hyde, R. T., Wing, A. L., I-Min Lee, M. B., Jung, D. L., and Kampert, J. B. (1993). The association of changes in physical activity level and other lifestyle characteristics with mortality among men. *The New England Journal of Medicine,* 328, 538-545.

Parker, S. D., Will, C., and Burke, C. L. (1989). *Activities for the elderly: A guide to quality programming.* Owings Mills, MD: National Health Publishing.

Pate, D. W. and Pierce, E. F. (1993). Mood alterations in older adults following exercise. *Journal of Aging and Physical Activity,* 1(1), 107.

Penner, D. (1990). *Elder fit: A health and fitness guide for older adults.* Reston, VA: American Alliance for Health, Physical Education, Recreation, and Dance.

Pepe, M. V. (1993). Payoff index that can predict older women's involvement in physical activities, with suggestions for programming. *Journal of Aging and Physical Activity,* 1(1), 107.

Perri, S. and Templer, D. I. (1985). The effects of an aerobic exercise program on psychological variables in older adults. *International Journal of Aging and Human Development,* 20(3), 167-171.

Pescatello, L. Murphy, D., and Costanzo, D. (2000). Low-intensity physical activity benefits blood lipids and lipoproteins in older adults living at home. *Age and Ageing,* 29(5), 433-439.

"Psychosocial factors and exercise in Japan" (1995). *Journal of Aging and Physical Activity,* 3(1), 111-112.

Puggaard, L., Larsen, J. B., Stovring, H., and Jeune, B. (2000). Maximal oxygen uptake, muscle strength and walking speed in 85-year-old women: Effects of increased physical activity. *Aging,* 12(3), 180-189.

Ross, C. E. and Hayes, D. (1988). Exercise and psychologic well-being in the community. *American Journal of Epidemiology,* 127(4), 762-771.

Schafer, W. (1990a). Exercise and smarts in later years. *Stress and Health Report,* November/December, p. 1. Chico, CA: Enloe Hospital Stress and Health Center.

Schafer, W. (1990b). Fitness and aging. *Stress and Health Report,* September/October p. 1. Chico, CA: Enloe Hospital Stress and Health Center.

Sharon, B., Boyette, L. W., Anderson, K. A., and Brandon, L. J. (1993). Effects of strength training on muscle fitness development in older women. *Journal of Aging and Physical Activity,* 1(1), 109-110.

Shephard, R. J. (1994). Determinants of exercise in people aged 65 years and older. In Dishman, R. K. (ed.), *Advances in exercise adherence* (pp. 343-360). Champaign, IL: Human Kinetics.

Sherwood, T. (1991). *The effect of intergenerational sports and games on the attitudes of college students and elders toward each other.* Chico, CA: California State University, Chico. Master's thesis.

Spirduso, W.W. (1983). Exercise and the aging brain. *Research Quarterly for Exercise and Sport,* 54(2), 208-210.

"Strength and mobility relationships in the elderly" (1995). *Journal of Aging and Physical Activity,* 3(1), 110-111.

"Study shows a stroll by elderly adds years" (1998). *The New York Times,* January 8, p. A15.

"Study shows exercise reduces falls by the aged" (1995). *The New York Times,* May 3, p. B9.

Teague, M. L. (1989). The 1990 PHS exercise objectives for older adults: Should they be changed? *Activities, Adaptation, and Aging,* 13(1/2), 107-115.

Thompson, S. (1993). PIPERS—Seniors leading seniors to good health. *Journal of Aging and Physical Activity,* 1(1), 110.

Toole, T. and Abourezk, T. (1989). Aerobic function, information processing, and aging. In Ostrow, A. C. (ed.), *Aging and motor behavior* (pp. 37-65). Indianapolis: Benchmark Press.

Toth, M. J., Gardner, A. W., Ades, P. A., and Poehlman, E. T. (1995). Contributions of body composition and physical activity to age-related decline in peak VO2. *Journal of Aging and Physical Activity,* 3(1), 110.

Wannamethee, S. G., Shaper, A. G., and Walker, M. (2000). Physical activity and mortality in older men with diagnosed coronary heart disease. *American Health Association Journal,* 102(12), 1358-1363.

Weiss, J. C. (1990). The "Feeling Great!" wellness program for older adults. *Activities, Adaptation, and Aging,* 12 (3/4), 1-59, 103-199.

Whitehouse, F. A. (1977). Motivation for fitness. In R. Harris and L. J. Frankel (eds.), *Guide to fitness after fifty* (pp. 171-190). New York: Plenum.

Work, J. (1989). Strength training: A bridge to independence for the elderly. *Physician and Sports Medicine,* 17(11), 134-140.

"Work out at 80? Experts see the gains" (2001). *The New York Times,* February 13, p. D8.

Chapter 13

Adapted Dance for Older Adults

INTRODUCTION

This chapter provides an overview of adapted dance for older adults, including program rationale and guidelines for leading and planning adapted dance sessions. A brief review of literature is presented in order to clarify the values and benefits of adapted dance, followed by guidelines for leading an adapted dance session. This section includes a description of the components of an adapted dance program and important considerations in leading a session for impaired elders. In the last section, actual adapted dance programs are presented, including examples of adaptations for folk, square, ballet, tap, and modern dance.

LEARNING OBJECTIVES

The learning objectives of this chapter are to be able to

1. understand the importance and benefits of adapted dance for elders,
2. select appropriate activities for an adapted dance session including opening, warm-up, creative dance patterns, and cooling off activities,
3. lead breathing and relaxation exercises and incorporate these exercises appropriately into an adapted dance program,
4. adapt and lead folk dances suitable for various groups of elders,
5. adapt and lead square dances suitable for various groups of elders,
6. conduct a class in simple ballet techniques for elders,
7. adapt and lead tap dances for various groups of elders, and
8. incorporate modern dance into activity programming and effectively adapt modern dance techniques to fit an older population.

RATIONALE

Adapted dance can be defined as the use of movement as a means of self-expression and communication that promotes a healthy relationship between mind and body. Adapted dance utilizes movement to provide outlets for expression and socialization that can lead to increased feelings of self-worth (Caplow-Lindner, Harpaz, and Samberg, 1979).

The physical and psychosocial benefits of exercise discussed in the previous chapter also apply to adapted dance as it is a form of exercise. A unique benefit of dance is improved nonverbal communication skills. According to Wapner (1981), communicating through movement patterns during an adapted dance session can improve psychological well-being. Through the use of nonverbal communication, interactions can occur among participants of the dance group that might not have been possible through verbal means. This communication can help to redirect an individual's focus away from self-absorption to an orientation more focused on the external environment.

Other benefits can be derived from adapted dance. Through movement, tension is released, which, in turn, reduces stress. Caplow-Lindner, Harpaz, and Samberg (1979) suggested that emotions, both positive and negative, are expressed through movement. Adapted dance is especially suited for elders in that it provides reality orientation and the older adult is encouraged to utilize both long- and short-term memory skills, adjust to reality, and gain new interests or remotivate old interests.

Participation in an adapted dance program provides opportunities to improve socialization skills. The group setting of an adapted dance program encourages a sense of unity, feelings of empathy and support, responses of acceptance, and develops interpersonal relationships (Caplow-Lindner, Harpaz, and Samberg, 1979).

The challenge for leisure services providers working with elders is how to enable impaired elders to reap the benefits of dance, thus the emphasis in this chapter on adapting dance for participation by elders in a seated position. Most elders cannot only participate in, but can excel in many dance forms. Horosko (1990) describes the success of dance-performing groups such as the Forever Young Dancers, the Twiliters, and the Dancers of the Third Age, all of which are comprised of dancers from ages sixty to ninety and are able to maintain rigorous performing and touring schedules. Spilner (1993) discusses the benefits of line dancing for elders and describes the Dancin' Grannies of Sun Lakes, Arizona, a group of twenty-seven women, ages fifty-nine to seventy-two, who perform vigorous, high-kicking line dancing and who tour nationally and have appeared on television.

GUIDELINES FOR LEADING
ADAPTED DANCE PROGRAMS

An adapted dance session should have four components: (1) the opening—participants get acquainted and are oriented to the upcoming activity; (2) the warm-up—the body is prepared for exercise through light movements; (3) the adapted dance patterns—adaptations of folk, square, ballet, tap, or modern dance sequences are taught; and (4) the cool-off—light movements are executed to relax and return the body to a relaxed state.

Opening

The adapted dance leader should welcome the participants, make introductions, and give a brief overview of the upcoming adapted dance activity.

Warm-Up

The purpose of the warm-up is to promote participant involvement in movement from a relaxed state. Through the use of light movements, the energy level is raised, respiration is increased, and circulation is stimulated. Eight basic actions that utilize imagery to encourage movement and are appropriate for the warm-up list that follows. (The list is based on Wethered's [1973] book on movement therapy.)

1. Thrusting (hammering and punching)
2. Pressing (pushing and pulling)
3. Wringing (screwing and unscrewing a jar lid)
4. Slashing (cutting wheat or cracking a whip)
5. Flicking (brushing off dust)
6. Dabbing (patting on powder)
7. Gliding (smoothing a tablecloth, ironing clothes)
8. Floating (moving like a feather in a breeze)

The warm-up should utilize body movements with variations of space, time, and energy. The following techniques are also appropriate for a warm-up period. (Refer to pages 19-21 of Wethered's [1973] book on movement therapy):

1. *Stretching:* Stretching all muscle groups causes a limbering up of body parts. Directions, levels, time variations (fast and slow), and en-

ergy variations (strong and weak) can all be explored by stretching various muscles.

2. *Swinging:* Swinging allows individuals to discover the relationship between release and control of different body parts. Swinging aids in exploring one's own natural rhythm.
3. *Slapping and rubbing:* Slapping and rubbing different body parts stimulate the circulation and boost the energy level.
4. *Clapping:* Clapping hands using different space patterns (up and down, side to side, forward and backward, etc.) increases the movement range. Various forms of energy can also be explored through clapping (heavy and light, etc.).

Breathing exercises and massage are appropriate during the warm-up phase of an adapted dance program but should also be interspersed throughout the adapted dance patterns phase of the session in order to allow participants to rest periodically throughout the session. The breathing, massage, and relaxation exercises described below are based on Caplow-Lindner, Harpaz, and Samberg's (1979) work on expressive movement.

Breathing Exercises

The following are examples of breathing exercises:

1. *Abdominal breathing:* Inhale through the nostrils, lowering the diaphragm and pushing out the rib cage. On the exhalation, say "HA," forcing the air from the lungs, raising the diaphragm, and contracting the abdomen. On the exhalation, breathe out as much air as possible.
2. Inhale through the nostrils and push out the abdomen. Exhale slowly through pursed lips.
3. Breathe slowly and deeply through the nose.

Relaxation Exercises

In a supine or sitting position, participants are instructed to progressively relax muscle groups starting from the feet and working toward the head or vice versa. The leader instructs the participants to relax specific body parts. Relaxation exercises can be accomplished by squeezing and releasing muscles, shaking body parts, raising and lowering body parts, or curling and uncurling body parts.

Massage

The use of massage during an adapted dance session stimulates circulation and improves skin and muscle tone. Massage can be by the leader, partner, or self. To effectively stimulate circulation, massage should include stroking, kneading, or tapping.

Adapted Dance Patterns

Adapted dance patterns incorporate creative or expressive experiences through movement. This portion of the adapted dance program can include adapted folk, square, ballet, tap, or modern dance. Examples of adapted dance patterns are explained in detail later in the chapter.

Cool-Off

Perform movements of decreasing intensity. Slow, controlled movements stretch and relax the muscles and cool down the body (Lopez, 1983).

Some examples of cooling-off exercises follow:

1. *In a seated position:*
    a. reach up with one arm high overhead while the other arm is relaxed and bent at the elbow with the hand touching the shoulder;
    b. alternate arms by reaching up with the bent arm and bringing the stretched arm back to the shoulder;
    c. perform this stretching motion for eight counts while concentrating on breathing and stretching;
    d. then, doing this for eight counts, bring both hands to the back of the head, elbows out, and gently rotate the head and spine while allowing the upper torso to relax;
    e. do this motion for eight counts; and
    f. repeat complete exercise three more times.
2. *In a seated position:*
    a. inhale and extend arms high overhead;
    b. exhale and bring arms back down to sides; and
    c. repeat three more times.

End the dance session with a relaxation exercise.

SPECIAL CONSIDERATIONS
IN PLANNING ADAPTED DANCE SESSIONS

When planning adapted dance sessions for older adults, use individual needs to create a more meaningful experience for the participants. The use of repetition and nonstrenuous movement will improve the older adult's ability to succeed in performing the dance patterns. Providing relaxation and breathing exercises will loosen muscles and reduce fatigue. Massage is another beneficial diversion, creating feelings of relaxation and reducing stress.

Total body exercise should be an objective for a session of adapted dance. As many body parts as possible should be involved in a single dance.

When adapting movement patterns of a dance, an infinite number of variations exists for each step. The dance leader should not feel limited to maintaining a similarity between the original and adapted movements; however, when feasible, it is desirable to do so.

Adapted dance programs for elders should facilitate a social and supportive atmosphere. A special consideration in developing adapted dances is, when possible, allowing for personal contact. Personal contact is an integral component of folk and square dance.

A final consideration in programming adapted dance sessions is to avoid unnecessary accidents. Caution is advised to prevent wheelchairs from colliding, participants from falling, and overexertion. The elders should be moving, not their wheelchairs.

ADAPTED DANCE PATTERNS

Modified versions of folk, square, ballet, tap, and modern dance are presented in this section.

Adapted Folk Dance

Folk dance provides specific movement patterns that may be more appropriate for people who feel inhibited with spontaneous movement. The basic nature of folk dance requires a cohesive group setting that creates a group identity and a sharing of experiences. Sharing and being part of a group enhance verbal and nonverbal communication (Feder and Feder, 1981).

Folk Dance Objectives

The following are folk dance objectives as presented by Feder and Feder (1981):

1. The scope of movement patterns is broadened by learning new movement sequences.
2. Body consciousness is heightened as one sees how he or she moves in relation to other group members.
3. An individual's own body alignment can be improved by observing other people's movement styles.
4. Tensions are reduced through movement.
5. Socialization skills can be improved by belonging to a group and sharing interactions with group members.

How to Adapt Folk Dance for an Older Population

High-functioning older adults may be capable of performing the actual folk dance steps without modification of movements. For moderately impaired and lower-functioning elders, adaptation of folk dance is necessary to enable participation. The following section focuses primarily on adaptations for folk dance for moderately impaired and lower-functioning older adults.

Adapted folk dance for impaired elders should be performed from a seated position in order to allow individuals with limited mobility to participate. Movements of all body parts should be incorporated into the adapted folk dance to accomplish total body involvement.

When teaching an adapted folk dance to impaired older adults, demonstrate the movements first without the music. The participants should have the opportunity to review the steps slowly, without the music, until they become familiar with the steps and are prepared to keep pace with the music. In addition, the adapted movements should be synchronized with the music.

Dances that are appropriately modified for the moderately impaired require further modification for lower-functioning elders, such as nursing home residents. Simple movements, which do not require a large range of motion, are appropriate. Fast movements should be replaced by movements that occur on every other beat so that participants are able to keep pace. More repetition is incorporated into the dance, making the dance easier to learn and perform.

A buddy or partner system that matches higher- and lower-functioning individuals should be established and facilitated through an appropriate seating arrangement. Consequently, the higher-functioning participants will be able to assist those individuals experiencing difficulty. If a sufficient number of volunteers or assistants is available, disperse them among the group members to offer help. Lower-functioning individuals may enjoy the activity as well as merely being part of the group, even though they are not able to keep pace with the movement sequences.

Folk dance is an especially appropriate dance form through which to incorporate physical contact. When seated in a close circle, participants can easily touch their neighbors.

Examples of some adapted folk dances are presented on the following pages. In order to clearly illustrate how to modify folk dances for elders, each dance has been presented in three columns:

1. *Dance steps:* The actual dance steps for the folk dance are listed in the left column.
2. *Adapted dance steps:* The adapted dance steps for performing the folk dance with moderately impaired elders (e.g., adult day care participants, retirement home residents, or frail elders attending multipurpose senior centers) are listed in the middle column.
3. *Simplified adapted dance steps:* A simplified version of the adapted dance steps is described in the third column. The simplified version in this column is geared toward the more severely impaired elders typically found in nursing homes.

The following abbreviations are used in the folk dance examples presented on the following pages:

(L) = left
(R) = right
CW = clockwise
CCW = counterclockwise

The following adapted folk dances are presented in Tables 13.1-13.5:

Table 13.1. Ve David (Israeli Mixer)
Table 13.2. Pata Pata (African)
Table 13.3. Mayim (Israeli)
Table 13.4. Ma Navu (Israeli)
Table 13.5. Troika (Russian)

TABLE 13.1. Ve David (Israeli Mixer)

Dance Steps	Adapted Dance Steps	Simplified Adapted Dance Steps
Record: Folk Dancer MH 1153		Music 4/4
Formation:	*Formation:*	*Formation:*
Couples	Seated in circle, facing center	Seated in a circle, facing center
Double circle facing counterclockwise	Chairs arranged close enough so that people can hold hands	Chairs arranged close enough so that people can hold hands
Woman on right side of man		
Both begin with right foot		
Steps:	*Steps:*	*Steps:*
1. Introduction	1. Introduction	1. Introduction
2. Couples walk counterclockwise—4 steps	2. Clap hands—count of 4	2. Clap hands—every other count—4 times
3. All join hands facing inward and form a single circle—walk back 4 steps	3. Clap hands high overhead—count of 4	3. Clap hands on knees—every other count—4 times
4. All walk in toward the center of the circle—4 steps	4. Stomp feet—count of 4	4. Thump heels on floor—every other count—4 times
5. All walk back—4 steps	5. Click heels together off the ground—count of 4	5. Snap fingers—every other count—4 times

317

TABLE 13.1 (continued)

6. Ladies walk in to the center—4 steps (men clap)	6. Step (R), Step (L), Step (R), Step (L)	6. All join hands and sway from side to side—8 counts
7. Ladies walk back—4 steps	7. Walk forward[1] (remain seated)—count of 4	End of sequence
8. Men walk in to the center—4 steps	8. Walk back[2]—count of 4	Repeat
9. Men make a sharp turn and walk 4 steps to the woman on the right of partner	9. Snap fingers—count of 4	
10. With new partners: do a buzz swing[3]—count of 8	10. All hold hands and sway from side to side—count of 8	
End of sequence	End of sequence	
Repeat	Repeat	

[1]Walk forward: Simulate small walking steps forward in a seated position.
[2]Walk back: Simulate small walking steps backward in a seated position.
[3]Buzz swing: right hips together, right foot carries weight of body and the left foot pushes. With each push, the left foot momentarily takes the weight. The left foot should not get ahead of the right foot. The right arm holds partner around the waist, left hand held high.
Adapted steps for Ve David include arm, leg, and upper torso movements; physical contact; and the ability to distinguish musical beats and rhythm.

TABLE 13.2. Pata Pata (African)

Dance Steps	Adapted Dance Steps	Simplified Adapted Dance Steps
		Music 4/4
Record: Reprise 0732		
Formation:	*Formation:*	*Formation:*
Performed individually	Seated in a circle	Seated in a circle
Standing facing (N)	Facing center	Facing center
Feet together	(Entire dance performed seated)	Hands in lap, palms together
(N) (W) (E) (S)		
Steps:	*Steps:*	*Steps:*
1. Touch (R) toe to floor to right side (about 12 inches)	1. Touch (R) toe to (R) side	1. Fling (R) hand to right
2. Bring (R) foot back	2. Bring (R) foot back	2. Bring (R) hand back
3. Touch (L) toe to (L) side	3. Touch (L) foot to (L) side	3. Fling (L) hand to left
4. Bring (L) foot back	4. Bring (L) foot back	4. Bring (L) hand back
5. Separate toes	5. Separate toes	5. Separate heels of hands
(L) (R)	(L) (R)	(L) (R)
6. Separate heels	6. Separate heels	6. Separate fingers
(L) (R)	(L) (R)	(L) (R)

319

TABLE 13.2 *(continued)*

7. Bring heels together (L) (R)	7. Bring heels together (L) (R)	7. Bring fingers together (L) (R)
8. Bring toes together (L) (R)	8. Bring toes together (L) (R)	8. Bring heels of hands together (L) (R)
(Feet are now back together)	(Feet are now back together)	(Hands are now back together)
9. Fling (R) knee up (hip level) and over diagonally left	9. Bring (R) knee up and over diagonally to left	9. Clap hands to knees 4 times
10. Bring (R) foot back to floor	10. Bring (R) foot back to floor	10. Clap hands together 4 times
11. Kick (R) foot across body diagonally left	11. Bring (L) knee up and over diagonally right	End of sequence
12. Step on (R) foot and pivot 1/4 turn to right (clockwise) to face (E)	12. Bring (L) foot back to floor	Repeat
13. Kick (L) foot out	13. Clap hands 4 times	
14. Step backward on (L) foot	End of sequence	
15. Step backward on (R) foot	Repeat	
16. Step backward on (L) foot		
End of sequence		
Repeat dance facing (E), then (S), then (W)		

This upbeat dance requires some degree of spatial awareness in order to perform the adapted and simplified dance steps correctly.

TABLE 13.3. Mayim (Israeli)

Dance Steps	Adapted Dance Steps	Simplified Adapted Dance Steps
Record: Folkraft 1108, 1475X45, LP-12		Music 4/4
Formation:	*Formation:*	*Formation:*
Single circle facing center, hands joined	Seated in a circle facing center	Seated in a circle facing center, holding hands
Steps:	*Steps:*	*Steps:*
1. Grapevine. Move clockwise. Cross (R) foot in front of left. Step (L) foot to side. Cross (R) foot behind left. Step (L) foot to side. Continue to count of 16	1. Step forward with (R) foot—count of 1	1. Step forward with (R) foot—count of 1
2. Run to center—count of 4	2. Step forward with (L) foot—count of 1	2. Step forward with (L) foot—count of 1
3. Scissor kick	3. Bring (R) foot back—count of 1	3. Bring (R) foot back—count of 1
4. Run backward—count of 3	4. Bring (L) foot back—count of 1	4. Bring (L) foot back—count of 1
5. Run to center—count of 4	5. Repeat this sequence 3 more times	5. Repeat this sequence 3 more times
6. Scissor kick	6. Raise arms overhead—count of 4	6. Drop neighbors' hands and raise hands to chin level—count of 4
7. Run backward—count of 4	7. Clap overhead—count of 1	7. Clap hands—count of 1
8. Four running steps clockwise	8. Bring arms down—count of 3	8. Bring hands back down to chair—count of 3
9. Face center. Hop on (R), touch (L) across front of (R) side. Hop on (R), touch (L) to side. Hop on (R), touch (L) in front of (R) side. Hop on (R), touch (L) to side	9. Bring arms up overhead—count of 4	9. Raise hands to chin level—count of 4

321

TABLE 13.3 (continued)

10. Hop on (L), touch (R) in front of (L) side. Hop on (L), touch (R) to side (arms out to sides shoulder high). Hop on (L), touch (R) in front of (L) side (hands clap overhead). Hop on (L), touch (R) to side (arms out to sides)	10. Clap overhead—count of 1	10. Clap hands—count of 1
11. Bring arms down—count of 3		11. Bring hands back down to chair—count of 3
12. Stomp both feet—count of 4		12. Shrug shoulders twice—count of 4
13. Arms out to sides, clap hands with neighbors—count of 8		13. Bring hands out to sides and clap hands with neighbors 4 times—count of 8
14. Holding neighbors' hands, make arm circles—count of 8		14. Holding neighbors' hands, make arm circles—count of 8
End of sequence		End of sequence
Repeat		Repeat
End of sequence		
Repeat		

This dance incorporates both leg and arm movements. An appealing aspect of the dance is the physical contact that occurs among the dancers.

TABLE 13.4. Ma Navu (Israeli)

Dance Steps	Adapted Dance Steps	Simplified Adapted Dance Steps
		Music ¾
Record: Tikva LP-T 100A		
Formation:	Formation:	Formation:
Circle, facing center; hands joined	Seated in a circle; hands joined	Seated in a circle; hands joined
Part I	Part I	Part I
1. Bring (R) foot forward 6 inches and touch floor—count "one"	1. Bring (R) foot forward 6 inches and touch the toe to the floor—count "one"	1. Bring (R) foot forward and touch the toe to the floor—count "one"
2. Touch (R) foot to (R) side—count "two"	2. Touch (R) foot to (R) side—count "three"	2. Touch (R) foot to (R) side—count "two"
3. Step (R) foot behind (L) foot—count "three"	3. Step (R)—count "three"	3. Step (R)—count "three"
4. Step (L) foot to (L) side—count "and"	4. Step (L)—count "and"	4. Step (L)—count "and"
5. Step (R) foot across in front—count "four"	5. Step (R)—count "four"	5. Step (R)—count "four"
6. Rock back on (L) foot—count "one and"	6. Point (R) toe forward 6 inches and touch floor, lift foot—count "one and"	6. Bring (R) foot forward and touch the toe to the floor, lift foot—count "one and"
7. Rock forward on (R) foot—count "two and"	7. Touch (R) toe again 6 inches forward—count "two and"	7. Touch (R) toe again—count "two and"
8. Rock back on (L) foot—count "three"	8. Bring (R) foot back to (L) foot—count "three"	8. Bring (R) foot back to (L) foot—count "three"
9. (R) foot forward, stepping in place—count "and"	9. Lift both heels off the ground—count "and"	9. Lift both heels off the ground—count "and"
10. Close (L) foot to (R) foot—count "four"	10. Bring heels back down to floor—count "four"	10. Bring heels back down to floor—count "four"

TABLE 13.4 (continued)

11. Repeat Part I, beginning with (L) foot	11. Repeat Part I, beginning with (L) foot	11. Repeat Part I, beginning with (L) foot
Part II	Part II	Part II
1. Yemenite step[a], (R)—count "one and two"	1. Step (R) foot to (R) side (about 6 inches)—count "one"	1. Drop neighbors' hands, raise hands up to shoulder level—count "one, two, three, and"
2. brush (L) foot across to (R), turning CCW—count "and"	2. Step (L) foot in place—count "and"	2. Snap fingers—count "four"
3. Step (R) foot—count "three"	3. Cross (R) foot over in front of (L) foot—count "two"	3. Bring hands down—count "one, two, three, four." Repeat Part II 3 more times
4. Close (L) foot—count "and"	4. Cross (L) foot over in front of (R)—count "and"	End of sequence
5. Step (R) foot—count "four"	5. Close (R) foot to (L) foot—count "three" across in	Repeat
6. Face center	6. Step (L) foot in place—count "and"	
Repeat Part II 3 more times	7. Step (R) foot in place—count "four"	
End of sequence	Repeat Part II 3 more times	
Repeat	End of sequence	
	Repeat	

aYemenite step = Step (R) foot to right side (about 6 inches) with a rocking motion. Step on (L) foot in place. Cross (R) foot in front of (L) foot.
Dancers hold hands throughout most of the dance. Thus, this dance provides a needed outlet for physical contact. The dance moves at a slower pace than the other dances and creates a peaceful atmosphere.

TABLE 13.5. Troika (Russian)

Dance Steps	Adapted Dance Steps	Simplified Adapted Dance Steps
Record: Folk Dancer MH 1059		Music 4/4
Formation:	*Formation:*	*Formation:*
Groups of 3, standing side by side holding hands	Groups of 3, seated in a triangle, one member identified as "center person"	Groups of 3, seated in a triangle, one member identified as "center person"
Face counterclockwise in a large circle		
Steps:	*Steps:*	*Steps:*
1. 8 forward running steps	1. Walk forward—8 counts	1. Clap hands every other count—4 times
2. 8 backward running steps	2. Walk backward—8 counts	2. Clap hands to knees every other count—4 times
3. 8 running steps in place; the person on the right goes through the front side of the arch formed by the center person and the person on the left, and back to the original position. The center person follows and makes a left turn under his or her own left arm	3. Center person joins hands with person on the right; then they clap hands together for 8 counts	3. Center person and the person on the right then join hands and push and pull—8 counts

325

TABLE 13.5 *(continued)*

4. The person on the left initiates the same sequence as above	4. Center person shifts toward person on the left; they join hands and clap hands together for 8 counts	4. Center person shifts to the person on the left; they join hands and push and pull—8 counts
5. Each trio joins hands, forming a circle of three, and does the grapevine (CW) for 12 counts, then jumps 3 times, shifting directions (left, right, left)	5. Trio joins hands and takes small steps to the left for 12 counts	5. Trio joins hands and takes six steps (step on every other count)
6. Trio does grapevine (CCW) for 12 counts, jumps 3 times, shifting directions (left, right, left)	6. Trio drops hands and claps their own hands 3 times	6. Drop hands and clap 3 times
7. Center person runs forward to join next group	7. Rejoin hands and side step back to the right for 12 counts	7. Trio rejoins hands and takes 6 steps (step on every other count)
End of sequence	8. Trio drops hands and claps 3 times	8. Trio drops hands and claps 3 times
Repeat	End of sequence	End of sequence
	Repeat	Repeat

This dance is different from the other dances in that groups of three dancers each join together to perform the dance. Consequently, the dance becomes a more intimate experience, involving the combined efforts of three people.

The record companies from which the music for each folk dance is available are identified at the top of each chart. A list of the record companies and their addresses appears at the end of the chapter.

Table 13.1 lists the movements for "Ve David," an Israeli folk dance. "Ve David" is a lively dance performed by couples in a circle formation. The adapted dance steps for impaired elders are designed to be performed from a seated position in a circle arrangement. A movement is performed on every beat. The simplified adapted dance steps for lower-functioning elders incorporate a smaller range of steps, and movements are performed on every other beat.

Table 13.2 lists the movements for "Pata Pata," an African folk dance. "Pata Pata" is performed individually. The adapted dance steps for moderately impaired elders are very similar to the actual dance steps, but they are performed from a seated position. The simplified adapted dance steps for lower-functioning elders incorporate only arm and hand movements; however, these movements are based on the actual leg movements.

Table 13.3 lists the movements for "Mayim," and Israeli folk dance. "Mayim" is a high-energy dance performed in a circle. The adapted dance steps for moderately impaired elders require a small stepping motion with the feet, arm movements, and combined movement efforts with individuals seated next to one another. The simplified adapted dance steps for lower-functioning elders utilizes leg movements similar to the adapted version. The arm movements, however, require a smaller range of motion.

Table 13.4 lists the movements for "Ma Navu," an Israeli folk dance. "Ma Navu" is a slow dance performed in a circle. The adapted dance steps for moderately impaired elders are performed in a seated position and are very similar to the actual steps. The simplified dance steps for lower-functioning elders are identical to Part I of the adapted steps. Part II requires a slow arm motion.

Table 13.5 lists the movements for "Troika," a Russian folk dance. "Troika" is a very fast-paced dance performed in trios. The adapted dance steps for moderately impaired elders require a quick stepping motion. It may be necessary to take very small steps to keep pace with the music. The simplified adapted dance steps for lower-functioning elders emphasize a movement on every other beat in order to allow participants to keep pace with the music. In forming trios, try to place the highest-functioning members of the group in trios with the lowest-functioning elders, so that the higher-functioning elders can help the lower-functioning participants to learn the dance.

Summary of Adapted Folk Dances

Adapted folk dance fosters feelings of group harmony and individual acceptance by the group members. The specific movement patterns inherent in folk dance may be more suitable for older adults who feel uncomfortable with spontaneous movement common to modern dance. The customary repetitive movements make adapted folk dance easy to learn.

Essentially, a folk dance is a series of movement patterns that are repeated several times throughout a song. The principles of creating adapted folk dances can be applied to creating chair dances synchronized to almost any music. For example, the following is a simple chair dance designed for lower-functioning elders, synchronized to the song "Put it There" (McCartney, 1989):

> Couples shake right hands (4 times, every other beat)
> Couples shake left hands (4 times, every other beat)
> Couples join hands and sway (4 times, every other beat)
> Right foot, heel-toe, then left foot, heel-toe (2 times)
> Repeat the entire sequence 4 times

Note: If the feet cannot be moved, then substitute hand clapping for the heel-toe step.

Similarly, a chair dance can be created for almost any song that has a steady beat. The key is to keep the dances simple (only a few different movements, repeated several times) when working with impaired populations. If the dances prove to be too simple, they can always be made more challenging by increasing the number of movements or the speed at which they are performed.

Exercise 13.1 asks you to select a song and create a chair dance synchronized to it.

You will find that folk dance is enjoyable for elders but tastes do vary, and some might prefer square dancing, described in the next section of the chapter.

Adapted Square Dance

Square dance is a desirable activity for elders because of its inherent social element. Social interaction is facilitated by the grouping of dancers into units of eight persons each. This unit is known as a square. The development of closer relationships is also fostered by the pairing of dancers into partners. The social nature of square dance can penetrate barriers and draw

EXERCISE 13.1. Creating a Chair Dance

Song: _____

Seating arrangement: _____

_____

_____

List of movements, number of repetitions for each movement: _____

_____

_____

_____

_____

_____

_____

_____

_____

_____

_____

Adaptations possible (if necessary): _____

_____

_____

_____

_____

_____

_____

_____

_____

_____

_____

_____

people out. Being accepted by the group can enhance an individual's psychological and emotional well-being.

Square dancing also contributes to physical fitness. Regular participation in a square dance program can help to develop rhythm, coordination, flexibility, and improve cardiovascular endurance. In addition, performing the skills and dance patterns can aid in memory recall and retention.

How to Adapt Square Dance for an Older Population

Non- or mildly impaired older adults may be capable of performing the actual square dance steps without modification of movements. For moderately impaired and lower-functioning elders, adapting square dance is necessary to enable participation. The following section focuses primarily on adaptations for square dance for moderately impaired and lower-functioning older adults.

A square dance can be adapted so that all the movements can be performed from a seated position. The square should be arranged closely so that each person can easily reach every dancer.

Use only a basic core of square dance movements; the use of too many movements may prove difficult to remember for elders with short-term memory problems. In addition, the movements should be reviewed with the participants numerous times before accompanying the dance with music; consequently, individuals with short-term memory impairment will have had much exposure to the new material.

When developing the lyrics for an adapted square dance, adequate time for performing the movement would be allotted after each call. Including gibberish (e.g., "weave the ring 'til the birdies sing") or phrases that do not dictate a movement allow time to perform the preceding movement.

When working with more impaired elders (e.g., nursing home residents) the sample adapted dances presented in the chapter will need to be simplified further. Delete some of the movement instructions and replace the instructions with gibberish lyrics. Also, try more repetitions of a smaller number of movements within a dance. These adaptations should facilitate the involvement of lower-functioning elders.

Last, when initially introducing adapted square dance to older adults, it may be helpful to have them wear numbered tags indicating the number for each couple.

A square consists of four couples. The lady sits on her partner's right. Couples are designated as 1, 2, 3, and 4. Couples 1 and 3 are called head couples. Couples 2 and 4 are the side couples. Couples 1 and 3 are opposites, as are couples 2 and 4. The corner is the person on the man's left and on the lady's right.

For an illustration of the formation of the square, see Figure 13.1.

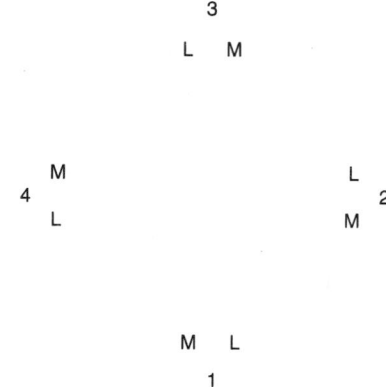

FIGURE 13.1. Formation of the Square (M = men; I = ladies)

Table 13.6 lists seventeen square dance calls and movements. The table includes the name of the movement, the actual movement description, and its counterpart adapted movement.

The adapted movements are designed to be performed from a seated position. The square consists of four couples seated closely together.

The following are sample adapted square dances utilizing the seventeen basic calls and movements. Lyrics were created to the tunes of old popular songs that can be sung and/or accompanied with musical instruments. There are two versions of each adapted square dance. The first version is designed for moderately impaired elders; the second version is designed for lower-functioning elders. The second version uses fewer movements and greater repetition.

Sample Square Dances

To the music of "He's Got the Whole World in His Hands"—the following dance is for moderately impaired elders and uses the following square dance movements:

- honors
- do-si-do
- circle left
- allemande left
- circle right
- weave the ring

- right hand star
- pass through
- promenade
- ladies chain
- star promenade
- allemande right

TABLE 13.6. Square Dance Movements

Name of Movement	Movement Description (Jensen and Jensen, 1973; Kraus, 1950)	Adapted Movement
1. Honors	1. Two people acknowledge each other, can be as simple as a tilt of the head or a curtsy and a bow	1. Man bows from the waist. Lady spreads her skirt with her hands, bends slightly and points her left toe toward her partner
2. Do-si-do	2. Two dancers face each other, walk forward and pass right as they pass back to back; they then pass left shoulders as they walk backward to their original positions	2. Place both hands behind the lower back and sway from side to side 4 times
3. Circle left or circle right	3. Dancers hold hands and move in a circle either clockwise or counterclockwise	3. All join hands, turn heads to the left if circling left, or right if circling right, and walk in place for 16 counts
4. Forward and back	4. The designated couples walk forward for 4 counts, then back 4 counts to original positions	4. The designated couples take three steps forward, reach forward and clap hands twice with opposite person. Take 3 steps backward
5. Promenade	5. Couples walk side by side counterclockwise around the square until they reach their original positions	5. Couples hold hands and sway from side to side
6. Allemande right	6. Partners face each other and walk around each other in a clockwise circle with right shoulders together	6. Couples join right hands and slowly lift arms up high, then bring arms back down again
7. Allemande left	7. Face the corner, join left hands with corner, walk in a counterclockwise circle, then back to original position	7. Corners join left hands, raise arms up high, then bring arms back down again

8. Courtesy turn

8. Partners join left hands. The man places his right arm around the lady's waist and the couple turns counterclockwise halfway around. This can be used as an ending for different movements

9. Weave the ring

9. Beginning with an allemande left, ladies move clockwise, men move counterclockwise, pass right shoulders with your partner, left shoulders with the next dancer, right with the next and so on until dancers meet their original partners

10. Ladies chain

10. Two opposite ladies move across the square to the opposite man and are turned with a courtesy turn

11. Right hand star

11. This movement is done by any combination of four people (i.e., ladies, men, head couples, side couples). Four people walk to the center of the square, join right hands, advance in a clockwise circle until they meet their partners. A left hand star is done to the left

12. Star promenade

12. The four men form a left hand star and place right arms around their partners' waists. Couples move side by side counterclockwise until they return to original positions

13. All around your left hand lady

13. Similar to "do-si-do your corner," except the couples continue walking forward keeping right shoulders together

8. Lady's left foot touches the man's right foot and, keeping their feet together, they form a circle with their feet

9. Designated couple shakes hands with each of the other couples

10. Two opposite ladies reach forward and shake hands

11. Four designated people reach forward, join hands and take eight walking steps

12. Four men reach forward and join left hands, hold their partners with their right hands and all take eight walking steps

13. Corners join both hands and rotate arms in a big circle

TABLE 13.6 *(continued)*

14. Pass through	14. Two opposite couples walk forward, then pass to the right of the person they face. Couples move to their new positions
14. Allemande that star	15. Men form a right hand star position and hold their partners with a left forearm grip. The men are on the inside of the star facing clockwise. The ladies are on the outside of the star facing counterclockwise. The star rotates in a counterclockwise direction, men moving backward and women moving forward
16. Split the ring	16. One couple moves forward and "passes through" the couple facing them. The lady turns right, the man turns left and both continue around the outside of the circle, then back to the original position
17. Grand circle	17. Dancers form two circles; ladies form a circle inside the square and move clockwise; men form a circle outside the square and move counterclockwise. Dancers walk around the circle back to their original positions

14. Opposite couples take four walking steps forward, left legs straight out and touch feet with opposite person. Take four walking steps backward
15. Men form a right hand star while women stomp their feet for eight counts
16. The designated couple claps hands together, then reaches forward, and claps hands with the opposite person, then partners clap hands again
17. Men join hands; ladies join hands. Men stomp their left feet and women stomp their right feet for eight counts

   It is necessary to review these movements numerous times before teaching the actual dance. After learning the individual movements, it may be helpful to break the dance down into subparts and master one section at a time before attempting the dance from start to finish.

>   Honor you partner, if you please
>   And honor your corner, everyone please
>   Turn toward your partner and do-si-do
>   Now, circle left and here we go
>
>   Now when you get through with your circle left
>   Turn toward your corner for an allemande left
>   Now that we're here we may dance all night
>   Let's join hands for a circle right
>
>   Couple #1, please weave the ring
>   Shake everyone's hand 'til the birdies sing
>   Now couple #2, go and weave the ring
>   And now we've all had a little fling
>
>   Come on, ladies, make a right hand star
>   Bet you didn't know you could go so far
>   Couples 2 and 4, let's see you pass through
>   Then promenade, go two by two
>
>   Couples 1 and 3, let's see the ladies chain
>   Now all together let's do a star promenade
>   There's one last thing we'll do tonight
>   And that's one more allemande right

   The following dance is for lower-functioning elders and utilizes the following square dance movements:

- honors
- do-si-do
- allemande right
- circle right
- promenade

>   Honor your partner if you please
>   Just sit right there and enjoy the breeze
>   And honor your corner, everyone please
>   We're gonna do this dance with ease

Turn toward your partner and do-si-do
Look at those dancers just lettin' it flow
Turn toward your corner for another do-si-do
Get ready, 'cause here we go

Let's join hands for a circle right
We may just stay and dance all night
Look at our feet movin' oh so light
These dancers are quite a sight

Couples, get ready, we're gonna promenade
It feels so nice in the cool shade
Now corners I bet you can promenade, too
See us dancing proud and true

Turn toward your partner for an allemande right
I know we can do it without a fight
What a nice day 'cause we all won
This dance has sure been fun

To the music of "Camptown Races"—the following dance is for moderately impaired elders and utilizes the following square dance movements:

- allemande left
- allemande right
- circle grand
- promenade
- do-si-do
- ladies chain
- forward and back
- circle left
- weave the ring
- pass through

Allemande left to your left hand,
doo-da, doo-da

Right to your own and a circle grand
Oh, doo-da-day

Meet your partner, promenade
doo-da, doo-da

Do-si-do, we've got it made
Oh, doo-da-day

Couples 1 and 3, pass right through
doo-da, doo-da

Ladies chain, couples 4 and 2
Oh, doo-da-day

Couples 1 and 3, go forward and back
doo-da, doo-da

Circle left but don't go far
Oh, doo-da-day

Couple #4 will weave the ring
doo-da, doo-da

Let's go back home and we will sing
Oh, doo-da-day

The following dance is for lower-functioning elders and utilizes the following square dance movements:

- allemande left
- allemande right
- grand circle
- forward and back
- circle right
- pass through

Allemande left to your left hand
doo-da, doo-da

Right allemande to your own man
Oh, doo-da-day

Let's all form a circle grand
doo-da, doo-da

We're the best in all the land
Oh, doo-da-day

Couples 1 and 3, pass right through
doo-da, doo-da

And couples 2 and 4 will pass through, too
Oh, doo-da-day

Couples 1 and 3, go forward and back
doo-da, doo-da

Now couples 2 and 4, go forward and back
Oh, doo-da-day

Circle right as we sing along
doo-da, doo-da

Now we end this old song
Oh, doo-da-day

The song "If You're Happy and You Know It" readily lends itself to the creation of an adapted square dance and would be good for intergenerational participation. The inclusion of some of the original ("jibberish") lyrics of the song provides ample time for the dancers to go from one movement to the next. For example:

If you're happy and you know it, *circle grand*
If you're happy and you know it, *circle grand*
If you're happy and you know it
Then your face will surely show it
If you're happy and you know it, *circle grand*

If you're happy and you know it, *weave the ring*
If you're happy and you know it, *weave the ring*
If you're happy and you know it
Then your face will surely show it
If you're happy and you know it, *weave the ring*

Similarly, additional square dance movements can be added, with plenty of transition time between movements by incorporating the original lyrics of the song. If the dance is being performed by an intergenerational group, some of the original instructions of the song can be included (e.g., "clap your hands," "stomp your feet," etc.).

Older adults who like music from the 1960s might enjoy the following adapted square dance, to the tune of "Twist and Shout" (Russell and Medley, 1960):

Well *honor your partner* now
Honor your partner
Twist and shout
Twist and shout

Come on and *honor your corner* too
Honor your corner
Come on and work it on out
Work it on out

Well let's *weave the ring* right now
Let's weave the ring
You know you look so good
Look so good
You know you got me goin' now
Got me goin'
Just like I knew you would
Like I knew you would

Well let's *allemande right* right now
Let's allemande right
Twist and shout
Twist and shout
Come on and *allemande left* now
Allemande left
Come on and work it on out
Work it on out

You know you should *circle right* now
Circle right
You know you look so fine
Look so fine
Come on and twist a little closer now
Twist a little closer
And let me know that you're mine
Let me know you're mine

Note: During the instrumental part, dancers can be instructed to join hands, slowly raise them up, then shake their hands over their heads during the "shrieking" part of the song.

Well *head couples pass through* now
Head couples pass through
Twist and shout
Twist and shout
Come on and *side couples pass through* too
Side couples pass through

Come on and work it on out
Work it on out

You know you should *circle left* now
All circle left
You know you look so fine
Look so fine
Come on and twist a little closer now
Twist a little closer
And let me know that you're mine
Let me know you're mine

Note: During the last part of the song, dancers can be instructed to "shake," just as the original lyrics state.

An adapted square dance can be created from almost any song. Exercise 13.2 asks you to select a song and create your own adapted square dance.

To the music of "Red River Valley"—the following dance is for moderately impaired elders and utilizes the following square dance movements:

- allemande left
- circle right
- weave the ring
- courtesy turn
- promenade
- grand circle

Oh, do an allemande left with your corner
And a circle right all the way round
When you meet up with your partner in the valley
Then promenade her to this pretty sound

Now the first couple go weave the ring
And let's see that big old grand circle
Don't forget to laugh, smile, and sing
And courtesy turn with your Red River Girl

The following dance is for lower-functioning elders and utilizes the following square dance movements:

- allemande left
- circle right
- star promenade
- do-si-do

EXERCISE 13.2. Creating an Adapted Square Dance

Song: _____

Lyrics/square dance movement instructions: _____

_____

_____

_____

_____

_____

_____

_____

_____

_____

_____

_____

_____

_____

_____

_____

_____

_____

Changes/adaptations (if needed): _____

_____

_____

_____

_____

_____

Oh, do an allemande left with your corner
And hold her tight as you swing her round
Let's go a big circle right in the valley
Now let's sit and listen to this pretty sound

All four couples form a star promenade
That's the best star we've ever made
Find your own partner for a do-si-do
Now that's the end of our song and show

In working with impaired elders, these seventeen adapted square dance movements may be a sufficient number to learn. Even if the elders know the traditional movements, relearning the adapted movements may prove to be a challenge. Working repetitively with a basic core of movements is desirable when working with elders, especially those with short-term memory deficits.

Summary of Adapted Square Dance

Square dance helps to sharpen socialization skills because of the interaction that naturally occurs due to the physical setting of the square. In addition, the physical activity involved in participating in adapted square dance contributes to improved fitness.

Adapted Ballet

Older adults can restore vitality and release tension by practicing ballet exercises. Simple ballet techniques are an effective form of exercise to improve posture and feel physically and mentally fit. Ballet strengthens the body and allows older adults the opportunity to discover their own inner rhythms. Ballet helps to reshape and control the body (Welles, 1982).

How to Adapt Ballet for an Older Population

Unlike folk and square dance, the adapted movements presented for ballet are very similar to the actual movements. The movements presented are not strenuous but are performed while standing, and can be accomplished by most elders. However, unlike adapted square and folk dance, it would be more difficult to adapt ballet to enable participation by more seriously impaired elders (e.g., nursing home residents). Set up a barre, or horizontal pole, about waist high. During exercise, one hand is placed on the barre for support. Each exercise sequence is performed on both sides, with one hand on the barre.

Adapted Ballet Exercises

The material presented in this section is based on Welles' (1982) book on ballet for women of all ages.

1. First position—heels are together and legs are rotated outward to form a *V* with the feet. The weight of the body is forward over the balls of the feet. The body is erect and extended; the abdomen is pulled in, and the buttocks are squeezed together. One hand is supported by the barre, and the other arm is lifted to the side and slightly ahead of the body.
2. Second position—feet are twelve inches apart, legs are rotated outward. The body and hand positions are identical to first position.

The following twelve exercises are sample adapted ballet exercises for older adults with moderate to good mobility. These exercises are also based on Welles' (1982) work on ballet for women of all ages.

Demi-plié and relevés in first position. These exercises warm up muscles and tendons and increase flexibility.

1. Bend the knees outward. Keep heels on the floor and the spine erect. The center of the knee should go directly over the foot. Three counts.
2. Straighten the knees and stretch the muscles in the legs. Three counts.
3. Relevé: Raise the heels off the floor. Weight should be evenly distributed over all ten toes. Raise the arm and look up simultaneously. Three counts.
4. Heels are lowered gently back to the floor. Arm returns to side. Three counts. Repeat three more times, then repeat this movement four more times on the other side.

Pliés in second position. This movement stretches the inner thighs.

1. Place feet about twelve inches apart; rotate legs outward.
2. Bend the knees directly over the toes, keeping the heels on the floor. The seat remains exactly in line between the feet; the spine is held straight. Six counts.
3. Straighten knees slowly and pull up thigh muscles. Squeeze buttock muscles together. Six counts. Repeat three more times, then repeat this movement four more times on the other side.

Battements tendus to the front. The following battements are performed in first position. This exercise strengthens abdominal and back muscles. Knees are pointed outward, away from each other in a turned-out position. The working leg refers to the leg away from the barre and the supporting leg is next to the barre.

1. Slide the heel on the working leg forward until the foot is entirely stretched and the toes are slightly touching the floor and the heel is naturally forced upward. Two counts.
2. Lift and extend the leg, toes pointed. Two counts.
3. Gently bring the toes back to the floor, keeping the knee straight. Two counts.
4. Slide the foot back to first position without bending the knees. Lift up on the supporting leg so the working leg fits back easily. Two counts.

Repeat three more times, then repeat this movement four more times on the other side.

Battements tendus to the back. The torso must remain facing straight ahead and not tilted to either side. The body should lean slightly forward as the leg is lifted back to avoid strain on the lower back.

1. Begin in first position. Slide the foot back and point the toes. Two counts.
2. Lift the leg. Two counts.
3. Bring the foot back down to a point. Two counts.
4. Bring the foot back to first position. Two counts.

During this exercise, hold the free arm extended forward. Repeat three more times, then repeat this movement four more times on the other side.

Battements tendus to the side. Keep the supporting knee straight and the spine erect. If the torso sinks, then the kick is too high.

1. Begin in first position. Slide the foot out to the side in the direction the toes are already pointed until the foot is fully stretched with toes pointed. Two counts.
2. Keep thighs in a turned-out position and lift the leg. Two counts.
3. Gently lower the leg back down to the floor with the foot still pointed. Two counts.
4. Return the foot to first position. Two counts.

Repeat three more times, then repeat this movement four more times on the other side.

Battements tendus en croix. This movement strengthens abdomen, back, and thigh muscles. Tighten the buttock muscles, point the toes and stretch the knees and ankles.

1. Two battements tendus to the front.
2. Two battements tendus to the side.
3. Two battements tendus to the back.
4. Two battements tendus to the side.

Repeat on the other side.

Grand battements. This movement strengthens the back and abdominal muscles and tones the thighs. If the torso buckles during this exercise, the kick to too high.

1. To the front. (In first position.) Legs are straight and turned out. Swing the working leg up with the knee pointing to the side of the room. Three counts.
   * Return leg to first position. Three counts. Repeat three more times.
2. To the side. Keep the torso straight and facing forward. During the kick, the knee should point upward and the toes should be pointed.
   * Kick the leg out to the side. Three counts.
   * Repeat three more times.
   * Repeat entire exercise on the other side four times.

Forward port de bras. Begin in first position. This exercise tones abdominal muscles, stretches the backs of the thighs and the spine.

1. Simultaneously:
   * Bend and reach forward, legs straight.
   * Bring the chin to the chest.
   * Contract abdominal and buttock muscles. Six counts.
2. Gently roll back up. Six counts.
3. Continue into a relevé, bringing the arm overhead. Slightly arch backward, keeping all muscles tight. Six counts.
4. Gently lower the heels back to the floor while slowly bringing the arm back to the side. Six counts. Repeat on the other side.

Balancoiré (leg swings). This exercise increases flexibility in the legs. Keep torso erect and stretch the entire working leg. Maintain a turned-out position. Begin in a lunge position (supporting knee bent, working leg straight), but as the leg swings forward and up, straighten the supporting leg throughout the exercise. Swing the leg forward and back four times on each side.

Attitude kicks (thigh lifts). This exercise tones the thighs. Keep the spine erect; the supporting leg is straight but the working leg is slightly bent.

1. Begin in first position. Swing the leg up and outward, bending the knee sideways; raise the heel upward and point the toes. Two counts.
2. Bring the leg back to first position. Two counts. Repeat three more times.
3. Swing the leg sideways; the knee is slightly bent, and the toes are pointed downward. Two counts.
4. Return leg to first position. Two counts. Repeat three more times. Repeat the exercise twice on each side.

Side port de bras and stretch. This exercise tones abdominal muscles and firms waistline.

1. Begin with feet in parallel position on the balls of the feet. Lean sideways away from the barre. With the free arm, reach up and over the head in the direction of the barre until the arm forms an arch. Thighs are touching. Six counts.
2. Bring the arm back to the side while gently lowering the heels back to the floor. Six counts.
3. Bring the free hand to the center of the chest with fingers pointed upward. Extend the arm straight up. Look at the hand moving upward. Lift up on the toes as the hand is raised. Six counts.
4. Allow the arm to drop and let the chin drop to the chest. Allow the knees to bend slightly. Contract abdominal muscles. Six counts.
5. Slowly roll back up to starting position and bring the heels back down to the floor. Six counts.

Repeat two more times; then repeat this movement three more times on the other side.

Battements facing center. This exercise tones the thighs. The legs and spine should remain straight; if the torso buckles, then the kick is too high.

1. Begin in first position with the back to the barre, holding on to the barre with both hands.
   - To the front: In a turned-out position, kick straight ahead, point the toes. Two counts.
   - Bring foot back to first position. Two counts.

2. To the side: Kick out to the side, toes pointed, turned-out position. Two counts.
- Return the foot to first position. Two counts.
- While kicking to the side, pull the opposite side of the body in the direction opposite the kick, which will create a two-way stretch. Buttock muscles should remain tight.
- Kick four times to the side. Repeat the entire exercise on the other side.

Summary of Adapted Ballet

Adapted ballet for older adults has both physical and mental benefits. Ballet strengthens and tones the body and simultaneously helps to create a more accurate self-concept. Adapted ballet is different from adapted folk and square dance in that it is performed standing and is very similar to the classical movements.

Adapted Tap Dance

High-functioning elders may be able to perform the actual tap movements without modification. For moderately impaired and lower-functioning elders, adaption of tap dance is necessary to enable participation. The following section focuses primarily on adaptations for tap dance for moderately impaired and lower-functioning elders.

Tap dance is especially suitable for older adults. The basic steps can be performed whether one is standing or seated. The special appeal of tap, the sounds the feet make, remains the same. Tap dance is noisy, expressive, and rhythmic. Tap dance utilizes many of the senses, and most dancers can actually hear if the steps are correct.

Taps can be purchased and attached to leather-soled shoes. The purchase of tap shoes is not essential.

How to Adapt Tap Dance for an Older Population

All the basic movements of tap dance can be adapted to a seated position. For older adults with limited mobility, tap dance can be performed sitting in a chair wearing tap shoes. An inexpensive alternative to tap shoes is cardboard tap attachments made in the following way: (1) cut out two cardboard pieces in the shape of a pair of shoes; (2) make one small hole on each side of the insole at the widest part of the foot; (3) make two more holes on each side of the instep; (4) run pieces of yarn or string through the holes and tie the string onto the foot; and (5) attach metal buttons onto the toe and heel areas of the piece of cardboard.

For elders who do not have use of their legs, adapted tap dance can still be done by making sounds with hands. With the use of tap socks, tap sounds can be simulated with the hands. Wear a sock on each hand and attach metal buttons to the finger and heel areas. A small board or tray placed on the lap of each individual will enable tap sounds to be produced. Use the same terminology as listed. The tap on the fingertips is the counterpart to the toe, and heel on the hand is the counterpart on the foot (see Photos 13.1 and 13.2).

The following are basic movement patterns categorized according to the number of sounds each step produces, based on Nash's (1969), Atwater's (1971), and Hungerford's (1939) works.

1. One-sound movements
   * brush (forward): Brush the ball of the foot on to floor as the foot moves forward. This movement can also be done to the side;
   * brush (backward): brush the ball of the foot on the floor as the foot moves backward;
   * step: transfer the weight to the entire foot;
   * toe: transfer the weight to the toe;
   * heel: transfer the weight to the heel;
   * stamp: same as a step, but use more force to create a louder sound;
   * leap: both feet momentarily lose contact with the floor: otherwise, it is the same as a step. Prepare one foot to take off; both feet lose contact with the floor; then the other foot lands on the floor;
   * jump: similar to the leap in that there are three parts—take off with one or two feet, a moment in the air, then land on two feet;
   * double heel: take off with both feet, knees bent and a moment in the air; land on heels with toes up;
   * heel click: hit the inside of the heels together while both feet are off the floor; can occur along with a leap, hop, or jump;
   * hop: take off and land on the same foot; no transfer of weight from one foot to the other;
   * heel thump: lift the heel, then bring the heel back down to the floor;
   * chug: lift the heel; then bring the heel back to the floor as the toe slides forward;
   * heel touch: touch the heel of the free foot to the floor;
   * toe touch: bend knee of free leg and touch the toe to the floor;
   * heel toe brush: no transfer of weight; the sound is made by hitting the shoes together. Hit the heel of the free foot against the toe of the other foot as it moves forward and diagonally across supporting foot; and

- toe heel brush: hit the toe of the free foot against the heel of the other foot as it moves diagonally backward across the supporting foot.

2. Two-sound movements
   - shuffle: brush forward, then backward; no change of weight;
   - flap: toe, then step while walking forward; weight change occurs on second sound;
   - heel-toe: transfer the weight on the second sound; touch the heel to make the first sound, then the toe;
   - toe-heel: transfer the weight on the second sound; touch the toe to make the first sound, then the heel;
   - ball change: shift the weight from one foot to the ball of the other foot; then shift the weight immediately back again to the first foot;
   - heel change: shift weight from one foot to the heel of the other foot; then shift immediately back again to the first foot; and
   - drawback: while moving backward-toe, then step; transfer of weight.

3. Three-sound movements
   - triple: shuffle, then step.

PHOTO 13.1. Man Performing Seated Tap Dance

PHOTO 13.2. Volunteer Teaching Seated Tap Dance

The following adapted tap dances are presented in Tables 13.7-13.10. These exercises are for older adults with moderate to good mobility:

Table 13.7. "Love Makes the World Go 'Round"
Table 13.8. "Sidewalks of New York"
Table 13.9. "Five Foot Two, Eyes of Blue"
Table 13.10. "Won't You Come Home?"

These dance sequences are to be read from left to right in each row. The lyrics are found on the first line matched with the tap movement and count or beat on the second and third lines.

Table 13.7 lists the movements for an adapted tap dance to the music of "Love Makes the World Go 'Round." The dance incorporates five basic steps for the hands or feet:

- brush forward
- brush backward
- step
- heel touch
- toe touch

TABLE 13.7. "Love Makes the World Go 'Round"

LOVE			MAKES		THE	WORLD		GO
(R) brush forward	(R) step	(L) step	(L) brush forward	(L) step	(R) step	(R) brush backward	(R) step	(L) step
1	2	3	1	2	3	1	2	3

ROUND			LOVE	MAKES	THE	WORLD		GO
(L) brush backward	(L) step	(R) step	(R) heel touch	(L) heel touch	(R) heel touch	(L) toe touch	(R) toe touch	(L) toe touch
1	2	3	1	2	3	1	2	3

ROUND			--------			SOME-	BODY	SOON
(R) heel touch	(L) heel touch	(R) heel touch	(L) toe touch	(R) toe touch	(L) toe touch	(R) brush forward	(R) step	(L) step
1	2	3	1	2	3	1	2	3

WILL			LOVE		YOU	--------		
(L) brush forward	(L) step	(R) step	(R) brush backward	(R) step	(L) step	(L) brush backward	(L) step	(R) step
1	2	3	1	2	3	1	2	3

351

TABLE 13.7 (continued)

Word	Action	Count	Word	Action	Count	Word	Action	Count
IF	(R) heel touch	1	NO	(L) heel touch	2	ONE	(R) heel touch	3
LOVES	(L) toe touch	1		(R) toe touch	2	YOU	(L) toe touch	3
NOW	(R) heel touch	1		(L) heel touch	2	SOME	(R) heel touch	3

Word	Action	Count	Word	Action	Count	Word	Action	Count
------	(L) toe touch	1		(R) toe touch	2		(L) toe touch	3
HIGH	(R) brush forward	1		(R) step	2		(L) step	3
IN	(L) brush forward	1		(L) step	2		(R) step	3

Word	Action	Count	Word	Action	Count	Word	Action	Count
SI	(R) brush backward	1		(R) step	2		(L) step	3
SKY	(L) brush backward	1		(L) step	2		(R) step	3
LOVE	(R) heel touch	1		(L) heel touch	2	A	(R) heel touch	3

Word	Action	Count	Word	Action	Count	Word	Action	Count
SIL	(L) toe touch	1		(R) toe touch	2	VER	(L) toe touch	3
SONG	(R) heel touch	1		(L) heel touch	2		(R) heel touch	3
--------	(L) toe touch	1		(R) toe touch	2		(L) toe touch	3

Beat 1	Beat 2	Beat 3
MAK- (R) brush forward 1	ING THE (R) step 2	EARTH (L) step 3
-------- (L) brush forward 1	(L) step 2	WHIRL (L) step 3
SOFT (R) brush backward 1	- (R) step 2	LY (L) step 3

Beat 1	Beat 2	Beat 3
LOVE (R) heel touch 1	MAKES (L) heel touch 2	THE (R) heel touch 3
-------- (L) brush backward 1	(L) step 2	(R) step 3
WORLD (L) toe touch 1	(R) toe touch 2	GO (L) toe touch 3

Beat 1	Beat 2	Beat 3
ROUND (R) heel touch 1	(L) heel touch 2	(R) heel touch 3
-------- (L) toe touch 1	(R) toe touch 2	(L) toe touch 3

This tap dance can be performed as slowly as is appropriate to allow the dancers to keep pace.

TABLE 13.8. "Sidewalks of New York"

	1	2	3
EAST	(R) triple · · · · · · ·		
SIDE	(L) Triple · · · · · · ·		
WEST	(R) triple · · · · · · ·		
SIDE	(L) triple · · · · · · ·		
ALL / A-	ALL — (R) heel thump	(R) heel thump	A- — (R) heel thump
ROUND / THE	ROUND — (L) heel thump	(L) heel thump	THE — (L) heel thump
TOWN	TOWN — (R) toe touch	(L) toe touch	(R) toe touch
THE	THE — (L) toe touch	(R) toe touch	(L) toe touch
TOTS	TOTS — (R) hop	(R) hop	(R) hop
SANG	SANG — (R) hop	(R) hop	(R) hop
RING / A	RING — (L) hop	(L) hop	A — (L) hop
ROS / IE	ROS — jump	- — jump	IE — jump
LON / DON	LON — leap	- — leap	DON — leap

Measure 1

heel toe brush . . .

	BRIDGE	IS		FALL	-	ING	DOWN		
Foot	to (R)	(L) step	(L) step	to (L)		(R) step	(L) step	(R) step	(L) step
Count	1	2	3	1	2	3	1	2	3

Measure 2

	------			BOYS		AND	GIRLS		TO-
Foot	(R) step	(L) step	(R) step	(R) triple			(L) triple		
Count	1	2	3	1	2	3	1	2	3

Measure 3

	GETH	-	ER	------			ME		AND
Foot	(R) triple			(L) triple			(R) heel	(R) heel	(R) heel
Count	1	2	3	1	2	3	1	2	3

Measure 4

	MA-	MIE	O'	ROURKE			------		
Foot	(L) heel thump	(L) heel thump	(L) heel thump	(R) toe touch	(L) toe touch	(R) toe touch	(L) toe touch	(R) toe touch	(L) toe touch
Count	1	2	3	1	2	3	1	2	3

TABLE 13.8 *(continued)*

TRIPPED		THE	LIGHT		FAN-	TAS-	TIC	
(R) hop	(R) hop	(R) hop	(L) hop	(L) hop	(L) hop	jump	jump	jump
1	2	3	1	2	3	1	2	3

ON		THE	SIDE-		WALKS	OF		NEW
leap	leap	leap	heel toe brush to (R)		(L) step	heel toe brush to (L)		(R) step
1	2	3	1	2	3	1	2	3

YORK	-				
(L) step	(R) step	(L) step	(R) step	(L) step	(R) step
1	2	3	1	2	3

This adapted tap dance uses more steps and less repetition than the dance in Table 13.7; consequently, the dance may be more challenging.

TABLE 13.9. "Five Foot Two, Eyes of Blue"

FIVE	FOOT	TWO	
(R) flap...		(L) flap...	
1	2	3	4

EYES	OF	BLUE,	BUT
(R) drawback...		(L) drawback...	
1	2	3	4

OH	WHAT	THOSE	FIVE
(R) flap...		(L) flap...	
1	2	3	4

FOOT	COULD	DO	HAS
(R) drawback...		(L) drawback...	
1	2	3	4

AN-	Y	BOD-	Y
heel click...		heel click...	
1	2	3	4

SEEN		MY	
(R) heel	(L) heel	(R) heel	(L) heel
1	2	3	4

GIRL?			
(R) toe	(L) toe	(R) toe	(L) toe
touch	touch	touch	touch
1	2	3	4

......			
jump	jump	jump	jump
1	2	3	4

TURNED-UP		NOSE	
(R) flap...		(L) flap...	
1	2	3	4

TURNED-DOWN		HOSE	
(R) drawback...		(L) drawback...	
1	2	3	4

NEV-	ER	HAD	NO
(R) flap...		(L) flap...	
1	2	3	4

OTH-	ER	BEAUS	HAS
(R) drawback...		(L) drawback	
1	2	3	4

TABLE 13.9 (continued)

GIRL?			
(R) toe touch	(L) toe touch	(R) toe touch	(L) toe touch
1	2	3	4

SEEN		MY	
(R) heel thump	(L) heel thump	(R) heel thump	(L) heel thump
1	2	3	4

AN-	Y	BOD-	Y
heel click			heel click . . . .
1	2	3	4

FIVE	FOOT	TWO	
(R) drawback . . .	(L) drawback . . .		(L) drawback . . .
1	2	3	4

RUN	IN	TO	A
(R) flap . . .		(L) flap . . .	(L) drawback . . . .
1	2	3	4

NOW	IF	YOU	
jump	jump	jump	jump
1	2	3	4

DIA-	MOND	RINGS	AND
heel click		heel click . . .	
1	2	3	4

FUR	-------		
(R) drawback	(L) drawback		(L) drawback . . . .
1	2	3	4

COV-	ERED	WITH	
(R) flap . . .		(L) flap	
1	2	3	4

IS-	N'T	HER	BUT
jump	jump	jump	jump
1	2	3	4

BET-	CHA	LIFE	IT
(R) toe touch	(L) toe touch	(R) toe touch	(L) toe touch
1	2	3	4

ALL	THOSE	THINGS	
(R) heel thump	(L) heel thump	(R) heel thump	(L) heel thump
1	2	3	4

COULD SHE LOVE?

1	2	3	4
COULD	SHE	LOVE?	
(R) flap ...		(L) flap ...	

COULD SHE WOO?

1	2	3	4
COULD	SHE	WOO?	
(R) drawback ...		(L) drawback ...	

COULD SHE COULD SHE

1	2	3	4
COULD	SHE	COULD	SHE
(R) drawback ...		(L) drawback ...	

COULD SHE COO? HAS

1	2	3	4
COULD	SHE	COO?	HAS
(R) drawback ...		(L) drawback ...	

AN-Y BOD-Y

1	2	3	4
AN-	Y	BOD-	Y
heel click ...		heel click ...	

SEEN MY

1	2	3	4
SEEN		MY	
(R) heel thump	(L) heel thump	(R) heel thump	(L) heel thump

GIRL?

1	2	3	4
GIRL?			
(R) toe touch	(L) toe touch	(R) toe touch	(L) toe touch

1	2	3	4
-----			
jump	jump	jump	jump

This lively dance includes basic movements that can be performed with either the hands or feet.

TABLE 13.10. "Won't You Come Home?"

Box 1

WON'T	YOU		COME	WON'T	YOU		COME
(R) brush to side	(L) step	(R) step		(R) brush forward	(L) step	(R) step	
1	2	3	4	1	2	3	4

Box 2

HOME	BILL	BAI-	LEY	SHE	MOANS		THE
(L) brush to side	(L) step	(R) step	(L) step	(R) brush backward	(R) step	(L) step	(R) step
1	2	3	4	1	2	3	4

Box 3

WHOLE	DAY		DAY	LONG			
(L) brush backward	(R) step	(L) step	(R) step	(R) toe-heel…	(R) toe-heel…	(R) toe-heel…	(R) toe-heel…
1	2	3	4	1	2	3	4

Box 4

I'LL	DO		THE	I'LL	PAY		THE
(R) heel-toe…	(L) heel-toe…	(L) heel-toe…	(L) heel-toe…	(R) heel-toe…	(L) heel-toe…	(L) heel-toe…	(L) heel-toe…
1	2	3	4	1	2	3	4

RENT				COOK-	IN'	DAR-	LING
(R) heel-toe…	(L) heel-toe…			(R) stamp	(L) stamp	(R) stamp	(L) stamp
1	2	3	4	1	2	3	4

Line 1 — "I KNOW I'VE DONE YOU WRONG"

Lyric	I	KNOW		I'VE	DONE		YOU		WRONG			
Foot	(R)	(L)	(R)	(L)	(R)	(L)	(R)	(L)				
Move	stamp	stamp	stamp	stamp	stamp	stamp	stamp	stamp	Jump	jump	jump	jump
Count	1	2	3	4	1	2	3	4	1	2	3	4

Line 2 — "------ 'MEMBER THAT RAINY EVE THAT"

Lyric					'MEM-	BER		THAT	RAIN-	Y	EVE	THAT
Foot					(R) brush	(L)	(R)	(L)	(L) brush	(L)	(R)	(L)
Move	jump	jump	jump	jump	to side	step	step	step	to side	step	step	step
Count	1	2	3	4	1	2	3	4	1	2	3	4

Line 3 — "I DROVE YOU OUT WITH NOTHIN' BUT A"

Lyric	I	DROVE		YOU	OUT		WITH		NOTH-	IN'	BUT	A
Foot	(R) brush	(L)	(R)	(L)	(L) brush	(R)	(L)	(R)	(R) brush	(L)	(R)	(L)
Move	forward	step	step	step	forward	step	step	step	backward	step	step	step
Count	1	2	3	4	1	2	3	4	1	2	3	4

Line 4 — "FINE TOOTH COMB?"

Lyric	FINE	TOOTH			COMB?						I	
Foot	(L) brush	(L)	(R)	(L)	(R) toe-heel…	(L) toe-heel…	(R) toe-heel…	(L) toe-heel…	(R) toe-heel…	(L) toe-heel…	(R) toe-heel…	(L) toe-heel…
Move	backward	step	step	step								
Count	1	2	3	4	1	2	3	4	1	2	3	4

TABLE 13.10 *(continued)*

KNOW	I'M		TO	BLAME		WELL		AIN'T		THAT	A
(R)	(L)	(R)	(L)	(R)	(L)	(R)	(L)	(R) heel-toe....		(L) heel-toe....	
stamp	stamp	stamp	stamp	stamp	stamp	stamp	stamp				
1	2	3	4	1	2	3	4	1	2	3	4

SHAME?		BILL		BAI-	LEY	WON'T YOU		PLEASE		COME	
(R) heel-toe....		(L) heel-toe....		(R)	(L)	(R)	(L)	(R)	(L)	(R)	(L)
				stamp	stamp	stamp	stamp	stamp	stamp	stamp	stamp
1	2	3	4	1	2	3	4	1	2	3	4

HOME				-----	
jump	jump	jump	jump	jump	jump
1	2	3	4		

This dance incorporates only two movement sequences. The movements within each sequence are repetitious and easy to learn.

A simple sequence of steps is repeated four times.

Table 13.8 lists the movement for an adapted tap dance to the music of "Sidewalks of New York." The dance incorporates eight basic steps for the hands or feet:

- triple
- heel thump
- toe touch
- hop
- jump
- leap
- heel toe brush
- step

A basic sequence of steps is repeated two times.

Table 13.9 lists the movements for an adapted tap dance to the music of "Five Foot Two, Eyes of Blue." The dance incorporates six basic movements for either the hands or feet:

- flap
- drawback
- heel click
- heel thump
- toe touch
- jump

A basic sequence of movements is repeated four times.

Table 13.10 lists the movements for an adapted tap dance to the music of "Won't You Come Home?" The dance incorporates six basic movements for either the hands or feet:

- brush
- step
- toe-heel
- stamp
- heel-toe
- jump

A basic sequence of movements is repeated two times.

Summary of Adapted Tap Dance

Adapted tap dance is an appropriate activity for the elderly because the basic steps remain unchanged regardless of whether one is standing or sitting. For elders with limited mobility, adapted tap dance can be performed with the feet, in a seated position. For elders without the use of their legs, tap sounds can be simulated by the hands with the use of tap socks.

Adapted tap dances can be created to almost any music. Exercise 13.3 asks you to create your own adapted tap dance to the song of your choice, following the format of the tables of adapted tap dances presented in this chapter.

Adapted Modern Dance

Modern dance can help the older adult gain increased awareness of the sensation of motion within his or her own body. It aids in the ability to express oneself creatively and can expand the movement potential. Modern dance allows the individual the freedom to create his or her own unique movements: through this physical involvement, a sense of well-being is fostered.

How to Adapt Modern Dance for an Older Population

High-functioning elders may be able to perform modern dance without modification. For moderately impaired and lower-functioning elders, adaptation of modern dance is necessary to enable participation. The following section focuses primarily on adaptation of modern dance for moderately impaired and lower-functioning older adults.

Adapted modern dance allows for spontaneity of movement. There are no right or wrong steps. Ideas or themes are suggested and each individual has the liberty to create movement patterns within his or her own unique framework. A supportive and accepting atmosphere must exist to eliminate inhibitions and to encourage this type of sharing.

Adapted Modern Dance Patterns

The following modern dance patterns are based on Caplow-Lindner, Harpaz, and Samberg's (1979) and Wethered's (1973) works. These patterns

EXERCISE 13.3. An Original Adapted Tap Dance

Follow the format of the "tap dance tables" presented in the chapter. In the boxes below, write in the lyrics of the song of your choice, with corresponding tap dance instructions and beat counts. Be sure to keep it simple and incorporate repetition to maximize the chances for success.

illustrate the potential for using a theme to stimulate movement in modern dance.

1. Movement sequences are created where different body parts come together, meet, and then part again, e.g., finger to toe, nose to knee, etc. This basic theme can be expanded to include meeting and clashing, meeting and passing, and meeting and joining to create another movement. This movement exercise can be done alone or with partners.

2. Explore movement principles such as free flow and controlled flow, light and strong energy, direct and indirect movement, body-oriented and environment-oriented movement, and simultaneous and successive movement.

3. Create movement patterns using different verbs, e.g., turning, exploding, digging, zigzagging, climbing, etc. This theme is called "Word-Movement Association."

4. Create a sequence of movements to develop a whole scene, e.g., a basketball game, an orchestra, a fishing trip, etc.

5. Explore locomotor movements, e.g., walk, slide, gallop, hop, etc. These movements can be done seated.

6. Experiment with movements as they relate to sounds, e.g., clicking, whistling, tapping, etc.

7. Use adjectives to elicit movement, e.g., scary, gooey, hot, etc.

8. Recite poems and/or stories to the group to stimulate movement.

9. Use sensory recall that evokes energy, space, and rhythm to elicit movement, e.g., raking leaves, walking in mud or snow, etc.

10. Use oppositional movement factors as an impetus to create movement, e.g., toward and away, high and low, large and small, slow and fast, open and closed, etc.

11. Use hand dancing as a form of self-expression to elicit movement. Two people face each other and place their palms together. One is designated as the leader and guides the movement of the other. The action can be performed in place, sitting or standing, and with changing levels and directions. Due to the physical contact that occurs between the pairs, this activity may be especially rewarding.

12. Try using a mirror image. One person initiates movement, while others mirror the movement. This activity can be performed in a partner situation or small groups. The passive and active roles should be reversed.

Exploring themes in modern dance may help to elicit imagery that can spark impetus for movement. Ideas for themes are limitless. Creating themes based on individuals' backgrounds in the group may stimulate movement and simultaneously induce interaction through a sharing of interests and experiences.

Dynamics of movement is often studied in modern dance classes. The degree of force and energy a dancer expends in his or her movements allows for variety and contrast in the quality of those movements (Duffy, 1982). Table 13.11 lists the common categories of energy, approaches to each category, and adapted versions of each approach for impaired older adults.

Summary of Adapted Modern Dance

Adapted modern dance fosters creativity and spontaneity for elders. The freedom to invent and express original movements helps to expand movement potential. Themes, movement principles, sound, props, and poems are a few of the aids that can be used in adapting modern dance.

SUMMARY

Participation in dance in later life can have both physical and mental benefits. It can enhance coordination, muscular strength, flexibility, and cardiovascular efficiency. Mental health can be improved through the opportunity for creativity and self-expression. Folk, square, tap, ballet, and modern dance can provide rewarding experiences for older adults if adapted appropriately. Using the guidelines presented, a limitless number of adapted dances can be created.

TABLE 13.11. Modern Dance: Dynamics of Movement

Name of Movement		Sample Movement		Sample Adapted Movement
1.	Sustained movement: Occurs with a smooth, continuous release of energy. There is a strong sense of control from beginning to finish.	1.	Move an imaginary heavy box across the floor. Midway, switch from moving the box with arms to moving the box with the legs.	1. Sitting in a circle, pass a very heavy imaginary box around the circle. One at a time, each person lifts the box from his or her lap and places it on a neighbor's lap. Continue this motion around the circle.
2.	Percussive movement: Uses a lot of energy, starts and stops suddenly. The movements are strong, sharp, and explosive.	2.	Simulate a baseball game using percussive movements.	2. In a seated position, experiment with motion by percussively moving each finger, one at a time. After each finger is involved, try it with the whole hand.
3.	Swinging movement: A small movement begins the momentum, then gravity takes control, which causes a swinging motion, a suspension in the motion, then uncontrolled flow again until finally the movement stops.	3.	Swing different body parts: legs, arms, head, torso, and in different combinations, creating as much space as possible.	3. While seated in a circle, have each person find a different body part that can swing; allow the whole group to try the same motion. Have another person demonstrate swinging a different body part, then the group will imitate. Continue until everyone has had a chance to lead the motion.

4. Vibratory movement: A succession of many quick and pulsating movements.	4. While walking across the floor, try quivering or shaking a series of body parts, beginning with the head and working progressively down toward the feet.	4. Pass a prop around the circle, e.g., scarf, paper cup, book, etc. As the prop touches a person's hands, that person's hands and arms begin to vibrate as he or she is passing it to the next person. After the object is passed, the vibrations cease.
5. Collapse: The body gives into gravity by releasing energy.	5. The total body or isolated body parts can be involved. Collapse to the ground from an erect position, then from a squatting position. Allow one body part to collapse while another body part is vibrating.	5. In a seated position, experiment with collapsing different body parts. Raise one arm and allow it to collapse, raise the other arm and experience its collapse, then raise both arms. Try the same thing with the legs, head, torso.
6. Ballistic movement: An explosive, vigorous movement, used to gain speed or power, ending with a follow-through. This forceful movement is usually directed at an object.	6. Pass around various props, e.g., a ball, a hat, a broom, etc., so that each individual can create a ballistic movement using the prop, then collapse to the floor.	6. Begin by powerfully pointing with both arms and feet at a person in the group and yelling out his or her name, then collapse in the chair. This person must initiate the next explosion by pointing with arms and legs and yelling out someone else's name, then collapsing. Continue until everyone has had a turn.

REFERENCES

Atwater, C. (1971). *Tap dancing: Techniques, routines, terminology.* Rutland, VT: Tuttle.

Caplow-Lindner, E., Harpaz, L., and Samberg, S. (1979). *Therapeutic dance movement: Expressive activities for older adults.* New York: Human Sciences Press.

Duffy, N. W. (1982). *Modern dance: An adult beginner's guide.* Englewood Cliffs, NJ: Prentice-Hall.

Feder, E. and Feder, B. (1981). *The expressive arts therapies.* Englewood Cliffs, NJ: Prentice-Hall.

Horosko, M. (1990). Senior adults: Your new pupils? *Dance Magazine,* April, pp. 60-61.

Hungerford, M. J. (1939). *Creative tap dancing.* Englewood Cliffs, NJ: Prentice-Hall.

Jensen, C. R. and Jensen, M. B. (1973). *Square dancing.* Provo, UT: Brigham Young University Press.

Kraus, R. (1950). *Square dances of today and how to teach and call them.* New York: A. S. Barnes.

Lopez, T. (1983). Guidelines for using dance with older adults. *Journal of Physical Education, Recreation, and Dance, 54,* 44-45.

McCartney, P. (1989). Put it there. Original sound recording on the cassette *Flowers in the Dirt,* by MPL Communications Ltd. under exclusive license to Capitol Records, Inc.

Nash, B. (1969). *Tap dance.* Dubuque, IA: W. C. Brown.

Russell, B. and Medley, P. (1960). Twist and shout. In *The Compleat Beatles,* Volume 1. Greenwich, CT: Cherry Lane Music Co., Inc.

Spilner, M. (1993). Dancing grannies! A chorus line keeps these seniors on their toes! *Prevention,* December, pp. 77-81.

Wapner, E. B. (1981). Recreation for the elderly. Great Neck, NY: Todd and Honeywell.

Welles, L. (1982). Ballet body book. Indianapolis/New York: Bobbs-Merrill.

Wethered, A. G. (1973). *Movement and drama in therapy.* Boston: Plays.

Chapter 14

Recreational Techniques and Activities

INTRODUCTION

A wide range of recreational activities can work successfully with elders. The purpose of this chapter is to foster a greater awareness and understanding of some of the diverse recreational activities and techniques possible with elders. Information on a variety of recreational activities and techniques is presented in this chapter, including massage, clowning, drama, reminisence and life review, music, arts and crafts, horticulture therapy, pet therapy, and the uses of humor and laughter with elders. Enough information is available on some of the techniques (e.g., arts and crafts, horticulture therapy, music, and drama) to write an entire textbook on that one topic. Thus, the discussion of some of these techniques is not intended to be a thorough overview. Rather, the intention is to increase awareness and understanding of the use of these techniques with elders, and to identify resources for obtaining further information and specific program ideas.

LEARNING OBJECTIVES

The learning objectives of this chapter are to be able to identify the benefits of and procedures for a variety of types of recreational activities for elders, including massage, clowning, drama, reminisence and life review, music, arts and crafts, horticulture, pet therapy, and laughter and humor.

MASSAGE

Massage is an exceptionally beneficial and enjoyable leisure activity for elders. The information presented in this section is intended to prepare you to be able to perform introductory massage activities with elders. A massage training course and certification is a necessity for someone interested in being a massage therapist. Also, the books on massage listed in the references at the end of the chapter are recommended as a reference for techniques.

Massage is defined as a systematic form of touch found to give comfort or promote good health. It involves stroking, kneading, and pressing the soft tissues of the entire body in order to facilitate relaxation (Lidell, 2001). There are many different types of massage, such as Swedish massage, shiatsu, aromatherapy, reflexology, and Reiki (Claire, 1995).

In the first subsection, the benefits of massage are described in order to foster a clear understanding of the value and importance of massage to elders. In the second subsection, general considerations in massaging elders are discussed. In the last subsection, specific massage techniques and strokes are explained.

Benefits of Massage

The benefits of massage for elders are impressive. Massage is a unique form of nonverbal communication. It is an effective way of expressing caring and warmth. Through massage, deeper levels of communication can be established between two individuals.

Massage is one of the more relaxing leisure activities. Relaxation is especially important for elders' health, given the stress many elders face (e.g., retirement, widowhood). Unlike most drugs used as sedatives and relaxants, massage has a relaxing effect without any harmful side effects (Downing and Rush, 1972).

Massage, especially facial massage, can have cosmetic benefits. Massaged areas have a less wrinkled, smoother, and more youthful appearance. This cosmetic benefit of massage often leads to enhanced self-esteem and a greater sense of well-being.

The emotional benefits of massage are significant. In addition to enhanced self-esteem and general sense of well-being, the experiencing of such a pleasurable, enjoyable leisure activity contributes to higher morale and happiness.

The physiological benefits of massage are equally impressive. Massage has the following general effects: increased circulation and respiration; relaxed and toned muscles; soothed nervous system; stretched connective tissue of joints; improved digestion; facilitated sleep; and relieved pain.

In particular, massage can help relieve the pain of arthritis, an ailment that affects many older adults. According to Jayson and Dixon (1974), massage can relieve arthritic pain because firmly rubbing in a liniment massages the underlying tissue and relieves the muscle spasm that produces the aches and pains.

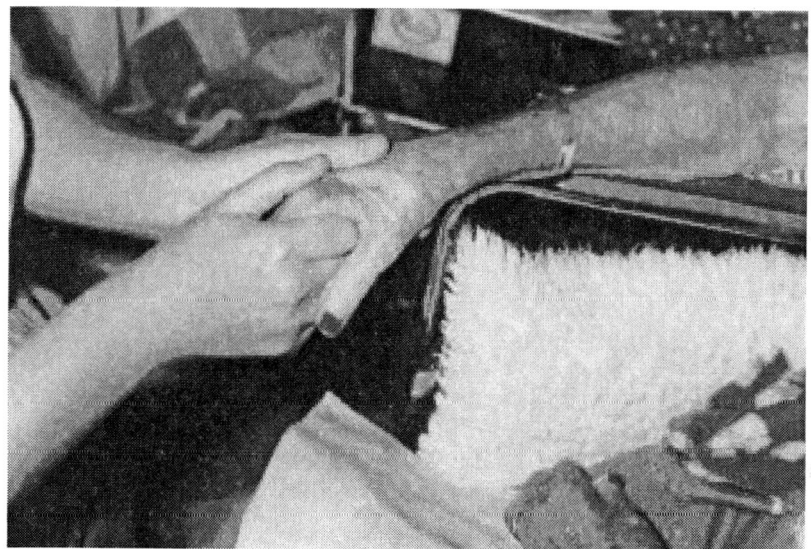

PHOTO 14.1. Hand Massage

According to Atkinson (2001), hand and foot massage relieves pain and stiffness in the hands and feet and also has the following benefits (Photo 14.1):

1. a greater ability to fight infections due to a strengthened immune system;
2. better skin and nail condition and color;
3. improved removal of waste products and excess fluid to reduce puffiness;
4. warming of the fingers and toes due to improved blood circulation (many elders suffer from cold fingers and toes);
5. improved mobility in the joints in the hands and feet; and
6. an increased awareness of the importance of caring for hands and feet, which can help prevent many common hand and foot disorders from occurring.

General Considerations

Downing and Rush (1972) identify numerous considerations and helpful hints for making massages more effective and more enjoyable:

1. The least expensive, yet most effective, liniment to use is a mixture of vegetable oil with some fragrance (e.g., a few drops of musk). Be sure that the oil is at least room temperature or warmer. For easy use, pour the oil into a plastic container with a narrow opening.

2. If the recipient of the massage feels awkward, or a group massage activity is being conducted, the massage recipients can remain seated in wheelchairs or chairs, fully clothed. However, the optimal conditions for a massage are to have the recipient partially undressed, lying on a massage table or gurney (usually available in a nursing home). Massage on a bed could be effective primarily for the face, arms, hands, legs, and feet, but not for the back, abdomen, and other body parts because of the lack of underlying support. Massage on the floor is also possible (use a foam pad for comfort and sheets to prevent staining the floor or carpet), but it tends to strain the massager's back.

3. The room temperature should be warm (over seventy-two degrees). People are difficult to warm once they are chilled.

4. The massager's hands should be warm, and fingernails should be short.

5. Do *not* use bright lighting.

6. Experiment with using soft, relaxing music in the background, but if the massager and/or the recipient seem to focus more on the music than on the massage, try massaging without music. Regardless of whether music is used, the environment should be quiet, relatively private, and free from distractions.

7. Talk as little as possible during the massage. However, sometimes (especially when working with nursing home residents) the recipients become extremely friendly, uninhibited, and expressive. Perhaps a reasonable compromise is to request silence and concentration on the sense of touch during some of the strokes, and allow free-flowing conversation at other times.

8. Ask the recipient for feedback during the massage in order to know whether to apply more pressure, less pressure, or whether to massage a particular area for a shorter or longer duration of time.

9. Hairy body areas require more oil.

10. Apply oil only on the body part immediately to be massaged.

11. Try never to lose contact with the recipient's body during the massage. When pouring oil, keep one arm or hand on the body, and pour the oil with the other hand into the hand on the recipient's body.

12. Relax hands, and apply pressure by using body weight, *not* muscles.

13. Involve the whole body in the massage, not just the hands.

14. If the massager is standing, try to keep the back straight, feet apart, and knees bent.
15. The speed and pressure used during the massage can vary once in a while to avoid monotony but, in general, maintain a flowing, even speed and degree of pressure.
16. Mold hands to fit the contours of the body parts over which they are passing.
17. Be especially gentle with very dry, chapped, injured, or sensitive body parts.
18. Prolonged, gentle pressure can loosen and relax tight and constricted body parts (e.g., curled fingers and toes can be straightened).
19. Do *not* force a joint to move.
20. Hands should be clean—wash with warm water and soap before beginning the massage.
21. Allow approximately forty-five minutes for the massage. The last few minutes of the massage should be devoted to silent thought and self-awareness of how the recipient's body parts feel.
22. As identified in the following section, a variety of strokes can be utilized. Try to use as many of these different strokes as possible. Because older adults often have thin, dry, or fragile skin that can easily be damaged, keep pressure light and use plenty of long, sweeping strokes. Also, avoid strong pressure on delicate bones and on stiff, painful, or swollen joints (Atkinson, 2001).

Massage Techniques/Strokes

There are numerous different massage strokes:

1. Massage the muscles with the ball of the thumb.
2. Move the fingertips in circles.
3. Knead the body with the fingers and hand.
4. Rake the body with the fingers.
5. Stroke the muscles with the heels of the hands.
6. Stroke the muscles with the undersides of closed fists.
7. Drum the muscles with the fingertips.
8. Move the undersides of the forearms in large sweeps and circles.
9. Press tightly over the muscles with the flat part of the elbow.
10. Lightly slap the body with cupped hands.

The following is a suggested sequence for a forty-five-minute massage session. The session begins with facial massage because (1) people identify themselves more by their face than any other part of their body and (2) touching the face is less taboo than touching other body parts (Downing and Rush, 1972). However, sometimes elders are apprehensive about someone touching their face. Others are hesitant to have anyone put any kind of liniment anywhere on their body, even on their hands. Therefore, it is sometimes best to begin the massage session with the back and shoulders (clothed), without the use of liniment. For others, it is best to begin with hand massage, so the recipient can see what you are doing and talk to you face to face. In a situation where college students or other volunteers are conducting a massage session for the first time, it is usually easiest and least threatening to do just hand massages.

The session outlined next can be adapted for a group of nursing home or assisted living residents in wheelchairs by allowing them to remain dressed, merely taking off shoes and socks for foot massage, rolling up pant legs for lower leg massage, and rolling up shirt sleeves for arm massage. The back and shoulders can be massaged gently without oil if the massage recipient remains clothed.

The massage session should involve only the back and shoulders, hands, and possibly the neck and face if either the massager or the recipient feels awkward about massaging other body parts. For the last activity of the semester, I (MJL) sometimes bring my students to a local nursing home or retirement home to give massages to the residents. Most students say it was the most therapeutic and enjoyable activity of the semester. However, some semesters, most students in the class are hesitant about being involved in any kind of massage activity and we do a different activity instead. The forty-five- to fifty-minute session usually consists of a getting reacquainted period, fifteen to twenty minutes of back and shoulder massage, ten to fifteen minutes of hand massage, a fifteen-minute facial (optional), time for elders to massage my students (I have received some excellent massages from women in their eighties and even nineties!), and time for closing discussion. During the massage session, elders usually open up to my students and vice versa, talking more freely than they have during any other activity during the semester. My students usually comment that the massage activity should have been done early in the semester, because it seems to be such a simple yet effective activity. However, the activity requires the elders to trust the students and the students to have confidence in themselves, which is why it is a good end-of-semester activity.

The different reactions of elders to a massage activity are interesting. Some are simply overjoyed at the idea of getting a massage for *free,* and are tickled by the idea that a student would be willing to take the time to massage them. Others are suspicious: Why would someone be giving them a massage? It must cost something! Some are afraid that the students don't know what they are doing, that the massage will injure them or hurt them. There are also those who simply do not understand or misconstrue the activity, they think that they will need to get undressed and lie on a table. Thus, some elders will adamantly refuse the offer of a massage, but will sit in the activity room, curious to see what will happen. After seeing their fellow residents enjoying back and shoulder and hand massages for a while, most of these skeptics are eager to receive a massage themselves. Those who are reluctant to use liniment should be encouraged to smell it and see how it feels on their hands. Student massagers should be reminded to use liniment sparingly, and exercise extreme caution at all times. If in doubt, massage lightly!

Suggested Sequence

    A. *Facial massage* (optional)
        1. Massage the forehead with the thumbs.
           a. Begin with the thumbs flat on the center/top of the forehead.
           b. Exert firm pressure, bringing the thumbs across the forehead in a horizontal line.
           c. Bring the thumbs down to the temples, and massage the temples *very lightly.*
           d. Repeat this procedure until the entire forehead has been massaged.
        2. Massage the cheeks with the fingertips.
           a. Begin massaging the lower area of the face.
           b. Gradually work upward to the eyes.
           c. Fingers should rotate in tiny circles as they move slowly up the face.
        3. Similarly, massage the neck and chin with the fingertips, working upward to the chin.
        4. Massage just the neck with the hands.
           a. Begin with the hands on the neck.
           b. Move the hands in circles around the entire neck area.
    B. *Shoulder and back massage* (for a recipient sitting in a chair, clothed, no liniment being used)
        1. Begin with the neck and shoulders.
        2. Focus on one area at a time; do not jump back and forth from one area of the neck and shoulders to the other.
        3. Begin with thumb circles, applying gentle pressure.
        4. Ask for feedback and adjust the amount of pressure according to your recipient's desires.

     5. Use as many of the ten different strokes listed as possible.

     6. Ask your recipient which strokes feel best and spend more time on those strokes.

C. *Arm massage* (optional)

     1. Massage the forearms.

        a. Place the person's elbow on the armrest and bring forearm to a vertical position.

        b. Place both hands on the wrist.

        c. Move hands down the forearm toward the elbow. Apply a great deal of thumb pressure.

        d. Repeat this motion several times.

     2. Similarly, massage the upper arms.

        a. Lift upper arm and bring the person's hand to the opposite shoulder.

        b. Place both hands on the elbow.

        c. Move hands down the upper arm toward the shoulder. Apply a great deal of pressure.

        d. Repeat this motion several times.

D. *Hand massage* (Atkinson, 2001)

     1. Make a hand sandwich.

        a. Place the recipient's hand in between both of the massager's hands.

        b. Gently squeeze the hand and hold in this position for a minute; ask the recipient to take some deep breaths and relax.

        c. Repeat with the other hand.

     2. Gentle stretch.

        a. Put some oil or cream on one hand.

        b. The recipient's hand is facing palm downward.

        c. Place your hands on either side with fingers curled underneath and thumbs on top.

        d. Draw thumbs out to the sides to create a rolling and stretching action over the back of the hand.

        e. Repeat several times.

     3. Stroking the back of the hand.

        a. The palm of the recipient's hand is facing downward.

        b. Wrap your hands around it, thumbs on top and fingers beneath.

        c. Use the pads of the thumbs to make alternate strokes across the top of the hand, going from the fingers to the wrist.

        d. Repeat six times or more with each hand.

4. Finger stretch.
    a. Palm faces downward; clasp the recipient's hand with one hand.
    b. With the other hand, work on one finger at a time.
    c. Hold the finger between the thumb and forefinger.
    d. Make gentle circular movements along the finger, working from the base to the top.
    e. Repeat several times on each finger; begin with the little finger and end with the thumb.
5. Palm stretch.
    a. Palm faces up; support the back of the hand with your hands.
    b. Place your thumbs on the palm, pointing toward the wrist.
    c. Push thumbs gently out to the sides to spread and stretch the palm.
    d. Hold the stretch for a count of five, then release and repeat twice or more.
6. Palm stroking and kneading.
    a. Palm faces up.
    b. Fingers support sides of hand, thumbs are in the palm.
    c. Knead the palm with the thumbs.
    d. Add some sliding strokes, going from the base of the fingers to the wrist.
    e. Repeat ten times or more.
7. Finishing touch.
    a. Palm faces downward, one hand is beneath it, the other one on top.
    b. With the fingertips of the free hand, stroke the top of the hand with a featherlike touch, working from the wrist to the fingertips.
    c. End with a hand sandwich (see #1).
E. *Leg massage* (optional)
    1. Massage the front of the lower leg.
        a. Place both hands on the recipient's skin, palms down, fingers facing in opposite directions.
        b. Glide hands up the lower leg, including the sides.
        c. Repeat with the other leg.
    2. Massage the knee.
        a. Crisscross thumbs over the knee.
        b. Move thumbs in opposite directions, making a circle around the knee cap.
        c. Repeat with the other knee.

   3. Massage the back of the leg (similar to the front of lower leg massage).
   4. Massage the calf by rotating the thumbs in tiny circles.
F. *Foot massage* (optional)
   1. Make a foot sandwich (similar to the hand sandwich).
   2. Thumb circles—work your thumbs in circles across the sole of the foot, going from the heel to the base of the toes. Repeat several times.
   3. Sole stretch.
      a. Rest the flat of one hand on the top of the foot.
      b. Make a loose fist with the free hand and place your knuckles just under the ball of the foot.
      c. Stroke the fist firmly down the sole of the foot toward the heel so that the backs of your fingers press into the skin.
      d. Repeat several times.
      e. Make firm, circular movements around the arch of the foot.
   4. Toe stretch—similar to the finger stretch.
   5. Finishing touch—similar to #7 under hand massage.

Summary

The massage sequence described in this chapter can be adapted for elders in a variety of settings. In a nursing home or assisted living community, massages can be given to bedridden elders on an individual basis, omitting some of the strokes if the elder remains clothed. Higher-functioning nursing home and assisted living residents can be massaged in a group setting (seated in wheelchairs and clothed), hopefully with a 1:1 or 1:2 ratio of staff and volunteers to elders. Groups that are composed of a mixture of high-functioning and low-functioning elders can utilize the higher-functioning elders as aides to staff in massaging low-functioning elders. The high-functioning elders can also be trained to massage one another, or perform self-massage (see Brown's [1996] book for techniques of self-massage). Thus, elders of almost any functioning level can enjoy the benefits of massage.

CLOWNING

Benefits of Clowning (Towsen, 1976)

   Another beneficial and enjoyable recreational activity for elders, though not usually associated with them, is clowning. Clowning is not only amusing; it is also an excellent activity for improving the mental and physical functioning of impaired elders. In the physical domain, clowning can help improve coordination, balance, and reduce stress. The psychological benefits are numerous.

1. Communication skills are improved, especially nonverbal communication skills such as body language and eye contact.
2. Mental stimulation is provided, especially for mentally impaired elders.
3. Because clowning is so unusual, it can prod the memory of someone with poor short-term memory.
4. Clowning can be a creative outlet for elders if they dress up and put on makeup to be clowns themselves.
5. Clowning can provide an outlet for the expression of emotions.
6. Many times, withdrawn elders are seemingly miraculously drawn out.

Clowning also promotes group interaction and socialization. Certainly, clowning is a desirable activity for elders because of its potential benefits. Guidelines for leading a clowning activity with elders are presented in the next subsection.

Guidelines (Towsen, 1976)

There are three different types of clowns:

1. *The mime:* This clown is white-faced, and not much makeup is used. The clown acts out stories and expresses emotions nonverbally.
2. *The traditional clown:* This clown has a big smile and rosy cheeks, and usually a baggy, funny costume.
3. *The character-type clown:* This clown dresses up to play a specific comedic role. For example, rodeos often have clowns dressed as cowboys.

The procedures described next pertain more to traditional clowns than to mimes or character clowns.

Materials Needed (Towsen, 1976)

1. Ping-Pong balls
2. Brightly colored nail polish
3. Funny hats

4. Brightly colored baggy clothes
5. Mirrors
6. Balloons
7. Strings
8. Pictures of different clowns
9. Skin lotion
10. Water-based clown white (face makeup)
11. Grease paints

Becoming a Clown (Towsen, 1976)

The clown-to-be should put on the makeup and costume in front of the participants so that they can see the transformation take place, and possibly become motivated to be clowns later during the activity. First, the clown should put on the funny clothes. Next, skin lotion should be applied, as this application of lotion makes it easier to take off the makeup later. The clown white should then be applied, followed by the colorful grease paints. Make funny noses by cutting Ping-Pong balls in half and painting them with nail polish. For finishing touches, attach funny-shaped balloons and wear unusual hats and wigs.

Once the clown has completed dressing and applying makeup, elders should be encouraged to get dressed up as clowns. One motivational technique is to show elders pictures of different clowns and ask them which one they would like to be made up to look like. Assure people that the makeup is easy to remove. Sit people in front of mirrors so that they can enjoy seeing themselves being transformed into clowns.

Once people have been transformed into clowns, a drama session can be conducted. Pantomimes and short humorous skits are effective because clowning tends to allow people to more freely express emotions, play roles they normally do not play in day-to-day life, laugh, and generally be less inhibited. Clowning can also be a well-received intergenerational activity. Young children are fascinated to watch elders transform themselves into clowns, and then are very amused by humorous performances by a group of clowns.

Summary

Clowning is a beneficial and enjoyable activity for elders. It allows elders to use their imagination and creativity, and it enables them to express their individuality. Above all, clowning can generate quite a few laughs!

DRAMA

In this section, drama activities for elders are discussed (see Photo 14.2). Topics covered include the benefits of drama for elders, components of a drama program; and special considerations in leading a drama session.

Benefits

The following are emotional and psychological benefits of drama for elders (Burger, 1980; Thurman and Piggins, 1982):

1. Reduces feelings of loneliness, isolation, and depression
2. Promotes social interaction
3. Validates personal experiences by remembering past events
4. Establishes a bridge between the past and the present
5. Enhances self-esteem
6. Boosts morale

Clark and Osgood (1985) report that research on the effects of a ten-month applied theater program with over 100 elders in Virginia indicates that the program participants were significantly less lonely and were happier than a matched control group of elders who did not participate in the program.

Thus, the benefits of drama activities for elders are significant. In the next subsection, components of a drama program are discussed.

Components of a Drama Program (Thurman and Piggins, 1982)

There are six components or phases of a drama program for elders: the introduction; sensory exercises; movement and pantomime; imagination

PHOTO 14.2. Drama with Elders

stretchers; improvisations; and session plans with a unifying theme. In addition, five to ten minutes at the end of each session should be allotted for a discussion of participants' impressions of the session. All drama sessions should include both the introduction and time for the concluding discussion, with any combination of the other phases enacted in between. The sensory exercises, movement and pantomime, imagination stretchers, and improvisations are most appropriate for the first few meetings of a drama group. Session plans with a unifying theme should be attempted after the group has met a few times and seems ready to try something more difficult. The session plans with a unifying theme are more involved and should be rehearsed several times until the group is able to master the session plan.

Introduction to the Session

The introductory phase of the session is designed to gain the group's interest. Open-ended questions are asked relevant to the upcoming theme of the session. To encourage participation, all responses are accepted; no answers are considered wrong.

Icebreakers can also be used as an element of the introductory phase to help the group members get acquainted and feel comfortable interacting with one another. Icebreakers are effective in heightening concentration, increasing the attention span, creating a supportive environment, and increasing energy levels.

An example of an appropriate icebreaker for the introductory phase of a drama session is the activity "How Do You Feel About . . ." Participants should sit in a small circle, facing one another. The leader begins by reciting a phrase such as "I feel . . . ," "I like . . . ," "My pet peeve is . . . ," etc. and then looks to the nearest participant to complete the phrase by briefly and openly expressing whatever comes to mind. Every person in the group is called upon to give his or her answers. Similar responses among different individuals help to validate personal feelings. Humorous responses elicit laughter, which in turn makes the group more relaxed and less inhibited.

Sensory Exercises

Many older adults experience a decline in their ability to distinguish sensory stimuli, resulting in a loss of self-esteem. By practicing sensory exercises, the ability to recognize senses can be heightened, renewing self-reliance in daily functioning.

An example of an appropriate sensory exercise is "Sleuth."
Exercise: "Sleuth" (Thurman and Piggins, 1982)
Objectives: To increase concentration and ability to focus on visual stimuli

Directions:
1. Pair all participants with a partner.
2. Direct the partners to observe each other for sixty seconds, carefully noticing each other's appearance (e.g., clothes, jewelry, hair, etc.).
3. At the end of one minute, ask the partners to turn their backs on each other and change three things about themselves.
4. Ask the partners to turn and face each other and share the changes they detect.

"Sleuth" can be especially challenging and humorous if partners make very subtle changes in appearances (e.g., remove a ring, unfasten one button).

Movement and Pantomime

These activities increase the energy level, enhance body awareness and coordination, and stir the imagination. Pantomime involves the use of imagery and characterization.

An example of a movement and pantomime activity is "Adverbs."
Exercise: "Adverbs" (Thurman and Piggins, 1982)
Objectives: To communicate ideas through actions and observe and discriminate among different qualities of movement
Directions:
1. Divide the group in half.
2. Group A decides on an adverb and keeps it a secret from group B. Some examples of adverbs are *lazily, nervously, intensely, cautiously,* and *frantically.*
3. Group B decides on actions they want group A to perform.
4. Group B tells group A what action they would like group A to perform.
5. Group A performs the action in the manner of the chosen adverb.
6. Group B tries to guess what adverb group A has chosen.
7. After a few attempts, the groups can reverse roles.

Imagination Stretchers

The imagination of elders will diminish if it is not exercised. Imagination stretcher activities involve sharing memories, associations, and ideas in a supportive environment and, most important, force people to use their imaginations.

An example of an imagination stretcher is "Transformation of Real Objects."

Exercise: "Transformation of Real Objects" (Thurman and Piggins, 1982)
Objectives: To exercise the imagination and share ideas
Directions:
1. The leader presents an object (e.g., rope, yardstick, cup, etc.) and demonstrates its normal use.
2. Through movement, the leader transforms the object to have a different use. For example, one can hold and swing a ruler so as to transform it into a baseball bat.
3. The leader passes the object around to each person in the group to pantomime a different use for the object.
4. The rest of the group members try to guess the pantomime.
5. The activity continues until all group members have had an opportunity to transform at least one object.

Improvisations

Individuals become emotionally involved in the activity while they actually become part of the scene. The group members are asked to experiment with dramatic principles, sensory skills, and create an impromptu scene incorporating interaction and movement. The higher the emotional involvement, the higher the level of belief.

An example of an improvisation is "Living Pictures."

Exercise: "Living Pictures" (Thurman and Piggins, 1982)
Objectives: To explore feelings through body language and experience a common group effort
Directions:
1. Divide the group into groups of four or five people each.
2. Present a picture title (e.g., the Wedding, the First Baby, the Picnic, etc.) to each group.
3. Direct the group to physically arrange themselves according to the theme of the picture. Each group decides on the setting, relationships, body positioning, etc. of their picture.
4. Each group presents their picture while the other groups try to guess the title of the picture.

Another example of an improvisation is "Stuck In" (Clark and Osgood, 1985). Participants are asked to develop a scene with a beginning, middle, and end on the general theme of being stuck in something (e.g., an elevator, a traffic jam, a bad relationship, etc.). If the larger group is divided into smaller groups, when each group does their improvisation, the other groups can be asked to try to guess what the acting group is stuck in.

An improvisation that can be adapted for intergenerational groups is "Reverse Role-Playing" (Weisberg and Wilder, 1985). Elders and youth would first discuss situations in which their generations might be in disagreement or conflict. The young people then act as they imagine the elders would act, and the elders act as they imagine the young people would act. In addition, women can play the part of men and vice versa. The results can be quite humorous! Exercise 14.1 asks you to develop some ideas for a "Reverse Role-Play" improvisational skit.

Session Plans with a Unifying Theme

This component is more involved than the other components. The session plan with a unifying theme should be a dramatic activity that needs to be rehearsed several times in order to master. Hopefully, once the session plan has been mastered, a performance can be arranged (e.g., at a nursing home or as a performance for children). The following are some ideas for session plans:

- A melodrama involving audience participation. The audience cheers, boos, and makes other noises in response to cue cards while the characters act out a comedy/drama, perhaps a spoof of a western hero/villain story.
- An enactment of a popular television show or movie. The memories of group members can be stimulated to write a script for the simulation of a familiar old movie or television show.
- A reader's theater activity is an excellent choice for elders with poor short-term memory. In the reader's theater, characters are not required to memorize their lines but rather expressively read and act out their parts. Numerous books are available in most libraries that have appropriate plays for a reader's theater activity.
- A biblical role-play is another appropriate type of session plan. The biblical role-play either can be in the format of a reader's theater (characters read expressively and play the parts of characters in a familiar story in the Bible) or can be an improvisational activity if the group members are very familiar with the story.

Videotaping the drama session can add of excitement to the session. Videotaping can be a motivational force during rehearsals. Playback of the vid-

EXERCISE 14.1. Reverse Role-Playing

*Cast of characters:*_____

_____

_____

Introduction/background to the situation/conflict: _____

_____

_____

_____

_____

_____

_____

_____

Description of opening scene: _____

_____

_____

_____

_____

_____

_____

Ideas on different directions the improvisation can go: _____

_____

_____

_____

_____

_____

_____

eotape at the end of the session can be an image booster, as well as a laughter-inducing stimulus.

Concluding the Drama Session

Allow five to ten minutes at the end of the session for individuals to share their impressions of the drama session.

Special Considerations in Leading a Drama Session (Burger, 1980; Thurman and Piggins, 1982)

The leader of a drama session for elders must create a warm, supportive atmosphere to reduce inhibitions and foster feelings of acceptance. The use of physical contact can be helpful in creating this type of environment. In addition, sensory input should be offered to individuals with impaired eyesight and/or hearing.

The leader of a drama class should always overplan the session. The drama class will appear much more invigorating when there is not quite enough time to finish all the material, rather than running out of material when time remains in the session.

A variety of stimuli should be incorporated into each session. Various props, music, sounds, mentally challenging activities, and opportunities for movement exploration enhance the success of drama session. At times, the drama leader may feel the need to share personal experiences to spark an interchange for others to relate their own personal experiences.

As in any other recreational activity for elders, match the pace of the activity to the pace of the group members and be prepared to adapt activities according to the functioning level of the participants. A major challenge for the leader is maintaining the interest of higher-functioning group members while slowing the pace of the activity to ensure the full participation of lower-functioning group members.

REMINISCENCE AND LIFE REVIEW

According to Weiss (1993), reminiscing is an enjoyable activity for elders. It enables the review of lifetime feats and adventures and provides an opportunity to receive acknowledgement from others. Weiss (1993) advocates focused reminiscing as opposed to freewheeling reminiscing, because it reduces ambiguity, fosters more depth and continuity, and enhances confidence because elders can pick the topics to discuss with which they feel most comfortable.

According to Magee (1988), life review is a form of reminiscence in which individuals reflect upon their personal history and accept responsibility for it. It focuses on the connection of the past to the present, thereby enabling elders to deal with current stressors in life by drawing on the skills and self-confidence that helped them in similar situations in the past. Magee (1988) discusses how poetry can be used to aid in life review: First, anthologies of poetry are distributed to group members; elders look through the poetry and are asked to select poems which express themes that have been prominent in their lives. The group then meets to discuss the poems and themes they have chosen.

Similarly, other activities can assist in reminiscing and life review. Drama activities that involve a recollection of past events are one example. Singing old songs or listening to old music can also facilitate reminiscing and life review. Even gardening and pet activities can lead to discussions on past experiences with animals, farms, and gardens. As Weiss (1993) states, reminiscing can be viewed as part of the recreational entity—contemplation.

MUSIC

Music is one of the most universally enjoyable and beneficial forms of recreation. People of all ages and functioning levels can be positively affected by music. The possibilities for utilizing music with elders are endless. In this section, the use of music with elders is examined briefly (further reading and musical training is strongly recommended). Topics discussed in this section include the benefits of music and ideas for music activity sessions.

Benefits

Wapner (1981) identifies several benefits of music:

1. Music can have a relaxing, stress-reducing effect.
2. Music can have a stimulating, energizing effect.
3. Musical activities can provide much-needed sensory stimulation, which can contribute to higher functioning of senses such as hearing, speech, and touch (if rhythm instruments are used).

In addition, Douglass (1978) states that music can

1. motivate even depressed elders to participate in activities,
2. stimulate social interaction and improve socialization and communication skills,

3. provide a creative outlet for individuals,
4. allow individuals to physically and emotionally express themselves, and
5. help elders feel better about themselves and enhance one's self-concept.

Thus, musical activities are very beneficial for elders. You only need to think of how enjoyable and integral an aspect of your life music is in order to appreciate the benefits of musical activities for elders.

Program Ideas

A selected few of the many musical activity possibilities for elders are described in this section. For additional musical activity ideas, consult Douglass' (1978), Schulberg's (1981), and Wapner's (1981) books. Also, refer to the chapter in this book on intergenerational recreational activity for ideas on intergenerational musical activities. Some of the more popular musical activity possibilities follow:

Listening Activities

- Live performances by either a visiting performer, or a field trip to a performance can be extremely entertaining. Even very confused elders are drawn out and hum along to familiar tunes.
- Listen to and critique or discuss recorded music.
- Listen to different types of music or music of various countries as an appreciation activity.
- Listen to and analyze the meaning of song lyrics. Songs dealing with a specific topic (e.g., love, aging, or social issues) can be listened to in order to generate discussion. Such an activity can prove to be enlightening and mentally stimulating.

Singing Activities

- For higher-functioning elders, a choral group with regularly scheduled rehearsals and performances can be formed.
- An intergenerational singing group can be formed, as depicted in the award-winning film, *Close Harmony.*
- One of the most enjoyable yet simplest activity to conduct with elders of any functioning level is a sing-along. All that is needed is a musician who can play songs familiar to the elders in the group. Conduct

the activity *without* song sheets, and select songs that most elders are familiar enough with to sing from memory. Song sheets tend to inhibit social interaction during the activity, because the participants are looking down at their sheets, rather than at one another or the leader. Also, the song sheets can be clumsy and difficult for impaired elders to hold. Another option is to have lyrics on overhead transparencies, projecting the words on a big screen in the front. The advantage is that everyone is looking in the same direction, but a disadvantage is that the lights would need to be dimmed. Children's songs/camp songs should be avoided, as elders might be offended by being asked to sing songs they perceive as being childish. Patriotic songs (e.g., "Yankee Doodle Dandy") and old standards (e.g., "You Are My Sunshine") are good choices for sing-alongs. Exercise 14.2 asks you to generate a list of appropriate songs for a sing-along in a retirement home. If you have trouble thinking of more than ten songs, ask an elder for help!

Playing Musical Instruments

- High-functioning elders might be interested in forming a performing ensemble.
- High-functioning elders might also be interested in taking music lessons in order to learn how to play the guitar, piano, recorder, and other instruments.
- Moderately impaired or lower-functioning elders not able to play a band instrument or learn how to play an instrument can still enjoy being part of a rhythm band, accompanying a pianist, guitarist, or recorded music with simple rhythm instruments (e.g., sandpaper blocks, triangles, bells, maracas, and tambourines).

Composing Activities

- An excellent creative outlet is the composing of original music and lyrics. This activity is intellectually stimulating and can enhance self-esteem.
- A creative and humorous activity is the composing of satiric lyrics to replace the existing lyrics of a popular song.

Movement to Music

A variety of music (various tempos and rhythmic patterns) should be utilized in order to elicit different types of movements.

EXERCISE 14.2. Sing-Along Song List

1. _____

2. _____

3. _____

4. _____

5. _____

6. _____

7. _____

8. _____

9. _____

10. _____

11. _____

12. _____

13. _____

14. _____

15. _____

16. _____

17. _____

18. _____

19. _____

20. _____

Musical Games

- Musical bingo is a great favorite (I led a two-hour game in a nursing home—the participants did not want to quit even after two full hours of playing the game). There are several versions of this game; the directions for one of the more popular versions follow:
  - Players receive regular bingo cards and chips.
  - The leader calls out the numbers.
  - As each number is called, players that have the number on their card notify the leader.
  - An excerpt from a popular song is hummed or played on an instrument. The players must correctly guess the title of the song in order to place a chip on their card.

  Naturally, the rules of this game can be made more flexible when working with a lower-functioning population.
- A variety of musical quiz games are possible, such as musical tic-tac-toe, musical baseball, musical anagrams, and others (refer to Douglass' [1978] and Schulberg's [1981] books).

Summary

This section presented a small sample of musical activity possibilities. It is important to remember to utilize music that is suited to the interests of the group you are leading.

People in different age groups tend to prefer music from different time periods. Because teenagers and young adults tend to be the most avid followers of popular music, elders tend to be most familiar with music and performers more popular during the time period when they were in their teens and twenties. Thus, a person age sixty-five in the year 2004 might be most familiar with the music of the 1950s and early 1960s. Meanwhile, a person age ninety-five in the year 2004 would probably be most familiar with the music of the 1920s and 1930s. Thus, the varying musical interests of different age groups of elders must be considered in selecting music for musical activities. Just think: People ages sixty to sixty-five in the year 2015 will probably be most interested in rock and roll music.

ARTS AND CRAFTS

In this section, an overview of arts and crafts activities for elders is presented. Many books have been written on this topic. The aim of this section is not to provide an in-depth discussion of arts and crafts for elders that has already been completed in other books. Rather, this section is intended to give the reader a basic understanding of arts and crafts activity possibilities and practical guidelines for leading them. Wilkinson and Heater's (1979), Williams' (1962), Merrill's (1967), Fish's (1971), and Wapner's (1981) books are recommended as resources for further information on arts and crafts for elders. This section has been divided into several subsections: goals and objectives of arts and crafts for elders; benefits of arts and crafts; guidelines in programming arts and crafts activities; special considerations; and a listing of arts and crafts activities.

Goals and Objectives

Arts and crafts activities should augment other programs occurring at the facility or institution. A unifying theme involving other events may provide motivation and a purpose to participate (e.g., making decorations for an upcoming party or creating special place mats for a family luncheon). The gathering of needed materials is an integral part of an arts and crafts session and participants can be involved in the planning and budgeting of materials (Wapner, 1981).

An effective arts and crafts program for elders is concerned with the creative and productive process of the group members (Wilkinson and Heater, 1979). In addition, the group members should be allowed to demonstrate their individuality in the arts and crafts they produce (Wapner, 1981). This allows the opportunity for self-expression, which can enhance emotional growth.

Another objective of an arts and crafts program is to utilize elders' inherent capacities and interests (Wilkinson and Heater, 1979). Consequently, varying levels of abilities and interests are accounted for in planning the arts and crafts sessions.

An important objective of an arts and crafts program is to improve skill levels. Skill levels are enhanced as a consequence of working on different projects. This is achieved by the necessity to focus on the project and utilizing cognitive, perceptual, and motor capacities in a constructive fashion.

Participation in an arts and crafts program gives elders a lasting object of personal value (Wapner, 1981). Thus, the participant may experience a sense of achievement and productiveness.

Benefits of Arts and Crafts (Fish, 1971; Wilkinson and Heater, 1979; and Wapner, 1981)

Participation in an arts and crafts program enhances physical, cognitive, social, and emotional growth.

1. Physical benefits
   a. Strengthens and tones muscles
   b. Increases range of motion
   c. Heightens tactile stimulation
   d. Improves manual dexterity
   e. Improves eye/hand coordination
2. Cognitive benefits
   a. Enhances perception
   b. Increases concentration
   c. Provides reality orientation
   d. Increases the attention span
   e. Increases concentration
   f. Evokes color identification
   g. Enhances the ability to adhere to directions
3. Social benefits
   a. Promotes social interaction
   b. Creates an opportunity for service to others
   c. Promotes group cohesion
4. Emotional benefits
   a. Channels energy
   b. Enhances self-esteem
   c. Provides an outlet for creativity
   d. Recognizes individual achievement
   e. Allows for ego satisfaction
   f. Provides an avocational interest

Guidelines in Programming Arts and Crafts

The following are practical guidelines in programming arts and crafts for elders:

1. Sufficient time should be allotted to set up and clean up art activities.
2. Specific tasks should evolve from simple procedures to more complex (Wilkinson and Heater, 1979).
3. Discuss the activity ideas with the participants prior to their occurrence.
4. Specific tasks should be broken down into basic steps to allow for greater participation (Wapner, 1981).
5. Plan projects that are economical, since funding for activities is usually limited (Wapner, 1981).

Special Considerations in Programming Arts and Crafts

The following are special considerations when programming arts and crafts activities for elders:

1. Special attention is required for very confused elders in a group arts and crafts setting. These individuals must be observed to avoid the possibility of them injuring themselves or digesting the art materials.
2. Crafts projects should not be so simple that they are boring and, on the other hand, they should not be too difficult so as to be frustrating (Wapner, 1981).
3. A higher degree of involvement can be obtained by allowing elders' input into choosing the crafts projects (Merrill, 1967).
4. Crafts that are very fine or intricate in detail may be difficult for elders with impaired vision (Williams, 1962).
5. The availability of a specific crafts room can generate the involvement of individuals working on their own time.
6. The use of bright colors may be helpful.
7. A discussion of the meaning of the project may increase motivation to participate.
8. Demonstrations, combined with clear instructions, are most effective. Try to relate one step at a time (Fish, 1971).

Arts and Crafts Activity Ideas

Place mats	Mobiles	Painting
Collage	Stuffed animals	Papercraft
Stained glass	Mosaics	Metalwork
Plaques	Sewing	Quilting
Table decorations	Signs and posters	Calligraphy
Bookmarks	Sketching	Ceramics
Greeting cards	Woodworking	Weaving
Decorated flowerpots	Caning	Cloth flowers
Wreaths	Knitting	Doormats
Holiday decorations	Hooked yard rugs	
Costume jewelry	Leathercraft	

The activity ideas listed represent oniy a small range of the arts and crafts activities possible in working with elders. The books cited in this section of the chapter should be consulted for arts and crafts activity ideas.

HORTICULTURE THERAPY

In this section, an overview of horticulture therapy for elders is presented. This section is intended to enhance the reader's awareness and understanding of the use of horticulture therapy with elders. Further reading on this topic is strongly recommended for those interested in incorporating horticulture therapy into a therapeutic recreation program for elders. This section has been divided into several subsections: benefits of horticulture therapy; background of horticulture therapy; and a listing of horticulture activity ideas.

Benefits of Horticulture Therapy

Horticulture activities can be used for therapeutic purposes. Such services as physical therapy, occupational therapy, recreational therapy, and vocational therapy can incorporate horticulture as a rehabilitative mechanism. Manual dexterity, the ability to understand instructions and follow directions, and the ability to concentrate are important skills utilized in horticulture therapy (Olszowy, 1978).

Horticulture as therapy is unlike many other therapies in that the focus is on living beings. Research indicates (Olszowy, 1978) a symbiotic relationship between humans and plant life.

Plants seem to thrive best with human care and, likewise, a psychological need in people is fulfilled through horticulture because a bond is created with the environment.

Caring for plants fulfills different needs in different people. For some, caring for plants poses a challenge; for others it becomes a responsibility and a desire for accomplishment. Caring for plants also provides an exposure to coping with loss (Olszowy, 1978). In addition, it can be a means of increasing "current concerns" (Riordan and Williams, 1988). Instead of dwelling on losses and other life changes, gardening can keep an older adult focused on the present by providing ongoing tasks and responsibilities.

Another therapeutic value of horticulture therapy is that it teaches patience. Waiting for the seed to germinate, the cutting to root, or the plant to flower requires patience (Olszowy, 1978).

Horticulture therapy can occur in a group setting conducive to social interaction, thereby helping to fill a void in the lives of socially isolated elders. Caring for plants also helps elders feel a greater sense of control over the environment. This is an important benefit because a loss of control over the environment is a concern for many elders (Olszowy, 1978).

The following are intellectual, emotional, and physical benefits of horticulture therapy (Olszowy, 1978; Riordan and Williams, 1988):

Intellectual Benefits

1. New skills are learned.
2. Vocabulary and communication skills are enhanced.
3. Curiosity is heightened.
4. Observation skills are increased.
5. Sensory perception is improved.
6. Training for vocational and prevocational opportunities are provided.

Emotional Benefits

1. Confidence and self-esteem are enhanced.
2. Outlets for aggressive behavior are provided.
3. Opportunities for self-expression are offered.
4. Activities arousing interest in the future are provided.

Physical Benefits

1. Basic motor skills are enhanced.
2. Outdoor activities that improve physical and mental health are participated in regularly.
3. Bone density is improved and thereby osteoporosis is prevented, according to a research study involving over 3,000 women ages fifty and older ("Tending your garden means tending your bones," 2003).

Background of Horticulture Therapy (Olszowy, 1978; Riordan and Williams, 1988)

For hundreds of years, garden activities have been used as a form of preventive medicine. Before the science of psychiatry was developed, physicians advocated working in the garden for patients with emotional problems. In 1798, Benjamin Rush prescribed digging in the soil as a curative agent for the mentally ill. Agricultural activities were viewed as helpful to mental patients in Spain dating back as early as 1806. In the early 1900s, garden activities were established in many hospitals and institutions for therapeutic purposes. After World Wars I and II, many veterans' hospitals developed garden therapy programs for their patients.

Today, many diverse institutions across the country have incorporated horticulture therapy into their activity programs, including schools, hospitals, arboreta, community centers, correctional institutions, rehabilitation facilities, and other institutional settings. The growth in horticulture therapy is expected to continue producing many new innovative programs that can be adapted for elders.

Activity Ideas

The following is a brief overview of activity ideas for a horticulture program for elders (Olszowy, 1978):

1. Drying plants and flowers
2. Flower arranging
3. Terrariums
4. Window box gardening
5. Growing herbs
6. Hanging baskets
7. Forcing bulbs
8. Vegetable gardening
9. Flower gardening

Alvarez (1992) discusses the advantages of hydroponic gardening for elders. Hydroponics, also known as soilless gardening, involves the growing of plants in a mineral solution instead of in soil. It is advantageous for elders in that the beds can be raised, making them wheelchair accessible and eliminating the need to stoop and bend, and the garden can be placed in any sunny spot, including patios, terraces, courtyards, and rooftops.

In addition to Olszowy's (1978) book, the following books and organizations should be consulted for additional information on activity ideas using horticulture therapy.

American Horticultural Therapy Association <www.ahta.org>.
Chaplin, M. (1978). *Gardening for the physically handicapped and elderly.* London: B.T. Batsford, Ltd.
Hill, C.O. and Relf, P.D. (1982). Gardening as an outdoor activity in geriatric institutions. *Activities, Adaptation, and Aging,* 3(1), 47-54.
Moore, B. (1989). *Growing with gardening: A twelve-month guide for therapy, recreation, and education.* Chapel Hill: University of North Carolina Press.

Relf, P.D. (1989). *Gardening in raised beds and containers for the elderly and physically handicapped.* Blacksburg: Cooperative Extension Service, Virginia Polytechnic University.

Rothert, E. and Daubert, J. (1981). *Horticultural therapy for senior centers, nursing homes, and retirement living.* Glencoe, IL: Chicago Horticultural Society.

Summary

Horticulture therapy is a rapidly expanding field, and this growth is expected to continue (Olszowy, 1978). Horticulture is a valuable therapy for older adults due to the many benefits derived from participation in such a program.

PET THERAPY

Another therapy which focuses on living beings is pet therapy (see Photo 14.3). According to Bustad (1980) and Cusack and Smith (1984), the benefits of companion animal association are especially significant for elders. An overview of the benefits of, considerations in, and program ideas for the use of pets with elders is presented in this section.

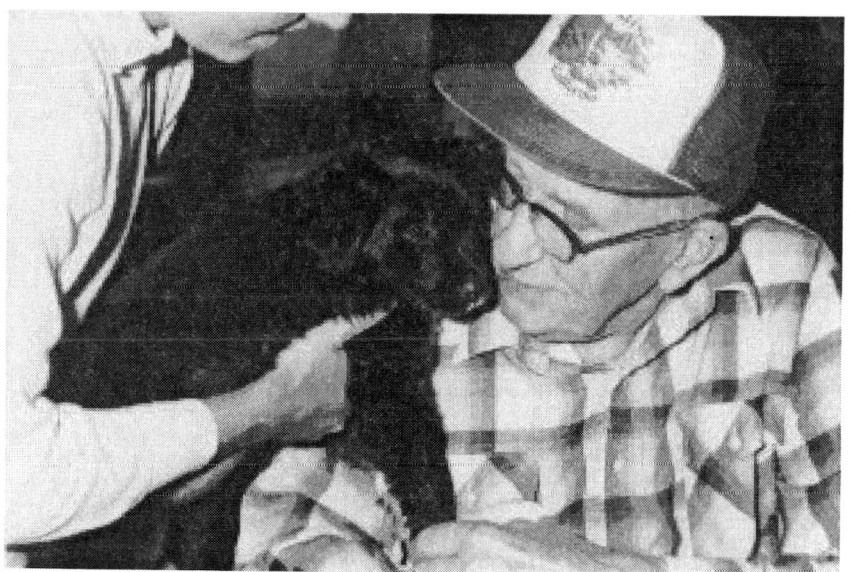

PHOTO 14.3. Pet Therapy with Elders

Benefits

Cusack and Smith (1984) cite research studies which indicate that pets can physiologically benefit people in several ways:

1. Pet ownership stimulates and facilitates recovery from illness.
2. Interaction with pets lowers blood pressure.
3. People who care for a pet tend also to take better care of themselves with regard to nutrition, hygienic and health conditions, adequate shelter, and creating a caring living environment.

Pets can also psychologically benefit elders in several ways:

1. Pets provide a much-needed outlet for affectionate, cuddling behavior (Corson and Corson, 1981).
2. Pets can allay anxiety and relieve depression ("Elderly Berliners Respond to Pet Therapy," 1992).
3. Pets provide the opportunity to be involved in a loving relationship with minimal risks for the elder. In a relationship with an animal, the person can choose the rules for the relationship and choose the degree of closeness, without fear of rejection (Cass, 1981).
4. Pets provide companionship and can reduce feelings of loneliness and isolation (Cusack and Smith, 1984).
5. Pets can help elders feel safer and more secure, especially in novel situations (Cusack and Smith, 1984).
6. Caring for a pet's needs provides elders with daily responsibilities and activities that can enhance reality orientation (Cusack and Smith, 1984).
7. Animals provide elders with amusing and entertaining experiences. Pets can induce laughter, prompt a sense of humor, and generally improve morale (Cusack and Smith, 1984).

According to Cusack and Smith (1984), pets can positively affect elders' social behavior:

1. Activities with pets can occur in a group setting conducive to forming new friendships.
2. Pets are an excellent topic for conversation, and can help people ease into social interaction.

Cusack and Smith (1984) also discuss how pets can facilitate a variety of activities:

1. Animals often motivate elders to engage in higher levels of physical activity and exercise. For example, the responsibility of needing to walk a dog can cause people to walk much more than they would if they did not have a dog.
2. Animals are sometimes able to prompt noncommunicative elders to speak.
3. Pets can stimulate creativity (e.g., in terms of grooming or decorating a pet for display).
4. Pets can stimulate elders to engage in educational activities (e.g., research aspects of pet care).

Thus, elders can benefit in numerous ways from interaction with animals. In the following section, recreational program ideas involving animals are discussed.

Program Ideas

Numerous types of animals can be utilized in a pet program for elders, such as dogs, cats, caged birds, rabbits, small caged mammals, aquarium fish, and vivarium reptiles and amphibians. Dogs are perhaps the most popular pets because of the numerous activities possible with dogs, such as:

1. A dog show, in which elders groom, decorate, and display their dogs. The local humane society will often be able to provide puppies for such an activity. Local pet stores might be able to loan grooming brushes for the activity. The dog show activity gives elders an opportunity to have a great deal of much-needed tactile contact with a living being. The activity can also stimulate creativity in decorating the dog and enhance self-esteem in displaying the dog.
2. A dog obedience show can be a stimulating and entertaining activity. Local dog fanciers clubs or pet shops are often willing to provide assistance for such an activity.
3. A "dog day" special event can be held, in which staff, program participants, and their families bring their dogs to the center or nursing home for a dog show and social activity.
4. Humorous activities possible with dogs include trying to teach the dogs to do tricks, puppy races, and a person/pet look-a-like contest (be

sure to introduce this activity properly so that it will not offend anyone).

Activities with pets must be carefully planned in order to be successful.
Exercise 14.3 asks you to plan a pet therapy session in a nursing home, retirement home, senior day care center, or senior center.

According to Corson and Corson (1981), the best types of dogs to use in a
pet program for elders are wirehair fox terriers, small poodles, border col-
lies, Labrador retrievers, Dobermans, cocker spaniels, dachshunds, and
some mongrels. Dogs can be utilized with elders in several ways: as occasional visitors, as individual pets, and as group mascots.

Considerations

Cusack and Smith (1984) identify several considerations in establishing
a pet program for elders:

1. The estimated yearly upkeep costs for different types of pets are $500-
   $700 for large dogs, $150-$200 for cats, and $150-$400 for large
   birds.
2. Allergic reactions of some elders to certain types of hair and fur
   should be considered.
3. The death of a pet can be devastating. Try to select young and healthy
   animals for mascots and individual pets, animals which are likely to
   outlive the people caring for them.
4. Legal restrictions regarding pets (especially relevant to institutional
   settings) must be considered.
5. A staff member must be responsible for overseeing that program participants properly care for the pet.

Summary

A variety of recreational activities and programs for elders involving animals are possible. As discussed earlier, pet activities and programs have
great potential physical, psychological, and social benefits for elders.

LAUGHTER AND HUMOR

Humor and laughter inducement have been cited as important benefits of
many of the recreational activities, programs, and techniques previously

EXERCISE 14.3. Pet Therapy Session Plans

Number of elders in your group: _____

Number of pets needed: _____

Number of staff/volunteers needed: _____

Type(s) of pets to be involved: _____

Where pets will be obtained: _____

How the pets will be transported to and from the facility: _____

_____

Activities to be attempted, and approximate time needed for each one:

_____

1. _____

_____

2. _____

_____

3. _____

_____

4. _____

_____

5. _____

_____

6. _____

_____

7. _____

_____

discussed. The purpose of this section is to further clarify the importance and benefits of laughter and humor for elders.

Laughter and humor are expressive and social outlets. Laughter is also an outlet for releasing excess energy. Thus, laughter can have a relaxing, stress-reducing effect on people.

According to Moody (1978), laughter and humor can be valuable in facilitating interaction between doctors and their patients. Similarly, humor and laughter can open avenues of communication between senior center, day care, hospice, or nursing home staff and their elderly clients.

Laughter can also produce impressive physiological benefits including

1. relief of tension headaches through laughter's relaxing effect on the tightened muscles in the back of the head and neck, which cause the pain associated with tension headaches (Moody, 1978);
2. laughter's pain-relieving, stress-reducing, and relaxing effects on the body in general (Scheele, 1979); and
3. increased oxygen saturation levels caused by sustained laughter. The increased oxygen saturation levels lend support to the old adage "Laughter is the best medicine" (Scheele, 1979).

A striking example of the physiological benefits of laughter is the story of Norman Cousins (Moody, 1978). Norman Cousins was suffering from a devastating terminal illness and decided to take control of the treatment of his illness. A major component of Cousins' treatment program was several hours per day of laughter-inducing activities, such as watching humorous films. Cousins found that one hour of laughter allowed him to enjoy two hours of painless sleep. This much-needed deep rest, along with the positive emotions brought about by laughter, seemed to make a great contribution to Cousins' miraculous recovery.

In summary, laughter and humor can enhance the physical, mental, and emotional health of elders. Some of the most effective laughter-inducing activities are intergenerational games, drama, clowning, and pet activities. Watching television comedies and films are generally less effective, although some shows and films can induce a great deal of laughter. In general, the more physically and mentally active your program participants are, the better. A good activity leader can inject humor into almost any situtation.

SUMMARY

This chapter presented information on a variety of recreational activities and techniques that can be successful with elders in a variety of settings.

Further reading and instructional classes on these topics are recommended in order to effectively be able to provide these activities and programs. Taking a course in massage therapy or taking guitar lessons are examples of personally enriching activities that can also be used professionally in recreational work with elders.

REFERENCES

Alvarez, E. A. (1992). A hydroponic garden in the Hospicio San Vicente de Paul: A productive aging project. *Aging International,* 19(2), 22-25.

Atkinson, M. (2001). *Hand and foot massage.* London: Carlton Publishing Group.

Brown, D. W. (1996). *Teach yourself massage.* Chicago: NTC Publishing Group.

Burger, I. B. (1980). *Creative drama for senior adults.* Wilton, CT: Morehouse-Barlow.

Bustad, L. K. (1980). *Animals, aging and the aged.* Minneapolis: University of Minnesota Press.

Cass, J. (1981). Pet facilitated therapy in human health care. In B. Fogle (ed.), *Interrelations between people and pets* (pp. 124-145). Springfield, IL: Charles C. Thomas.

Claire, T. (1995). *Bodywork: What type of massage to get, and how to make the most of it.* New York: William Morrow.

Clark, P. and Osgood, N. J. (1985). *Seniors on stage: The impact of applied theater techniques on the elderly.* New York: Praeger Publishers.

Corson, S. A. and Corson, E. O. (1981). Companion animals as bonding catalysts in geriatric institutions. In B. Fogle (ed.), *Interrelations between people and pets* (pp. 146-174). Springfield, IL: Charles C. Thomas.

Cusack, O. and Smith, E. (1984). *Pets and the elderly: The therapeutic bond.* Binghamton, NY: The Haworth Press.

Douglass, D. (1978). *Happiness is—Music! Music! Music! Music activities for the aged.* Salem, OR: LaRoux Enterprises.

Downing, G. and Rush, A. K. (1972). *The massage book.* Berkeley, CA: The Bookworks.

Elderly Berliners respond to pet therapy. (1992). *Ageing International,* 19(2), 20.

Fish, H. U. (1971). *Activities programs for senior citizens.* West Nyack, NY: Parker Publishing Company, Inc.

Jayson, M. and Dixon, A. (1974). *Understanding arthritis and rheumatism.* New York: Pantheon Books.

Lidell, L. (2001). *The book of massage.* New York: Simon and Schuster, Inc.

Magee, J. J. (1988). Using poetry as an aid to life review. *Activities, Adaptation, and Aging,* 12(1/2), 91-101.

Merrill, T. (1967). *Activities for the aged and infirm: A handbook for the untrained worker.* Springfield, IL: Charles C. Thomas.

Moody, R. A. (1978). *Laugh After laugh: The healing power of humor.* Jacksonville, FL: Headwaters Press.

Olszowy, D. R. (1978). *Horticulture for the disabled and disadvantaged.* Springfield, IL: Charles C. Thomas.

Riordan, R. J. and Williams, C. S. (1988). Gardening therapeutics for the elderly. *Activities, Adaptation, and Aging,* 11(1/2), 103-111.

Scheele, S. C. (1979). Humor and tension: The effects of comedy. In T. J. Scheff (ed.), *Catharsis in healing, ritual, and drama* (pp. 183-203). Berkeley, CA: University of California Press.

Schulberg, C. (1981). *The music therapy sourcebook: A collection of activities categorized and analyzed.* New York: Human Sciences Press.

Tending your garden means tending your bones (2003). *Tufts University Health and Nutrition Letter,* April, p. 8.

Thurman, A. H. and Piggins, C. A. (1982). *Drama activities with older adults: A handbook for leaders.* Binghamton, NY: The Haworth Press.

Towsen, I. N. (1976). *Clowns.* New York: Hawthorn Books.

Wapner, E. B. (1981). *Recreation for the elderly: A leadership, theory, and source book.* Great Neck, NY: Todd and Honeywell, Inc.

Weisberg, N. and Wilder, R. (eds.) (1985). *Creative arts with older adults: A sourcebook.* New York: Human Sciences Press.

Weiss, C. R. (1993). Capture the moments: Preserving the memories of older adults. *Journal of Physical Education, Recreation and Dance,* 64(4), 41-44.

Wilkinson, V. C. and Heater, S. L. (1979). *Therapeutic media and techniques of application: A guide for activities therapists.* New York: Van Nostrand Reinhold Co.

Williams, A. (1962). *Recreation in the senior years.* New York: Association Press.

PART IV:
ISSUES IN PROVIDING LEISURE SERVICES FOR ELDERS

Chapter 15

The Role of Recreation in Hospice Care

INTRODUCTION

According to the National Hospice Organization (NHO, 1988), hospice is a coordinated interdisciplinary program of supportive services and pain and symptom control for terminally ill people and their families. It is a concept of care, not a specific place of care. The purpose of hospice is to provide support and care to those in the final phase of a terminal disease so that they can live as fully and comfortably as possible.

As stated by the U.S. Department of Health and Human Services (1994), hospice focuses on care, not cure. Its emphasis is on helping patients make the most of each hour and each day of remaining life. Hospice care is an area of concern to the fields of recreation and gerontology in that 68 percent of male patients and 72 percent of female patients are age sixty-five and older (NHO, 1993), and as stated by the National Hospice Organization (NHO, 1979), "one of the greatest problems of the dying is the boredom that comes out of not doing anything" (p. 1). The purpose of this chapter is to develop an understanding of how recreation can play a role in hospice care, especially in caring for its older adult patients.

LEARNING OBJECTIVES

Upon successful completion of this chapter, the student will be able to

1. understand the purpose and philosophy of hospice care,
2. cite statistics on the growth of hospice care in the United States,
3. identify at least three benefits of hospice care,
4. identify at least three benefits of recreation for hospice patients, and
5. identify appropriate leisure activities for various examples of older adult hospice patients.

OVERVIEW OF HOSPICE CARE

Hospice care has been expanding rapidly in the United States. Only a handful of programs were in existence prior to 1972, but by 1980, a National Hospice Organization directory identified 138 member organizations providing services (Buckingham, 1983). By 1992, the number of operational hospice programs in the United States had increased dramatically to 1,935, up from 1,529 in 1989 (NHO, 1993). Estimates indicate that 540,000 people were served by 3,100 hospice programs in the United States in 1998 (HFA, 2003). Dr. Cicely Saunders started the hospice movement in 1967 when she opened St. Christopher's Hospice in London (NHO, 1988). Her work with the St. Christopher's Hospice has been the inspiration for many of the newly formed hospice groups in the United States (Stoddard, 1978).

Although the modern hospice movement has its origins in England, traces of the hospice philosophy can be found in the ancient Greek and Roman "healing places." Similar to modern hospices, these Greek and Roman places of healing emphasized "total treatment" of the individual—maximization of comfort, physical and mental stimulation, as well as medical treatment. However, dying and terminally ill persons could not take advantage of these healing places because such persons were felt to have little value to the state. On the other hand, modern hospices are specifically designed to help terminally ill and dying persons live as fully as possible until death, and to die peacefully. Unlike the Greek and Roman philosophy of value to the state, Dr. Saunders states that people matter up until the last moments of their lives (quoted in Stoddard, 1978).

Because Dr. Saunders and the St. Christopher's Hospice have been so influential in the evolution of the hospice movement, a description of the St. Christopher's program can facilitate a better understanding of hospice care.

St. Christopher's Hospice is a freestanding facility, surrounded by beautiful landscaping. There is a reflecting pool and flower beds, a lawn, chapel, study center, and outpatient clinic. Large paintings are found on most walls inside the buildings. Staff, visitors, and patients of all ages are found; the sound of laughter fills the air (Stoddard, 1978).

St. Christopher's is perhaps a "model" hospice program; there is great variation among hospice programs. Some are freestanding facilities, such as St. Christopher's, and others are part of a hospital or nursing home. Hospice programs can offer services to dying and terminally ill people in the patient's place of residence (private home or institution) or in the hospice facility (on an inpatient or outpatient basis) (Osterweis and Champagne, 1979). According to the National Hospice Organization (NHO, 1993), 77 percent of hospice patients die in their own personal residence, 14 percent die in an acute inpatient facility, and 9 percent in another institution. A majority of patients (55 percent) live with their spouse, 20 percent live with children, 10 percent live with a significant other, 10 percent live alone, and 5 percent live with parents (NHO, 1993).

The goals and objectives of hospice programs vary, but some generally applicable goals and objectives are to help terminally ill and dying persons maintain a personally acceptable quality of life until death; to help patients maintain and/or improve their mental and/or physical functioning so as to promote their independence; to keep pain to a minimum and comfort at a maximum for patients; to help patients find meaning in their life and death; and to facilitate patients' families to respond *appropriately* to their family member's death (Alsofrom, 1977; Cunningham, 1979; National Hospice Organization, 1979; Osterweis and Champagne, 1979; U.S. DHEW, 1979).

Hospice programs include an array of services designed to meet the aforementioned goals and objectives. Some of the components of hospice care are pain control through the use of drugs and comfort maximization; home health care or inpatient care including physician services, skilled nursing, and psychiatric consultation; physical, speech, and occupational therapy; day care for the patient; homemaker services; meal preparation at home; transportation to and from treatment centers; education about death; emotional counseling; spiritual support; and bereavement services after the patient has died. Above all, an essential aspect of hospice care is loving kindness (Osterweis and Champagne, 1979; Stoddard, 1978; U.S. Department of Health and Human Services, 1994).

Some of the staff needed in a hospice program are a hospice administrator, a medical director, a director of patient/family services, a pastoral counselor, volunteers and a volunteer coordinator, and a medical records consultant. In addition, an interdisciplinary hospice team should include a physician, registered nurse, social worker, nutritionist, occupational therapist, and other rehabilitation therapists (NHO, 1979; U.S. DHEW, 1979).

RESEARCH AND CASE STUDIES

Value of Hospice Care

Hospice care is a more desirable means of caring for the terminally ill for several reasons. Economic savings is one clear-cut benefit of hospice care. Wald (1979) states that the New Haven Hospice was serving patients for an average time of seventy-six days for slightly more than $1,000, whereas a hospital in New Haven was charging patients $285 per day. According to the National Hospice Organization (NHO, n.d.), 1992 statistics indicated that for every dollar spent on hospice care, Medicare saved $1.26, a significant savings considering that Medicare spent more than $40 billion in 1992 caring for people in their last year of life (almost 50 percent of these costs are expended in the last two months of life).

Although economic benefits are fairly easy to document, it is more difficult to find clear-cut evidence that hospices actually help dying patients enjoy life more or maintain better physical and mental health in their last days. Hospice care is an area that does not readily lend itself to well-controlled, experimental study, thus the difficulty in inferring cause-and-effect relationships based on the literature.

However, case studies of hospice programs support the notion that hospice care is beneficial for its patients and their families (Ingles, 1974; Wentzel, 1976; Stoddard, 1978; Ward, 1978; and Wald, 1979). Ingles's article provides insight into the value of hospice through an in-depth description of the St. Christopher's Hospice program. According to Ingles, St. Christopher's provides the love, kindness, and attention that dying patients so desperately need. The well-being of patients is enhanced through the provision of activities and services such as discussion groups; arts and crafts; group sing-alongs; flowers and plants in patients' rooms; television and radio; preparation of patients' favorite foods; and, above all, companionship.

Wentzel's (1976) description of the St. Christopher's Hospice also indicates that hospice care has a positive effect on terminally ill persons. According to Wentzel, many patients at St. Christopher's feel better than they have in years. Wentzel's article indicates that patients at St. Christopher's are relatively free of pain, and surrounded by love. Both Wentzel's and Ingles's articles create the impression that St. Christopher's hospice patients are living their last days to their fullest.

Stoddard (1978) presents an overview of the Marin Hospice in California and the New Haven Hospice in Connecticut. Both of these hospice programs emphasize a humane approach toward treatment of terminally ill persons. Similar to St. Christopher's, the Marin and New Haven hospices attempt to enrich the lives of their patients through the devoted efforts of paid staff and volunteers.

In a related vein, Ward (1978) describes the development and implementation of a hospice home care program connected with Overlook Hospital in Summit, New Jersey. The intent of this program is to help terminally ill persons live in their own homes for as long as possible. Ward concludes that through an expansion of home care services, the hospital was better able to meet the needs of terminally ill patients and their families.

Wald's (1979) article conveys the value of hospice care through quotes from hospice patients and staff of the New Haven Hospice, Hospice Orlando, and Hospice of Central Pennsylvania. According to a spokesperson for the New Haven Hospice, something can always be done to make the patient more comfortable. This statement accurately sums up the rationale for hospice care.

Although the aforementioned studies provide evidence that hospice care can be beneficial for dying persons and their families, more scientific evaluation research on hospice care is needed (Buckingham and Foley, 1978). Evaluation research is also needed on specific components of hospice care. One such component is recreation.

Value of Recreational Activity to the Dying

Several case studies and programs discussed in the literature lend support to the notion that recreation and related activity therapies can work well with dying patients. Rogers (1978) cites the need to support the creativity of dying patients. Rogers describes the value of creative activities such as poetry writing, music, arts and crafts, dance, and drama to patients of the Hillhaven Hospice in Tucson, Arizona. According to Rogers, artistic stimuli helped create a more relaxed atmosphere for the Hillhaven Hospice patients.

According to Gilbert (1977), music therapy is a potentially beneficial resource for terminally ill patients and their families. Gilbert states that music is an activity that helps draw people closer together and that music therapy can open lines of communication between patients and their families.

Similarly, Cannon (1974) states that recreation can help an individual find meaning in one's death. Furthermore, Lovelace (1974) points out that in play, one's ego can feel superior to time, space, and social and physical limitations (all of these limitations are particularly relevant to terminally ill persons).

Both Newman (1974) and Cannon (1974) describe how recreational activity can help improve the quality of life of a dying person in the final stages of life. Newman states that recreational activity can help dying persons keep their minds off their diseases; recreation gives a person something to do and talk about. Cannon cites an example of how recreation activity can be adapted for a terminally ill person in poor physical condition. The author describes how a sportsminded boy too sick for participation in active sports became the "sports editor" of his hospital ward—the boy collected sports information from newspapers, television, and radio sports reports and wrote a sports newsletter for the other patients on his floor.

RECREATIONAL ACTIVITIES
FOR ELDERLY HOSPICE PATIENTS

The case studies and programs discussed in the previous section lend support to the notion that recreation can benefit hospice patients. Theory also dictates that recreation can benefit elderly hospice patients. According to hospice philosophy, the health, overall functioning, morale, life satisfaction, and self-esteem of clients are all very important concerns. Research indicates that recreation can effect positive change in these areas of elders' lives. Thus, why not provide recreational activities and programs for dying and terminally ill elders?

An often-cited argument against providing recreational activities and programs for older adult hospice patients is that dying and terminally ill elders have very limited abilities or desires to recreate. As illustrated in the following examples, this argument is false. Almost any person in a conscious state can enjoy and benefit from recreational activities.

Example #1

The Client

Mr. C. is sixty-eight years old, a cancer patient diagnosed to have only a few months left to live. He is in a weakened state and is unable to walk. He is able to sit up in a chair, but usually for no longer than two hours at a time. Mr. C. still has use of his arms, although his muscles are deteriorating due to lack of use. His favorite leisure activity throughout his life has been tennis. Unfortunately, he is physically unable to play tennis due to his weakened state.

Appropriate Activities

Based on Mr. C.'s love for the game of tennis, and considering his level of functioning, he could enjoy numerous appropriate recreational activities.

1. Adapted forms of wheelchair tennis, for example:
    a. Play on a regulation-size tennis court, modifying the rules and boundaries to enable a desirable level of success. If the tennis racket is too difficult to manipulate, a small wooden paddle can be tried.
    b. Play an adapted version of tennis on a smaller court with a lower net.

c. Mr. C. could practice hitting tennis balls against a backboard, or hit balls driven at him by a ball machine, tossed gently to him by someone, or even practice hitting a stationary tennis ball attached to a string.

2. Mr. C. might enjoy playing a tennis video game, while sitting in his wheelchair, or sitting up in bed (if a portable unit is available).

3. Giving bedside tennis lessons could enhance Mr. C.'s self-esteem and provide much-needed mental stimulation. Mr. C. could demonstrate proper grips and explain strokes to tennis students.

4. A simple yet physically beneficial activity would be to periodically squeeze tennis balls, in order to increase arm and hand strength.

5. Tennis-related spectator activity might also be stimulating. Mr. C. could watch tennis matches on television and keep abreast of tennis news by reading newspapers and magazines. Mr. C. might also enjoy going to nearby tennis courts to watch some local players in action.

6. Mr. C. might enjoy playing racket sports similar in nature to tennis, such as table tennis and badminton. Such sports could probably be performed at a higher skill level than tennis by a person in a weakened state. Also, playing new sports and learning new activity skills can be an exciting challenge.

Thus, Mr. C. could enjoy a variety of recreational activities, based on his love for tennis, and adapted to his level of functioning.

Example #2

The Client

Mrs. A. is seventy-five years old, suffering from lung cancer, and diagnosed to have only a few months to live. She has been widowed for the past fifteen years and has one daughter who lives 2,000 miles away.

Mrs. A. lives in an assisted living community and receives assistance with most of her personal care needs. She spends most of her time lying in bed or sitting up in a chair, because she suffers from shortness of breath with the smallest amount of exertion. Mrs. A. has had very few recreational interests throughout her life. She was a dedicated housewife and mother who "never had time to do much else." She never sought a career and had few friends. However, one aspect of housework Mrs. A. always enjoyed was cooking. She said it was always important to her to serve her family good, nutritious meals.

Appropriate Activities

Based on Mrs. A.'s interest in cooking, and considering her level of functioning, she could enjoy numerous recreational activities.

1. Writing a cookbook would be a time-consuming, involving activity that could enhance Mrs. A.'s self-esteem and maintain her interest for a sustained period of time. Mrs. A. could dictate the recipes from her bedside; the recipes could then be typed and placed in a folio. The cookbook project would be exciting and challenging, yet it would be an activity Mrs. A. could definitely engage in, despite her poor physical condition.
2. An excellent activity for strengthening the fingers and hands would be to help knead bread as part of a bread-baking activity.
3. Mrs. A. could act as a consultant for meal planning for the impaired elders residing in the personal care home.
4. Home economics students from a local school could visit with Mrs. A. for tips on bread baking or other aspects of cooking.
5. Mrs. A. could be involved with a local nursing home in helping to plan the refreshments to be served to the residents for parties.
6. Mrs. A. could subscribe to various nutrition magazines and be informed of any cooking or nutrition-related television programs that might be of interest to her.
7. Mrs. A. could assist in the preparation of simple snacks or meals at the personal care home.

Obviously, Mrs. A. could enjoy numerous recreational activities, based on her interest in cooking, and adapted to her level of functioning.

Exercise 15.1 presents another client example and asks you to use your imagination to identify appropriate activities for this person.

SUMMARY

Through recreational activity, a new dimension of meaning can be added to the final stages of life. Recreation can serve as a major motivational force to continue living. Is life worth living if it means an existence of pain, devoid of enjoyment? Recreational activity not only provides enjoyable experiences and laughter, which can be a motivational force to continue living, but it can also give an individual feelings of competence and self-esteem.

Both theory and practice indicate that recreational activity can greatly benefit hospice patients. Recreational therapists, volunteers, and even family members can employ leisure activities as a tool in improving the lives of hospice patients.

EXERCISE 15.1. Identifying Appropriate Leisure Activities for an Elderly Hospice Patient

The Client

Mrs. B. is eighty years old, a cancer patient diagnosed to have only a few months left to live. She is able to sit up in a chair for short periods of time, but spends most of her time in bed. Her favorite activities when she was younger were playing the piano and dancing. List and describe at least ten activities that would be appropriate for this patient.

Appropriate Activities

1. _____

_____

2. _____

_____

3. _____

_____

4. _____

_____

5. _____

_____

6. _____

_____

7. _____

_____

8. _____

_____

9. _____

_____

10. _____

_____

REFERENCES

Alsofrom, J. (1977). The hospice way of dying. *American Medical News,* February 21, pp. 7-9.

Buckingham, R.W. (1983). *The complete hospice guide.* New York: Harper and Row Publishers.

Buckingham, R.W. and Foley, S.H. (1978). A guide to evaluation research in terminal care programs. *Death Education,* 2(1/2), 127-141.

Cannon, K.L. (1974). Death and attitudes toward death—Implications for therapeutic recreation service. *Therapeutic Recreation Journal,* 8(1), 38-41.

Cunningham, R.M. (1979). When enough is enough. *Hospitals,* July 1, pp. 63-64.

Gilbert, J.P. (1977). Music therapy perspectives on death and dying. *Journal of Music Therapy,* 14(4), 165-171.

Hospice Foundation of America (HFA) (2003). What is hospice? <www.hospicefoundation.org/what_is/>.

Ingles, T. (1974). St. Christopher's Hospice. *Nursing Outlook,* 22(12), 759-763.

Lovelace, B.M. (1974). The role of the recreation therapist with the terminally ill child. *Therapeutic Recreation Journal,* 8(1), 25-28.

National Hospice Organization (NHO) (1979). *Frequently asked questions about hospice: A working paper.* Vienna, VA: NHO.

Newman, B. (1974). The role of paramedical staff with the dying adult patient. *Therapeutic Recreation Journal,* 8(1), 29-33.

NHO (1988). *The basics of hospice.* Arlington, VA: NHO.

NHO (1993). 1992 stats show continued growth in programs and patients. *NHO Newsline,* October, pp. 1-2.

NHO (n.d.). *Hospice care: Dollars & sense.* Arlington, VA: NHO.

Osterweis, M. and Champagne, D.S. (1979). The U.S. hospice movement: Issues in development. *American Journal of Public Health,* 69(5), 492-496.

Rogers, B.L. (1978). Using the creative process with the terminally ill. *Death Education,* 2(1/2), 123-126.

Stoddard, S. (1978). *The hospice movement.* New York: Vintage Books.

United States Department of Health, Education and Welfare (U.S. DHEW) (1979). *Hospice.* Washington, DC: U.S. DHEW.

U.S. Department of Health and Human Services (1994). *Medicare hospice benefits: A special way of caring for the terminally ill.* Washington, DC: U.S. GPO Publication No. HCFA 02154.

Wald, M. (1979). Hospices give help for dying patients. *The New York Times,* April 22, p. 45.

Ward, B.J. (1978). Hospice home care program. *Nursing Outlook,* 26, 646-649.

Wentzel, K.B. (1976). Dying are the living: St. Christopher's Hospice, London. *American Journal of Nursing,* 76, 956-957.

Chapter 16

Sexuality in Later Life

INTRODUCTION

A favorite topic of jokes is sex and older adults. However, the topic is no laughing matter. Sexual activity has been well documented as a uniquely beneficial leisure activity for elders (Butler et al., 1994). Unfortunately, myths and stereotypes regarding sexuality in later life are prevalent and have inhibited the free sexual expression of elders (Kaye, 1993). According to Weg (1983), one means of enhancing the sexual expression of elders in the future is to ensure that health professionals (including recreation therapists) working with elders be well informed on this topic so that they will be able to effectively advise elders in sex-related matters. Furthermore, educating health professionals regarding the sexuality of elders can help to improve their attitudes toward sex for older adults, an important concern in that the negative attitudes of staff in settings such as nursing homes have been cited as contributing to an atmosphere that inhibits the free sexual expression of elders (Corby and Zarit, 1983). Therefore, the purpose of this chapter is a very important one: to provide information on sexuality in later life that will educate recreation professionals and enable their counseling of elders on sex-related matters, and to enhance their attitudes regarding sex for elders in the hopes that positive attitudes of staff toward sex will result in a more conducive social environment for elders to sexually express themselves.

In the first section of the chapter, the value and benefits of sexual activity for elders are discussed. In the second section, the current status of sex in later life is examined, including a discussion of research studies on the sexual behavior patterns of elders. In the third section, factors affecting the sexual behavior of elders are explored, including an examination of physiological considerations and psychosocial factors. In the last section, a variety of ideas are presented regarding how to improve the ability of elders to sexually express themselves, including a discussion of treatments to alleviate physiological limitations and solutions to psychosocial limitations on the sexual behavior of elders.

LEARNING OBJECTIVES

The learning objectives of this chapter follow:

1. Identify at least four benefits of sexual activity for elders.
2. Identify five common physical changes that affect sexuality in later life.
3. Identify at least three psychosocial barriers to sexual fulfillment in later life.
4. Identify at least five ideas for overcoming physical and psychological barriers to sexual fulfillment in later life.
5. Cite accurate facts on the level of interest and activity of older adults in sexual behavior.

VALUE OF SEXUAL ACTIVITY FOR ELDERS

According to Hodson and Skeen (1994), sexual activity can be physically, psychologically, and emotionally beneficial for elders. One physical benefit of sex is improved circulation. Another physical benefit of sex is reduced tension, as documented by Dr. West's experience in a rural nursing home (Weg, 1983). Sexual intercourse can help arthritics maintain a greater range of motion of joints and limbs (Hodson and Skeen, 1994).

Research (Altman, 1997) indicates that regular sexual activity might help people live longer. Based on an analysis of death rates of nearly 1,000 men in a Welsh town, researchers concluded that sexual activity has a protective effect on men's health, perhaps reducing the risk of death by about half. The researchers even suggested that it might be beneficial to promote the benefits of an active sex life, similar to the campaigns to promote exercise and better eating habits for good health.

The psychological and emotional benefits of sexual activity for elders are also impressive. According to Hodson and Skeen (1994), sexual activity can enhance elders' sense of well-being, improve their life satisfaction, and provide elders with a unique, pleasurable experience that is shared with another individual. The psychological and emotional lift that sex can provide is especially important to elders, in light of the loss of life roles many elders experience (Weg, 1983). For men, sex can counteract a loss of prestige and self-confidence in the work world. For women, sexual activity can enhance self-esteem by reaffirming physical attractiveness and desirability after menopause (Weg, 1983). Thus, with the elimination of some of older person's outlets for pleasure, ego satisfaction, and sensual expression, sexual activity can be even more vital to the well-being of some elders than it is to that of younger persons.

SEXUAL BEHAVIOR OF ELDERS

According to research studies cited by Kaye (1993), interest in sexual activity is maintained throughout the life span to a greater degree than is commonly believed. Although interest in sex does decline, it is a *gradual* decline, and many people in their nineties still report having sexual desires.

Bandon (1997) reports that survey research found that 40 percent of older adults are sexually active and have sex an average of 2.5 times per month (compared to seven times per month for those under age sixty-five). The same survey found that 17 percent of elders reported having a "high sex drive" and 25 percent described their lovemaking abilities as excellent or very good. About 50 percent of those in committed relationships say they are satisfied with the quality of their sex lives.

There are differences in level of sexual activity within the older population. In the sixty to seventy-four age group, 31 percent of men and 24 percent of women report having sexual intercourse about once a week or more (Toner, 1999). However, among those age seventy-five and older, only 19 percent of men and 7 percent of women report having sexual intercourse about once a week or more. A major factor influencing these statistics is having a partner. The same study found that among those age seventy-five and older who had a partner, more than 25 percent reported having sexual intercourse once a week. Another factor that seems to be an accurate predictor of the level of sexual activity in later life is the level of sexual activity earlier in life (Weg, 1983).

Another study on this topic found more good news: The percentage of adults who view their partners as romantic and/or physically attractive seems to increase with age, with almost two-thirds of older adults saying that they are extremely or somewhat satisfied with their sex lives ("You Can't Teach an Old Dog New Tricks," 2002).

However, there are some distressing research findings, especially with respect to women. More than two-thirds of women ages seventy-five and over said that they had experienced no sexual kissing or hugging in the past six months, and more than 50 percent said that they no longer had sexual thoughts (Toner, 1999). Among men ages seventy-five and over, 38 percent reported being completely impotent. Another interesting study on this topic was conducted from 1955 to 1964 with 260 persons ages sixty to ninety-four by the Duke Center for the Study of Aging and Human Development (Weg, 1983). The major findings of this study were (1) interest in sex declined, although 50 percent of the people age eighty and older interviewed still had an interest in sex; (2) approximately 20 percent of male subjects age eighty and older remained sexually active; and (3) approximately 14 percent of the males and 24 percent of the females cessated. The most common reason cited by males for cessation was health; females most commonly attributed cessation to the lack of a male partner.

With regard to the sexual behavior of elders, it is also interesting to note findings on the prevalence of masturbation among elders. According to Hodson and Skeen (1994), 43 percent of men and 33 percent of women age seventy and over masturbate. Weg (1983) cites a study that found that for males, masturbation peaks in the teenage years and declines thereafter, but for women, research findings indicated that 58 percent of older women masturbate while only 20 percent of younger women masturbate. The explanation of these findings is that the sociosexual outlets for older women tend to be limited, and that possibly older women have profited from their experiences and understand the pleasurableness of masturbation. According to Weg (1983), masturbation is an important sexual outlet that can help reduce stress, stimulate sexual desires, and contribute to well-being.

Another form of sexual behavior that can stimulate sexual desires and heighten pleasure is sexual daydreaming. Unfortunately, research indicates that the prevalence of sexual fantasies and daydreams declines in later life (Weg, 1983). However, "fantasy romance" can be an adaptive way for elders to continue a connection with the romantic and sexual part of themselves (Rose and Soares, 1993).

A positive aspect of sexual behavior in later life is the seemingly prevalent trend toward being less goal oriented toward orgasm but rather being more gentle, caring, warm, and loving during sexual intercourse (Weg, 1983). Therefore, even though the frequency of sexual activity might be lower for elders than for younger people, the enjoyment of sexual activity might be even greater for many elders.

FACTORS AFFECTING SEXUAL BEHAVIOR

The previous section presented an overview of sexual behavior patterns of elders. It is important to understand the factors affecting these behavior patterns, which is the purpose of this section of the chapter. Physiological factors that affect the sexual behavior of elders are discussed first, followed by an overview of psychosocial factors.

Physiological Factors

Common physical changes related to sexual functioning are typically associated with aging; however, these physical changes do not necessitate cessation of sexual activity. It is unfortunate that the physiological changes discussed next have caused many elders to mistakenly believe that they should cease physical activity.

Physical Changes in Women

According to Weg (1983), the following are sex-related physical changes that most older women experience:

1. Significantly lower levels of estrogen are produced.
2. Fullness of breasts is diminished.
3. The cervix and ovaries become smaller.
4. Vaginal capacity for expansion is reduced, and elasticity diminishes.
5. Less vaginal lubrication is present.
6. The clitoris becomes slightly smaller.
7. Due to a depletion of sex steroids, vaginitis (an infection caused by yeast organisms) becomes more prevalent after menopause. Vaginitis can cause one to experience pain during intercourse.
8. A thinning of the vaginal walls, combined with decreased lubrication, not only causes sex to be painful but it can make penetration difficult and cause bleeding.
9. Painful cramping becomes common.
10. The bladder and urethra become more susceptible to inflammation and irritation.
11. Intercourse sometimes causes urination and/or a burning sensation.
12. Intensity of physiological responses to stimulation are decreased.
13. The duration of the orgasm is reduced.
14. Resolution after orgasm is faster.

On the other hand, two physical characteristics of older women that contribute to their enjoyment of sexual intercourse are

1. the multiorgasmic capacity of the younger years is retained, and
2. because older women are released from the fear of pregnancy, they often experience a heightened interest in sex and reduced inhibitions.

Do not despair at the long list of negative sex-related physical changes older women often experience. According to Weg (1983), sexual disorders and dysfunction among elders are just as treatable as those among younger persons. Furthermore, as discussed in the last section of the chapter, specific treatments (e.g., hormone replacement therapy) can partially prevent, reverse, or retard the aforementioned physical changes.

Physical Changes in Men

According to Weg (1983), the following are sex-related physical changes that most older men experience:

1. Fewer sperm are produced due to lower testosterone levels.
2. A reduction in sex steroids causes a reduction in muscle tone and strength.
3. The testes are smaller and more flaccid.
4. The prostate enlarges.
5. Contractions are weaker.
6. Aching testes or sharp discomfort at the distal end of the penis may be experienced.
7. The force of ejaculation is weaker due to a reduction in the viscosity and volume of seminal fluid.
8. A longer period of time is needed for the penis to become erect.
9. More direct stimulation of the penis is generally required to reach an erection.
10. The loss of the erection after orgasm is faster.
11. A positive change is the ability to maintain an erection for a longer period of time, thereby increasing the potential for arousal and orgasm for the partner.

Again, do not to despair at the long list of negative changes, because specific treatments to prevent, reverse, or retard many of the aforementioned physical changes are available. These treatments are discussed in the last section of the chapter. Also, it is important to remember that often the despondency over the physical changes inhibits sexual activity more than the changes themselves.

Physical Conditions Affecting Males and Females

Weg (1983) discusses the effects of common physiological problems on the sexual activity of elders:

1. Diabetes can affect sexual activity in several ways:
   a. Vaginal lubrication is sometimes delayed and more scant.
   b. The diabetic male sometimes has less control over ejaculation and will occasionally ejaculate prematurely.
   c. The diabetic male sometimes is unable to attain an erection.
2. Pelvic surgery's effects on sexual activity appear to have the potential to be either positive or negative. Weg (1983) cites a study in which 34 percent of the women studied had heightened sexual responsiveness after a hysterectomy, and 37 percent of the women studied felt that their sexual relationship deteriorated after the hysterectomy. Although the removal of prostate tumors and hysterectomies sometimes depresses sexual desires and interferes with the capacity for climax, these are not inevitable results of surgery. Also not inevitable, but a very serious problem, is the feeling of some women after surgery that they have been defeminized.
3. Cardiovascular disease and hypertension often inappropriately inhibit elders from engaging in sexual activity due to myths about sex being a strenuous and dangerous form of exercise. In reality, only between 0.3 and 1 percent of all sudden coronary deaths are caused by sexual activity (Weg, 1983). Furthermore, sex can probably do more to prevent heart attacks (due to its stress-reducing effects) than to cause them. However, drugs commonly taken for hypertension can cause a loss of erective ability.
4. Drug use can have a negative effect on sexual capacities. Tranquilizers commonly used by elders (e.g., Librium and Mellaril) often weaken the erection and delay ejaculation. Continued use of these drugs can result in impotence. Similarly, the use of alcohol, marijuana, and other drugs can adversely affect sexual capacities.
5. Kaye (1993) cites research by Masters and Johnson indicating that overindulgence in food and drink, especially alcohol, can lead to a loss in sexual responsiveness.

Psychosocial Factors

As mentioned previously, attitudes toward sex-related physical changes can inhibit sexual activity more so than the actual changes themselves. According to Weg (1983), changes in reproductive functioning are especially ego damaging and feared. These changes tend to have a more negative impact on self-concept than most other types of physical changes.

Furthermore, Weg (1983) asserts that elders have been assigned to a special category—"sexually inert, uninterested, and dysfunctional" (p. 40). As a result, elders who want to fulfill their sexual desires often feel apprehensive and guilty, because of the societal attitude that sexual activity among elders is abnormal.

Robinson (1983) identifies several psychosocial constraints on the sexual behavior of elders:

1. Stigmas commonly attached to old age
2. The negative attitude of adult children toward their parents engaging in sexual activity
3. The barriers imposed by institutional living arrangements (approximately 1.5 million elders are institutionalized)
4. The numerous obstacles older women face, such as the unbalanced ratio of females to males, the high proportion of older women unmarried and thus without a sanctioned partner, the poor chances of remarriage, the tendency of husbands to be older than wives (thus often leaving women without a partner or one with limited sexual capabilities due to health problems), sex roles (especially those of previous generations) that have discriminated against women freely expressing their sexuality, and the double standard of aging, which portrays aging men as sexually desirable and aging women as sexually undesirable.

Constraints are also imposed by attitudes. One concern is that the attitudes of nursing home staff and the nursing home environment in general are not supportive of sexual expression. According to Wringer (1988), many nursing home administrators hold the view that any sexual activity among residents "causes problems," even if those involved are husband and wife. Meanwhile, a study of older women's attitudes toward sexually active elders indicated an expectation that elder sexual expression was acceptable in nursing homes (Hodson and Skeen, 1994).

In a related vein, Kassel (1983) expressed concern that elders in institutions are deprived of outlets for sexual expression, even though they are greatly in need of such outlets. However, there seem to be some positive changes in this area of concern. For example, at the Hebrew Home for the Aged in Riverdale, the Bronx (New York), a set of procedures and policies concerning sexual expression and the nursing home resident were introduced in 1995, stating that "residents have the right to seek out and engage in sexual expression, including words, gestures, movements or activities that appear motivated by the desire for sexual gratification" (Villarosa, 2002, p. D6). At the nursing home, residents have the right to obtain for private use materials with sexually explicit content and have the right of access to private space in support of sexual expression. On a lighter note, the recreation director of an assisted living facility in New Jersey helped a resident celebrate her 105th birthday by organizing a "dating game" for her, similar to the television show by that name, except that the participants were older (Kelley, 2003). In this case, the bachelorette chose a younger man—who was only age eighty-five. It seems that part of the attitudinal problem regarding sexuality in later life concerns the myths about sexuality and aging that younger persons, as well as elders, believe to be true. According to Croft (1982), these myths include the following:

1. Sexual intercourse is harmful to health and can cause death.
2. One can stay sexually active later in life through abstinence when one is young.
3. Only disturbed elders masturbate; it is a childish activity.
4. Coital satisfaction decreases after menopause.
5. Older women who enjoy sex were probably nymphomaniacs when they were younger.
6. Most older men lose the ability and desire to have sex.
7. Older men tend to be sexually deviant (e.g., child molesters and exhibitionists).
8. Sexual ability and performance remain the same throughout life.
9. A person cannot have sex if he or she has not engaged in sexual activity for several years.
10. A senior citizen who has a chronic illness or disability should not have sex.

Many of the factors affecting the sexual behavior of elders that were discussed in this section are limiting factors. The next section of this chapter focuses on how some of these limiting factors can be counteracted.

SUGGESTIONS FOR ENHANCING SEXUAL EXPRESSION IN LATER LIFE

This final section has been divided into two subsections: in the first, suggestions for overcoming some of the psychosocial limitations on sexual expression in later life are discussed; in the second subsection, treatments designed to counteract specific sex-related negative physical changes associated with aging are discussed.

Overcoming Psychosocial Barriers

In the previous section of this chapter, the environment of institutional settings was identified as a barrier to the free sexual expression of those elders living in those settings. Corby and Zarit (1983) write that the creation of a "heterosexual living space" within the institution is an excellent solution to this problem. In addition, the creation of the heterosexual living space in one particular nursing home was documented as resulting in men grooming themselves better and limiting their use of profanity. Furthermore, Corby and Zarit (1983) claim that institutions that permit the free expression of sexual behavior have less of a problem with inappropriate behavior.

An innovative program designed to help nursing home residents reactivate their sexual interest was implemented by psychologist Mary Ann Sviland. Barrow (1989) reports that in the program, couples were sent to X-rated movies and bookstores that sold sex handbooks, and then participated in group discussions on individual fantasies and goal setting for shedding inhibitions and expanding sexual repertoires. According to Sviland (cited in Barrow, 1989), positive changes in attitudes and behavior included the initiation of romantic pleasantries such as candlelight dinners and love notes, and a renewed interest by the program participants in making themselves attractive to their mates.

Croft (1982) identifies several suggestions for enhancing sexual opportunities for elders:

1. Communal living, in which groups of elders band together to share housing and form a family unit, could facilitate outlets for sexual expression as well as improve other aspects of life (e.g., shared responsibilities in cleaning, cooking, etc.). This concept has already been implemented by a Florida organization called Share-A-Home, and in an apartment building in San Francisco called Merrill Court.
2. Polygynous marriages, according to Kassel (1976), would have many advantages for elders such as
   a. the uneven sex ratio would be somewhat remedied;
   b. women could be a part of a meaningful family unit;
   c. elders could pool their incomes and thus live better;
   d. better nutrition would result (more incentive to cook for several people than for just one or two people);
   e. older women would have a regular sexual partner;
   f. older men would have a variety of sexual partners;

g. better grooming and appearance would result from the competition for attention; and

h. loneliness and depression would be reduced.

3. There could be a greater acceptance of women fulfilling their sexual desires through sexual relationships with other women.
4. There could be a greater acceptance of masturbation as a sexual outlet.
5. There could be a greater societal acceptance of older women marrying younger men.

Hodson and Skeen (1994) and Weg (1983) offers some additional suggestions for enhancing sexual capacity in later years:

1. Sex counseling can help remove inhibitions restricting an older person's sexual behavior.
2. Sex education throughout the life span will improve the sexual capacity of future generations of senior citizens.
3. Placing emphasis on the quality of the sexual relationship, rather than performance, will make the experience of sexual activity more enjoyable for elders.
4. As identified at the beginning of the chapter, one means of improving the sexual expression of elders is the education of health professionals in this area in order to improve their attitudes toward sex in later life and facilitate their ability to counsel elders in sex-related matters.
5. Greater research efforts to extend the male's life span, in order to reduce the life expectancy advantage of women over men, thereby reducing the problem of older women not having a partner for sexual activity.
6. Provide elders in nursing homes with staff members who model comfortable attitudes toward sexuality.
7. Encourage regular participation in exercise, as it can enhance libido.

Overcoming Physiological Barriers

There are several ways to prevent, treat, or reduce the effects of common negative sex-related physiological changes associated with aging, such as the following:

1. Hormone therapy in women can correct vaginal conditions that may inhibit intercourse. Women suffering from vaginal dryness after menopause can benefit from hormone replacement therapy ("You Can't Teach an Old Dog New Tricks," 2002). Chisholm (2002) reports

that a substance called "Dream Cream" has been developed to help women's arousal and enjoyment of sex.

2. The use of lubricants can reduce the problem with friction during intercourse that can cause sex to be painful for women (Beedy-Morrison, 1989).

3. Hormone therapy in men can treat gonadal problems (Valenta and Elias, 1983).

4. Surgical procedures can overcome erection problems (Valenta and Elias, 1983).

5. An intriguing hypothesis has been presented by Leiblum et al. (1983), who state that their studies indicate that females who tend to be more sexually active have less vaginal atrophy. In other words, continued sexual activity throughout life may prevent undesirable changes in the vagina. Leiblum et al. (1983) point out that although a cause-and-effect relationship has not yet been proven, their test results should stimulate further study.

6. Other possible methods of overcoming physiological obstacles to sexual performance and enjoyment in later life include nutrition, vitamin supplementation, and the use of drugs (Pearson and Shaw, 1982).

7. Last, but certainly not least, is the Viagra revolution. Many older men are using Viagra to overcome erection problems. The long-range implications of Viagra will be interesting. For now, the use of Viagra is certainly making sexual intercourse possible for many older adults, and is also increasing interest in sex. It also seems to have sprouted a new wave of jokes related to sex in later life!

SUMMARY

In many cases, recreation therapists are the ones that elders confide in regarding personal matters such as sex. Therefore, recreation therapists should be aware of the various medical, psychological, and social approaches to maintaining and enhancing sexual activity in later life. If recreation therapists are more knowledgeable in this area and thus can help enhance sexuality in later life, they will be making a great contribution to improving the life satisfaction and general well-being of elders.

REFERENCES

Altman, L. K. (1997). More orgasms, more years of life? *The New York Times,* December 23, p. C7.

Bandon, A. (1997). Longer, healthier, better. *The New York Times Magazine,* March 9, pp. 44-45.

Barrow, G. M. (1989). *Aging, the individual, and society* (Fourth edition). St. Paul, MN: West Publishing Co.

Beedy-Morrison, D. (1989). Sexual assessment and the aging female. *Nurse Practitioner,* 14(12), 35, 38, 39, 42, 45.

Butler, R. N., Lewis, M. I., Hoffman, E., and Whitehead, E. D. (1994). Love and sex after 60: How physical changes affect intimate expression. *Geriatrics,* 49(9), 20-27.

Chisholm, C. (2002). The new sexual revolution. *The Herald Sun,* February 11, p. B6.

Corby, N. and Zarit, J. M. (1983). Old and alone: The unmarried in later life. In Weg, R. B. (ed.), *Sexuality in the later years: Roles and behavior* (pp. 131-145). New York: Academic Press.

Croft, L. H. (1982). *Sexuality in later life: A counseling guide for physicians.* Boston: John Wright.

Hodson, D. S. and Skeen, P. (1994). Sexuality and aging: The Hammerlock of myths. *The Journal of Applied Gerontology,* 13(3), 219-235.

Kassel, V. (1976). Sex in nursing homes. *Medical Aspects of Human Sexuality,* 10, 126-131.

Kassel, V. (1983). Longterm care institutions. In Weg, R. B. (ed.), *Sexuality in the later years: Roles and behavior* (pp. 167-189). New York: Academic Press.

Kaye, R. A. (1993). Sexuality in the later years. *Aging and Society,* 13, 415-426.

Kelley, T. (2003). The art of dating (a younger man). *The New York Times,* March 29, p. D7.

Leiblum, S., Bachmann, G., Kemmann, E., Colburn, D., and Swartzman, L. (1983). Vaginal atrophy in the postmenopausal woman: The importance of sexual activity and hormones. *Journal of the American Medical Association,* 249(16), 2195-2198.

Pearson, D. and Shaw, S. (1982). *Life extension: A practical scientific approach.* New York: Warner Books.

Robinson, P. K. (1983). The sociological perspective. In R. B. Weg (ed.), *Sexuality in the later years: Roles and behavior* (pp. 82-103). New York: Academic Press.

Rose, M. K. and Soares, H. H. (1993). Sexual adaptations of the frail elderly: A realistic approach. *Journal of Gerontological Social Work,* 19(3/4), 167-178.

Toner, R. (1999). A majority over 45 say sex lives are just fine. *The New York Times,* August 4, p. A9.

Valenta, L. J. and Elias, A. N. (1983). Pituitary-gonadal function in the aging male: The male climacteric. *Geriatrics,* 38(12), 67-76.

Villarosa, L. (2002). At elders' home, each day is Valentine's Day. *The New York Times,* June 4, pp. D6, D10.

Weg, R. B. (1983). The physiological perspective. In Weg, R. B. (ed.), *Sexuality in the later years: Roles and behavior* (pp. 40-80). New York: Academic Press.

Wringer, P. (1988). Sex and the elderly. *The Futurist,* July/August, p. 53.

"You can't teach an old dog new tricks" (2002). *Tufts University Health and Nutrition Letter,* 20(3), 1, 4-5.

Chapter 17

Global Perspectives on Leisure and Aging

INTRODUCTION

The purpose of this chapter is to provide global perspectives on leisure and aging. All of the previous chapters examined issues related to leisure and aging from an American perspective. Most of the statistics cited were relevant to elders in the United States. In this chapter, leisure and aging in other countries is explored. The chapter does not attempt to provide a comprehensive overview of leisure and aging throughout the world (an entire book would be needed for that!) but rather is a presentation of facts, research, ideas, and examples of programs in various countries for the purpose of better understanding leisure and aging in the world today.

LEARNING OBJECTIVES

The learning objectives of this chapter are

1. to be able to cite statistics on the growth in the older population in the world today and in selected countries,
2. to be able to compare leisure and aging in the United States and selected countries, and
3. to be able to cite facts, research, ideas, and examples of recreation programs for elders in various countries.

The next section of the chapter presents a demographic overview of leisure and aging in the world today. The rest of the chapter is divided into sections for various regions and countries.

DEMOGRAPHIC OVERVIEW

According to McPherson (1999), there were 328 million elders worldwide in 1990, and projected figures for 2005 were 475 million, and by the year 2025, 822 million. Segrist (1999) states that the United Nations (UN) projects the worldwide population of elders to be 1.42 billion in the year 2050, representing an increase in the proportion of elders in the global population from 6.8 percent in 1999 to 15.1 percent in 2050. The fastest growing age group in the world is people over eighty, according to the UN (Crossette, 2002). The UN projects that there will be 2 million people age 100 or older in the world by the year 2050 ("U.N. Offers Action Plan for a World Aging Rapidly," 2002).

Developing countries are projected to experience a rapid increase in the proportion of older adults in their population in the next twenty years (Braun, 2002). Most of these countries are not prepared to provide for the needs of their rapidly aging populations.

Approximately 30 percent of U.S. elders live alone, compared to 40 percent in Sweden and only 9 percent in Japan. In most of the developed nations, 25 to 35 percent of elders live alone, whereas in most undeveloped nations, less than 10 percent of elders live alone (National Institute on Aging, 1992).

Older men in the United States have a suicide rate that is several times the overall average rate of suicide (Barrow, 1989). Curiously, this pattern is not evidenced in other countries. According to Stenback (Barrow, 1989), the peak rate for suicide in men occurs between the ages of thirty and sixty in Canada, Finland, Norway, and Poland. One possible explanation for this difference between the United States and other countries is a greater emphasis on work in the United States, causing retired men in the United States to feel a greater sense of loss of status and meaning in later life than do their counterparts in other countries, particularly in Western Europe. Americans work 350 hours (nine weeks) more than Western Europeans (de Graaf, 2003). It seems that whereas Americans (particularly men) place a greater emphasis on work, Europeans have made a choice to live simpler, more balanced lives and work fewer hours. While Western Europeans average five or six weeks of paid vacation a year, workers in the United States average only two weeks. European men have an advantage over American men in adjusting to the extensive free time of the retirement years because during their working years, they experienced large blocks of free time (five or six weeks of vacation time), whereas many American men have not.

Many European countries also have an advantage over the United States in terms of health life expectancy (the number of years a person can expect to live in good health). According to a study conducted by the World Health Organization (Braun, 2001), the top ten countries in terms of health life expectancy are Japan (seventy-five years), Australia, France, Sweden, Spain, Italy, Greece, Switzerland, Monaco, and Andorra. The United States ranked only twenty-fourth but, of course, was far ahead of the bottom ten countries (from sub-Saharan Africa). The health life expectancy in Sierra Leone is only twenty-six years.

In summary, aging is indeed a global issue. The rest of this chapter examines leisure and aging in various countries and regions.

EUROPE

Harahousou and Kabitsis (2002) summarize the status of leisure activity programs for elders in Europe as follows:

1. Many of the programs offered emphasize physical activities to promote good health and quality of life.
2. The training of professionals to provide these programs is an important issue in most countries. Training courses have been developed in Holland, Switzerland, Germany, Spain, Finland, and Poland.
3. Retired volunteers are increasingly being utilized in program implementation efforts.
4. The participation rate of older adults in these programs seemed to have improved throughout the 1990s in most European countries.
5. Programs and participation, although improved, are still insufficient.
6. Water exercise and dancing are popular activities.
7. Most of the participants in general exercise classes and dance are women.
8. Bicycling is popular in Denmark, Belgium, and the Netherlands, whereas hill walking is more popular in Britain, Switzerland, France, and Italy.

Harahousou and Kabitsis (2002) also discuss some of the special events and promotional activities offered to elders in various countries.

1. England and other countries have implemented health promotion courses. An innovation in Britain, according to Harahousou (2001), is "short tennis" for elders. The game is played on a badminton court with a low net and a special ball that moves slowly.
2. In France, physical activity programs for elders have been organized and implemented by older adults themselves.
3. In Italy, The University of the Elderly offers programs for older adults in many accessible locations.
4. In Finland, a program designed to increase physical activity among nursing home residents is ongoing.

5. In Greece, a project has been implemented in which physical education teachers are involved in providing fitness and recreation classes for older adults.

Harahousou (2001) also reports on a variety of leisure activities enjoyed by elders in various countries in Europe:

1. In Germany, adapted volleyball is popular. Also popular are golf, archery, and bowling because they are self-paced activities.
2. Poland offers the University for Elders, with courses ranging from physical education to gerontology.

Obviously, there are many countries in Europe and many programs that are being offered. A few countries are highlighted on the following pages, beginning with Denmark.

Denmark

Adults ages sixty and over constitute approximately 20 percent of the population in Denmark. A system of twenty-four-hour home care services was developed in Denmark as an alternative to nursing homes, and it is widely considered to be one of the best care systems available for elders (Karel, 2003).

The participation of older adults in sports has been increasing. In 1975 only 12 percent participated in sports or physical exercise, but by 1993 the proportion had more than doubled to 27 percent. All of the increase occurred in the sixty to seventy-nine-year-olds age group, with the participation of those ages eighty and over remaining unchanged. The majority (58 percent) of participants are women. The most popular activities are general gymnastics, other physical exercise, swimming, tour biking, and walking/marches. An extensive system of sports clubs facilitates participation in these activities. Denmark, with a population of about 5 million people, has over 22,000 sports clubs (Povlsen and Larsen, 1999).

Research in Denmark documents some of the benefits of these programs. For example, a study by Puggaard et al. (2000) on the effects of regular training on eighty-five-year-old women found that the program reduced blood pressure, improved VO2 maximum by 18 percent, increased strength, and resulted in a 17 percent gain in maximal walking speed.

In summary, Denmark offers extensive recreational programs for older adults. Similarly, extensive programs are offered in Great Britain.

Great Britain

A study on the leisure lifestyles of older women living in the inner city in Leeds, England (Watson, Scraton, and Bramham, 1996), found three important characteristics that described these women:

1. *resilience,* meaning having the ability to recover quickly after a setback;
2. *ritual,* meaning having a regular routine of activities (including leisure activities such as hobbies and social gatherings); and
3. *resourcefulness,* meaning having the ability to adapt activities to suit individual needs.

These three characteristics probably apply to successful aging for men and women in most countries. Another study on the topic of leisure and urban older women in England (Hague, Thomas, and Williams, 2000) focused on some of the problems this population faces:

1. *fears over personal safety,* particularly in the city center after dark;
2. *affordability,* or not being able to pay for expensive activities such as theater tickets;
3. *accessibility,* a concern especially for those depending on public transportation; and
4. *identity,* a complex issue involving changes in the city center that cause some older adults to feel that it is no longer a familiar place and that the people are not familiar either. For example, if old shops that had been familiar landmarks are taken over by new businesses catering to a younger clientele, some elders feel that they can no longer identify with the area as a familiar place.

Again, these problems probably are relevant to older men and women in many countries. Another study (Morgan et al., 2000) in Great Britain with relevance to elders in many countries focused on comparing exercise and diet of urban and rural elders. This study found that urban elders spent more time walking than rural elders. Although the rural elders had a healthier diet, the greater level of physical activity of the urban elders might give them greater protection from heart disease.

Further insight into the leisure interests and activities of elders in Great Britain can be gleaned from a study on the destination behavior of older travelers (You and O'Leary, 1999). Common traits of older travelers included very low participation in physically demanding activities, and high participation in shopping, dining in restaurants, sight-seeing in cities, and getting to know local people. Destination safety and environmental quality were reported to be important destination attributes. According to Grabowski (1999), older adult U.K. tourists are also concerned about health. Health-related concerns include the demands that older tourists put on local health services, finding medical health provision in less-developed countries that meets the standards found in developed countries, and holiday insurance. Again, these concerns seem to be relevant to elders in many countries, not only those in Great Britain.

Greece

Recreational activities of Greek elders tend to be sedentary. According to Harhousou (1999) the following are some of the reasons for the low rate of participation in physically active recreation:

1. Most Greek adults lead sedentary lives.
2. Women's participation in sports has been discouraged over the years.
3. Greek ideology or beliefs about older people discourage sports participation.
4. High rates of crime, insufficient transportation, and environmental pollution restrict elders' leisure and limit their participation to home-based activities.
5. Many lack experience with physical education in school (e.g., among rural females, 66 percent had no physical education classes in school).
6. Greeks have strong bonds to traditional values as opposed to modern attitudes.

The most popular physical activities of Greek older women were walking, swimming, and country dancing. The most popular leisure activities were watching television, visiting friends, attending religious services, gardening, and excursions. The favorite activities of older men are reported to be work around the house, repairing things, care of the garden, relaxing, listening to the radio, watching television, reading or writing, walking, going to the local coffeehouse, or going to church. In Greece, sitting in a coffee shop is a form of leisure viewed as suitable for men only (Harahousou, 1999).

A positive feature of leisure in the lives of Greek elders is the extensive network of "centers for the care of senior citizens. According to Laios, Theodorakis, and Martinidis (2002), there are 530 such centers in Greece, offering a variety of services and programs including a cafeteria, excursions, theater, lectures, library, dances, arts and crafts, painting, physiotherapy, occupational therapy, and other health-related services. The centers try to keep older adults in their home environments under the best possible living conditions.

ISRAEL

Israel, similar to Greece, has an extensive network of senior centers and adult day care centers. The centers provide a variety of activities and services for elders, much like the centers in the United States. I conducted research (Leitner, Scher, and Shuval, 1999; Leitner and Scher, 2000) with Israeli Arab and Jewish elders that gave me insight into the centers and the elders that attend them.

The purpose of my research was to see if participation in an intergenerational recreational activities program could foster more positive attitudes between Israeli Arab and Jewish elders. The research findings indicated that the program did improve attitudes of Israeli Arab and Jewish elders toward one another, and that the positive attitude changes were still in effect even one year later.

For the most part, Israeli Arab and Jewish elders are segregated; the Arabs go to their centers and the Jews go to theirs. For my study, Jewish elders came on buses from their centers to the Arab senior center. There was an initial resistance to the idea of bringing the two groups together. After briefly talking with the elders about the program, the response was overwhelming, with many more elders volunteering to participate in my program than I needed (see Photo 17.1).

Appearances can be deceiving. Judging by the conservative dress of the Arab women, it did not seem that they would be willing to engage in or enjoy the fun, active games that were planned. However, they laughed, smiled, and enjoyed the activities as much as any group of elders. They were also very hospitable, always wanting to serve food to my students and me. In summary, the study gave me an optimistic feeling about the prospects for peace in the region. If older adults, with deeply rooted attitudes, could become more positive in their outlook through participation in a recreation program, then surely positive change must be possible with Arabs and Jews in general.

There are other interesting aspects of leisure in later life in Israel. For example, group tours for elders are popular. I was fascinated to see a group of fifty to sixty elders, primarily in their eighties and nineties, at a resort area on a vacation. They enjoyed a number of activities together, including swimming, visiting historical sites, eating meals, and attending lectures.

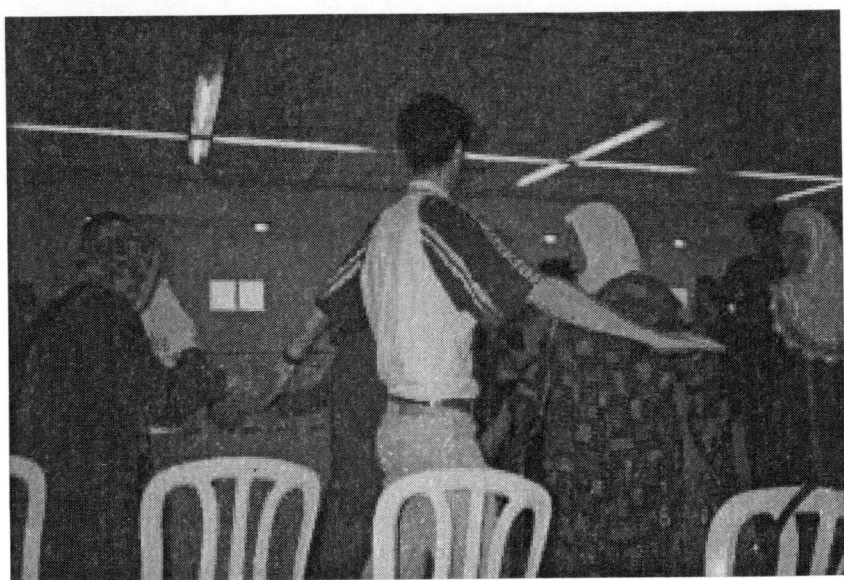

PHOTO 17.1. Joining hands, older Israeli Arabs and Jews folk dance together.

The group was composed of retired members (and their spouses) of a union. In Israel, it is fairly common to go on trips and tours with co-workers. Because of the high rate of taxation in Israel, a group trip is often offered as a perk for workers instead of a pay raise. Consequently, it seems that camaraderie develops among co-workers, and this friendship often continues through later life.

A unique aspect of life in Israel is the kibbutz. Although only a small percentage of Israelis live on kibbutzim, the life of elders on the kibbutz is noteworthy and can be a useful model for maximizing the quality of life of elders. The kibbutz is a communal living arrangement in which all members share in the work and the profits of the industry of the community. For example, some kibbutzim have agriculture as their main industry. Kibbutzim have been sensitive to the needs of their elders, giving them work more suitable to their needs and abilities (e.g., working in the café or tutoring children), keeping them integrated in kibbutz life. At many kibbutzim, older residents can be seen traveling about the safe, quiet streets of the community in three-wheel or motorized bicycles.

Traditional culture seems to encourage respect for elders in Israeli society. However, older immigrants from other countries pose a special challenge. For example, Israel has absorbed many thousands of immigrants from Ethiopia since the 1980s. In Ethiopia, the elders are highly respected and have a great deal of authority. In Israel, these elders have difficulty learning the language and adapting to the modern lifestyle, whereas the youth go to school, learn the language, and become integrated in society. This creates an awkward situation where the elders are dependent on the youth for helping them with many things. To some degree, elders from other immigrant groups (e.g., the former Soviet Union) also experience a loss of status.

Also related to the large number of immigrants Israel has absorbed from numerous countries is the challenge of programming recreational activities in senior centers and in other settings for a diverse population. Many elders do not know how to speak the national language (Hebrew) well. One center, can have elders from Ethiopia, Russia, France, Germany, England, Argentina, Yemen, Iraq, Iran, and other countries.

The following section on exercise habits of older adults in Israel was written by Gilad Scher, an exercise specialist who works with older adults in Israel. He leads exercise groups and also is involved in planning and designing exercise facilities for older adults.

Exercise Habits of Older Adults in Israel

In the past two decades, there has been a substantial increase in the awareness and the amount of exercise of the older population in Israel. Approximately 40 percent of older adults participate in some form of exercise at least twice a week.

The variation in the amount and quality of activity is big and depends mostly on socioeconomic status and gender. The higher socioeconomic populations and women tend to be more active, and the variety of their activities is greater. At the top of the list is walking. You can see hundreds of older people walking in the streets, gyms, parks, and beaches. Another popular activity is swimming, although not all know how or can afford it. A common form of exercise is a group class such as a physical activity sitting on chairs (most common in senior centers and nursing homes) and exercising lying on mats, doing Feldenkreis, yoga, or different forms of gymnastics. More men participate in the individual exercise activities such as walking and swimming, whereas in the group classes, the majority are women.

Another new and growing field is gyms that are designed to be especially suitable for older adults. For example, Eshel, the Israeli organization for promoting and developing programs for elderly, has over 1,000 people over the age of sixty participating in ten gyms (fitness rooms) that were built all over the country, side by side with the adult day care centers of Eshel.

Hiking and Israeli folk dancing are popular as well with Israeli older adults. Tennis and golf are popular activities with English speaking older adults who immigrated to Israel from Australia, South Africa, England, and the United States.

In summary, Israel is a small country (approximately 6 million people) facing many challenges in the provision of leisure services to its elders. On the other hand, India is one of the largest countries in the world, and challenges are also discussed.

INDIA

The following section on India was written by Dr. Shalini Singh. Dr. Singh has written extensively in the areas of leisure and tourism in general, and has expertise related to older adults in India as well.

Leisure for Seniors in India:
Glimpses Through the Cultural Frame

Overview of Senior Population in India

In the year 2003, approximately 8 percent of the total population of India was age sixty and over. Of these, almost 8 percent are age eighty and over. Interestingly, 59 percent of senior men and almost 18 percent of senior women continue to contribute to India's huge and productive labor force. This number belongs largely to the organized sector. A massive number of seniors work in the unorganized sector, usually in the rural sector, whose contribution is unrecognized. They are the ones who may be working for survival reasons. Few among these may engage in tasks of their free will. A special mention must be made of women, both in the rural and urban sectors, whose productivity and work are taken for granted and who never retire, unless they are too physically debilitated to undertake work any longer.

These facts partly explain the status of leisure in later life in India. At the same time, the philosophy of life (which follows) is a major contributory factor in the near absence of exclusively overt leisure time and activities.

The picture is not so grim for the few urban dwelling seniors who can afford to engage in a variety of leisure activities ranging from visiting friends and relatives in the country and even abroad, golfing, clubbing, sightseeing/touring, eating out, or participating in events and festivities. In terms of passive leisure such as reading, watching TV, listening to music, or even reading, most urban seniors do find time for these. This engagement is possible due to availability of free time, access to media, and inclination to take time off.

National Policy for Older Persons (Highlights)

The well-being of older persons is the goal of the national policy, which will be achieved by securing them their place in society so that they live this phase of life with purpose, dignity, and peace. The policy states that action is necessary

- to help the elderly, offer them protection from abuse and exploitation, and create opportunities for them to improve the quality of their lives;
- to ensure the rights of the elderly, giving them their share of development funds to ascertain that elderly women are not subject to the triple evil of age, widowhood, and gender;
- to regard life as a continuum and the age after sixty another phase. As such, there should be opportunities to lead an active, creative, and satisfying life;
- to create an age-integrated society in which there are strong bonds between the generations and conditions are suitable for the elderly to stay with their families;
- to acknowledge the potential of the elderly and to use them like other human resources;
- to empower the elderly so that they can take decisions concerning themselves, having regard for the fact that they constitute 12 percent of the electorate;
- to provide more money for the well-being of the elderly with contributions from the community and society; and
- to do more for the rural old who constitute 75 percent of the aged population and are terribly neglected.

The *concept of leisure* for an average Indian is derived generally through the Vedic philosophy for life (lifestyle). The traditional view to leisure is in sharp contrast to the Western philosophy of work–leisure–work. Vedic philosophy does not place leisure within the brackets of "work." Neither does it perceive leisure to be separated from work in the temporal and/or spatial dimensions. For most Indians, leisure occurs "in the here and now" of daily living. This makes the understanding of leisure, in the Indian context, pertinent.

Coming to seniors, the Hindu *"dharma"* (interpreted as duties and obligations toward self and society), advocates renunciation of the world in the fourth, and last, stage of life. Most people methodically followed this concept in the past, whereas some who are religiously inclined may take this option either for religious reasons or to escape certain trying circumstances. However, due to the changing social values and, moreover, because of the extremist approach of this ideology, most elderly take the moderate path of visiting religious places, in varying time limits, while keeping contact with home, extended families, and related social groups. Pilgrimages thus constitute a substantial form of leisure and recreation of Indian seniors. Interestingly, today's pilgrimages have an increasing sight-seeing component as opposed to the sanctity element (Kaur, 1985).

Opportunities for leisure in the contemporary social context (eating out, senior travel, senior/health clubs, libraries, and the like) are rather few and are affordable only to those with surplus incomes. Among those, not all have an inclination to avail such options.

Conventional Indian lifestyles, however, provide quaint opportunities for leisure (and sometimes recreation when health permits it), within the family and small social groups of the elderly (Anandlakshmy, 1998). Visiting family and relatives and religiocultural journeys usually find a major place in the leisure spectrum of Indian seniors, though this is largely dependent upon the surplus income factor. The fairs and festivals that mark the occasional holidays provide some spaces for "improvised leisure." Otherwise, the elderly are happy to engage themselves in the fun and frolic of everyday living, since it fits comfortably within the contemporary interpretations of religious and the Vedantic frames, which have been modified sufficiently to avoid inconveniences accruing from extremism (Srinivasan, 1998).

The ideas expressed by Singh are reinforced by research in India on this topic. It is pertinent to note that older men and women are inextricably linked with the family wherein both the young and the old engage in need-based reciprocity of care and affection (Bali, 2001). For example, Prakash (1999) writes that older women in India become free from work routines only due to changes in their roles (e.g., children growing up and leaving home) or ill health. Women do not view their time as something that they can actively structure to fulfill classic definitions of leisure. Their time is structured around their household. Television and radio seem to be the most popular leisure activities of both older women and older men.

Similarly, a study of rural older adults in the Punjab state of India (Singh, Gupta, and Aggarwal, 1994) found that most elders keep busy in the work they have done all their life. The most popular leisure activities were playing cards, gossiping, and reading newspapers.

India will be one of the most important countries in the world to watch during the next fifty years regarding developments in leisure and aging. As one of the most populous countries in the world, it will have a very high percentage of the total population of older adults in the world. Only 8 percent of its population today is age sixty and over, but this figure is likely to rise sharply.

Similarly, China, with its large population of elders, is an important country to follow in terms of developments in leisure and aging.

PEOPLE'S REPUBLIC OF CHINA (PRC)

China has a vast population and a vast older population, estimated to grow to 16 percent of the country's population in 2030 and 23 percent by 2050 (Braun, 2000). The city of Shanghai hosted the World Leisure and Recreation Association's Conference on Leisure and the Older Person in April 2001. Representatives from many countries shared information on leisure in later life in their countries, and it was an opportunity for people around the world to learn about leisure in later life in China.

Leisure services for older adults are a major undertaking in China due to the size of the older population. If all of the older adults of China broke away to form their own country, it would be the eighth largest country in the world! There are over 100,000 senior centers and clubs in China, with almost 9 million members. Life expectancy in China is 78.44; for women it is 80.53, and for men it is 76.38 (Shanghai Municipal Information Office, 2000). In the city of Shanghai alone, there are over 2 million adults age sixty and over (18.27 percent of the population) and almost 300,000 adults over age eighty (Zhenming, 2000). Shanghai has over 4,000 senior centers, 3,600 sports clubs, and 1,500 social clubs for elders. Every day, approximately 100,000 elders in Shanghai are attending over 5,000 different clubs and centers (Derong, 2001). In addition, there is a network of almost 3,000 schools for older adults in Shanghai, with an enrollment of almost 300,000 students (Lingli, 2001). Courses offered emphasize "delight, leisure, and health."

The authors had the pleasure of visiting the Shanghai University for the Elderly in April 2001. We will never forget the exceptionally warm greeting that the students and instructors of the university gave us when we visited. The university, established in 1985, had nearly 4,000 students in 2001, with an additional 18,000 students in twenty-three branches. Similarly, there are Universities for the Elderly, with satellite branches located in cities throughout China. According to Cangping (2001), the Society for Senior Colleges in China includes 17,000 colleges serving 1.5 million students. The university in Shanghai boasts a computer room, language lab, piano room, digital piano room, painting and calligraphy room, cooking room, multifunction room, fourteen standard classrooms and big rooms, reading room, body-building corner, indoor bodybuilding room, exhibition room, and speech room. Courses offered include various forms of art, such as calligraphy, painting, and crocheting, Internet (see Photo 17.2), health and aging, legal protection, cooking, social-psychology of aging (see Photo 17.3), music (see Photo 17.4), dancing (see Photo 17.5), English, chorus, and piano. In addition, the university offers online courses and "University for the Elderly on Air" on the Shanghai Education TV station (each course has 30,000 students).

Equally impressive are the early morning exercise groups in the parks in Shanghai and in other cities. In one park we visited (Fuxing Park in Shanghai), many different types of exercise were going on in different parts of the park simultaneously. Besides tai chi (see Photo 17.6), there was a group doing ballroom dancing, another group doing exercise with swords (see Photo 17.7), a group exercising with colorful scarves, a group exercising with fans, one group that seemed mainly to be clapping, another group dancing with sticks, a group doing breathing exercises, and a singing group as well. At 7:30 a.m., the park was very busy with people doing exercise. We were told that some people come as early as 5:00 or 5:30 a.m. to begin their activities and that about 10,000 people come to the park in the morning each day to exercise. According to Cangping (2001), an association for Sport Activity for the Elderly was formed in China in 1983, and over 50 million elders in China are engaged in different forms of exercise. Almost 40 percent of elders in China participate in outside exercise in the parks. In Beijing, the participation rate is about 60 percent.

A different form of leisure activity is offered by the Chengdu Old People's Health Club (Eckholm, 2003). The group was formed in the 1980s as a bicycle club for retirees. It has evolved into a motorcycle club that organizes three or four tours each month that last anywhere from a day to more than a week. Once on the road, the motorcyclists stay in small lodges and inns and spend their evenings enjoying one another's company.

Apparently, the motorcyclists aren't the only elders in China making some loud noises. Smith (1996) reports that elders in Beijing, participating in dance in the streets, have annoyed many young people with their noise. Beijing officials estimated that 60,000 elders were filling the streets each night, dancing to the loud clashing of cymbals and banging of drums. Police estimated the decibel level to be about equal to that of a freight train. The city received 1,652 noise complaints (mostly from young people trying to study or work) over a four-day period. This seems like a bit of role reversal, with the older generation dancing and making noise to the frustration of the younger generation.

PHOTO 17.2. Computer Class at Shanghai University for the Elderly

PHOTO 17.3. Psychology Class at Shanghai University for the Elderly

PHOTO 17.4. Music Class at Shanghai University for the Elderly

PHOTO 17.5. Dance Class at Shanghai University for the Elderly

PHOTO 17.6. Tai Chi Exercise Group at Fuxing Park in Shanghai

PHOTO 17.7. Exercise Group with Swords at Fuxing Park in Shanghai

However, overall, intergenerational relations appear to be stronger than they are in the United States. For example, many of the students at the Shanghai University for the Elderly leave in the midafternoon to pick up their grandchildren from school, bring them home, cook them dinner, and care for them until the parents (the elders' children) come home from work. Changes are occurring and there are assisted living and nursing home facilities, but it is less common for elders to live in these settings than it is in the United States.

In summary, the level of publicly provided recreational services for elders in China seems to far exceed that in the United States. The system of colleges and universities for older adults is excellent, and the exercise groups in the parks in the mornings would be well worth copying in the United States. Differences and similarities exist in the leisure activities of elders in China's neighbors, as discussed in the next section.

HONG KONG, TAIWAN, AND SOUTH KOREA

The PRC officially assumed control of Hong Kong in 1997. Up until that time, Hong Kong had been much more modern and developed than the PRC. There are still some differences between Hong Kong and the rest of the PRC.

Sivan (2002) conducted extensive research on leisure participation of older adults in Hong Kong. Several trends in participation were found:

1. There is a high level of involvement of older adults in physical activities in comparison to other age groups. Similar to the PRC, many elders participate in morning exercise in the parks.
2. There has been an increase in using new technologies, including computers.
3. The use of mass media seems to increase and social activities seem to decrease in later life. Watching television and reading newspapers, magazines, and books are all popular leisure activities.
4. Older adults continue to participate in activities they participated in during their earlier adulthood.

Taiwan (Chinese Taipei) is still independent from the PRC but, similar to Hong Kong, is modern and industrialized. According to Chen (2001):

1. Only 25 percent of older adults in Taiwan are happy with their lives. Much needs to be done to improve the quality of their lives through leisure services.

2. The main leisure activities of Taiwanese elders are watching TV, chatting with friends, and walking.
3. Physically active recreational activities included walking, jogging, hiking, and mountain climbing.
4. An increasing number of elders feel alienated from the society.
5. Elders prefer doing exercise with friends, going places close to where they live, and participating in free activities.
6. On holidays, many older adults participate in mountain climbing and hiking.
7. There has been an increase in the number of older couples living alone, apart from their children. Still, only 1 percent of older adults live in institutions. A person "loses face" if he or she sends an older parent to a senior citizen apartment building, even though these places might be offering better services than what is available to older adults living at home with their adult children.

South Korea, similar to its neighbors, is experiencing a rapid growth in its older population. However, according to Cho, Jun, and Cho (2002), many older adults in South Korea are inactive because of a lack of available active recreation, sports, and physical fitness opportunities. More recreation, sports, and physical fitness opportunities need to be provided, especially in hospitals. Passive or sedentary recreation opportunities, such as board games and watching TV, seem to be abundant in the nursing homes, senior centers, and senior schools.

Cho, Kim, and Kang (2000) studied the level of knowledge of college students regarding demographic trends, diet and medication, and physical health of older adults. The students seemed to be knowledgeable in the areas of aging and demographic trends, diet and medication, and physical health, but not so well informed regarding aging and mental health. One reason for the high level of knowledge in most areas is that over 60 percent of the students indicated that they had experience living with grandparents as part of their family household. Similar to Chinese culture, South Korean culture has been very family centered, with the responsibility for taking in and caring for elders being an unquestioned familial duty. This tradition might be changing, as urbanization and modernization has seen a rise in nuclear-family-style apartment complexes. Japan, the most modern country in all of Asia, is the next country discussed in this chapter.

JAPAN

The Japanese have the longest life expectancy in the world, and one of the youngest retirement ages.* Therefore, it is probably the number-one country in the world for postretirement life expectancy!

Retirement at age fifty-five is fairly common. It used to be that those who retired at age fifty-five started work at another job. However, because of the economic problems Japan has experienced, companies are encouraging retirement at age fifty-five, and it is difficult for these young retirees to find work again after retirement. This situation is difficult for many men to deal with because they do not have any identity outside of work. They often have never developed a social life outside of work. Many men do not know what to do with their free time and so they follow their wives around most of the day. However, in Japan, men and women tend to have very separate lives. Women have their own friends and activities. So when the husband tries to tag along, he is often referred to as "wet leaves," meaning that no matter what the wife does, she cannot sweep him away.

One popular leisure activity for older adults in Japan, especially for women, is attending classes at outreach colleges and other educational programs. Many noncredit courses are offered at schools, community centers, and even at department stores. Popular courses include English, computers, dance (including hula dance and ballroom dancing), music, art, writing, and painting. Other popular recreational activities for older adults in Japan include walking and swimming.

The concept of elders being highly respected is changing, due to the emergence of the nuclear family. Many young people do not want to live with their parents or grandparents. However, in some areas of the country, tradition is still strong. For example, in most rural areas the first son is still expected to take care of the parents. But, overall, older adults have become more independent from their children and some very nice retirement communities and assisted living facilities are found in Tokyo and in other cities.

An innovative facility is the Togoshidai special nursing home and Togoshidai Junior High School in Shinagawa City. This special consolidated facility houses a nursing home, other care facilities for elders, and a junior high school. Intergenerational events are held regularly to promote friendly contact between the elders and the children. These events include concerts and athletic festivals performed by the students and attended by the elders, and a joint exhibition of handicraft works by the elders and the children.

---

*This section is based on information from Dr. Harumi Karel and Dr. Nozomi Sato of The Center on Aging at University of Hawaii at Monoa.

An interesting program designed to prevent psychosocial withdrawal of elders in Japan is described by Chiba (2001). The program includes hiking, singing of nostalgic songs, games, and lectures from "super-aged people" who are good examples of leading a vivacious life in their advanced years. The program also includes games such as Japanese chess and karaoke, intended for "keeping youth of the mind." Exercise and sports are also important aspects of this program.

Harada (1999) reports that sports and exercise are popular among Japanese elders. Examples of popular physical activities among the older population are walking (the most popular activity), exercising in private fitness clubs (participation has doubled since 1993), and swimming (travel is the only activity that ranks higher in terms of potential demand).

In summary, Japan is a country where leisure in later life is an important concern given the long life expectancy and early retirement age of its people. In fact, whereas retirement used to be referred to as "extra life," a leisurely bonus of time at the end of a career, it is now referred to as "second life," meaning it is a time when many people try new careers and new hobbies ("Japanese Pursue 'Second Life' Instead of Retirement," 1999). Similarly, the life expectancy in Australia is one of the highest in the world, and it is common for people to retire when they are in their fifties.

AUSTRALIA

The older adult population in Australia is growing rapidly, and the government and private sector realize the need for expanding leisure services for elders. The government published a thirty-one-page guide (NSW Sport and Recreation, 2000) advising elders on how to become more active. The guide advocates walking, gentle exercise classes in group settings, swimming, aqua aerobics, golf, weight training, tai chi, and gardening as healthy recreational activities for older adults.

According to Dyer (2001a), the government is involved in ensuring that adequate recreational opportunities for older adults are offered in residential care settings through its accreditation of all aged care facilities program. Recommended leisure facilities in residential care communities for elders include a swimming pool, spa, gym, library, shuffleboard, dance floor, entertainment areas, pianos for concerts and for practice, gardens, golf/crochet putting greens, and a bus for touring.

Trends in leisure activity participation among older adults include studying at universities and using technology. There are community-based universities in Australian towns and cities specifically for older adults that are called Universities of the 3rd Age (Dyer, 2001b).

Aside from exercise, perhaps the most important type of recreational activity for older adults in Australia is travel and tourism. A study on the motives of Australian older adults to travel (Cleaver et al., 1999) found that the most common motives were nostalgia (32 percent), socialization (22.7 percent), and learning (18.9 percent). Other motives included escape, contemplation, status seeking, and physical exertion.

One type of travel that is popular with older adults in Australia is long-distance touring with a private automobile. According to research (Pearce, 1999), the following factors are apparently important to Australian elders in planning self-drive long distance touring vacations: ease of access; that the activity be engaging and purposeful; having a companion or companions with whom to share the experience; and traveling at a leisurely pace that enables a reflective experience.

Research (Moscardo and Green, 1999) on travel behavior and activity participation of older adults at the Great Barrier Reef region of Australia found that elders were even more satisfied with their experiences than were adults in other age groups. Elders tended to participate less in nightlife and entertainment and outdoor physical nature-based activities.

In contrast, some older adults in Australia are enthusiastic about adventure-based recreational activities and have formed a club called Adventurers (James and Riordan, 1994). The club participates in activities such as cycling, horse and camel riding, bushwalking, camping, abseiling, gliding, and white-water canoeing. They also run an annual overnight camp for homebound elders.

In summary, there are many similarities in in leisure in later life in Australia and the United States. The older adult populations of both countries are growing rapidly, and many new recreational programs are being developed.

SUMMARY

Many countries were discussed in this chapter but, obviously, many were not. For example, African countries were not discussed. Actually, in Africa, only 3 percent of the population is age sixty-five or older (Braun, 2000), which is a far lower percentage than most of the countries discussed in this chapter. The older adult population is not growing in every country. Braun (2000) reports that life expectancy in the Ukraine has dropped more than three years between 1989 and 1997, largely due to deepening poverty.

Nevertheless, leisure and aging is a major concern in most countries of the world, not just in the United States. The sharing of information on leisure in later life in different countries can help to improve the quality of recreational programs offered for older adults. The Commission on Leisure and Later Life of the World Leisure and Recreation Association is spearheading efforts to improve recreational opportunities for older adults around the world. Information is available at their Web site: <www.worldleisure.org>.

REFERENCES

Anandlakshmy, S. (1998). Ageing gracefully? *The Hindu* (daily), October 18, p. 4.

Bali, A. P. (2001). Care of the elderly in India—Changing configurations. Indian Institute for Advanced Study, Shimla.

Barrow, G. M. (1989). *Aging, the individual, and society* (Fourth edition). St. Paul, MN: West Publishing Co.

Braun, K. L. (2000). National/International news. *AGHE Exchange,* 24(2), 15.

Braun, K. L. (2001). International news. *AGHE Exchange,* 24(4), 10.

Braun, K. L. (2002). Aging is a global issue. *AGHE Exchange,* 25(3), 11.

Cangping, W. (2001). Studies on quality of life of older persons in China. Paper presented at The World Leisure Shanghai 2001 Conference on Social Development, Leisure, and the Older Person in Shanghai, China, April.

Chen, H. H. (2001). Leisure activities of the older persons in Chinese Taipei. Paper presented at The World Leisure Shanghai 2001 Conference on Social Development, Leisure, and the Older Person in Shanghai, China, April.

Chiba, Y. (2001). The organization and program development of preventative group operation against psycho-social withdrawal of the elderly in Japan. Paper presented at The World Leisure Shanghai 2001 Conference on Social Development, Leisure and the Older Person in Shanghai, China, April.

Cho, M-H., Jun, J-K., and Cho, B-J. (2002). Availability of recreation, sports, and physical fitness opportunities for elderly people in South Korea. *World Leisure Journal,* 44(1), 29-38.

Cho, M-H., Kim, D-K., and Kang, K-H. (2000). Community sports and recreation students' knowledge and stereotypes of aging. *World Leisure Journal,* 42(4), 43-47.

Cleaver, M., Muller, T. E., Ruys, H. F. M., and Wei, S. (1999). Tourism product development for the senior market, based on travel-motive research. *Tourism Recreation Research,* 24(1), 5-11.

Crossette, B. (2002). United Nations report shows rapid aging of populations around globe. *The New York Times,* March 1, p. A9.

de Graaf, J. (2003). Workweek woes. *The New York Times,* April 12, p. A12.

Derong, S. (2001). Pay close attention to community leisure in later life and promote the elderly undertakings in Shanghai. Paper presented at The World Leisure Shanghai 2001 Conference on Social Development, Leisure, and the Older Person in Shanghai, China, April.

Dyer, L. (2001a). Leisure programs for the elderly in retirement homes: A workshop with an Australian perspective. Paper presented at The World Leisure

Shanghai 2001 Conference on Social Development, Leisure, and the Older Person in Shanghai, China, April.

Dyer, L. (2001b). Leisure and recreation as a social service for the elderly. Paper presented at The World Leisure Shanghai 2001 Conference on Social Development, Leisure, and the Older Person in Shanghai, China, April.

Eckholm, E. (2003). The good bikers of Sichuan roar off. *The New York Times,* February 18, p. A10.

Grabowski, C. P. (1999). Elderly travelers and health. *Tourism Recreation Research,* 24(1), 80-81.

Hague, E., Thomas, C., and Williams, S. (2000). Political constructions and social realities of exclusion in urban leisure: The case of elderly women in Stroke-on-Trent, England. *World Leisure Journal,* 42(4), 4-13.

Harada, M. (1999). Aging and leisure in Japan. *World Leisure and Recreation,* 41(3), 30-32.

Harahousou, Y. (1999). Elderly people, leisure and physical recreation in Greece. *World Leisure and Recreation,* 41(3), 20-24.

Harahousou, Y. (2001). The European model. Paper presented at The World Leisure Shanghai 2001 Conference on Social Development, Leisure, and the Older Person in Shanghai, China, April.

Harahousou, Y. and Kabitsis, C. (2002). European models of leisure policies and physical activity programs for elderly people. *World Leisure Journal,* 44(1), 3-10.

James, K. and Riordan, P. (1994). "Rocking chair rebels": A model of adventure-based recreation for mature aged people. *World Leisure and Recreation,* 36(3), 18-23.

"Japanese pursue 'second life' instead of retirement" (1999). *The Jerusalem Post,* July 15, p. 6.

Karel, H. S. (2003). Elder care in Denmark. *AGHE Exchange,* 26(3), 13.

Kaur, J. (1985). *Himalayan pilgrimages and the new tourism.* New Delhi: Himalayan Books.

Laios, A., Theodorakis, N., and Martinidis, K. (2002). Structure, organization, and function of the Greek centres for the care of senior citizens. *World Leisure Journal,* 44(2), 42-45.

Leitner, M., Scher, G., and Shuval, K. (1999). Peace-making through recreation: The positive effects of intergenerational activities on the attitudes of Israeli Arabs and Jews toward each other. *World Leisure and Recreation,* 41(2), 25-29.

Leitner, M. and Scher, G. (2000). A follow-up study to peace-making: The positive effects of intergenerational recreation programs on the attitudes of Israeli Arabs and Jews. *World Leisure and Recreation,* 42(1), 33-37.

Lingli, X. (2001). A new dimension in leisure for older persons—Study activities in full swing among the elderly. Paper presented at The World Leisure Shanghai 2001 Conference on Social Development, Leisure, and the Older Person in Shanghai, China, April.

McPherson, B. D. (1999). Population aging and leisure in a global context: Factors influencing inclusion and exclusion within and across culture. *World Leisure and Recreation,* 41(3), 5-10.

Morgan, K., Armstrong, G., Huppert, F., Brayne, C., and Solomou, W. (2000). Health ageing in urban and rural Britain: A comparison of exercise and diet. *Age and Ageing,* 29(4), 235-242.

Moscardo, G. and Green, D. (1999). Age and activity participation on the Great Barrier Reef. *Tourism Recreation Research,* 24(1), 57-68.

National Institute on Aging (1992). *Global aging: Comparative indicators and future trends.* Washington, DC: U.S. Department of Commerce.

NSW Sport and Recreation (2000). *Physical activity for older adults.* North Sydney, NSW (Australia): NSW Sport and Recreation.

Pearce, P. L. (1999). Touring for pleasure: Studies of the senior self-drive travel market. *Tourism Recreation Research,* 24(1), 35-42.

Povlsen, J. and Larsen, K. (1999). Aging and leisure in Denmark. *World Leisure and Recreation,* 41(3), 25-29.

Prakash, I. J. (1999). Senior women's perception of leisure in India. *Tourism Recreation Research,* 24(1), 82-85.

Puggaard, L., Larsen, J. B., Stovring, H., and Jeune, B. (2000). Maximal oxygen uptake, muscle strength and walking speed in 85-year-old women: Effects of increased physical activity. *Aging,* 12(3), 180-189.

Segrist, K. (1999). AGHE: An association with an international flavor? *AGHE Exchange,* 22(3), 1, 15.

Shanghai Municipal Information Office and Shanghai Municipal Statistics Bureau (2000). *Shanghai Basic Facts.* Beijing: China Intercontinental Press.

Singh, H., Gupta, M., and Aggarwal, B. K. (1994). Leisure among aged rural people in India. *World Leisure and Recreation,* 36(2), 29-31.

Sivan, A. (2002). Leisure participation of Hong Kong elderly: Policy and practice. *World Leisure Journal,* 44(1), 11-18.

Smith, C. S. (1996). Old folks in Beijing dance in the streets, annoying the young. *Wall Street Journal,* May 5, pp. A1, A6.

Srinivasan, S. (1998). Productive ageing. *The Hindu* (daily), October 18, p. 5.

"U.N. offers action plan for a world aging rapidly" (2002). *The New York Times,* April 14, p. A5.

Watson, B., Scraton, S., and Bramham, P. (1996). Leisure lifestyles, elderly women and the inner city. *World Leisure and Recreation,* 38(4), 11-14.

You, X. and O'Leary, J. T. (1999). Destination behavior of older UK travelers. *Tourism Recreation Research,* 24(1), 23-34.

Zhenming, Z. (2000). *2000 Shanghai Basic Facts.* Beijing: China Intercontinental Press.

Chapter 18

Leisure in Later Life in the Future

INTRODUCTION

The purpose of this chapter is to explore how leisure services for elders might need to change in the future in response to demographic changes and various societal trends. Were planners so smart in the year 1900 or even in 1950 to predict that the older population would grow so much and that there would be a corresponding need for increased leisure services and other services and facilities for elders? Unfortunately, they were not. If they had been, some of the inadequacies in service provision today would not exist. Although the future is difficult to predict, some trends which are fairly obvious and point toward action that should be taken today to alleviate potential problems. Also, speculating and planning for the future can enable a better response to future changes when they do occur or as they emerge. At a minimum, this chapter should stimulate you to think about your leisure in later life and what you can do today to prepare for it.

LEARNING OBJECTIVES

The learning objectives of this chapter are to be able to

1. understand the implications of demographic changes on leisure services for elders,
2. identify ideas for improving leisure services provision for elders in the future, and
3. identify ways to personally prepare for leisure in later life.

DEMOGRAPHIC CHANGES

Growth in Older Population

As discussed in Chapter 1, elders are the fastest-growing segment of the population and are projected to represent 20 to 25 percent of the U.S. population by the year 2050, but could possibly grow to 50 percent of the U.S. population if the birth rate stays low and significant advances are made in cancer and heart disease research. It sounds incredible, but it is possible: a society in which one out of every two persons is over age sixty-five!

One of the implications for leisure services is that activities which cater mainly to a younger clientele *must* become popular with elders in order to stay in business! For example, Deckard (1992) predicts that elders will be patrons of amusement parks in the future, and that services need to be varied and improved for this age group.

Programs for elders at colleges and universities, such as Elderhostel (see Chapter 11) are already experiencing great popularity and have been growing, but even more growth will be necessitated by the aging of society. All educational facilities (schools as well as colleges and universities) will need to offer programs for elders. Perhaps many of the senior centers and day care centers of the future will be located in schools and colleges? Perhaps a majority or at least nearly 50 percent of all college students in the future will be age sixty-five or older?

Another certain growth area within the field of leisure services for elders is travel and tourism. The present population of elders figures prominently in the travel market, but the elders of the future will surely be a much bigger segment of this market. House-swapping, house-sitting, and other programs to enable low-cost travel will be even more desirable, as might vacations for single elders (à la "Club Med"?). As discussed in the next section, due to advances in medical research, elders of the future might be stronger and more capable of adventure travel and other strenuous forms of recreational activity.

Health Status, Life Span Improvements

Because the over eighty-five age group is the fastest-growing segment of the older population and most of the gains in life span have been in the *disability life span,* not the healthy life span, there is strong need for increased therapeutic recreation services (e.g., in senior day care centers and nursing homes) to serve impaired elders. However, medical breakthroughs may lead to greatly improved health status among elders, enabling a revolution in leisure services for elders.

Kolata (2002) discusses research on the antiaging effects of daily injections of human growth hormone. The treatment is controversial because although many patients report remarkable aging reversal effects (e.g., loss of body fat, muscle mass gains, increases in bone density and skin thickness, and improved sexual functioning), negative side effects have also been reported (e.g., development of diabetes, aching joints, and swollen tissue). There is also concern over negative long-term effects, such as promoting the growth of cancers and arthritis.

Weiss (1993) reports that other hormones, such as testosterone, melatonin, and DHEA, are being experimented with as potential antiaging supplements. As with human growth hormone, there may be negative side effects as a result of treatments, but there are also indications that treatment with these hormones can improve memory, help strengthen muscles (when combined with exercise), eliminate insomnia, boost the immune system, prevent cancer, and increase the life span. Although none of these treatments has as yet been perfected, research in this area might unlock the secrets of the "fountain of youth" in the near future. At least one man, Wallace Steinberg, chairman of the Healthcare Investment Corporation, is willing to bet his money on it. Kolata (1992) reports that Mr. Steinberg has invested millions of dollars in research devoted to turning back the biological clock. He believes that it should be possible to stop aging by creating a continuous supply of new body cells and by reviving aging cells.

However, a group of fifty-one top scientists published a position paper that attacked antiaging medicines and warned consumers that "anti-aging medicine is an industry intended to make money for those who are selling the products" (Pope, 2002, p. 3). They strongly urged the general public to avoid buying or using products from anyone claiming that they will slow, stop, or reverse aging.

Actually, part of the fountain of youth has already been discovered, and it is no secret: regular, enjoyable, vigorous exercise. As discussed in previous chapters, exercise enhances both mental and physical fitness and can help to prevent the onset of many of the health problems generally associated with aging. If more people were to exercise regularly and vigorously, there would no doubt be a general improvement in the health and fitness of elders. It also appears that people would live longer if they exercised regularly and vigorously. In the search for the fountain of youth, exercise is better and cheaper than growth hormone, and it is safer as well ("Growth Industry: Seeking the Fountain of Youth," 2003).

Lazar (1987) discusses other possibilities for extending the life span. Some evidence supports the idea that a calorie-restricted, nutritionally adequate diet can increase life span. Also, DNA experiments and freezing are being explored as possibilities for extending the life span.

So, people might someday be living well past the age of 200 or 300, and they might have the strength and vitality of a twenty-year-old, but will these fit 200-year-olds of the future look incredibly old and wrinkly? Probably not, at the rate that skin care products are improving. Brink (1994) reports that new wrinkle cream products are succeeding in wiping out wrinkles by thickening deep layers of the skin. The products are still not 100 percent effective and are expensive, but great progress has been made in recent years.

Therefore, it seems possible that in the future, the life span will be extended, and that there will be many strong and vital people well over 100 years old, alert and youthful in appearance. Perhaps these "super-centenarians" will not want to participate in special recreational programs for their age peers but will prefer to integrate with people of all ages. It just might be that the good-looking woman that you meet at the club and ask to dance with you is 105! Perhaps chronological age will become completely irrelevant!

The ideas discussed in this section of the chapter are not intended as predictions of the future, but rather are presented as possible scenarios. Perhaps the life span will never be significantly increased, and maybe the fountain of youth will never be discovered. However, do not assume that aging and old age in the future will be the same as it is today; the possibilities for change are endless. The key is to be open-minded to change, to adjust attitudes to changing times and new developments.

Work, Leisure, and Later Life

Whether elders of the future will have more or less free time than today's elders is questionable. Levy (1992) discusses some emerging patterns of work, education, and leisure that will affect the free time and leisure activities of elders:

1. Phased retirement, which allows older workers to gradually reduce their work hours in order to ease the strain of the last years of work and adjust to retirement. When combined with retirement education programs, phased retirement can help to expand activities and interests in later life by exposing people to new activities. However, it can also reduce free time in later life by pushing back the age of full retirement.
2. Permanent part-time work is another option that can have the effect of reducing free time in later life by pushing back the age of full retirement. It has a positive effect on the free time of younger people by enabling workers to spend fewer hours on the job.

3. Similarly, voluntary reduced work time enables younger workers to reduce their working hours and have more free time, perhaps helping them to be better prepared for retirement and leisure in later life.

Therefore, the changing patterns of work, education, and leisure might infringe on the free time of future elders by increasing their work hours in their retirement years, but might also help to expand their leisure activities by giving them an opportunity to develop new interests during early and middle adulthood. Similarly, a decline in the economy could work to increase free time in later life or infringe on it. Having less work available might necessitate an earlier retirement age. However, economic woes could also force more elders to return to work in order to supplement inadequate pensions and social security income.

Another factor that could have both negative and positive effects on leisure in later life in the future is the relative size of the baby boom generation. As Kuhey (1989) speculates, because the baby boom generation is larger than the generation that followed it, it will continue to have a great influence on the media and social norms when they are over sixty-five, just as they influenced society in the 1960s and 1970s. Thus, entertainment, travel, resorts, sports facilities, and other recreational enterprises might cater more to the needs of elders in the future because elders will represent such a large percentage of the market for their services. However, the relative size of the baby boom generation could infringe on the free time of these future elders, because with fewer offspring to care for elders, it will be more the responsibility of siblings to provide care in the absence of a spouse or significant other.

One of the biggest questions regarding the free time of future elders is the prominence of the work ethic. It appears that the work ethic was stronger among today's elders than it is among the baby boomers, yet evidence suggests a resurgence in the work ethic (Leitner and Leitner, 2004). Whether the influence of the work ethic declines or increases will affect the amount of free time of future elders and their ability to enjoy it.

Positive Changes in Leisure in Later Life

Some trends will certainly have a positive impact on leisure in later life, one being increasing levels of education. Many more of the future older population would have attended college than did today's elders. As discussed in Chapter 1, higher levels of education are generally associated with more varied leisure interests.

In addition, youth and adults of today have been exposed to many more leisure activities than were today's elders when they were younger. Therefore, future elders will have more varied leisure interests than today's elders.

Technological advances will also have a positive impact on the leisure opportunities for elders in the future, enabling new activities and the participation of those with impairments. Already, advances in physical conditioning and exercise are enabling elders to participate and excel in sports that were previously associated only with young adults.

What do you envision for your leisure in later life, and what can you do now to ensure that it is the best it can be? Exercise 18.1 asks you to explore these questions.

SUMMARY

Leisure in later life in the future will likely be vastly different from what it is today. The key is to be open-minded, not bound by preconceived notions of aging and old age. One thing is certain, however: Leisure and aging is a growing field, one that has great opportunities for future employment. For further information, contact the National Association of Activity Professionals, <www.thenaap.com>.

REFERENCES

Brink, S. (1994). The dewrinkling of America. *U.S. News and World Report,* June 6, p. 79.

Deckard, L. (1992). IAAPA panel: Variety livens theme park entertainment. *Amusement Business,* December 7, pp. 8-9.

"Growth industry: Seeking the fountain of youth" (2003). *University of California, Berkeley Wellness Letter,* 19(9), 1-3.

Kolata, G. (1992). Laying pipe for the fountain of youth. *The New York Times,* November 1, p. F7.

Kolata, G. (2002). Growth hormone changed older bodies, for better and worse. *The New York Times,* November 13, p. A26.

Kubey, R. (1989). The aging of Aquarius. *This World,* April 2, pp. 9-12.

Lazar, J. (1987). Do you dare to live forever? *California Magazine,* July, pp. 48-51, 96-97.

Leitner, M. J. and Leitner, S. F. (2004). *Leisure enhancement* (Third edition). Binghamton, NY: The Haworth Press.

Levy, J. (1992). Leisure and retirement in the new age wave society. *World Leisure and Recreation,* 34(1), 5-9.

Pope, E. (2002). 51 top scientists blast anti-aging idea. *AARP Bulletin,* June, pp. 3-4.

Weiss, R. (1993). A shot at youth. *Health,* November/December, pp. 39-47.

EXERCISE 18.1. My Leisure in Later Life in the Future

My projected retirement age: _____

My projected healthy life span: _____

My projected disability life span: _____

My projected health and fitness at age seventy-five: _____

_____

My projected leisure activities at age seventy-five: _____

_____

_____

_____

How I am currently preparing for leisure in later life: _____

_____

_____

_____

What I can do to better prepare for leisure in later life: _____

_____

_____

_____

_____

Index

Order a copy of this book with this form or online at:
http://www.haworthpress.com/store/product.asp?sku=5198

LEISURE IN LATER LIFE
Third Edition

_____in hardbound at $69.95 (ISBN: 0-7890-1535-8)

_____in softbound at $49.95 (ISBN: 0-7890-1536-6)

Or order online and use special offer code HEC25 in the shopping cart.

COST OF BOOKS_____

☐ **BILL ME LATER:** (Bill-me option is good on US/Canada/Mexico orders only; not good to jobbers, wholesalers, or subscription agencies.)

☐ Check here if billing address is different from shipping address and attach purchase order and billing address information.

POSTAGE & HANDLING_____
(US: $4.00 for first book & $1.50 for each additional book)
(Outside US: $5.00 for first book & $2.00 for each additional book)

Signature_____

SUBTOTAL_____

☐ **PAYMENT ENCLOSED: $_____**

IN CANADA: ADD 7% GST_____

☐ **PLEASE CHARGE TO MY CREDIT CARD.**

STATE TAX_____
(NY, OH, MN, CA, IL, IN, & SD residents, add appropriate local sales tax)

☐ Visa ☐ MasterCard ☐ AmEx ☐ Discover
☐ Diner's Club ☐ Eurocard ☐ JCB

Account # _____

FINAL TOTAL_____
(If paying in Canadian funds, convert using the current exchange rate, UNESCO coupons welcome)

Exp. Date_____

Signature_____

Prices in US dollars and subject to change without notice.

NAME_____

INSTITUTION_____

ADDRESS_____

CITY_____

STATE/ZIP_____

COUNTRY_____ COUNTY (NY residents only)_____

TEL_____ FAX_____

E-MAIL_____

May we use your e-mail address for confirmations and other types of information? ☐ Yes ☐ No
We appreciate receiving your e-mail address and fax number. Haworth would like to e-mail or fax special discount offers to you, as a preferred customer. **We will never share, rent, or exchange your e-mail address or fax number.** We regard such actions as an invasion of your privacy.

Order From Your Local Bookstore or Directly From
The Haworth Press, Inc.
10 Alice Street, Binghamton, New York 13904-1580 • USA
TELEPHONE: 1-800-HAWORTH (1-800-429-6784) / Outside US/Canada: (607) 722-5857
FAX: 1-800-895-0582 / Outside US/Canada: (607) 771-0012
E-mailto: orders@haworthpress.com

For orders outside US and Canada, you may wish to order through your local
sales representative, distributor, or bookseller.
For information, see http://haworthpress.com/distributors

(Discounts are available for individual orders in US and Canada only, not booksellers/distributors.)
PLEASE PHOTOCOPY THIS FORM FOR YOUR PERSONAL USE.
http://www.HaworthPress.com   BOF04